William Hugh Ferrar

A Comparative Grammar of Sanskrit, Greek and Latin

William Hugh Ferrar

A Comparative Grammar of Sanskrit, Greek and Latin

ISBN/EAN: 9783742813961

Manufactured in Europe, USA, Canada, Australia, Japa

Cover: Foto ©Andreas Hilbeck / pixelio.de

Manufactured and distributed by brebook publishing software (www.brebook.com)

William Hugh Ferrar

A Comparative Grammar of Sanskrit, Greek and Latin

A COMPARATIVE GRAMMAR

OF

SANSKRIT, GREEK, AND LATIN.

BY

WILLIAM HUGH FERRAR, M.A.,

FELLOW AND TUTOR OF TRINITY COLLEGE, DUBLIN.

IN TWO VOLUMES.

VOL. I.

LONDON:
LONGMANS, GREEN, READER, AND DYER.
DUBLIN: WILLIAM M^cGEE, 18, NASSAU-STREET.
1869.

PREFACE.

Most of those writers on Philology to whose works I am indebted are mentioned either in the text or notes of this book, and I have here only to express my especial obligations to the writings of Bopp, Schleicher, Corssen, Curtius, and Bücheler, and to several valuable essays in Kuhn's Zeitschrift by Ebel, Grassmann, Dietrich, Walter, and others.

I have also to thank Dr. C. Lottner, Professor of Sanskrit in the University of Dublin, for helping me in the revision of the proof-sheets, and for many valuable suggestions supplied during the progress of the work.

The abbreviations occurring in the text do not require much explanation, and the following only require to be noticed:—

A. S.,	. . Anglo-Saxon.	Gr.,	. . . . Greek.
Ch. Sl.,	. . Church-Slavonic.	Ir.,	. . . . Irish.
E.,	. . . . English.	It.,	. . . . Italian.
Fr.,	. . . . French.	I. E.,	. . . Indo-European.
G.,	. . . . German.	Kel.,	. . . Keltic.
O. H. G.,	. Old High German.	L.,	. . . . . Latin.
Goth.,	. . . Gothic.	O. L.,	. . . Old Latin.

Lith.,	. . . Lithuanian.	Sp.,	. . . . Spanish.
O. N.,	. . . Old Norse.	U.,	. . . . . Umbrian.
O.,	. . . . . Oscan.	O. U.,	. . . Old Umbrian.
O. O.,	. . . Old Oscan.	Wall.,	. . . Wallachian.
O. P.,	. . . Old Prussian.	W.,	. . . . Welsh.
O. S.,	. . . Old Saxon.	Z.,	. . . . . Zend.
Skr.,	. . . . Sanskrit.		

Sanskrit and Zend nouns are generally given in their crude forms, except when the case-ending is separated by a hyphen from the stem, or when the sign of equality is added, as in Skr. *as'vas* = L. *equus*. Curtius Essay "Zur Chronologie der Indo-Germanischen Sprachforschung," appears in the fifth volume, "der Abhandlungen der Philologisch-historischen Classe der Königl. Sächsischen Gesellschaft der Wissenschaften."

I refer to the second series of Max Müller's Lectures on the Science of Language, as Max Müller, Vol. II. K. Z. stands for Kuhn's "Zeitschrift für vergleichende Sprachforschung auf dem Gebiete des Deutschen, Griechischen und Lateinischen."

I have been delayed in the publication of this book for more than a year through a severe attack of illness.

The Second Volume of this Work will, I hope, be ready for publication in January, 1872.

WILLIAM HUGH FERRAR.

33, TRINITY COLLEGE, DUBLIN,
   September 1, 1869.

CONTENTS.

		Page.
CHAPTER I.	The General Alphabet, ...	1
CHAPTER II.	The Indo-European Language, ...	19
CHAPTER III.	Grimm's Law, ...	26
CHAPTER IV.	The Sanskrit Alphabet, ...	39
CHAPTER V.	The Greek Alphabet, ...	55
CHAPTER VI.	The Latin Alphabet, ...	102
CHAPTER VII.	Roots and Stems, ...	178
CHAPTER VIII.	Substantives, ...	199
CHAPTER IX.	Adjectives, ...	299
CHAPTER X.	Numerals, ...	306
CHAPTER XI.	Pronouns, ... , ...	315

APPENDIX. The Cerebrals, . . . 335

ADDENDA ET CORRIGENDA.

COMPARATIVE GRAMMAR.

CHAPTER I.

THE GENERAL ALPHABET.*

§. 1. THE physiology of the human voice is the true basis upon which all inquiries into the origin of language and the mutual connexion of languages should be built.

§. 2. All that the human ear is sensible of may be divided into *noises* and *sounds*. Examples of the former are the howling of the wind, and the splashing of water. Sounds, on the other hand, are produced by musical instruments or the human voice. Noises are caused by rapidly changing and irregular impulses communicated to the air; sounds, by its periodic vibrations. The human voice, which is only a stream of air, emitted from the lungs, becomes sound by the vibration of the vocal chords, which thus put the air passing through them into a state of vibration.

§. 3. An exact description of the vocal organs is not part of my present plan. For such a description I refer the reader

---

* For further information on this subject the following works may be consulted:—"Essentials of Phonetics," by Ellis; Max Müller's "Survey of Languages," also his "Lectures on the Science of Language," Second Series; Lepsius' "Standard Alphabet;" "Grundzüge der Physiologie und Systematik der Sprachlaute," by Brücke; "die Lehre von den Tonempfindungen," by Helmholtz; also various articles, by Ebel and others, in Kuhn's Zeitschrift.

to any good book on anatomy; merely adding here, that the vocal organs may be said to consist of the *lungs*, which by being dilated or compressed act like a pair of bellows, the *windpipe*, the *larynx*, and the upper cavities of the *pharynx*, *mouth*, and *nose*. The larynx, the true organ of voice, is placed at the upper part of the windpipe. It is narrow and cylindrical below, but broad above, where it presents the form of a triangular box. Its cavity is traversed by an elastic membrane, which is divided into two parts, called the vocal chords, by a narrow fissure called the *rima glottidis*. When sound is produced, the vocal chords almost touch, and their edges at the same time vibrate, rapidly for high, and slowly for low notes. We see, then, that the vocal organs form a wind instrument, in which the vibrating apparatus consists of the vocal chords.

§. 4. In the impression made by a sound on the ear three things can be distinguished—*loudness*, *pitch*, and *quality*. The loudness depends on the amplitude of the oscillations of the vibrating body. The pitch depends on the duration of these oscillations. Now, notes of the same loudness and the same pitch can be produced by different musical instruments, and also by the human voice. The same note, however, of the violin differs from that of the trumpet, and that from the same note of the voice, and so on. This difference had already been supposed to depend solely on the form of the vibrations of the air, as it could not depend on either their amplitude or duration. This has now been proved directly by Helmholtz. The quality, therefore, is due solely to the form of the vibrations of the air.

§. 5. THE ELEMENTS OF LANGUAGE.

The phonetic elements (στοιχεῖα) are threefold—vowels (φωνήεντα), breathings, and consonants (σύμφωνα). The consonants are divided, according to their *duration*, into mutes and semivowels, these latter including liquids (ὑγρά), nasals, and sibilants (flatus); according to their *hardness*, into surds (sharp, stosslaute, tenues, ψιλά, Skr. aghosha, vivûras'vâsâghosha), and sonants (blunt, drucklaute, mediæ, μέσα, Skr. goshavant, samvâranâdaghosha); and according to their *aspiration* into aspirated (δασέα, Skr. mahâprûṇa) and unaspirated (Skr. alpaprûṇa). In Sanskrit the term *ûshman* is also applied to the sibilants and *h*, *spars'a* to the mutes and nasals, and *antaḥsthá* to *y, r, l, v*, as intermediate between the former and the latter.

The mediæ differ from the tenues in this, that in the former the glottis is somewhat narrowed to enable it to sound.

The mediæ were so called because they were pronounced by the Alexandrian grammarians with more aspiration than the tenues, and with less than the aspirates. To us, however, and most probably to the Greeks of the classical period, *g* is as little aspirated as *k*.

The term consonant means " sounding along with," and, as Ellis writes, " is said to be given to these letters because they have no sound of their own, but sound* with vowels." If, however, we consider *s, f, r*, &c., to be consonants, all consonants do not require the aid of a vowel to enable us to pronounce them; for we can pronounce the nasals, liquids, and sibilants without the help of any vowel. The Sanskrit name for a consonant is *vyañg'ana* (Sâv. 5: 25), from *vyañg'*, to make clear.

The Arabic grammarians call a vowel, *motion*, and a consonant, a *barrier*, because in forming vowels the voice is not interrupted, but only modified by the position of the tongue and lips, whereas in forming consonants the voice is stopped at certain fixed positions. Brücke, on the other hand, considers the vowel-signs to be properly marks of rest, and the consonantal signs to be marks of motion, because the

* Ellis remarks (p. 57), that this definition reads very like a bull.

latter signifies both the closing of the barrier and the opening of it.

The consonantal signs were originally marks for syllables, as the Devanâgarî and Semitic alphabets prove.

§. 6. The Vowels.

Vowels are composed of vocalized breath. The difference between the various vowels is due to the form of the vibrations of the air emitted from the lungs, which vibrations depend upon the form of the buccal tubes.*

The three primary vowels are A, I, and U, pronounced as in German or Italian.

In forming A the mouth assumes a position gradually widening itself from the guttural point, like a funnel. The lips are in this position wide, and the tongue lies flat in the mouth.

U is formed by rounding the lips, so as to leave the opening between them as narrow as possible, and by drawing down the tongue, so that the cavity of the mouth is enlarged as much as possible. The mouth in this position is like a bottle without a neck.

I is formed by narrowing the lips and raising the tongue towards the hard palate. Thus a bottle with a narrow neck is formed, the body of which is in the throat, while the neck lies between the hard palate and the upper surface of the tongue. The length of this neck, according to Helmholtz, is six centimètres.

All the other vowels are formed between these three pri-

---

* "In der That sind die Vocale der menschlichen Stimme Töne membranoser Zungen, nämlich der Stimmebänder, deren Ansatzrohr, nämlich die Mundhöhle, verschiedene Weite, Länge, und Stimmung erhalten kann, so dass dadurch bald dieser, bald jener Theilton des Klanges verstärkt wird." Helmholtz, p. 163.

mary ones. The following tabular view of them is that given by Brücke:—

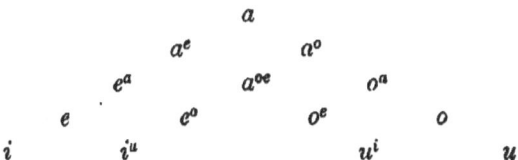

In forming *o* we open the lips wider and elevate the tongue more than in forming *u*. In proceeding from *a* to *i* we gradually change the buccal tubes from the *a* to the *i* position; and similarly in proceeding from *a* to *u*. In forming u^i we give the lips the *u*, and the tongue the *i* position; while in forming i^u the lips take the *i*, and the tongue the *u* position. In u^i the length of the canal, which was six centimètres in *i*, is now eight (Helmholtz, p. 170).

a is long in E. *farm, calm,* and short in E. *Sam.*

i is long in E. *wheel, ravine,* and short in E. *knit.*

u is long in E. *flute, fool,* and short in E. *full.*

a^e is the German *ä*, the French *è*. It is short in the Cockney pronunciation of *man, fat.*

a^o is long in E. *nought, water,* and short in E. *hot, not.*

e^a is the German *e* in *echt*, the French *è*.

a^{oe} occurs in Fr. *veuve, sœur, peur.*

o^a is heard in the Fr. *encore.*

e is long in G. *ewig,* E. *hay,* and short in G. *werden.*

e^o is a common sound in the Wallachian language. Brücke says that it is heard in G. *zwölf.*

o^e is the G. *ö* in *Konig,* Fr. *peu.*

o is long in E. *ago,* and short in G. *sonne.*

i^u is heard in G. *Myrte* and *Physik*. It is the Slavonic hard *i*. This sound is of Tataric origin, and traces of it are still found in the Dravidic languages of Southern India.

u^i is the G. *ü*, long in *Thür*, and short in *dürr*. It is the Fr. *u* in *sûr* and *sur*. It is also the Dutch *uu* and the Scotch *ui*.

Lepsius inserts another vowel sound between a^e and a^o, which, he says, is heard in the E. *but, son*.

§. 7. The Original Vowel.

In addition to the vowels noticed in the last section, we have another vowel, called variously, the *indefinite*, or *neutral*, or *original* vowel, *Urlaut, Urvocal.* This is a sound that exists in all languages, and from it, according to Ellis, all the other vowels are derived. Willis says that it 'seems to be the natural vowel of the reed.' All unaccented vowels in our European languages have a tendency to return to this sound; e. g. E. beggar, nation, Paddington (for -town), G. lieben, Fr. tenir. This vowel sound is formed by leaving the tongue in its most natural position, opening the mouth easily, and emitting vocal breath. Lepsius says that this sound comes among the clear sounding vowels next to a^{oe}, but that it is capable of various shades, sometimes approaching *a*, sometimes *e, i, o, u*, being distinguished from all these by the absence of that clear resonance, which is lost by either partially closing or shutting the mouth. The French *e muet* and the Welsh *y* approach this sound very nearly. Brücke considers that Lepsius is wrong in stating, that this vowel is inherent in all soft fricatives and nasal explosives,* for the indistinct vowel sound here is merely the tone of the voice. Moreover, the only actual examples of the amalgamation of a vowel and consonant are *uw* and *iy*.

Max Müller is wrong in supposing that we hear this sound in E. *el-m, mar-sh*; for, in proceeding from *l* to *m*, or *r* to *sh*, we do not require to interpose any vowel.

* These terms will be explained farther on.

This indistinct vowel, when combined with r and l, forms the two Sanskrit vowels ṛ and ḷ. This Sanskrit vowel ṛ differs from E. r, as heard in *her, steward*, in this, that it is pronounced at the cerebral,* whereas the E. r is pronounced at the guttural point of the mouth.

§. 8. The Nasal Vowels.

The nasalization of the vowels is produced by allowing the air to vibrate in the nasal cavities as well as in the mouth. The air need not pass through the nose, for by closing the nose we may increase the nasal twang.

Nasalization is an alteration solely within the vowel itself, no consonantal element being brought into play. This, as Lepsius points out ("Standard Alphabet," p. 9), was rightly understood by the Indian grammarians, who express the nasalization by a vowel-like sign, viz., a dot over the letter. It is theoretically possible to give all the vowels the nasal twang, but few receive it. Miklosich remarks that in all the languages known to him, only a, a^e, o^e, and o were nasalized. Ellis says that the Portuguese have both a nasal i and a nasal urvocal.

§. 9. Diphthongs.

When two vowels follow each other so rapidly as to melt into one sound, we obtain a diphthong. Now, we know that a is formed at a point in the mouth before i and u, and therefore it alone of the three primary vowels can form a true diphthongal base. Moreover, as e and o are also formed in the mouth farther back than i and u, they may serve as bases. We can make a both long and short. We have, therefore, eight proper diphthongs, which are moreover capable of receiving different shades of pronunciation.

---

* These terms will be explained further on.

We see at once that we cannot form any proper diphthongs with *i* and *u* as bases; for if we try to pronounce *ia* and *ua* very rapidly we do not form diphthongs, but merely the syllables *ya* and *wa*. In Welsh we find the improper diphthongs *ia* and *ua*, and in French we find improper *u* diphthongs frequently as in *oui*, which is not pronounced as *we* in English.

§. 10. THE BREATHINGS.

These are classed by some writers among the consonants, as by Lepsius, who gives them the name Faucal,* and classifies them thus:—

Explosive fortis, Arabic ع, *ain*.
Explosive lenis, Arabic *Hamzeh*, Greek *Spiritus Lenis*.
Fricative fortes, Arabic ح, *hha*, and English *h*, as in *hand*, which is not as strong an aspiration as *hh*.

There can be no nasal breathing, for the canal of the nose is closed during the formation of a Faucal sound.

Ellis and others separate the breathings from the consonants, and form them into a distinct class.

The pure aspirate, however, as I believe, does not belong to any special organ, though it appears to have some connexion with the gutturals. Accordingly, while we find *h* representing frequently an original *gh*, we sometimes find it developed from an original *dh* and *bh*.

§. 11. THE CONSONANTS.†

These are produced under the following conditions:—

A. No air is allowed to pass into the nasal cavities, and the canal of the mouth is closed at some definite point. Thus are formed the *Explosive* sounds, both *tenues* and *mediæ*.

---

* See Brücke in K. Z. vol. xi., p. 265.
† In this section I have followed Brücke very closely.

B. The air is still prevented entering the nasal cavities; but, in place of closing the canal of the mouth at any point, a narrow passage is left, so that the air comes forth with a sound of friction. Thus are formed the *Fricatives*, including h, y, v and the *Sibilants*. The *L*-sounds are fricatives; but they differ from the other letters of this class in this, that the passage for the emission of the air does not lie in the centre of the canal of the mouth, but on each side, between the edges of the tongue and the grinders.

C. The nasal cavities are still closed, but some portion of the canal of the mouth is made to vibrate, thus causing the vibration of the air passing out. Thus arise the *R*-sounds.

D. The mouth is closed, and the nasal cavities are open. Thus we have the *Resonants*, or *Nasals*. The nasals and vowels are the sounds easiest to be heard from a distance. Thus words such as *Mamma, mine, no*, can be heard very far away.

§. 12. The four classes are divided again under three heads, according to those parts of the canal of the mouth that approach each other.

I. The under lip may approach the upper lip or the upper teeth. These sounds are the *Labials*. They are the most constant sounds in all languages.

II. The fore part of the tongue may approach the teeth or the palate. These sounds are the *Dentals* and *Cerebrals*. Bühler has demonstrated that the existence of the cerebrals in Sanskrit is not due to Dravidian influences, but that they were independently developed in that language. The Arabic linguals differ from the Sanskrit cerebrals solely in this, that in the latter the tongue is more contracted than in the former. The name cerebral is not quite correct, but its use has become so general that it is better to retain it. The Sanskrit name for these letters is *mûrddhanya*, from *mûrddhan*, which means the highest point in the roof of the palate, and not the brain.

It is absurd to say that any letter is pronounced in the brain (cerebrum).

III. The middle or hinder part of the tongue may approach the palate. Thus we have the *Palatals* and *Gutturals* (Skr. g'ihvâmûlîya). The term guttural* is not exactly correct, for these letters are not produced in the *guttur*, but by contact between the tongue and the *soft* palate. By pushing this point of contact forwards to the *hard* palate, we get the palatals. These palatal sounds have a tendency to assume a shade of *y*, which frequently becomes independent, and developes itself into a full *y*. This is easily accounted for by the fact that in the palatals the tongue is raised very nearly into the *y*-position. Thus we can explain the fact that original gutturals often become sibilants; for the guttural *k* became the palatal; this again became *ky*, this *ty*, this *ts*, and sometimes *s*. For example, the L. *cantus* became E. *chant* (palatal tenuis), and Fr. *chant* (palatal sibilant); L. *canis*, Fr. *chien*; L. *quatuor*, Skr. *k'atvár*; L. *que*, Skr. *k'a*; Gr. κοῖλον, L. *cœlum*, It. *cielo*; L. *caseus*, E. *cheese*; L. *causa*, Fr. *chose*.

This tendency of the palatals to develope *y* after themselves also explains how an original guttural sometimes becomes a dental; thus τίς has been developed from κις the groundform of which was *kvas*, whence Skr. *ka-s*, Goth. *hvas*, L. *quis*; similarly τίσσαρες is derived from an original *kvatváras*, whence come L. *quatuor*, Skr. *k'atvár*, Lith. *keturi*, &c.

"Such transitions," writes Lepsius ("Stand. Alph.," p. 72), "in the history of languages never take place suddenly, but always gradually. It is a very common phenomenon that the explosive letters first produce the corresponding fricative sounds behind them, and afterwards pass entirely into them,

---

* Consult a paper by Lepsius in K. Z. vol. xi., p. 442.

and that at the same time the gutturals advance constantly towards the anterior part of the mouth."

§. 13. THE LABIALS.

A. *The Explosives.*

The tenuis p (p^1) is formed by simple contact of the lips: it is a surd consonant, for the glottis is wide open. The media b (b^1) is formed similarly, except that now the glottis is narrowed. In modern Greek, where β is pronounced as ν, the sound b is expressed by μπ, where μ merely tells us that the glottis is now contracted; similarly ντ is used to express the sound d. Thus, *barber* would be written μπάρμπερ, and *dreadful* ντρείτφουλ, for ντρεντφουλ.

We can form a second p (p^2) by bringing the upper lip and lower teeth together.

B. *The Fricatives.*

F is formed by bringing the under lip towards the upper teeth (f^2); or by bringing the lips towards each other (f^1). V is related to f, exactly as b is to p. F^2 is the f in *life*; v^2 is the v in *live*. Brücke says that we find v^1 in G. *quelle*, and v^2 in G. *wie;* but Ellis separates the sounds of the G. *w* and E. *v* from each other. The former he writes, '*v*, and thus describes its formation—" the lips are brought into the position for *w*, and the contact at the edge is slackened, while the inner surfaces are brought close together and flattened." The E. *w*, he says, arose from a cross between this '*v* and the Fr. *u*. No other European language possesses the E. *w*, and hence it has been supposed by some that this *w* is properly the vowel *u*. But this is wrong; for we can make this sound surd in *wheel, which;* and the fact that the words *woo* and *wood* are monosyllabic proves that *w* is a true consonant.

C. *The R-sound.*

If we place the lips in the p^1 position and then let them vibrate, we form two sounds, the one surd, and the other sonant, which are related to each other as p to b. We find this labial *r* in the Kretan τρέ for τϝε = Skr. *tvâm*, in δεδροικώς for δεδϝοικως, unless δεδρόκως, i. e. δεδορκώς, be the correct reading, in Kr. ῥίγα (σιώπα) for σριγα from σϝιγα, and perhaps in ἄτρεγκτος (ἄβροχος) from τέγγω, if Goth. *thvaha* be from same root. This *r* only appears in Greek in the Kretan dialect. In the following Latin words *r* has perhaps been developed out of an original *v* :— L. *cras* = Skr. *s'vas*, L. *creta* beside Skr. *s'veta* (white), L. *cresco* beside Skr. *s'vi* (to increase). This interchange of *r* and *v* occurs also in some German dialects (see K. Z., vol. xv., p. 320).

D. *The Resonants.*

If we close the lips as in b^1, and allow the air to vibrate in the nasal cavities, we form m^1. M^2 is not used: The nasals are closely connected with the mediæ—*m* with *b*, *n* with *d*, and *ñ* with *g*. Hence we find L. *flamma* for *flañma* from *flagma*; Sp. *Inez* for *Agnes*, L. *hibernus* beside χειμερινός; L. *puber* beside Skr. *pumâns*. In northern climates the nasals are frequently omitted; as in Ir. *coic* (quinque), *cet* (centum), O. N. *gêck* for *gênck*.

§. 14. THE DENTALS AND CEREBRALS.

A. *The Explosives.*

By pressing the fore part of the tongue against the palate and teeth we form a *t*-sound, of which there are four kinds.

T^1. *Alveolar.* The sides of tongue touch the upper grinders, and the point of tongue lies on upper internal gums, thus forming an air-tight receptacle.

T^2. *Cerebral.* The tongue is now convex, and its lower side touches the palate. This *t* has been called *lingual;* but I prefer the term cerebral, because the other term is applied in Arabic to a different class of letters, and moreover it does not suffice to distinguish this sound, as all *t*s are pronounced by means of the tongue.

T^3. *Dorsal.* The tongue is still convex, but its upper side now touches the palate, and its tip rests on lower teeth.

T^4. *Dental.* The tongue now merely touches the teeth.

We have four *d*s related to these four *t*s as *b* is to *p*.

B. *The Fricatives.*

We have four *s*s related to the four *t*s, as *f* is to *p*, and four *z*s related to the four *s*s as *v* is to *f*.

S^1 is the Arabic *Sad*, and is nearly the same as the *s* in E. *sin, seal.*

S^2 is a more rushing sound than s^1.

S^3 is the sharp hissing *s* in E. *sharp*, Fr. *chose.*

S^4 is the E. *th* in *thin*, the Mod. Gr. θ. This θ has become *f* in Russian: this change is easily explained, for the edge of the upper teeth, which in θ lies between point of tongue and under lip, now merely has to approach the latter.*

Z^1 is the Arabic *za*, and is nearly the same as *z* in E. *breeze.*

Z^3 is found in E. *pleasure, giraffe,* Fr. *jeune,* according to Lepsius.

Z^4 is E. *th* in *other*, Mod. Gr. δ. In English, when z^4 is initial, we generally say d^1z^4; and when it is final, z^4s^4 instead of it; thus, for *breathe* we say $breaz^4s^4$, and not $breaz^4$. In this respect the Spanish pronunciation of z^4 differs from ours; for final z^4 in Spanish is always pronounced purely. Neither s^4 nor z^4 exists in Sanskrit.

* Consult a paper by G. Michaelis, in K. Z., vol xiii., p. 223.

If in the four *t*-positions we allow an opening to be left at each side of the tongue between its edges and the grinders, we form from the four *t*s four λs, and from the four *d*s four *l*s.

L^1 is the common *l* in E. *leave*.

L^2 is the Vedic *l*.

L^3 occurs in *l mouillé*.

L^4 is used by those who lisp.

L^1 often becomes vocal in English, as in *apple, double*, which Ellis writes *ap'l*, &c. The surd λ^1 is unknown in English, but is very common in Welsh, where it is written *ll*, as in *Llangollen*. This surd λ^1 takes the place of *le* in conversational French, in such words as *able, possible*, which Englishmen pronounce as *ab'l*, &c. This *ll* is Ellis' whispered *l*. In his terminology, *surd* consonants are *whispered*, and *sonant, spoken* or *voiced*. Whisper differs from voice solely in this, that in whispering there is no vibration of the vocal chords, whereas in voice there is.

C. *The R-sound.*

The alveolar *r*, when sonant, is our common *r*. When surd, it occurs in Welsh, and in French as in *tendre*. This surd *r* is scarcely to be distinguished from *s*, the only difference being a small ripple of the whisper. This accounts for the fact that *s* and *r* frequently interchange (Ellis, p. 50).

The Sanskrit grammarians treat *r* as a cerebral, and therefore deduce it from *d*^{2}; but they are wrong, for it is impossible to make the tongue vibrate from the cerebral position.

As they did not distinguish the alveolar position, they had to treat *r* as either a dental or a cerebral; and they chose the latter, probably on account of the point of the tongue being directed upwards (Brücke, p. 42).

D. *The Resonants.*

We have four *n*s, corresponding to the four *d*s, exactly as *m* to *b*. N^3 is contained in *n mouillé*.

§. 15. The Gutturals and Palatals.

A. *The Explosives.*

In forming k the middle or hinder part of the tongue touches the middle or hinder part of the palate, while in forming t the fore part of the tongue touches the fore part of the palate. Hence the articulation of t begins where that of k ends; yet in the cerebral t we may go backwards across the k limit, and still pronounce a t. This, however, cannot be done in the case of the dorsal t. Two ks may be formed—one on the hard palate (k^1 *palatale*), and one on the soft palate (k^2 *velare*).

The It. *ch*, in *chiesa*, *chiaro*, is formed at the front limit of the hard palate; the Arabic *Caf* at the hinder limit, and the G. *k*, in *wickeln* between these two. The k^2 in G. *stock* is formed at front limit of soft palate. The Arabic *Kaf* is formed farther back than any other k sound.

G^1 and g^2 are related to k^1 and k^2, as b is to p. G^1 is the It. *gh* before i; the G. *g* in *geben* is formed a little farther back than It. *g*, but it is still palatal.

B. *The Fricatives.*

In these the stream of air strikes the palate, as in the *s* sounds it struck the teeth. They are related to the k sounds as f is to p.

The palatal flatus, χ^1, is the G. *ch* after *e* and *i*, as in *Recht*, *ich*, and the Mod. Gr. χ before *i* as in χείρ. The initial sound of the E. *hew*, *human* very nearly approaches this χ^1. This is the whispered form of the *y* in E. *yea*, *year*.

The guttural flatus is the G. *ch*, after *a*, *o*, *u*, the Mod. Gr. χ before *a*, *o*, *v*, *ω*.

Another χ sound, χ^3 can be formed so far back that no k sound corresponds to it. This is the Swiss *ch* in *ach*, and is common in Arabic.

There are three ys, related to the three χs exactly as w is to f.

Y^1 occurs in E. *yea;* and y^2 is the G. *g* in *Tage, Lüge,* and the Mod. Gr. γ before *a, o, ω*.

C. *The R-sound.*

If we make the uvula vibrate, we form the *uvular r*. This is distinguished from the dental *r* by the fact, that in the latter it is the tip of the tongue that vibrates. The *l* and *r* sounds are commonly called *Trills*. They differ in this, that in the *r*s the stream of air is periodically *interrupted*, but in the *l*s there are no interruptions, but merely *oscillations* produced in the emitted air.

D. *The Resonants.*

We form two *n*s (ν^1, ν^2), related to g^1 and g^2 as *m* is to *b*. ν^1 occurs in G. *Bengel;* ν^2 in G. *Wange*.

The French *n* in *un, en,* is now merely a sign of the nasalization of the preceding vowel, and is therefore no consonant at all. From a comparison, however, with Latin and Italian, we see that it has been developed out of an *n* sound which was neither ν^1 nor ν^2, but ν^3.

§ 16. THE ASPIRATES.

These are classed by some writers among the fricatives, by others among the explosives. They are, according to Lepsius, "those explosive sounds which are pronounced with a simple but audible breath." Three different methods of pronouncing the *tenues aspiratæ* have been proposed:—(1), the tenuis and spiritus asper may be pronounced separately; (2), the spiritus asper may be changed into the corresponding flatus, and then *ph, th, kh,* become *pf, ts* and *kch,* respectively;

(3), the tenuis and the spiritus asper may melt into one sound. The first of these methods is said to prevail at present among the Brahmans; it is compared to the pronunciation of *ph*, *th*, and *kh*, in the English words *haphazard*, *anthill*, *inkhorn*; but this is incorrect—for in these words the tenuis and the spiritus asper belong to different syllables, whereas in Sanskrit they belong always to the same syllable.

The *mediæ* are aspirated by allowing the spiritus lenis to be heard immediately after the explosion. In Sanskrit the mediæ aspiratæ were always pronounced as one sound; for we find words beginning with the following combinations, *ghn, dhm, ghr*, &c.

We must carefully remember that the Sanskrit *h* does not form part of the aspirated tenuis; for it is a sonant letter, and therefore cannot form part of the aspirated tenuis, which is surd.

The original aspirates in process of time lost their true character, and gradually changed into other sounds. Thus, in Greek, they became the corresponding fricatives; *e. g.* χ, which was originally a tenuis aspirata, became the fricatives, χ^1 and χ^2.

§. 17. Concrete Consonants.

These are those sounds which are formed by the vocal organs being placed at the same time in two different consonantal positions. The G. *sch* and the Fr. *j* are concrete consonants. These concrete sounds are perfectly distinct from groups of consonants, such as *x*, *ψ*, which Brücke calls *compositæ*. The G. *sch* is equivalent to $[s^1\chi^1]$: we first place the vocal organs in the χ^2-position, and then bend the tongue upwards into the s^1-position. The It. *c* in *ciceri* is equivalent to $t^1 \, [s^1\chi^2]$, while the E. *ch* in *church* is more nearly $t^1 \, [s^1\, \chi^3]$. The Fr. *j* in *jamais* is related to the G. *sch* as *b* is to *p*. It is therefore $[z^1y^2]$. The E. *j* in *joy* is similarly related to the

It. c in *ciceri*. It is therefore d^1 [z^1 y^2]. Max Müller differs from these views of Brücke; he says that *ch* in *church* does not consist of two consonants, but merely of half t and half *sh*, and therefore that it is merely equivalent to one whole consonant.

CHAPTER II.

THE INDO-EUROPEAN LANGUAGE.

§. 18. THIS is the name given to that language from which the whole family of the Indo-European languages are derived, and which therefore stand to it in the same relation as the Romance languages do to the Latin. As we could approximate to the roots and grammatical forms of the Latin language, even if we had no monuments of it, from a comparison of the roots and grammatical forms at present existing in the Romance languages, so analogously we may approximate to the roots and forms of the language of the Indo-Europeans from a comparison of the languages spoken by their descendants. For example, if we take the case of the numerals, we see at once that the names for the first ten numbers in any Romance language are not derived from those in any other, but from the Latin. The Sp. *ocho*, Port. *oito*, It. *otto*, Wall. *optu*, Fr. *huit*, are all formed independently of each other from the L. *octo ;* and if the L. *octo* did not exist, we could infer its existence from a comparison of these forms with each other. Similarly the Skr. *k'atvâras*, Gr. τέσσαρες, Æol. πέσσυρες, L. *quatuor*, Umb. *petur*, Ir. *ceathair* (m.), *ceteora* (*f.*), Welsh *pedwar* (m.), *pédair* (*f.*), Goth. *fidvôr*, Lith. *keturi*, &c., are all independent of each other, but they all presuppose an Indo-European form *kvatvâras*, which is nearly the same as the L. *quatuor*.

§. 19. The sounds that in all probability existed in this language, immediately before the separation of the Asiatic branch from the European, are given in the following table :—

	MUTES.			SEMIVOWELS.				VOWELS.
	unasp.		asp.	Spirants.		Nasals.	R-sound.	
	surd.	son.	son.	surd.	son.	son.	son.	
Gutt.	k	g	gh			n̈		a, â
Pal.					y			i, î
Cer.							(r l)?	
Dent.	t	d	dh	s		n	r l	
Lab.	p	b	bh		v	m		u, û

At an older period the I. E. possessed probably no aspirates, and only the single vowel *a*, *i* and *u* being subsequently developed out of this *a* on the one side, and from the vocalization of *y* and *v* on the other.

The representation of an original *a* by *a*, *e*, and *o* distinguishes the European branch of the Indo-European from the Asiatic; thus we have, in the following cases, *a* in Sanskrit and Zend, and *e* or *i* in Greek, Latin, &c.; Skr. and Z. *das'an*, Gr. δέκα, L. *decem*, O. H. G. *zehan*; Skr. *sad*, Z. *had*, Gr. ἕδος, L. *sedeo*, Goth. *sita*; Skr. *madhya*, Z. *maidhya*, Gr. μέσος, L. *medius*, Goth. *midjis*. This change of *a* into *e* and then into *i* occurred in very early times, while the change into *o* and then into *u* is much later. This change is believed by Curtius* to have arisen at a time when the North-European branches had separated from the Southern ones; for the Greek and Latin frequently agree in representing an original *a* by *o*, in cases where the Gothic, Lithuanian, &c., preserve the *a*, or change it to *i*; as in

Gr. γιγνώσκω, L. *gnosco*, O. H. G. *knâu*.
Gr. ὄϊς, L. *ovis*, Goth. *avistr*.
Gr. ὀκτώ, L. *octo*, Goth. *ahtau*.
Gr. δόμος, L. *domus*, A. S. *timber*, O. H. G. *zimbar*.

In this respect the Keltic languages are more akin to the Greek and Latin than to the languages of Northern Europe. When *e* and *o* had been developed out of *a*, the greater num-

---

* Curtius, "Grundzüge," p. 85.

ber of the Greek dialects made no further change; but the
Æolic dialect and the Italic languages frequently change this
e and *o* into *i* and *u*.

§. 20. The Guttural *ṅ* is an uncommon sound, and only
occurs before gutturals. *M* is an older sound than *n* : thus,
Skr. *damam* (acc. sing.) and L. *domum* are older than Gr. δόμον,
and L. *decem* than Skr. *das'an*. The change of *m* into *n* is
very common : thus G. *boden* comes from O. H. G. *bodam*,
Fr. *rien* from L. *rem*, It. *con* from L. *cum*, Fr. *nappe* from
L. *mappa*, Wall. *furnice* from L. *formica*.

The converse of this change seldom occurs; but, as it is
sometimes found in modern languages, as in E. *ransom* from
Fr. *rançon*, we may from analogy infer that a similar interchange between *m* and *n* existed in the Indo-European.

§. 21. From the number of cases in which *l* in Sanskrit
corresponds to *l* in the European languages, we infer that *l*, as
well as *r*, existed, in the Indo-European, although the *r*-sound
vastly predominated. Thus we have,

Skr. *kalya*, Gr. καλός, Goth. *hails*, E. *whole*.
Skr. *sphal*, Gr. σφάλλω, L. *fallo*, O. H. G. *fallan*.
Skr. *mala*, Gr. μέλας, L. *malus*, Goth. *mail*.
Skr. *lis'*, Gr. ὀλίγος, Goth. *leihts*.
Skr. *lû*, Gr. λύω, L. *reluo*, Goth. *laus* (loose).
Skr. *lubh*, Gr. λίπτομαι, L. *lubet*, Goth. *liubs*.
Skr. *lôta* (loot), Gr. λεία, L. *lucrum*, Goth. *laun*.
Skr. *lash*, Gr. λάω, L. *lascivus*, Goth. *lustus* (lust).

On the other hand, there are many roots in which the
European languages present *l* where the Sanskrit has *r*; thus,

Skr. *ûrmi* (a wave), Gr. ἐλύω, L. *volvo*, Goth. *valvjan*.
Skr. *par*, Gr. πλήρης, L. *plenus*, Goth. *fulls*.
Skr. *ruk'*, Gr. λευκός, L. *luceo*, Goth. *liuhath*.
Skr. *rik'*, Gr. λείπω, L. *linquo*, Goth. *laiba*.

This is one of the facts from which Lottner (K. Z., vol. vii.,
p. 19), infers that, after the Europeans separated from the

parent stock, they remained for some time united together as
one people.

R always has had a tendency to become *l*, as we see from
the Romance languages: thus, It. *albero* comes from L. *arbor*,
It. *célebro* from L. *cerebrum*, Fr. *autel* from L. *altare*, It. *pellegrino* from L. *peregrinus*. The reverse change also occurs, but
much less frequently: we find it in Fr. *rossignol* from L. *lusciniolus*, Fr. *apôtre* from L. *apostolus*, Fr. *chapitre* from
L. *capitulum*, Fr. *esclandre* from σκάνδαλον, Wall. *poporu* from
L. *populus*, Wall. *firu* from L. *filum*. In some of these cases
dissimilation has favoured this change.

§. 22. The Indo-European B.

The chief proof that *b* existed in the Indo-European is the
fact that it forms the chief element in the original sound *bh*.
That it must have had a very limited sphere, is proved by the
few cases in which it seems to be original. These cases are
the following:—Gr. βραχύς, βρόγχος, Goth. *praggan* (to press),
the fundamental idea being "narrowness;" Skr. *lamb* (to fall),
L. *labi*, E. *slip* (Benfey compares E. *limp*), Goth. *slĕpan* and
E. *sleep* come perhaps from this root, the fundamental idea
being that of "sinking down to rest;" Gr. κάνναβις, O. H. G.
hanf, E. *hemp*; Skr. *kubg'a* (crooked), Gr. κύβος, Goth. *hups*,
O. H. G. *huf*, L. *cubare*, E. *hip* and *hump*; Gr. ῥόμβος, ῥέμβω,
Goth. *vairpan*, G. *werfen*.* *B* is original in some imitative
words; but, as Grimm's law does not apply to such words, it
remains unchanged: thus we have Gr. βληχή, L. *balare*,
O. H. G. *blâzan*, E. *bleat*; Skr. *barbara*, Gr. βάρβαρος,
L. *balbus*, E. *bubble*; Gr. βομβυλίς, L. *bullire*, E. *bubble*.

Initial *b*, as Grassmann has pointed out, has generally in
Sanskrit, Greek, and Latin, been developed from other sounds:
in Sanskrit from *p*, *bh*, *m*, and *v*, as *banig'* (a merchant) from

---

* Consult Bickell in K. Z., vol. xiv., p. 425; and Grassmann in K. Z.,
vol. xii., p. 122.

pan (to buy), *bal* from *bhal*, *brû* from *mṛû*, and *baṭ* from *vaṭ*; in Greek and Latin from *gv*, as in Gr. βαρύς, βαίνω = L. *venio* for *gvenio*; from *dv*, as in L. *bis, bellum, bonus*; from *v*, as in Gr. βούλομαι (Skr. *vṛ*, L. *volo*), βρίζα; from *m*, as in Gr. βροτός, βλώσκω, βραδύς = Skr. *mṛdus* (mild and slow) = L. *blandus* for *mlandus* (E. *mild*); *bucca* (Skr. *mukha*); from *bh*, as in Gr. βρέμω, L. *fremo*, βασκαίνω, L. *fascino*; and from *p*, as in Gr. βόσκω (?), L. *bibo, buxus*.

§. 23. Wherever we find fricative sounds corresponding etymologically to explosive, we believe that the latter are original, as they require a stronger articulation than the former. We find examples of this in the following changes:—*t* becomes *s*, in Gr. σύ, Dor. τύ, L. *tu*; *d* becomes *l*,* in L. *lacruma* = Gr. δάκρυ; L. *levir* = Gr. δαήρ, Skr. *devṛ* (a husband's brother); L. *calamitas*, from an older *cadamitas*; *d* becomes *r* in L. *arvorsum* = *advorsum*, L. *meridies* for *medidies*, Sp. *lampara* from acc. sing. of L. *lampas*; *b* becomes *v* in Fr. *avoir* = L. *habere*; *k* becomes a sibilant in Fr. *cent* from L. *centum*, Skr. *das'an* from I. E. *dakam*, Skr. *s'van* from I. E. *kvan*, Fr. *cheval* from L. *caballus*. The modern Greek spirants have been developed from the old aspirates, and the Latin spirants *h* and *f* from the old *gh* and *bh*.

There are some exceptions to this law: thus *gv* has been developed from *v* † in It. *golpe* from L. *vulpes*, Fr. *gâter* and It. *guastare* from L. *vastare*, Fr. *guêpe* from L. *vespa*. *V* has become *p* on account of the *s'* in Z. *s'pâ* = Skr. *s'vâ*. In the Lesbian dialect we find β for F before ρ; here either F became β, or else β was pronounced as F. The Romans disliked the group *vu*, and frequently used *bu*, as in *ferbui* from *ferveo*; similarly the Greeks said βούλομαι for Fουλομαι. *D* represents

---

* In the "Rigveda" the symbol ळ is employed to represent the *l*-sound, into which an older *ḍ* is sometimes changed. This sound must have been either *dl* or *ld*.

† See Max Müller, vol. ii., p. 265, *seq.*; and Curtius, "Grundzüge," pp. 386, 527.

an older *l* and *r* in some Norwegian dialects; thus in Sogndal *ll* becomes *dl*, as in *kadla* for *kalla*, *gudl* for *gull*, &c. In Danish we have *ld* for *ll*, as in *fuld* = E. *full;* and *fald* = E. *fall.*

§. 24. That the *weak* aspirates existed in the Indo-European, is proved by the fact that the Sanskrit *weak* aspirates are represented in Zend by the mediæ and mediæ aspiratæ; in Slavic, Lettic, Gothic, and Irish, by the mediæ; and in Latin sometimes by the mediæ. Thus, we have Skr. *dhâ* (to place), Z. *dâ*, L. *do* (in *condo*), Lith. *dedù*, E. *do, doom;* Skr. *bhar* (to bear), Z. *bar*, L. *fero*, Goth. *baira*, Lith. *bérnas* (a child), E. *burden;* Skr. *bhû* (to be), Z. *bû*, L. *fui*, Lith. *bùti* (to be), E. *be;* Skr. *bhrâtar*, Z. *brâtar*, L. *frater*, Goth. *brôthar*, Ir. *bráthir;* Skr. *madhya*, Z. *maidhya*, L. *medius*, Osk. *mefiai* (= *mediæ*), Ir. *medón*, Goth. *midjis ;* I. E. *dnambhas*,* Skr. *nabhas*, L. *nubes*, Sl. *nebo*, Ir. *neamh*, Lith. *debesis*. These examples are sufficient to prove the original existence of the mediæ aspiratæ; for, if they had been developed from the mediæ in Sanskrit, after it had become a distinct language, we should find them represented in Gothic, for example, by *k*, *t*, and *p*, and not by *g*, *d*, and *b;* and if they had been developed from the tenues aspiratæ, we should not find them represented in the cognate languages by the mediæ.

§. 25. Whether the Indo-European possessed the hard, as well as the soft, aspirates is still a disputed question.† The main argument brought forward in support of the opinion that it did, is the fact that the Greek aspirates, which are hard, correspond in many cases to the hard aspirates in Sanskrit. Now, in all these cases I believe that the tenuis was the original sound, and that the aspiration is generally due to the influence of neighbouring sounds, which have sometimes fallen

---

* According to Lottner, who compares Gr. ἔνοφος.

† Consult Curtius, "Grundzüge," p. 375; and Grassmann in K. Z., vol. xii., p. 109.

out. Moreover, in many of these examples we find in Greek side-forms with the simple tenuis, which evidently contain older forms of the roots. Thus, a sibilant has aspirated the tenuis in the following cases:—*sphar* (caus. to throw), σφαῖρα, also σπαίρω, ἀσπαίρω; *sphur* (= *sphar*), σφῦρα, σφυρόν; *sphal* (caus. with *â*, to strike), σφάλλω, A. S. *feallan*, Lith. *pùlti* (to fall), *sphurg'* (to thunder), σφάραγος, *sphaṇt* (to split), σφήν; *phalaka* (a bench), σφέλας; *k'hid* (to cut), σχίζω, L. *scindo*. In κόγχος = *s'aṅkhas* the aspiration is due to the nasal. *Khalīnas* (nom. sing.) is borrowed from χαλινός. The aspirate in the ending of the 2 sing. perf. -*tha* = -θα (οἶσθα = *vettha*) is due to the falling out of *v* from the pronominal stem *tva*. Grassmann compares μάχη with *makha* (a warrior), ἀθήρ with *athari* (the point of a lance), μόθος with *math* (to agitate), and asserts that the aspirated tenuis in all these cases is original; but *makha* comes from *magh*, ἀθήρ is connected with *andhas* (plant). We find the asp. tenuis developed from the asp. media in *nâth* (to ask aid) from *nâdh*, E. *need*, O. H. G. *nôt*; in *atha* (then) from *adha*; in *kha* (aër, cœlum), Gr. χάος, L. *halare*; in *phal* (to bear fruit), L. *flos*, Goth. *blôma*; in *nakha*, ὀνυχ-, L. *unguis*, *ungula*, Ir. *ionga*, O. H. G. *nagal*, Lith. *n'agas*. It is much more probable that the Sanskrit hard aspirates and the Greek aspirates arose either from the soft aspirates or the tenues, than that both rows of aspirates existed in the Indo-European, and afterwards coalesced in Greek.

CHAPTER III.

Grimm's Law.*

§. 26. The roots of the Indo-European languages are subject to two distinct classes of changes—irregular or sporadic, and regular. The regular changes permeate all the dialects of a language, while the irregular show themselves chiefly in some one dialect. Thus, in Greek, χ, θ, φ, in all the dialects represent the original *gh, dh, bh* ; but ἴκκος, κῶς, πόκα, ὄκα, δᾶ, ὀδελός, are sporadic varieties of ἵππος, πῶς, πότε, ὅτε, γῆ, ὀβελός. The regular changes are threefold :—(1), we have the splitting up of an original sound into several others, as when an I. E. *a* is represented in Greek and Latin by *a, e, o* ; (2), we have the loss of an original sound running through an entire language, as in the case of the disappearance of the aspirates in Latin ; (3), we have the remarkable law of the dislocation of the consonants, discovered by Grimm, and called by him *Lautverschiebung*, which we now proceed to enunciate and illustrate.

§. 27. This law, stated generally, is as follows :—If the same root exist in Sanskrit, Greek, Latin, Gothic, and Old High German, when Sanskrit, Greek, and Latin present the aspirate, Gothic presents the corresponding media, and Old High German the corresponding tenuis ; when the first three languages present the media, Gothic has the tenuis, and Old High German the aspirate ; when the first three languages

---

* "Deutsche Grammatik von Dr. Jakob Grimm," vol. i., p. 584. Consult also " Gesammelte sprachwissenschaftliche Schriften" von Rudolph von Raumer, and Max Müller, vol. ii., p. 198.

present the tenuis, Gothic has the aspirate, and Old High German the media. This law may be tabularly exhibited thus:—

```
Skr. Gr. L.  GH DH BH  |  G  D  B   |  K  T  P
Goth.         G  D  B  |  K  T  P   |  GH DH BH
O. H. G.      K  T  P  |  GH DH BH  |  G  D  B
```

These letters, of course, are only symbols; for in Latin we have no real aspirates, but merely the corresponding breathings, and moreover the dental breathing is wanting in Latin; in Greek we have only the hard aspirates; in Sanskrit H frequently takes the place of an older GH, DH, or BH; in Gothic the guttural and labial aspirates are replaced by H and F; and in Old High German for the expected guttural and labial mediæ we find H and F. Extending this law to Keltic, Slavic, and Lettic, we may add that these languages, though for the most part they stand on the same line as the Sanskrit, represent the soft aspirates always by the corresponding mediæ. Translating these symbols, then, into the actual consonants that represent them in each language, we have the following tables:—

I.

	(1).	(2).	(3).
I. E.	*gh*,	*dh*	*bh*
Skr.	*gh, h*	*dh, h*	*bh, h*
Z.	*g, gh, g', z, zh,*	*d, dh*	*b*
Gr.	χ	θ	φ
L.	*h, f, g,*	*f, d, b,*	*f, b*
Kel	*g*	*d*	*b*
Sl.	*g, z, ž*	*d*	*b*
Lith.	*g, ž,*	*d*	*b*
Goth.	*g*	*d*	*b*
O. H. G.	*k*	*t*	*p*

II.

	(1).	(2).	(3).
I. E.	*g*	*d*	*b*
Skr.	*g, g'*	*d*	*b*
Z.	*g, gh, g', z, zh*	*d, dh*	*b*
Gr.	γ	δ	β
L.	*g*	*d*	*b*
Kel.	*g*	*d*	*b*
Sl.	*g, ž, z,*	*d*	*b*
Lith.	*g, ž*	*d*	*b*
Goth.	*k*	*t*	*p*
O. H. G.	*ch*	*z, sz*	*f, pf*

III.

	(1).	(2).	(3).
I. E.	*k*	*t*	*p*
Skr.	*k, kh, k', s'*	*t, th*	*p, ph*
Z.	*k, kh, k', s'*	*t, th*	*p, f*
Gr.	κ	τ	π
L.	*c, q,*	*t*	*p*
Kel.	*c, ch,*	*t, th*	*p*
Sl.	*k, c, č , s*	*t*	*p*
Lith.	*k, sz,*	*t*	*p*
Goth.	*h, g*	*th, d*	*f, b*
O. H. G.	*h, g*	*d*	*f, v, b*

§. 28. Examples of Grimm's Law.*

I. (1). Skr. *dirgha* (long), Z. *darĕgha* (long), Gr. δολιχός, L. *longus*, Goth. *laggs*. Skr. *laghu* (light), Gr. ἐλαχύς, L. *levis* for *legvis*, O. H. G. *liht*, Kel. *lugu* in *Lugudunum*, another form of *Lugdunum*. Skr. *gharsh* (to rub), Gr. χρίω, L. *frio, frico.* Skr. *ghas* (to eat), L. *hostis*, O. L. *fostis, hospes* (qui ci-

---

* In these examples I have nearly always omitted the corresponding roots in Slavic, Lithuanian, and Keltic.

bum petit), Goth. *gasts*, E. *guest*, Lith. *gaspadù* (hospitium), and, according to Bopp, Gr. γαστήρ. Skr. *haryâmi* (I love), Gr. χαίρω, L. *gratus*, Goth. *faihu-gairns* (greedy of money), E. *yearn*, O. H. G. *kiri* (desire). Skr. *hyas* (yesterday), Gr. χθές, L. *heri, hesternus*, Goth. *gistra*, E. *yesterday*, O. H. G. *kestar*. Skr. *hansa* (a goose), Gr. χήν, L. *anser*, Goth. *gans*, E. *goose*, O. H. G. *kans*. Skr. *vah* (to carry), Gr. ὄχος, L. *veho*, Goth. *vigs* (via). O. H. G. *waggan* (currus), Gr. χόρτος, L. *hortus, cohors*, E. *garden, gird*, O. H. G. *karto*, Goth. *gards* (a house).

I. (2). Skr. *indh* (to burn), Gr. αἴθω, L. *æstus, ædes*, A. S. *ád*, O. H. G. *eit* (fire). Skr. *rudhira* (blood), Gr. ἐρυθρός, L. *ruber, rufus*, E. *red*, O. H. G. *rôt*. Skr. *dhê* (to drink), Gr. θῆσθαι, θηλή, L. *filius, femina*, Goth. *daddja* (lacto), O. H. G. *tâu* (lacto). Skr. *dharsh* (to dare), Z. *daresh* (to dare), Gr. θάρσος, L. *fortis*, Goth. *gadaursan* (to dare), O. H. G. *gitar*. Skr. *dhû* (to shake, blow), Z. *dunman* (vapour), Gr. θύω, θύελλα, θυμός, L. *fumus, suffio*, Goth. *dauns* (odor), E. *dust*, O. H. G. *tunst* (storm).

I. (3). Skr. *bhû* (to be), Z. *bû* (to be), Gr. φύω, L. *fui*, E. *be*, O. H. G. *pim* (I am). Skr. *bhrâtar*, Z. *brâtar*, Gr. φρατρία, L. *frater*, Goth. *brôthar*, O. H. G. *pruodar*. Z. *bar* (to bore), Gr. φάρος, φάραγξ, L. *forare*, E. *bore*, O. H. G. *poran*. Skr. *bhadra* (best), E. *better, best*. Skr. *bhang'* (to break), Gr. ῥήγνυμι, L. *frango*, Goth. *brikan*, O. H. G. *prechan*.

II. (1). Skr. *g'an* (to beget), Z. *zan* (to beget), Gr. γένος, L. *genus*, Goth. *kuni* (race), E. *kind, child*, O. H. G. *chind* (offspring). Skr. *gar* (to sound), Z. *gar* (to sing), Gr. γῆρυς, L. *garrio, gallus*, E. *call*. Skr. *guru* (heavy), Goth. *kaurs* (heavy), E. *care*. Skr. *bhug'* (to enjoy, endure), L. *fruor, fungor*, Goth. *brûkjan*, E. *brook*. Skr. *ganḍa* and *hanu* (gena), Gr. γένυς, L. *gena*, Goth. *kinnus* (chin), O. H. G. *chinni*.

II. (2). Skr. *druma* (wood), Z. *dru* (wood), Gr. δρῦς, δόρυ, δένδρον, Goth. *triu* (tree). Skr. *dam* (to tame), Gr. δαμάω, L. *domare, dominus*, Goth. *gatamjan* (to tame), O. H. G. *zami* (tame). Skr. *dis'* (to show), Gr. δείκνυμι, L. *dico*, Goth. *teiha* (nuntio), O. H. G. *zeigôm*. Skr. and Z. *das'an*, Gr. δέκα, L. *decem*, Goth. *taihun*, O. H. G. *zehan*. Skr. and Z. *dva*, Gr. δύω, L. *duo*, Goth. *tvai*, G. *zwei*. Skr. *vid* (to perceive), οἶδα = Goth. *vait* = Skr. *vêda*, L. *video*, O. H. G. *wizan*. Skr. *dant* (tooth), Z. *dañt*, Gr. ὀδούς, L. *dens*, Goth. *tunthus*, O. H. G. *zand*. Gr. ῥίζα for Ϝριδια, Lesb. βρίσδα, L. *radix*, Goth. *vaurts* (root), O. H. G. *wurza*.

II. (3). Consult § 22.

III. (1). Skr. *s'vas'ura* (socer), Z. *qas'ura*, Gr. ἑκυρός, Gr. *socer*, Goth. *svaihra*, G. *schwager*. Skr. *dars'* (to see), Gr. δέρκω, O. S. *torht* (bright), E. *torch*, O. H. G. *zoraht*. Skr. *as'ru* (a tear), Gr. δάκρυ, O. L. *dacruma*, Goth. *tagr*, O. H. G. *zahar*. Skr. *s'âlâ* (house), Gr. καλία, L. *cella, domi-cilium, celare*, E. *hall, hell, hole*. Skr. *kalya* (healthy), Gr. καλός, Goth. *hails*, E. *whole, heal*, G. *heil*. Skr. *s'î* (to lie), Gr. κεῖμαι, L. *quies, civis* = Osk. *kevs*, Goth. *haims* (village), E. *home, hamlet*. Gr. κλέπτω, L. *clepo*, Goth. *hliftus* = κλέπτης. Skr. *s'ru* (to hear), Gr. κλύω, κλέος = Skr. *s'ravas*, L. *cluo, cliens*, Goth. *hliuma* (ἀκοή), O. H. G. *hlût* (loud), Sl. *slava* (glory). Skr. *karsh* (to draw), L. *accerso*, E. *hearse, harrow*. Skr. *kâs* (to cough), E. *husky*, O. H. G. *huosto*.

III. (2). Skr. *tri*, Z. *thri*, Gr. τρεῖς, L. *tres*, Goth. *threis*, O. H. G. *drî*. Skr. *tarsh* (to thirst), Z. *tarshna* (thirst), Gr. τέρσομαι, L. *torreo, terra* (?), Goth. *thaurstei* (thirst), G. *durst*. Skr. *tar* (to cross), Z. *tarô* (across), Gr. τέρμα, L. *terminus, trans* = Umb. *traf*, O. N. *thröm* (margo), E. *through*, O. H. G. *drum* (finis). Skr. *pat** (to fly), *patra* (a wing), Gr. πέτομαι, πτερόν, L. *peto, penna* (O. L. *pesna*), *acci-piter, præpes*, O.H.G. *fedara* (a wing), E. *feather*. Skr. and Z. *tan* (to stretch), Gr. τείνω, L. *tendo, tenuis*, Goth. *thanja* (extendo), O. H. G. *dunni*

---

* Benfey deduces Skr. *patrin* (a mountain) and Gr. πέτρος from this root, remarking that in the old poetical language clouds and rocks are identified, and the clouds considered as wings of the mountains!

(thin). Skr. *tu* (to be powerful, to increase), Z. *tu* (to be able), Gr. τύλος, ταῦς μέγας (Hesych.), L. *tumeo, tuber, tueor, totus*, Umb. *tauta* (a city), O. Pr. *tauta* (land), Ir. *tuath* (people), Goth. *thiuda* (people), E. *thumb*, O. H. G. *dûmo* (thumb).

III. (3). Skr. *apa* (away), Z. *apa,* Gr. ἀπὸ, L. *ab,* Goth. *af,* O. H. G. *aba.* Skr. *saptan,* Z. *haptan,* Gr. ἑπτά, L. *septem,* Goth. *sibun.* Skr. *parâ* (away), Z. *para* (from), Gr. παρά, L. *per,* Goth. *fra-,* E. *from,* O. H. G. *far-,* N. H. G. *ver.* Skr. and Z. *par* (to bring over), Gr. περάω, L. *porta,* Goth. *faran* (to go), E. *fare,* G. *erfahren.* Skr. and Z. *par* (to fill), Gr. πίμπλημι, L. *plenus, populus,* E. *folk, full.* Skr. *prî* (to please), Z. *frî* (to love), Gr. πραΰς, E. *friend.* Gr. πύξ, L. *pugnus,* E. *fist.* Gr. πλίνθος, E. *flint* (?). Gr. παῦρος, L. *paucus,* E. *few.* Skr. *prath* (to extend), Gr. πλατύς, L. *Latium,* E. *flat.*

§. 29. No satisfactory explanation of the origin of the changes expressed by this law has ever been given. It has been suggested* that "this phonetic diversity is due to a previous state of language in which the two or three principal points of consonantal contact were not yet felt as definitely separated from each other." Each of the branches of the Indo-European family, it is maintained, modified this sound in its own way; hence we have different forms of the original vague sound. But, it is extremely unlikely† that such vague sounds existed in the original Indo-European language contemporaneously with the strong articulation which is peculiar to all old languages. If we thus account for the origin of Skr. *ap* and L. *aqua,* Æol. πίσυρες, and L. *quatuor,* &c., we will be forced from analogy to account for the origin of the Wallachian *apa, epa, patru*‡ from *aqua, equa, quatuor,* in

* By Max Müller, vol. ii., pp. 180, 181.
† Curtius, " Grundzüge," p. 366.
‡ Max Müller suggests, as an explanation of these forms, that the Legions which colonized Dacia were raised in the Oscan and Umbrian districts of Italy, where *p* represented the Latin *qu.* But, in addition to the obvious improbability of this account, it may be added that it does not

the same way, and to assert that these Latin words were pronounced with a vague and indistinct consonantal sound; this, however, is too absurd to be maintained for a moment.

The very example (Skr. *gharma*, Gr. θερμός, L. *formus*) given by Max Müller should have been sufficient to demonstrate the incorrectness of this theory; for what pronounceable sound can be imagined which could approximate to each of these guttural (*gh*), dental (θ), and labial (*f*) sounds, without being exactly any of them? Such divergencies arose, not from any vague articulation on the part of the Indo-Europeans, but from other causes. These were (1), the influence of neighbouring sounds; (2), the springing up of adventitious or parasitic sounds; (3), a psychological principle of differentiation, *i. e.*, a desire to keep up within the limits of the same language a difference between words or sounds that threaten to become identical, or to develope such a difference between words or sounds that are at a given moment identical. We find examples of (1) in the derivation of the Wall. *epa*, *apa* from *equa*, *aqua*; for the *u* (*v*) became *p* through the influence of the tenuis *q* (*k*). We find (2) exemplified in such forms as χθές, Skr. *hyas*, I. E. *ghyas*, where the *y* developed *d* before itself, as it frequently does, and then fell out, this δ afterwards becoming θ on account of the preceding χ.

We find numerous examples of psychological processes in all languages. Thus in Greek we have ἀμείνων, μείζων, τείνω, for ἀμενγων, λεγγων, τενγω, where the ι arises from the throwing back of the original *y* that once existed in the last syllable, and where this *y* must have been present to the mind before it was pronounced. This effect—called variously Hyperthesis, Infection, or Umlaut—appears in its complete form in Zend. We find it also in English, as in the verb *to fell*, the

seem to be borne out by the forms of the Wallachian language. The example (Osc. *pomtis* = L. *quinque*) adduced by himself overthrows this theory; for the Wallachian for five is *quinqué*, a word evidently of pure Latin origin.

causative of *to full*, where the *e* (*ai*) arises from *a* by hyperthesis. In Latin forms such as *scripsi* we also see the effect of Psychological influence, for as in the hyperthesis of *i* we think of the following *y*, so we think of the following *s*, and change the *b* of *scribo* into *p*, as *s* is a hard sound. We see a similar cause at work in the origin of the It. *buono, nuovo, fuora, fuoco*, from L. *bonus, novus, foris, focus*. The Italians had lost the distinction between the short and the long *o*, but they still felt that a distinction should be made between the *o* of *nŏvus* and the *o* of *nonus*; so, while they kept *o* wherever it was long, they employed *uo* to represent *o* when it was short.

In the old Norse imperfect indicative we find the *a* of the singular changed into *ö* in the plural, on account of the *u* of the final syllable, which therefore must have been present to the mind during the pronunciation of the first syllable; thus, sing. 1. *kalladha*, 2. *kalladhir*, 3. *kalladhi*; pl. 1. *kölludhum*, 2. *kölludhut*, 3. *kölludhu*.*

§. 30. The changes of sounds, noticed in the last section, arise from what has been called by Max Müller *Dialectic Growth*; but there are other changes that manifest themselves not only in some ancient languages, but also much more frequently in their modern representatives. These latter arise from what he calls *Phonetic Decay*;† and the cause of this decay he rightly traces to laziness, or want of muscular energy on the part of the speaker. Thus, as he remarks, nearly all the changes that have taken place in the transition from Anglo-Saxon to modern English belong to this class. We have *silly* from *sælig*, *woman* from *wifman*, *lord* from *hláford*, *king* from *cyning*, &c. Similarly we have *squire* from Fr. *escuier*,

* Aasen's "Norsk Grammatik," p. 224.

† Max Müller, vol. ii., pp. 176–178. Curtius calls this phenomenon *Verwitterung*, thus comparing it to the decay caused by the operation of the atmosphere.

L. *scutarius;* *stranger* from Fr. *estrangier,* L. *extraneus; sexton* from Fr. *sacristain; chapter* from Fr. *chapitre,* L. *capitulum; damsel* from Fr. *demoiselle,* L. *dominicella; Sir* from Fr. *sieur,* L. *senior.* In Greek the insertion of the mediæ between μ and ρ, or ν and ρ, is due to the same cause, ἄνδρες and γαμβρός being more easily pronounced than ἀνρες and γαμρος. We find similar insertions in English, as to *slumber* from A. S. *slumerian, cinders* from L. *cineres,* &c. In Goth. *hunds,* E. *hound* (L. *canis*), *d* has been added to facilitate the pronunciation. The *ds* in *gold* and *mind* have been explained in the same way, but wrongly so; for *gold* is the Gothic *gulth* = I. E. *ghar-ta* from I. E. and Skr. *ghar* (to shine), whence Skr. *hiraṇa, hiranya* (gold), Z. *zaranu, zaranya* (gold), Gr. χρυσός = χρυτγυς = I. E. *ghartyas,* χλουνός = χρυσός (Hesych.), Phryg. γλουρός χρυσός (Hesych.); and *mind* = L. *ment* in *mentis.* From this root *ghar* come also Skr. *hríku, hlíku* (tin), Gr. χαλκός, and L. *glisco.*

§. 31. Apparent Exceptions to Grimm's Law.*

The first class of these exceptions consists of natural sounds (naturlaute), onomatopœic, and imitative words; thus we have as natural sounds, Skr. *attâ* (mother), Gr. ἄττα, L. *atta,* Goth. *atta* (father); *ma* and *pa,* the words used by infants for their food and their parents, whence arise Gr. μάμμη, ἄππα, L. *mamma, mamilla, papilla,* G. *amme,* E. *mamma, papa, paps, pap;* Skr. *tâta* (dear, used chiefly by parents addressing their children, and children their parents), Gr. τέττα, τάτα, τίτθη, τιθήνη, L. *tata,* E. *tit, teat,* O. H. G. *tutto* (breast), *toto* (godfather), Lith. *teta* (aunt): as onomatopœic and imitative words, we have Skr. *hrésh* (to neigh), O. H. G. *hross,* E. *horse;* Skr. *hikkâ,* E. *hiccough;* Gr. ὑλακτῶ, E. *howl,* G. *heulen;* Gr. κλαγγή, L. *clango,* E. *clank, clatter, clap,*

---

* For the materials of sections 31 and 32 I am almost entirely indebted to the instructive articles of Lottner and Grassmann, in K. Z., vol. xi., p. 161; and vol. xii., p. 131.

O. N. *klaka* ; L. *grunnio*, E. *grunt* ; Gr. μυκᾶσθαι, μηκᾶσθαι, G. *meckern* ; Gr. λάπτω, L. *lambo, labrum*, E. *lap, lip.*

A second class consists of borrowed words. L. *tus* is borrowed from Gr. θύος; if it were genuine Latin, it would begin with *f*, as the root is Skr. *dhû.* L. *scalpo* and *sculpo,* along with the art of sculpture, were borrowed from the Greeks; for these words correspond to Gr. γλάφω and γλύφω, the *p* representing the hard φ; the words *glaber* and *glubo* are genuine Latin words, *b* being the exact equivalent of the Gr. φ. *Scribo* also exactly corresponds to γράφω, with the exception of the prefixed *s*, which proves either that writing was known to the Greeks and Italians while they still formed one people, or that *scribo* was borrowed from the Greeks in very early times, when φ was still soft. When a word belonging to any one of the three classes of languages, whose consonants are regulated according to Grimm's law, is similar in meaning and consonants to a word belonging to either of the other classes, we may lay down, as a general rule, either that one of these words was borrowed from the other, or else that there is no connexion between them. E. *husky* has nothing to do with Z. *huska* (dry) ; for *husky* is connected with Skr. *kâs* (to cough), and *huska* = Skr. *s'ushka* (dry, emaciated), Gr. σαυκός (dry), L. *siccus.* E. *go* is not from same root as Skr. *gâ*, but we find it in Skr. *hâ* (to go), I. E. *ghâ.* E. *look* is not the Skr. *lok* (to see), but rather *laksh* (to see) = *lag + s.* E. *whole* is not the same as Gr. ὅλος; for E. *h* represents an I. E. *k*, while the Greek aspirate represents an I. E. *s.* E. *call* is not connected with Gr. καλεῖν, nor E. *care* with L. *cura;* for E. *c* requires *g* in the corresponding Greek and Latin roots; E. *call* corresponds to Skr. *gar* (to praise), *gir* (a voice), Gr. γῆρυς, L. *garrio, gallus,* and E. *care* to Skr. *guru* (heavy), L. *gravis.*

A third class of exceptions arises from sounds having been irregularly changed within the same language: thus *h* in E. *heart* appears to represent *h* in Skr. *hrd*, but here the Skr. *h* has been developed from an I. E. *k*, as we see from the cognate forms, Gr. καρδία, L. *cor*, Ir. *cride*. The following cases are easily explained by supposing that the corresponding Indo-European roots began and ended with aspirates. Thus we have, I. E. *bhudhna*, Skr. *budhna* (depth), Gr. πυθμήν, L. *fundus*, O. H. G. *bodam*, E. *bottom;* I. E. *bhudh*, Skr. *budh* (to know), Gr. πυνθάνομαι, Goth. *biuda* (I know); I.E. *bhandh*, Skr. *bandh* (to bind), Gr. πενθερός, πεῖσμαι, L. *fascis*, *funis*, E. *bind;* I. E. *bhidh*, Gr. πείθω, L. *fido*, Goth. *bidja;* I. E. *bhâdh*, Skr. *bâdh* (to repel), Gr. πάσχω (for παθ-σκω), L. *fendo*, O. N. *böd* (a fight), A. S. *beadu;* I. E. *bhâghu*, Skr. *bâhu* (arm), Gr. πῆχυς, O. N. *bogr*, O. H. G. *buoc;* I. E. *bhaghu*, Skr. *bahu* (large), Gr. παχύς; I. E. *bhugh*, Skr. *baṅh* (to grow), Goth. *bagms* (tree), E. *beam;* I. E. *bhugh*, Skr. *bhug'* (to bend), Gr. φεύγω, L. *fugio*, Goth. *biuga* (I bend); I. E. *bhargh*, Gr. φράσσω (for φραγγω), Goth. *bairga* (I guard), *baurgs* (a town); I. E. *bhargh*, L. *flagellum*, Goth. *bliggvan* (to scourge); I. E. *dhûbh*, Skr. *dhûp* (to fumigate), Gr. τῦφος (smoke), τυφλός, Goth. *daubs* (deaf), *dumbs* (dumb), G. *taub ;* I. E. *dhigh*, Skr. *dih* (to smear), Gr. θιγγάνω, L. *fingo*, Goth. *deiga* (I form), *daigs* (dough), G. *teig;* I. E. *dhagh*, Skr. *dah* (to burn), Goth. *dags* (day), O. H. G. *tâht*, (a lamp-wick), G. *tag, docht;* I. E. *dhughatar*, Skr. *duhitar*, Goth. *dauhtar*, O. H. G. *tohtar:* this word comes perhaps from the next root, and means the "milker;" I. E. *dhugh*, Skr. *duh* (to milk, to enjoy), Goth. *dugan* (to be useful), E. *dug*, Ir. *diugaim* (I drink off), Scot. *deoghail* (mammas sugere); I. E. *dhrugh*, Skr. *druk* (to hurt), Gr. θέλγω (?) L. *frustra*, Goth. *driugan*, O. N. *draugr* (a ghost), Z. *drug'* (an evil spirit), O. H. G. *triugan* (to deceive), Ir. *droch* (bad); I. E. *ghabh*, Skr. *g'abh*, (to gape), E. *gape;* I. E. *ghardh*, Skr. *gardh* (to desire), Goth. *grédags* (hungry), E. *greedy*, O. H. G. *kir* (desire), G. *gier*, Ir. *gradh* (love). *D* in Skr. *dvâra* (a door), represents an I. E. *dh;* for we have Gr. θύρα, L. *fores*, Goth. *daur*, O. H. G. *tor.*, Ir. *dor* (a door). Gr. γε (Skr. *ha*, Ved. *gha*), may have arisen on European soil from an older χε, from same root as χι in ἥχι, Skr. *hi*. Bopp, however, connects with γε the *k* in Goth. *mik, thuk,* and the *h* in O. H. G. *unsih, iwih,* which can only be explained on the supposition of an original *g*. In Skr. *aham*, Gr. ἐγώ, L. *ego*, Goth. *ik*, Skr. *mahat*, Gr. μεγας, L. *magnus*, Goth. *mikils* = μεγάλος, Skr. *hanu* (jaw), Gr. γένυς, L. *gena*, Goth. *kinnus*, Skr. *laṅgh* (to jump), Gr. λαγώς, Goth. *laikan*, the Gothic and Greek forms point back to an I. E. *g*, while the Skr. *h* represents an I. E. *gh*. Hence we may infer either that the Indo-European possessed these roots in a double form before the separation of the Sanskrit from the other languages, or that the Sanskrit subsequently aspirated the original *g*, and then reduced it to *h*.

§. 32. ACTUAL EXCEPTIONS TO GRIMM'S LAW.

These exceptions occur in the consonantal groups *sk, st, sp*. Thus we have Skr. *k'had* (to conceal), from I. E. *skad*, Gr. σκότος, Goth. *skadus* (shadow), Ir. *scath* (shade); L. *piscis*, Goth. *fisks*; Skr. *k'hid* (to cut), from I. E. *skid*, Gr. σχίζω, L. *scindo*, Goth. *skaida* (separo), Ir. *scaithim* (I cut off); L. *hostis*, Goth. *gasts*; Skr. *târa* (star), Gr. ἀστήρ, L. *stella*, Goth. *stairnô*; Skr. *tud* (to strike), from I. E. *stud* (?), Gr. Τυδεύς (the striker—compare Charles *Martel* and Judas *Maccabæus*), L. *tundo, tudes* (hammer); Goth. *stauta* (I strike); Gr. στείχω, Goth. *steiga* (I ascend); Gr. πτύω, L. *spuo, pituita*, Goth. *speiva* (spuo).

An original tenuis sometimes appears as a media. Thus we have Gr. δάκρυ, Goth. *tagr*; L. *septem*, Goth. *sibun*; L. *quatuor*, Goth. *fidvôr*; Gr. κρατύς, Goth. *hardus*; L. *centum*, Goth. *hund*; L. *pater*, Goth. *fadar*; L. *mater*, A. S. *môdor* (Goth. *brôthar* and E. *father*, &c. are regular); Gr. κύτος, A. S. *hŷd* (hide).

In the present participle we have Goth. *-and* for Skr. *-ant*, Gr. *-οντ*, as Goth. *bairands* (nom. sing. masc.) = Gr. φέρων, E. *friend, fiend*. In the past participle we have Goth. *-d* for

Skr. *-ta*. This Goth. *d* must have arisen from an older *th*, of which traces are still found, as in *fads* and *faths* = Skr. *patis*, *kunths* (known) = Skr. *g'ñâtas* = Gr. γνωτός (whence E. *uncouth*), *bairith* and *bairid* = Skr. *bharati*.

We find the mediæ unchanged in the following cases:— Skr. *gar* (sonare), E. *nightin-gale;* Skr. *g'arbh* (aperire), Gr. γράφω, Goth. *graba* (fodio), E. *grave, grub*, Ir. *grabhaim* (I carve), *grafaim* (I write), *grafan* (a grubbing axe) ; Skr. *gras* (vorare), L. *gramen*, E. *grass* (unless *grass* be from I. E. and Skr. *ghar* (to shine) whence *harit* (green) Gr. χλόη, L. *holus*, E. *green) ;* Skr. *hlâd* (to be glad), Gr. κίχλαδα, E. *glad*. In many of the cases where a media is retained, this effect is due to the influence of a neighbouring *l, m, n*, or *r*.

The original tenuis is also unchanged in the following cases : Gr. τεταγών, L. *tango*, Goth. *têkan* (to touch), E. *take ;* Skr. *pathas* = Gr. πάτος, A. S. *pād*, E. *path*.

In the three following cases a Gothic *tenuis* corresponds to an I. E. aspirate : I. E. *magh*, Skr. *mah* (to be great), *mâmahyê* (macto), *makha* (a warrior), Gr. μάχομαι, L. *macto, macellum*, Goth. *meki* (a sword) ; I. E. *ghrabh*, Skr. *grah*, Ved. *grabh* (to seize), Gr. γρῖφος, Goth. *greipan* (to seize), E. *grip, grab*, Ir. *grabaim* (I devour) : Gr. σκάφος, σκάπτω for σκαφτω, Goth. *skip* (ship).

CHAPTER IV.

The Sanskrit Alphabet.*

§. 33. Tabular View of the Sounds.

MUTES.				SEMIVOWELS.			VOWELS.	
unasp.		asp.		Spirants.	Nasals.	r & l-sounds		
surd. son.		surd. son.		surd. son.				
Gutt. k g		kh gh		h̤ h	ṅ		a, â	
Pal. k' g'		k'h g'h		s' y	ñ		i, i } ê, âi	
Cer. ṭ ḍ		ṭh ḍh		sh	ṇ	(r, l) ?	(ṛ, ṝ, l) ? } ô, âu
Dent. t d		th dh		s	n	r, l	ṛ, ṝ, l
Lab. p b		ph bh		v	m		u, û	

Sanskrit writing is called by the native grammarians Dêvanâgarî, which means the nâgarî of the gods or brahmans. Nâgarî is the name applied to the current style of writing used by the Hindus, and is supposed to be derived from nagara (a city), thus meaning "the art of writing as practised in cities" (M. Müller's "Skr. Gr." p. 1). The names of the letters are formed by adding kâra (making) to each sound; thus a is called akâra, k, kakâra, as each consonant is supposed to have a short a inherent in it. R forms an exception, and is called rêpha (burring), from rêbh (to sound), Gr. ῥοῖβδος.

---

* Sanskṛta means properly "what is made fit;" hence it came to mean purified, as being made fit for sacred purposes. This is why this name is applied to the ancient sacred language of the Vedas. The local dialects of India are called Prâkṛta, i. e. "what has a type, or original" (Benfey's "Skr. Lex."), this type (prâkṛti) being Sanskrit. Sanskria is from sam (σύν) and skar (to cut), according to Lottner, who thinks that in this compound skar is mixed up with kar (to make).

§. 34. Anusvâra, Anunâsika and Visarga.

Anusvâra, ṅ (from *anu*, after, and *svâra*, sound), is a nasal after-sound, and is compared by Bopp to the Fr. *n* at the end of a syllable. It is, however, properly speaking, not an after-sound, but merely a modification of the preceding vowel (§. 10). Its pronunciation is very weak, for it does not prevent the euphonic influence of an *i* or *u* upon a following *s*; in prosody, however, it and Visarga make a preceding short vowel long, when the next syllable begins with a consonant. It occurs in the middle of words before the sibilants and *h*, as *dans'* (to bite), *hansa* (goose), *sinha* (lion). Before *y*, *r*, and *v*, in the middle of words it is only found in reduplicated syllables, as *yanyamyatê*. Another anusvâra is used for the nasals, merely "for the sake of neatness in writing," as Colebrook says. This must always receive the same pronunciation as the nasal in the place of which it stands. In Prâkrit a final *m* always, and, as is never the case in Sanskrit, the dental *n* become the anusvâra (Bopp's "Skr. Gr.," p. 17).

Anunâsika (from *anu*, after, and *nâsikâ*, the nose), is a still weaker nasal sound than Anusvâra; its weakness is shown from the fact that it can be followed by *l* and *r*. It is very nearly equivalent to the Fr. *n* in *genre*. Such a combination is generally avoided in French by inserting *d*, as in *viendrai:* compare ἀνδρός for ἀνρος.

Visarga, ḥ, is an euphonic change of final *s* and *r*. It may also take the place of *s* before the loc. pl. ending *su*. The Visarga that occurs before *k* and *kh* is formed by the root of the tongue and is called *G'ihvâmûlîya;* that occurring before *p*, *ph*, and a pause, by the palate, and is called *Upadhmânîya;* *s* therefore before labials, is equivalent to the blowing sound *f*. We see the same change in other languages: thus the Irish *s* sometimes corresponds to the Welsh *f*; we have in Greek the two forms φήρ and θήρ, and L. *rufus*, beside ἐρυθρός. We may explain on this ground the change of final *as* into *ô* in Sanskrit, through the steps *as, af, av, au, ô.*

§. 35. The Vowels.

Sanskrit had no short *e* or *o*, though the short *a* had both a clear and an obscure sound (*Pán.* VIII. 4, 68). Short *e* and *o* are similarly wanting in Gothic. Skr. *ă* is represented in Greek by ᾰ, ε, ο; and Skr. *â* by ᾱ, η, ω; in some cases Skr. *â* corresponds to Gr. ᾰ, ε, ο, as in *âgas* = ἄγος, *vâstu* = Fάστυ, the participial suffix *-mânas* = -μενος (L. *-minus*) and -μνος (L. *-mnus*) in μέδιμνος, μέριμνα (L. *alumnus, columna*), *dhâman* = θέμα, *dâru* = δόρυ, *g'ânu* = γόνυ (L. *genu*), *g'ag'âna* = γέγονα, *bhâras* = φόρος, *dâtâ* = δοτήρ, ο in ἔχομεν, &c. = *â* in *vahâmas*, &c. In Bengali *ă* has either become *o*, or been lost, as in B. *opotyo* = Skr. *apatya*; B. *ontor* = Skr. *antara*. $\mathcal{R}$ is pronounced as *ri* in *merrily*. It is never original, but has always been developed from *r*, preceded or followed by any vowel; thus we have *tṛtîya* (tertius) from *tri*, *stṛnômi* = στόρνυμι, *s'ṛinômi* (I hear) from *s'ru*, *bhṛkuṭi* (a frown) from *bhrû* (an eyebrow), *pṛk'h* from *prak'h* (to ask), *pitṛ* from *pitar*, *dâtṛ* from *dâtâr*, *pitar* and *dâtâr* being the original forms, as the accusatives *pitaram* = πατέρα, and *dâtâram* = δοτῆρα prove. The vowel $\hat{\mathcal{r}}$ is pronounced exactly as *rî*; it only occurs in nouns whose stems end in *ṛ*, and which lengthen this vowel after the analogy of other nouns, whose stems end in other vowels; thus, *pitṝn* = πατέρας, *duhitṝs* = θυγατέρας, *datṝnâm* = *datorum*. The vowel *ḷ* is pronounced as *li*. It has been developed from an older *ṛ*, and occurs only in the root *klp* (to create), which is derived from *kṛ* and the causal *p*, which is connected, perhaps, with the root of ποιέω. Bopp connects E. *help*, and Benfey L. *corpus*, with this root. The long *ḷ* vowel never occurs, and is merely an invention of the grammarians.

§. 36. Weight of the Vowels.

A is heavier than *u*, and *u* heavier than *i*; that is, *a* occurs in the lightest forms, *i* in the heaviest, and *u* in the intermediate. For instance, the terminations *-vas*, *-thas*, *-tas* are heavier than *-mi*, *-si*, *-ti*; hence we have *yunámi* (I bind), *yunási*, *yunáti*, but *yunívas* (we two bind), *yuníthas*, *yunítas*; similarly we have *a* weakened to *u* in *kurmas* (we make), beside *karómi* (I make), and in *-thus*, *-tus*, the terminations of the 2nd and 3rd dual of the reduplicated perfect, beside *-thas* and *-tas* of the present. As *e* is equal to *ai*, it is lighter than *a*, and heavier than *i*; hence we have *é'mi* = εἶμι, and *imás* = ἴμεν; similarly we have in Latin, *amicus*, *inimicus*; *cano*, *cecini*; *jacio*, *abjicio*; *tango*, *tetigi*; *lego*, *colligo*. In open syllables *a* becomes *i*, while in closed ones it either becomes *e* or remains *a*, as in *abjectus*, *inermis*, *expers*, *tubicen* beside *tubicinis*, and *contactus*, *exactus*. As *u* is lighter than *a*, and heavier than *i*, we have *calco*, *conculco*; *salsus*, *insulsus*; *fructifer* beside an older *fructufer*. As labials prefer *u*, we find *occupo*, *aucupo*, *nuncupo*, *contubernium*, &c. The vowel *u* in Latin frequently maintains its ground, and does not give way, as in *tutudi*, *pupugi*. As *ae* is heavier than *î* (= *ii*), and *au* than *û* (= *uu*) and *ô*, we have *quaero*, *acquiro*; *claudo*, *concludo*; *faux*, *suffoco*. Short *o* in Latin is lighter than *u*, as we see from *corpus*, *corporis*; *jecur*, *jecoris*. The oldest forms of words are therefore generally distinguished by the retention of the vowel *a*; for example, Skr. *k'atváras* and L. *quatuor* are older than Gr. τέσσαρες, πίσυρες, and Goth. *fidvôr*; Skr. *dadámi* than δίδωμι; Skr. *dadhámi* than τίθημι; Skr. *naktam* (by night) than νύκτα. Within the limits of the Sanskrit itself *a* is frequently reduced to *i* and *î*, *u* and *û*; thus *giri* (mons) and *guru* (heavy) from *gar*; *sthitas* = L. *status*, Gr. στατός; *sthitis* = Gr. στάσις; *hiraṇa* (gold), Z. *zaraná*; *pitá* = Gr. πατήρ; *puras* = Gr. πάρος; *stirna* from *star* (sternere); *pita* (part., præt. pars.) from *pâ* (to drink); *dirghas* = Z. *dareghas* = Gr. δολιχός; *púrṇas* = L. *plenus*, from *par* (to fill). *A* often vanishes completely, as in *santi* = L. *sunt*, from *as* (to be); *g'agmus* (3 pl. perf.) from *gam* (to go). After *v* and *y* this frequently occurs, and then these spirants are vocalized into *u* and *i*, respectively, as *ukta* (part. præt. pass.) from *vak'* (to speak) and *ishṭa* (part. præt. pass.) from *yag'* (to sacrifice).

§. 37. Guṇa and Vṛddhi.

Guṇa (quality) consists in prefixing a short *a* to any vowel, and *Vṛddhi* (increase) in prefixing a long *â*. We have therefore,

Primitive Vowels,	a	â	i	î	u	û	ê	âi	ô	âu	ṛ	r̄	l̥
Guṇa,	â	..	ê	ê	ô	ô	..	..	..	..	ar	ar	al
Vṛddhi,	â	..	âi	âi	âu	âu	âi	..	âu	..	âr	âr	âl

It is only from a comparison of grammatical forms that we can distinguish the guṇa of *a* from its vṛddhi; e. g. by comparing *papâta* (he fell) from *pat* with *vivês'a* (he entered) from *vis'*, we see that *â* in the former is the guṇa of *a*, as *ê* in the latter is the guṇa of *i*.

The guṇa of *i* is *ê*, as in *êmi* = εἶμι ; *vêda* = οἶδα; *vêsas* = Ϝοῖκος ; *s'êtê* = κεῖται from *s'i*, whence L. *civis*. The vṛddhi of *i* is *âi*, as in *vâis'ya* (a man of the third class), from *vis'* (to enter); *s'âiva* (a worshipper of Siva) from *s'iva*, &c.

The guṇa of *u* is *o*, as in *bubôdha* (he knew) from *budh*; *sûnôs* (gen. sing.) of *sûnu* (a son), &c. The vṛddhi of *u* is *âu*, as in *bâuddha* (a follower of the Bauddha religion) from *budh*; *Bâudha*, a son of *Budha*, &c.

These examples are sufficient to show what we mean, when we speak of the guṇa or vṛddhi of any vowel.

§. 38. The Gutturals.

Skr. *k* is = I. E. *k*: *kas* = L. *quis* = Goth. *hvas*, Gr. κῶς, κότερον, Ir. *cia*; *kâla* (time), Gr. καιρὸς, Goth. *hveila*; *kâla* (death), Gr. κήρ, Ir. *ceal*; *kârâ* (a prison), L. *carcer*; *kan* (to shine), L. *candela*, Goth. *skeina* (I shine), Ir. *cann* (the full moon). Bopp, Schleicher, and others have asserted that *p* frequently represents an I. E. *k*, and that consequently we find these sounds interchanged in Sanskrit and the cognate languages: thus we have, Skr. *kanth* (to mourn), Gr. πένθος, πέπονθα; Skr. *kars'* (attenuare), L. *parco, parcus, parvus;* Skr. *ka* (who), Gr. πό-τερον; Skr. *pâpa* (bad), Gr. κακός, L. *pejor* for *pepjor;* Skr. *pañk'an* = L. *quinque;* Skr. *pak'* (to cook), Gr. πέπτω, L. *coquo*. Now, I am fully convinced that *p* has never been thus developed from an original *k*; but that, wherever these sounds appear to be interchanged, either the original sound was *kv*, or else the change is due to assimilation, and perhaps in one or two cases to a false analogy. Thus Skr. *ka* must be derived from an I. E. *kva;* for we find Skr. *kva* (where), *kutra* (where), L. *quis* and Goth. *hvas*, all of which point back to an I. E. *kva;* Skr. *k'atvâras*, Gr. πίσυρες, Lith. *keturi*, point back to an I. E. *kvatvâras*, which we find in L. *quatuor;* Skr. *pañk'an*, may have been a reduplication of *kvan*, as L. *quinque*. In some cases an initial *p* may have been changed into *k* or *kv* by the assimilative power of a succeeding *k* or *kv*, as some assert to have been the case with L. *coquo* and *quinque:* from a comparison, however, of *coquo* with Lith. *kepejas* (a baker), and Gr. ἀρτοκόπος (a baker), it seems possible that the initial *k* or *kv* may be original: compare L. *coquina* = *popina, culina* for *cuclina*.*

Ksh (= *ks*) corresponds frequently to κτ in Greek; here either *kt* was original, and from it *ks* arose by weakening the explosive sound to a sibilant, or else *ks* was original, and *s* became *t* through the assimilating power of the preceding explosive sound. We have *rkshas* = ἄρκτος; *takshâ* = τέκτων; *kshan* (to hurt), κτείνω, κτά-μεναι; *kshi* (to rule), κτάομαι; *kshi*

---

* From the fact that this same root, meaning to *bake*, is found in Skr., Gr., and L., Mommsen appears to be mistaken in asserting that the Greeks and Latins did not practise baking till after they separated from the parent stock and from each other.

(to dwell), κτίζω ; *aksha* (the eye), ὄκταλλος. Sometimes also *ksh* corresponds in Greek to ξ, and sometimes *to* σχ, as *kshura* (a razor), ξυρόν ; *kshud* (conterere), ξύω, ξυστός, for ξυδτος ; *kshad* (to slaughter), σχάζω ; similarly we have *kshal* (to wash) beside Lith. *skalau* (I wash), and *kshubh* (to agitate) beside A. S. *be-scufan* (contrudere), G. *schieben*. *Sh* sometimes disappears, and leaves *k* or *kh*, as in *kshud* (conterere), L. *cudo, incus* ; *ksham* (to endure), κομίζω ; *kshudra* (small), Lith. *kudikis* (infans), Pers. *kûdek* (small) ; *khura* (a razor), another form of *kshura* ; *kshêtra* (campus), Goth. *haithi* (ager), G. *heide; kshaya* (a house), Ir. *cai* (a house). K also sometimes disappears, and leaves *s*, as in *kshubh* (to agitate), W. *hwbiau* (to make a sudden push), Sl. *sŭbati* (to agitate) ; and perhaps in *kshvêl* (se movere), O. H. G. *suillu* (turgeo). *Ksh*, when not initial, appears often as *g* in Gothic and English : we have *kânksh* (optare), E. *hunger; pakshin* (a bird), Goth. *fugls*, E. *fowl, aksha* (the eye), Goth. *augó*, E. *eye*. *Ksh*, according to Bopp, also appears as *kr* in Latin and Greek : we have *kshapas* (night), L. *crepus-culum* ; *kshi* (to rule), *urukshayas* = εὐρυκρείων ; *kship* (to throw), ρίπτω for κριπτω ; *kshipra* (celer), κραιπνός·

Kh has generally been developed from an older *k*, sometimes through the aspirating influence of a preceding *s*, which has afterwards disappeared : thus we have *khañg'* (to limp), Gr. σκάζω, O.H.G. *hinkan* ; L. *caligo* ; *khan* (to dig), Gr. χαίνω, L. *canalis, cuniculus*, O.H.G. *ginêm* (hio) ; *khad* (to slay), L. *clades*, with *l* inserted, as in Goth. *hlaha* (I laugh), G. *lachen*, E. *laugh*, beside Skr. *khakkh* (to laugh),* *khâd* (to eat), Ir. *caithim* (I eat). *Kh* also represents an I. E. *gh* in *kha* (air), Gr. χάος, L. *halare*, and *nakha* (a nail), Gr. ὄνυξ, Goth. *nagls*.

G = I. E. *g*: *gar* (to sound), Gr. γηρύω, γλῶσσα, L. *gallus, garrire*. Wherever Skr. *g* corresponds to *b* in Greek or

---

* *L* is perhaps inserted in L. *claudus*, Skr. *khôd* (to be lame) ; Ir. *glun*, Skr. *g'ánu* ; Ir. *dluimh* (smoke), Skr. *dhûma*.

Latin, the original sound must have been *gv:* thus we have I. E. *gvanâ*, Skr. *g'anî* (a woman), Gr. γυνή for γϜανα, Bœot. βανά, Ir. *bean* (a woman), E. *quean, queen;* I. E. *gvam*, Skr. *gam* (to go), Goth. *qvima* (I come), L. *venio* for *gvenio;* I. E. *gvar*, Skr. *gar* (to devour), Gr. βρώσκω, L. *gula, gurges, glutio, voro* for *gvoro;* I. E. *gvaru*, Skr. *guru* (heavy), Gr. βαρύς, L. *gravis;* I. E. *gvâ*, Skr. *gô* (a cow), Gr. βοῦς, γά in γα-λα (for γα-λακτ,* which, according to Bopp, meant *lac vaccinum*, λακτ being the same word as Skr. *dugdha*, milk), L. *bos, ceva;* I. E. *gvâ*, Skr. *gô* (the earth), Gr. γύα for γϜαα, γαῖα for γαϜια, γῆ for γαα.

Gh = I. E. *gh: stigh* (to mount up), Gr. στείχω, A. S. *staeger* (a stair); Skr. *gharma* (warm), Sl. *goreti* (ardere).

H is a sonant, and therefore cannot have the hard sound generally given to it by English grammarians, perhaps on account of its having a hard sound in Bengali. It never ends a word, and in any other position only stands before vowels, and semivowels, as in *hrêsh* (to neigh), *hnu* (to hide), *hlâd* (to be glad). When it comes before *t* or *th*, it changes them into *dh* or *ḍh*, as in *dugdha* from *duh* (to milk), L. *duco*, and *liḍha* from *lih* (to lick), Gr. λείχω. *H* represents an I. E. *gh* in *hima* (snow), Gr. χιών; *hari* (green), Gr. χλόη, *hyas*, Gr. χθές; an I. E. *dh* in *hitas* = θετός; an I. E. *bh* in *grah*, Ved. *grabh* and *mahyam* (mihi), beside *tubhyam* (tibi); and an I. E. *k* in the single case of *hrḍ* (the heart).

§. 39. The Palatals.

The palatal mutes and nasals have all arisen from the corresponding gutturals; and the palatal sibilant generally stands for an original *k*. It is not known how these letters were

---

* Max Müller assents to the first part of this derivation, and compares with it Gr. βούτυρον, and Ir. *bleachd* (milk) for *bo-leachd*, but he connects λακτ with Skr. *rag'as* (a clear fluid). The Homeric γλάγος would then be exactly equivalent to a Skr. *gorag'as*.

pronounced in ancient Sanskrit; k' may have been sounded either as *ty* or as *ky*, like the *c* in E. *card*, which is frequently pronounced as if it were written *cyard*.

$K' = $ I. E. *k*, *ká* = L. *que*, *pe*, in *quippe*, Goth. *uh*, *h* in *hvasuh* (quisque), *nih* (neque); *k'akshus* (the eye), Ir. *cais* (the eye); *k'añk'* (vacillare), L. *cunctari*, Ir. *ceangtha* (they go); *k'áurya* (furtum), Ir. *coire* (trespass); *k'and* (to shine), L. *candeo, accendo, scintilla*, Goth. *skeina* (I shine); *k'al* (to move), Gr. κέλομαι, κέλης, L. *celer, procella*, Ir. *caill* (a path); *k'al* (nugari), Ir. *cal* (a joke); *k'arman* (corium), Gr. χόριον, L. *corium, calceus* (?) Ir. *croicionn* (a skin). In reduplicated syllables *k'* takes the place of *k*, as in *k'akâra* (feci), from *kṛ*.

$K'h = $ I. E. *sk*, *k'hid* (to cut), Gr. σκίδνημι, L. *scindo*, Goth. *skaida* (I separate), Ir. *scaithim* (I cut off); *gak'k'hámi* (I go) for *ga-skámi* ; *prak'h* (to ask) from L. *precor*, I. E. *prask*.

$G' = $ I. E. *g*; *g'ánu* = Gr. γόνυ; *g'val* (to burn), Ir. *geal* (bright), *gual* (coal), E. *coal;* *g'var* (to be sick), L. *æ-ger*, Ir. *gurt* (pain); *g'ná* (to know), Gr. ἔγνων (γ)νοῦς, L. (*g*) *nosco, gnarus, i-gnoro*, E. *know, can*, Ir. *gnia* (knowledge); *g'ush* (to desire), L. *gustus*, Goth. *kiusu*, E. *choose*, Ir. *gus* (desire); *g'ash* (to kill), Ir. *gus* (death), and perhaps L. *vasto* for *gvasto*, as *vivo* for *gvivo* ; &c.; *g'an* (to produce), Gr. γίγνομαι, L. *gigno, genus*, E. *kin*, Ir. *genim* (I beget); *g'anaka* (father), from last root, G. *könig*, E. *king*. In reduplicated syllables *g'* takes the place of *g*, as in *g'igámi* = Gr. βίβημι.

S' nearly always represents an I. E. *k*, and consequently we find corresponding to it *k* in Greek and Latin, and *h* in Gothic. The Lettic and Slavic languages, on the other hand, nearly always present the sibilant, although the guttural is sometimes found, as in Lith. *akmen*, Sl. *kamen*, Skr. *as'man*. We have *nas'* (to perish), Gr. νέκυς, L. *nex, nox* (the dying away of day); *S'ri* (the deity of plenty), L. *Ceres;* *s'ravas*

---

* See Ellis' "Phonetics," p. 56; and Max Müller, vol. ii., p. 142.

= κλέος; *s'vas* (to sigh), L. *ques-tus*, E. *wheeze*; *s'véta* (white), Goth. *hveits*, E. *white*, *wheat*, "the white plant"; *s'ata* (a hundred), Gr. ἑκατόν for ἑν-κατον, L. *centum*, Goth. *hund*, W. *kant*; *s'iras* and *s'irsha* (the head), Gr. κόρση, κάρα, L. *cerebrum*; *s'roni* (the hip), L. *clunis* : *mrs'* (to touch), L. *mulcere*; *s'ad* (to fall), L. *cadere*; *as'man* (a stone), *as'mara* (stony), Gr. ἄκμων, O. N. *hamar* (saxum, malleus), E. *hammer*; *as'vas* = Gr. ἵκκος, ἵππος, L. *equus*, Goth. *aihvs*, O. S. *ehu*, Ir. *ech*; *ás'u* (quickly), Gr. ὠκύς, L. *ocius*, *accipiter*, *aquila*; *vis'* (a man), E. *wight*; *s'aṅk* (to doubt), L. *cunctari*; *bhrs'am* (quickly), L. *frequens*; *s'ana* (hemp), O. H. G. *hanaf*; *s'ans* (to say, praise), L. *censeo*; *s'apha* (a hoof), E. *hoof*; *s'van* (a dog), Gr. κύων, Lydian Κανδαύλης (σκυλλοπνίκτης), Median σπάκα, Z. *s'pánem* (acc. sing.), L. *canis*, Goth. *hunds*, E. *hound*. In some Sanskrit forms we see the original *k* kept as in *adikshat* = ἔδειξε from *dis'* (to point out); *dikshu*, loc. pl. of *dis'* (a region of the sky). *S'* sometimes takes the place of an original *s*. This is a change not easily explained, but in all cases I believe that it arises either from assimilation, or from the presence of a neighbouring guttural. The second *s'* in *s'as'a* (a hare), from *s'as'* (to leap), represents an original *s*, and has arisen from the assimilative power of the first *s'*; the I. E. form was *kasa*, whence G. *hase*, E. *hare*; yet we have the following gloss from Hesychius, κεκῆνας λαγωούς Κρῆτες, where the second *k* seems to point back to an I. E. *k*. In *s'vas'uras* = Gr. ἑκυρός, L. *socer*, the first *s'* is due to the assimilative power of the second *s'*. In the following cases *s'* has sprung from *s*, through the influence of the neighbouring guttural, *s'akṛt* (dung), Gr. σκώρ, σκατός, L. *stercus*; *s'ushka* (dry)*, Z. *huska*, L. *siccus*; *s'ambúka*, borrowed from Gr. σαμβύκη; *kés'a* (hair),

---

* Benfey explains the *s'* here by the assimilating influence of the following *sh*; but then how would he explain *s'akṛt*, &c.?

E. *hair;* *kês'ara* (juba leonis),* L. *cæsaries*. On this principle L. *sacer* has been connected with *s'ak* (to be able), but wrongly, if the O. N. *hagna* (prodesse) be from the latter root. The L. *saccharum* and E. *sugar* have been borrowed from Skr. *s'arkarâ* (gravel, clayed or candied sugar), in which *s'* = I. E. *k*, if L. *calculus, calx*, Gr. κρόκη, κροκάλη be connected with it. *S'* was pronounced either as *ch* in G. *mich*, or as *ssi* in E. *session*. "No simple *s* can be pronounced at the palatal point. The letter *s* is formed by the simple friction of the breath between the upper and lower teeth, and is in consequence always dental. The rushing sound of the English *sh* or the German *sch* is formed in the hollow space left between the teeth and the palatal point, and may thus be regarded both as a dental and as a palatal sound" (Lepsius' "Standard Alphabet," p. 70).

The palatal nasal was pronounced as *gn* in Fr. *campagne*, or as *n* in E. *new*.

§. 40. THE CEREBRALS.

The presence of the mutes and nasal of this class in Sanskrit has been generally ascribed to the influence of the Non-Aryan races of India, from whom these letters are supposed to have been borrowed. Bühler† has, however, completely overthrown this theory, and has pointed out that by far the greater number of these cerebrals is produced either by the direct change of *r*, *sh*, into them, or by the change of dentals into the corresponding cerebrals through the influence of *r*, *ṛ*, *ṝ*, *sh*, and consequently that cerebralization is entirely an Aryan proceeding, rooted in the ancient phonetic system of

---

* Bopp derives *hair* for *kês'ara* by throwing out the *s'*. He deduces *kês'a* from *kê*, loc. of *ka* (the head), which is found in Gr. κό-μη, L. *co-ma*, *ca-pillus*, and *s'a* for *s'aya* from *s'i* (to lie) ; *kês'a* would then be " quod in capite jacet." If this derivation be correct, *s'* is original here.

† Consult Appendix A.

the language. In Prakrit these cerebral sounds have frequently supplanted the corresponding dentals, as in *baḍi* = Skr. *prati* (προτί, ποτί); *paḍhama* (first) = Skr. *prathama*. In transcribing English words the Hindus at present substitute cerebrals for dentals, as in *Direktar*, *Gavarṇment*, &c. This shows us that the ordinary English pronunciation of these words is more cerebral than dental.

Ḍ has sprung from *sd* in *nîḍa* (a nest) from *ni* (under) and *sad* (to lie), and therefore means "what lies under;" L. *nidus*, E. *nest*, Ir. *nead*, W. *nyth*; *pîḍ* (to press) = *pisd* = *api-sad*, compare πιέζω = ἐπι-σεδγω; *bâḍ* and *vâḍ* (to bathe) = *vasd* = *ava-sad*, from *ava* (down), and *sad*.

Sh = I. E. *s*; *ush* (to burn), L. *uro* for *uso, us-si*; *tarsh* (to be thirsty), Gr. τέρσομαι, L. *torreo* for *torseo*, E. *thirst*. *Sh* before *s* becomes *k*, as in *dvêkshi* (thou hatest).

§. 41. THE DENTALS.

T = I. E. *t*; *ta*, Gr. τό, L. *is-te*; *tvam*, L. *tu*; *pat* (to fly), Gr. πέτομαι; *bharanti* = Gr. φέροντι, φέρουσι, L. *ferunt*.

Th = I. E. *t*; *sthag* (to cover), Gr. στέγω, L. *tego*; *sthâ* (to stand), L. *sto*; *prath* (to extend), Gr. πλατύς; *asthi* (a bone), Gr. ὀστέον; *ratha* (a car), L. *rota*, E. *rather*.

D = I. E. *d*; *pad* (a foot), Gr. πούς, ποδός; *das* (to lift), E. *toss*; *dar* (to tear), Gr. δέρω, E. *tear*; *dam* (to tame), Gr. δαμάω, L. *domo*, E. *tame*.

Dh = I. E. *dh*; *dhûma* (smoke), Gr. θυμός, L. *fumus*; *dhar* (to support), Gr. θρᾶνος, L. *firmus, fortis*; *dhrâkh* (arescere), L. *fraces* (lees of oil), *floces* (lees of wine), E. *dregs, dry*; *dhâ* (to place*), Gr. τίθημι, L. *con-do*, E. *do, doom*; *vadhû* (a wife), from a root which appears in Zend as *vad*

---

* The late Professor Siegfried derived from this root the Keltic *datl* (judicium), whence were borrowed, according to Lottner, E. *tattle*, G. *tadel*, the termination *-tl* being = Gr. -τρον, L. *-trum*.

(to lead), and which has in Lithuanian the sense of *to marry* (uxorem ducere), L. *vas, vad-is* (a contract, as marriage was perhaps the earliest kind of contract known), E. *wedding*. *Dh* is sometimes reduced to *h*, as in *hitas* (part. pret. pass. of *dhâ*) = θετός; *–hi* (termination of 2 pers. sing. imper. act.) for *–dhi* after vowels,* as *pâhi* (tuere), *–dhi* is still kept after consonants, as *addhi* (eat), and in Vedic as *s'rudhi* = κλῦθι.

S = I. E. *s*; *saptan*, L. *septem*; *svid* (to sweat), Gr. ἰδρώς, L. *sudo*, E. *sweat*; *as* (to be), L. *esse*. *S* is subject to many changes in Sanskrit; thus after *k, r*, and all the vowels, except *a* and *â*, it becomes *sh*. In certain other cases it is represented by *h, r*, and *s'*; but these need not be noticed here, as they properly belong to the special Sanskrit Grammar. The change of *s* into *r* occurs also in other languages. In the Laconian dialect, final σ became ρ, as τίρ, πίσορ, for τίς, πίθος; and in Latin *s* between two vowels became *r*, as *eram* for *esam, quorum* = Skr. *kêshâm* (*sh* for *s*, on account of preceding *e*), *quarum* = Skr. *kâsâm*. *S* has frequently an aspirating influence on a following consonant, as in *sthag*, Gr. στέγω; *sthâ*, L. *sto; sphây* (to increase), Gr. σπάω, L. *spatium; asthi*, Gr. ὀστέον.

R† = I. E. *r* : *mar* (to die), L. *mori*. It is sometimes omitted in Sanskrit after an initial consonant, as in *bhañg'* (to break), L. *frango; bhug'* (to enjoy and endure), L. *fruor*, E. *brook; g'hillî* (a cricket), L. *gryllus*, G. *grille*. We find a similar omission in other languages, as in Pkr. *padhama* = Skr. *prathama;* E. *speak* = G. *sprechen*.

L = I. E. *r, lup* (to break), L. *rumpo; lok'* (to see) from

---

* The exceptions are *êdhi* (be), *s'âdhi* (rule) *g'uhudhi* (offer). *Liḍhi* (lick) is for *liḍḍhi*.

† Schleicher and others place *r* and *l* among the cerebrals; but, as they appear to be closely connected with the dentals, it is perhaps better to place them among the latter. This question, however, requires a much more complete investigation than it has yet received.

ruch (to shine); *kalp* (to prosper), from *karp*. *L* = I. E. *l*; see §. 21.*

N = I. E. *n*; *nas'* (to die), νέκυς, L. *noceo;* *nara* (a man), ἀνήρ, L. *Nero*. *N* is frequently changed into another nasal for phonetic reasons; thus we have *purṇa* (full), where *ṇ* takes the place of *n*, on account of the preceding *r*, and in general the nasal belongs to the same class as the following consonant, as *yuṅg'anti* = L. *jungunt*, *lumpati* = L. *rumpit*.

§. 42. The Labials.

P = I. E. *p*; *pati* (a master), Gr. δεσπότης (lit. 'a master of slaves,' Skr. *dása*, a slave); *pitar*, Gr. πατήρ; *pá* (to drink),* Gr. πίνω, L. *potus;* *pyai* (to increase), *pívan* (fat), Gr. πίων, πῖαρ, L. *pinguis*, E. *fat; pis'* (to adorn), *pés'alas* (beautiful) = Gr. ποικίλος, *púy* (to putrefy), Gr. πῦος, πύθω, L. *pus*, *putris*, E. *foul; pri* (to love), Gr. πρᾶος, E. *friend; pas'u* (cattle), Gr. πῶϋ(?), L. *pecus*, Goth. *faihu*, A. S. *feoh*, E. *fee*.

Ph has generally arisen from an I. E. *p*, perhaps through the influence of a preceding *s*, as in *sphaṭika* (crystal), G. *spath; sphuṭ* (to burst), E. *split; sphur* (to tremble, to strike), Gr. ἀσπαίρω; Skr. *phēna* (foam), L. *spuma*, E. *foam; phala* (fruit) for *spala*, lit. 'what may be split,' or from *bhala*, L. *flos*, E. *bloom*.

B = I. E. *b* (§. 22), or = I. E. *bh* (§. 22).

Bh = I. E. *bh*; *bhar* (to bear), Gr. φέρω, L. *fero; bhid* (to cleave), L. *findo*, E. *bite; abhi* (towards), Gr. ἀμφὶ, E. *by*. *Bh* is in some cases reduced to *h*, as in *grah* (to seize), from Ved. *grabh*, *mahyam* (to me) = L. *mihi*, beside *tubhyan* = L. *tibi*.

---

* *L* does not exist in Zend. The Chinese, on the other hand, always use *l* for *r*, as *Eulopa* for *Europe*, *Killissetu* for *Christ*, *Yamelika* for *America*. The New Zealanders have no *l*. They say *Rota* for *Lot*, *Horomona* for *Solomon*.

† *P* here may represent an I. E. *bh*, if L. *bibo*, E. *beer*, be from this root. We have a trace of the *b* in Skr. *pibámi* (I drink).

V allows consonants to stand after it, which is hardly ever the case with *y*. It is frequently interchanged with *b*. In *drapsa* (a drop), from *drav* (*dru* gunated), the *v* is changed into *p* on account of the following hard *s*, as in Mod. Gr. ἔκλαψα from ἔκλαυσα. The interchange of *b* and *v* is of common occurrence, as L. *habere*, Fr. *avoir*, L. *cantabam*, It. *cantava;* *berber* (in Salian Hymn) = *fervere;* *Vesuvius* = Βέσβιος; *–ber* in *September*, Skr. *vára* (time); *Vesontio* = *Besançon*. Bopp considers that *v* has been hardened into a guttural in the following cases: Skr. *g'iv* (to live), L. *vivo*, *vixi*, E. *quick*, Skr. *bhâyavâmi* (I make to be) = L. *facio;* Skr. *dévaras* = L. *lévir*, A. S. *tâcor*, O. H. G. *zeihur;* Skr. *naus* = Gr. ναῦς, L. *navis*, A. S. *naca*, O. H. G. *nacho*. In this opinion he appears to be mistaken; and it is far more likely that an original guttural has fallen out in *levir* and *vivo*, than that *v* should have been hardened into one; as to *facio*, it is not from *bhâvayâmi;* and in the case of A. S. *naca*, we have a different termination from the *va* in *nâu*, which is for *snâ-va*. *V*, according to Bopp, is sometimes changed into *l*, as in L. *-lent* = Gr. -Φεντ = Skr. *-vant;* Skr. *svadus* (sweet) = Lith. *saldùs* (sweet); Skr. *svapnas* (sleep) = Gr. ὕπνος = E. *sleep*.* Similarly *v* becomes *r*, as in L. *cras* = Skr. *s'vas;* L. *ploro* = Skr. *plâvayâmi;* Kr. τρέ = Skr. *tvâm;* Goth. *driusan* (to fall) = Skr. *dhvaṅs;* O. H. G. *pirumes* = Skr. *bhavâmas;* O. H. G. *scrirumes* = Skr. *s'râvayâmas;* Ir. *raidim* (I say), Goth. *raṣda* (speech), Skr. *vad* (to speak).

M = I. E. *m*: *manas* = Gr. μένος, L. *mens;* *smar* (to remember, L. *memor;* *as'vam* = L. *equum;* *syâm* = L. *siem*.

§. 43. When one consonant follows another, the law that

---

* Notwithstanding the parallel case of Lith. *saldùs* = Skr. *svâdus*, the connexion of E. *sleep* with Skr. *svapna* is very unlikely, on account both of the long vowel (Goth. *slêpan* O. H. G. *slâfan*) and the *p*, which should be *f*, according to Grimm's law. Moreover, the root *svap* appears in O. N. *svefn* (somnus), O. H. G. *sweljan* (sopire), A. S. *swefian*. Lottner connects E. *sleep* with O. H. G. *slaph* (languidus).

governs them is this, 'sonants follow sonants only, and surds surds only :' thus *vâk'* (speech), inst. pl. *vâgbhis*, *yunag'mi* (I join), *yunakti* (he joins); *admi* (I eat), *atsi* (thou eatest). Only one consonant is permitted to end a word; when several consonants occur together, all but the first are thrown off: thus, *vâk'*, nom. sing. *vâk* for *vâksh*, and this for *vâk-s*. Tenues alone are allowed as final consonants, the mediæ and aspirates being changed into the corresponding tenuis; but when this final tenuis comes before a word beginning with a sonant or a vowel, it becomes the corresponding sonant, the tenues being therefore retained only before a pause and a following tenuis; thus *harit* (green), *mud* (joy), *yudh* (a fight), become *harit, mut*, and *yut* before a pause; but we have *harid bhavati* (viridus est), *mud bhavati* (gaudium est), *yud asti* (pugna est). For further information on this subject, the reader is referred to the special Sanskrit Grammar.

CHAPTER V.

The Greek Alphabet.*

§. 44. Tabular View of the Sounds.

	MUTES.		SEMIVOWELS.			VOWELS.
	unasp.	*asp.*	*Spirants.*	*Nasals.*	r & l-sounds.	
	surd. son.	surd.	surd. son.	son.	son.	
Gutt.	κ γ	χ	‘ ’	γ		$\left.\begin{array}{l}a\ \bar{a}\\ \iota\ \bar{\iota}\end{array}\right\}\iota\ \eta$
Pal.						
Cer.					(ρ, λ)?	$o\ \omega$
Dent.	τ δ	θ	σ (σ)	ν	ρ, λ	$v\ \bar{v}$
Lab.	π β	φ	F	μ		(ου)

Z, ξ, and ψ were called σύμφωνα διπλᾶ; but ζ differs from ξ and ψ in this, that it is a consonantal diphthong, being equivalent properly to *dy*, while ξ and ψ are merely signs for κς and πς. It is a mistake to suppose that ζ is equivalent to δσ; for such a combination is impossible, as δ is a sonant, and σ a surd. Before the introduction of the symbols ξ and ψ, the Greeks frequently used χσ and φσ instead of them. The Romans also must have aspirated the κ and π in their pronunciation of ξ and ψ; for Priscian* writes, "multo molliorem et volubiliorem sonitum habet ψ quam *ps* vel *bs*;" and again, "sicut ergo ψ melius (mollius?) sonat quam *ps* vel *bs*, sic *x* etiam quam *gs* vel *cs*." In Zend a similar phenomenon occurs; thus the nom. sing. of *ap* (aqua) is *áfs*, and of *vâk'* (vox), *vâkhs*. Σ seems in some cases to have been soft, as in σβέννυμι, ἄσβολος, μίσγω, ὕσγη, and the Æolic Σδεύς for Ζεύς, σδυγός for ζυγός, βρίσδα for ῥίζα. Plato placed σ among the ἄφωνα. He says, τὸ σῖγμα

---

* Böhtlingk (K. Z., vol. xv., p. 148), however, considers that Priscian means that ψ sounded as *bz*, and *x* as *gz*, as in Fr. *examen*.

τῶν ἀφώνων ἐστί, ψόφος τις μόνον, οἷον συριττούσης τῆς γλώττης. Ἄφωνα, however, in Plato's language, included both the semivowels (φωνήεντα μὲν οὔ, οὐ μέντοι γε ἄφθογγα), and the mutes (ἄφθογγα): consult Plato, Kratyl. 424, C.

§. 45. Pronunciation of the Vowels.

Υ was originally a pure *u*, but in early times it became *ü*. This was the first beginning of that tendency in Greek towards allowing the *i*-sound to predominate over the other vowels, which so strongly characterizes Modern Greek. When υ became *ü*, the pure *u*-sound was expressed by ου. This pure sound was retained by the Boeotians; they wrote τού, or τούν for σύ, κοῦμα for κῦμα, γλουκού for γλυκύ, &c. In the Laconian dialect we also find τούνη for συ, κάρουα for κάρυα, μοῦϊαι for μυῖαι, &c. In Mod. Gr. υ has the sound of *i*; but it could not have had this sound in classical Greek, for it was pronounced with contracted lips (μύοντες τὰ χείλη), and it is impossible to pronounce a pure *i* in that position. The old pure sound of υ was kept* in the diphthongs αυ, ευ, and ου; for these must have arisen in early times, before υ had become *ü*; and in the cases where υ represents F, it must have had the sound of the pure *u*. Moreover, if υ in these diphthongs had been pronounced *ü*, the Mod. Gr. pronunciation av, ev, ov, would be inexplicable. We find also on inscriptions φεογειν, Εὐεργέτης, αὀτούς, &c., for φεύγειν, Εὐεργέτης, αὐτούς, &c., which forms teach us the same fact. Ου in a later period lost its diphthongal pronunciation, and became a pure *ú*; this could not have happened, had υ in ου been pronounced as *ü*. This is corroborated by the fact that the junction of ο and υ never forms the diphthong ου, but that they are pronounced separately, as in ὀλιγόϋπνος. The old name of ὁ μικρόν was οὖ, and at Athens, before Ol. 100, ο was always written in place

---

* Dietrich, in K. Z., vol. xiv., p. 48.

of the later ου, where this ου arose either from contraction, or from mere lengthening, whether arising from the falling out of a consonant, or from any other cause, wherever, therefore, the Doric had ω: on the other hand, ου was written wherever υ was original, whether as representing F or for some other reason; thus we have τος for τούς, from τονς, εκ το κοινο for ἐκ τοῦ κοινοῦ, &c., but always οὐκ and οὗτος, in both of which words the Doric has also ου.* In early times o was used to express both the long and short clear o and the long and short obscure o. The latter sound became ú (ου), the former ω (= oo). The clear sound prevailed in early times, and hence we have λέων, λέγων, &c. for λεοντς, λεγοντς, &c.; for o was lengthened to compensate for the throwing out of the consonants at a time when it still had the clear sound. The augment ε before o coalesced with this o into ω, for this change likewise occurred at an early period. On the other hand, in τούς for τονς, λέγουσι for λέγοντι, the ν remained in long; and when it was thrown out o had become obscure, and therefore the u-sound (ου) took its place. Similarly in Old Latin, o had both a clear and an obscure sound: the obscure o became u, as in legunt, vulgus, from O. L. legont, volgus, while the clear o remained unchanged, as in colo, honestus. When o was succeeded by a vowel, it in some cases seems to have had the sound of w; thus we have, ὀά for the Persian wah, Ὄαξος for Fάξος, ὄασις from Ar. wadi, δοάν for δϜην, Κοίντιος for Quinctius, and perhaps in οἶστρος, the gadfly, so called from its *whizzing* noise.

As o was written ου before the Archonship of Eukleides, so ε was written for ει. Ει was however written in full wherever the ι was original, as in ἔχει, λεῖος, πόλει (dat. sing.); but where ει arose either from contraction or any other cause, ε is found, as in πολες for πόλεις, εργασται for εἴργασται, κλεγενες for κλειγένης, ενθεναι for ἐνθεῖναι. In this latter case the Æolians wrote η for ει, as in συμφέρην, χήρ, τρῆς. We

---

* Dietrich, in K. Z., vol. xiv., p. 53.

find one exception to this rule; for on inscriptions we find ειπεν for εἶπεν and εἰπεῖν, though the root Fεπ contains no ι originally; the Æolians also wrote εἴπην for εἰπεῖν. E had two sounds in early Greek, the one approaching a (e^a), the other approaching i (e^i); e^a, when lengthened, became η, and e^i, ει. The former sound was older than the latter; and hence, when phonetic changes requiring ε to be lengthened occurred in early times, it became η, whereas in changes of later origin e^i became ει. Thus we have ἤρχετο, ἤθελον, beside εἶχον (= εσεχον), εἰπόμην (= εFεπομην), εἴργασμαι (= FεFεργασμαι), for the consonants in these cases were not thrown out till late; -ηρ, -ην, -ης (in αἰθήρ, τέρην, εὐγενής), for -ερς, -ενς, -εσς, beside -εις (in χαρίεις, τίθεις), for -εντς, as in the former cases the nom. sing. σ was early lost, while in the latter ν remained in till a later period.

The Bœotic is a stage in advance of the Attic, for in it we find ει for η, as in ἐβδομείκοντα, where –μει– for –μα– must have passed through the stage –μη–, πένεις for πένης, τίθειμι for τίθημι; η for αι, as in κή for καί, τύπομη for τύπτομαι; and ι for ει, as in λέγις for λέγεις, ἠί for αἰεί. While ει in Greek, and ei in Latin gradually approached î in pronunciation, the English î conversely is pronounced as ei; similarly, while ου in Greek and ou in Latin approached û, the N. H. G. au has been developed from the M. H. G. û, as in *haus* from *hus*. H in classical Greek never could have had the sound of î, for the bleating of sheep is represented by βῆ. The diphthongs αυ and οι were probably pronounced as E. *ou* and *ee*; for in Aristophanes (Vesp. 903), a dog's bark is αὖ, αὖ, and a bird's note is ποῖ (Aves, 227), compare E. *pewit*.

§. 46 Pronunciation of the Aspirates.*

The aspirates were originally hard sounds; for before the introduction of the signs, θ, χ, φ, they were written, TH,

---

* Consult Raumer, "Gesammelte sprachwissenschaftliche schriften," p. 96; and Curtius, "Grundzüge," p. 370.

ΚΗ, ΠΗ, as in ΕΠΕΥΚΗΟΜΕΝΟΣ, ΕΚΠΗΑΝΤΟΙ, on the Columna Naniana; moreover, we find them reduplicated by the tenues, as in τίθημι, κέχυκα; and in addition, when the Ionic dialect separated from the parent stock, they must have been hard, for we frequently find them represented in it by the tenues. These hard aspirates were originally soft, and traces of this fact still manifest themselves, as in Φιδάκνη = Πιθάκνη, Τελχίνες = Θελγῖνες, φέβομαι for φεβίομαι, an irregularly reduplicated form of the same root as the Skr. *bhî* (timere). Curtius attempts to account for the origin of these hard aspirates from the I. E. *gh, dh,* and *bh,* by supposing that the *h* in these latter was hard, and that it assimilated to itself the preceding mediæ, just as β in R. βλαβ becomes π before τ in βλαπτός. This explanation is, however, perfectly untenable. The aspirates were also in classical Greek actually double sounds, as we see (1) from the moveableness of the aspiration in reduplicated syllables, in θρέψω from τρέφω, in Ion. ἐνθαῦτα = ἐνταῦθα, Ion. κιθών = χιτών, in ἀφ' οὗ from ἀπ' οὗ, &c.; (2) from the way in which Barbarians pronounced Greek, as αἰτρίαν, πυλάξι (Thesmoph. 1001, *seq.*), ὄρνιτο (Aves, 1678); (3) from the way in which they were transliterated in the older Latin, where *t* = θ, *c* = χ, *p* or *b* = φ, as in *tesaurus, Corintus, tiasus, calx* (= χάλιξ), *Nicomacus, Aciles, Poinos* (= Φοῖνιξ), *Pilemo* (= Φιλήμων), *Nicepor* (= Νικηφόρος), *purpura* (= πορφυρᾶ), *Burrus* (= Πύρρος), *Bruges* (= Φρύγες); (4) Dionysius of Halikarnassus states that in the case of the aspirates there was a προσθήκη τοῦ πνεύματος; (5) in Modern Greek in some cases the tenuis represents the old aspirate, which could not be accounted for if θ, χ, φ had been spirants, as ἕκω, στοκάζομαι, τεκνίτης in Rhodian dialect, τέλω = θέλω among Asiatic Greeks, and λευτερόνω = ἐλευθερόω, in the Peloponnesus. Those who disagree with the preceding view of the aspirates bring forward in support of their opinion, that they were not true aspirates, the fact that we find such combinations as φλ, χθ, φθ, χς (= ξ anciently), and ask how could these be pronounced if θ, χ, and φ were true aspirates. But this is a very unsafe foundation on which to build; for we are not likely to be good judges of what the ancient Greeks could pronounce, and the mere fact that we are unable to pronounce a certain combination of letters does not prove that others could not pronounce it. The statement of Priscian, that the only difference between *f* and φ was that φ was pronounced *fixis labris*, only proves that in his time φ had become a spirant—not, however, a labiodental like *f* and Mod. Gr. φ, but rather an interlabial.

§. 47. The Vowels.

An original α often vanishes, as in γίγνομαι for γιγενομαι, from R. γεν, Skr. *g'an*; πίπτω for πιπετω from R. πετ, Skr. *pat* (to fall); πατρός = Hom. πατέρος. It is generally retained, when it is initial, as in ἔσμεν = Skr. *smas* (we are), L. *sumus*; εἴην = Skr. *syâm*, L. *siem*.

ᾰ = I. E. *a*: ἀπὸ = L. *ab* = Skr. *apa* (away); ἄκων, L. *acus, acies*; δάκρυ, Skr. *as'ru* (a tear); ἄγω, L. *ago*, Skr. *ag'* (to go).

ᾰ = I. E. *am* and *an*: ἑπτά = Skr. *saptan*; ἐννέα = Skr. *navan*; δέκα = Skr. *das'an*; ἔδειξα = Skr. *adiksham*; πόδα = Skr. *padam*, πατέρα = Skr. *pitaram*.

ε = I. E. *a*: ἐστι = Skr. *asti*; φέρω = Skr *bharâmi*; τέτταρες = Skr. *k'atvâras*; φλέγω, L. *flagro*; πατέρα = Skr. *pitaram*; ἔχις, L. *anguis*. We find ε and α standing beside each other in many grammatical forms: τέμνω, ἔταμον; τρέπω, ἔτραπον; στρέφω, ἐστράφην; δέρκω, ἔδρακον; πάσχω, πείσομαι. In the dialects ε and α are frequently interchanged; στρέφω, Dor. στράφω; τέμνω, Dor. τάμνω; πιέζω, Dor. πιάζω; Ἄρτεμις, Dor. Ἄρταμις; ἱερός, Dor. ἱαρός; ὅτε, Æol. ὅτα; κράτος, Æol. κρέτος; θάρσυς, Æol. θέρσος; λεγόμεθα, Æol. λεγύμεθεν; βάραθρον, Arkad. ζέρεθρον, Ion. βέρεθρον; βάλλω, Arkad ζέλλω; ἄρσην, Ion. ἔρσην; ὁράω, Ion. ὁρέω. As Dor. ᾱ = Att. ε, so Doric ᾱ = Ion. and Att. η, wherever this η represents an original a. So also η = Skr. á, as τίθημι = Skr. dadhámi.

o = I. E. ă: νέϝος = Skr. navas (new); πάτος = Skr, pathas (a path); πόσις = Skr. patis (a master); μένος = Skr. manas (mind). In the dialects we find o and a frequently interchanged: είκοσι, Dor. ϝίκατι; τριακόσιοι, Dor. τριακάτιοι; όνειρον, Kret. άναιρον; τέσσαρες, Dor. τέτορες, where o perhaps represents the original ϝa; ὑπό, Æol. ὑπά; ἀνά, Æol. ὀν; βραχέως, Æol. βροχέως; ἑκατόν, Arkad. ἑκοτόν; καρδία, Kypr. κόρζα; ὀῤῥωδεῖν, Ion. ἀῤῥωδεῖν. Similarly we find λέαινα (= λεανγα) beside λέων, st. λεοντ; τέκταινα (= τεκτανγα) beside τεκτον; ἅμα beside ὁμός, &c. As Dor. a=Att. o, so Doric ā=Att. ω, as in Dor. πρᾶτος for πρῶτος, Dor. θεαρός for θεωρός. So also ω = Skr. á, as in δίδωμι = Skr. dadámi. In some cases ε and o are interchanged ὀδόντες, Æol. ἔδοντες; ὀδύνη, Æol. ἐδύνα; Κέρκυρα, Dor. Κόρκυρα; 'Απόλλων, Dor. 'Απέλλων; ὀβολός, Dor. ὀδελός; 'Ορχομενός, Bœot. 'Ερχομενός.

ι = I. E. i: ἴ-μεν, R. i, Skr. imasi (we go); λείπω, R. λιπ, Skr. rik' (to leave), L. linguo; ὀμιχεῖν, R. μιχ, Skr. mih (mingere).

ι = I. E. a: a then passed through the intermediate stage ε, and in many cases we find side-forms containing both ε and ι: thus we have ἴλλω beside ἐλύω, κίρνημι beside κεράννυμι, κτίννυμι beside κτείνω, κράμεναι, πίλναμαι beside πέλας, πιτνημι beside πετάννυμι, πίτνω beside πεσεῖν, ἴσθι beside ἐστί, νίσσομαι beside Νέστωρ, ἴζω beside ἔδυς. In the following cases these side-forms in ε do not exist: ἵππος = Skr. as'vas, L. equus; κρίνω beside L. cerno; ῥίζα beside L. radix. I = a in reduplicated present tenses, as τίθημι = Skr. dadhámi, πίπτω from R. πετ, τίκτω from R. τεκ for τιτκω. E and ι are frequently interchanged in the dialects: Bœot. ἰών = ἐών, R. ες; Lak. σία = θεά; Kret. θιός = θεός; Dor. ἱστία, Ion. ἱστίη = ἑστία; Arkad. ἰν = ἐν; χρύσεος and similar adjectives in −εος end in −ιος in Æolic. In Æol. τέρτος=τρίτος, and Æol. Πέρραμος for Πρίαμος, Ahrens considers that ι is changed into ε on account of the following ρ, as in L. *tertius*, and pronunciation of E. *third*. Although an I. E. *a* can thus be weakened to *i*, the converse never occurs; this rule has long been known; for in the "Etymologicum Magnum" we are told that οὐδέποτε τὸ ι εἰς α τρέπεται.

υ=I. E. *u*: φύω, Skr. *bhu* (to be); ὠκύς = Skr. *ás'us* (quick); ζυγόν = Skr. *yugam* (a yoke); κλύω, Skr. *s'ru* (to hear); suffix – τυ in βοητύς, &c., = Skr. Lith. and L. *-tu*.

υ = I. E. *a*: *a* then passed through the intermediate stage *o*, and in numerous examples *o* and *u* stand beside each other, while the Latin corresponding forms have sometimes not advanced beyond the *o*-stage, though, as we have already remarked, the Latin has generally advanced to the *u*-stage, even in cases where the Greek still keeps *o*; λύκος, L. *lupus*, from an I. E. *varkas*, as may be inferred from Skr. *vrka* (wolf); μορμύρω, L. *murmur*, Skr. *marmara* (murmur); μύλη, L. *molo*, Lith. *malunas* (a mill), which are all derived by Max Müller from an I. E. *mar* (to rub down), with which he also connects μάρναμαι, μῶλος Ἄρηος (the toil and moil of Ares), μώλωψ (a weal), L. *mors*, &c.; νύξ, L. *nox*, Skr. *naktam* (by night); σύν, ξύν, L. *con*, *cum*, Skr. *sam* (with); ὄνυξ, Skr. *nakha* (a nail); πανήγυρις beside ἀγορά; κύκλος = Skr. *k'akras* (a wheel); ἀνώνυμος beside ὄνομα, Skr. *nâman* (a name); the suffix –τυρ in μάρτυρ beside –τορ, nom. -τωρ, as in L. *daturus* beside *dator*; πρύτανις from προ (πρότανιος is found on a Lesbian inscription), the termination being found in ἐπηετανός, and L. *diutinus*. In γυνή υ represents an older Fα, as we see from Bœot. βανά. In Æolic υ frequently takes the place of ο: ὄνυμα = ὄνομα; ὕμοιος = ὅμοιος; ἀπὺ = ἀπὸ; Ὑδυσσεὺς = Ὀδυσσεὺς; Ὕλυμπος = Ὄλυμπος; ὔμφαλος = ὄμφαλος; ὔσδος=ὄζος; ὔρνις = ὄρνις; μύγις=μόγις; πύταμος = πόταμος; δεῦρυ = δεῦρο. In Æolic we also find υ for ω: τέκτυν = τέκτων; χελύνη = χελώνη (compare φώρ = L. *fur*): and οι for υ in the single case of χροισός = χρυσός. We find υ for α in Æol. σύρξ = σάρξ, and Lak. ἔγκυτα = ἔγκατα (entrails); and υ for ο in Ion. ῥυφέω = ῥοφέω. The Bœotic dialect often substitutes υ for οι, and ῳ, as in Fῦκος = Fοῖκος, δάμυ = δήμῳ: in these cases the o-sound became u, and then ui became ū. The old Latin *oitier* must similarly have passed through *uitier* in becoming *uti*: the only difference being that the Latin u is a true u, while the Greek υ is ū. It is remarkable that the Bœotic also agrees with the Latin in sometimes representing οι by οε, as in Διονύσοε = Διονύσῳ. We find υ for ο in the Arkadian genitive in -αυ (Ζαμιαυ) from -āο, -āος = Skr. -*áyás*.*

The old u having become υ (ū), in some cases advanced a step farther and became ι: φῖτυς (a father), φιτύω from R. φυ; σίαλος (a fat pig), from σῦς; ὑπερφίαλος beside ὑπερφυής; κίρκος (a ring), beside κύκλος, R. κυρ, from which root come also Κέρκυρα and κέρκος (a tail), ε arising from ι through the influence of the following ρ; ψιθυρός (slanderous), from ψύθος (a lie); μίτυλος and μύτιλος (curtailed), L. *mutilus*; δρίος (copsewood), from δρῦς; θίασος (a band), from R. θυ, with same suffix as in πέτασος; βίβλος from βύβλος (papyrus); ὀλιβρός (slippery), beside L. *lubricus*; μολιβδός beside μολυβδός; λίπτομαι (I am eager), R. λιφ, Skr. *lubhyâmi* (I desire), L. *lubet* and *libet*. We also find Æol. ἴψος, ἴπέρ, ἴπαρ for ὕψος, ὑπέρ, ὕπαρ.

§. 48. Guṇa and Vṛddhi.

The guṇa of ι is ει, and in a few isolated cases αι; its vṛddhi is οι, ο here representing a Skr. *á*. The guṇa of υ is ευ and αυ; its vṛddhi is ου and āυ. The I. E. *a* is represented in Greek by *a*, ε, ο; its guṇa is ο, ā, and η; its vṛddhi is ω.

	Primitive vowels	ε o a	ι	υ
	Guṇa	ο ā η	ει (αι)	ευ (αυ)
	Vṛddhi	ω	οι	ου (āυ)

* Curtius, "Grundzüge," p. 646.

The guṇa of ε of the root is ο: R. γεν, γένος, γόνος; R. φερ, φέρω, φόρος = Skr. *bháras* (a weight); R. τεκ, τεκέσθαι, τόκος; R. τρεφ, τρέφω, τροφή; R. δερκ, δέρκομαι, δέδορκα = Skr. *dadars'a*. In μέμηλα beside μέλει, R. μελ, η appears to be the guṇa of ε of the root.

The guṇa of α of the root is ā or η; R. λαθ, ἔλαθον, λέληθα; R. λαβ, ἔλαβον, εἴληφα; R. λακ, ἔλακον, λέλᾱκα, λέληκα; R. κλαγ, ἔκλαγον, κέκληγα; R. δακ, ἔδακον, δέδηχα.

The guṇa of ο is ā or η: νέος = Skr. *navas* (new), νεᾱ, Ion. νέη = Skr. *navā*, and similar cases.

The vṛddhi of α, ε, ο is ω: R. Ϝραγ, ῥήγνυμι, ἔρρωγα; R. πτακ, ἔπτακον, πτήσσω = πτηκϳω (beside πτα in κατα-πτή-την), πτώξ (cowering for fear); ἀρήγω, ἀρωγός; R. ἀγ, ἄγω, ἀγωγή; R. δο, δίδομεν, δίδωμι; R. ὀδ, ὀδμή, ὄδωδα; L. ἐδ (to eat), ἐδωδή.

The guṇa and vṛddhi of ι are ει and οι; R. ἰ, ἴμεν = Skr. *imas*, εἶμι = Skr. *emi*, οἶμος (a way); L. Ϝικ, ἔ-ϊκ-τον, εἰκών, ἔοικα; R. λιπ, ἔλιπον, λείπω, λοιπός; Κ. Ϝιδ, Ϝίδμεν, Ϝεῖδος, Ϝοῖδα; R. λιβ, λιβάς (a drop), λείβω, λοιβή; Κ. στιχ, ἔστιχον, στείχω, στοῖχος; R. κι, κεῖται = Skr. *s'été*, κοίτη; R. δυ, δίεσθαι (to flee, to be afraid), δείδω, δείδοικα; R. στιβ, ἔστιβον, στείβω, στοιβή; R. λιπ, λίπα, ἀλείφω, ἀλοιφή; R. λιχ, λιχμάω (I lick), λείχω. In αἴθεσθαι (to burn), αι is the guṇa of ι; for it is connected with Skr. *indh* (to burn), L. *æstus*, O. H. G. *eit* (fire). The vṛddhi of this root may be found in οἶστρος (the gadfly), as G. *bremse* (the horsefly), comes from *brennen* (to burn), and L. *tabanus* is connected with Skr. *tap* (to burn).

The guṇa and vṛddhi of υ are ευ and ου, but ευ nearly always takes the place of ου: R. ελυθ, ἤλυθον, ἐλεύσομαι, εἰλήλουθα; κέλευθος, ἀκόλουθος; R. ρυθ, ἐρυθρός, ἐρεύθω (I make red), ῥούσιος (reddish); R. λυκ, ἀμφιλύκη (the dawn), λευκός, λοῦσσον (the white pith of the fir tree); R. πνυ, πνέϜω, πνοϜή; R. φυγ, ἔφυγον, φεύγω, πέφευγα.

Schleicher considers αυ to be the guṇa of υ in αὔω (I kindle), for αὔσω, beside εὕω (1 singe), Skr. *ush* (to burn), *óshami* (I burn), L. *uro* for *uso;* in αὐγή (splendour) beside Skr. *óg'as* (strength and splendour); and in αὐξανω from R. υγ, beside Skr. *ug-ra* (strong). In the first two of these examples, however, he is probably wrong, and in the last certainly so; for Skr. *ush* is from an older *vas*, which is found in *vâsara* (a day), *óg'as* is from *vag'* (to strengthen), L. *vigere, vegere,* and αὐξάνω from R. Ϝαξ, Skr. *vakshâmi* (I grow), Goth. *vahsja* (I grow). In the first two cases the old Ϝα probably became αϜ by transposition, and then αυ, and in the last case we find Hom. ἀέξω = αὔξω, which points back to a form ἀϜεξω, where ε is merely a help-vowel, and where we find α and Ϝ already transposed. If ναῦς, Ion. νηῦς, comes from R. σνυ, Skr. *snu* (to flow), ᾱυ is here the vṛdhhi of υ: on the other hand, if it comes from R. σνᾱ, Skr. *snâ* (to bathe), it is formed like γραῦς, and ᾱυ is therefore not the vṛddhi of υ.* In the following cases ω appears to be the vṛddhi of υ ; ζωμός (broth) beside ζύμη (leaven), L. *jus;* ζώννυμι (I gird), from R. ζυ; χώννυμι (I heap up) from R. χυ. Curtius considers that ω arose from υ through the intermediate step οϜ. Schleicher's view is that, as we have Ion. πλώω for πλώϜω beside πλίϜω, and Dor. βῶς = βοῦς = Skr. *gâus*, and Ionic diphthong ωυ for αυ, so there once, as vṛddhi of υ, existed ωυ = Skr. *âu*, the first element of which gradually assimilated to itself the second, so that finally only the o-sound was heard.

We must carefully distinguish from the diphthongs arising from guṇa and vṛddhi, those which arise from contraction or from compensation for the loss of consonants or from the vocalization and hyperthesis of the original spirants *y* and *v*.

§. 49. When a consonant or consonants are thrown out of a word, the preceding vowel is generally lengthened, to compensate for the loss of the consonants. Thus *a* becomes

* Curtius, "Grundzüge," pp. 161, 281.

ᾱ in πύλᾱς (acc. pl.) = πύλανς, &c., ἱστάς = ἱσταντς, &c.; a becomes αι in the Lesbian Æolic acc. pl. term. -αις = Kret. -ανς, as ταίς = Kret. τάνς, also in Lesb. Æol. τάλαις = ταλανς, παῖς = πανς for παντς, ἀκούσαις = ἀκουσανς; υ becomes ῡ in δεικνύς = δεικνυντς; ε becomes η in πατήρ = πατερς, ποιμήν = ποιμενς, δυσμενής = δυσμενεσς; ε becomes ει in τιθείς = Kret. τιθένς for τιθεντς, εἰς = Kret. ἐνς, χείρ = χέρς, which is still found in a fragment of Timocreon, εἰμί (I am) = ἐσμι, Æol. ἔμμι, ὀρεινός = ὀρεσνος, Æol. ὄρεννος, ἔνειμα = ἐνεμσα, Æol. ἐνέμματο; ο becomes ω in τύπτων = τυπτοντς, ἡγήτωρ (a leader) = ἡγητορς; ο becomes ου in ἵππους = Kret. ἵππονς, &c., ὑπαρχούσας = Kret. ὑπαρχόνσας, ἄγουσι = Dor. ἄγοντι; ο becomes οι in the Lesb. Æol. acc. pl. term. -οις = Kret. -ονς, as τοίς = Kret. τούς, also in ἔχοισα = ἐχοντya, &c., κρύπτοισιν = κρύπτοντι, &c. We have already pointed out that, when a consonant was lost in early times, and compensation was made for it, ε became η, and ο became ω; but that, on the other hand, when the loss did not occur till a later period, ε became ει, and ο became ου. The examples from the dialects above quoted confirm this account of the matter; for we find that the consonants are frequently kept by them in the latter case, but never in the former.

§. 50. The vowels ι and υ, when coming after a semivowel, are frequently thrown back by hyperthesis. Thus, φέρεις = φερεσι = I. E. *bharasi*; ὑπείρ = ὑπερι = Skr. *upari* (above), Z. *upairi* (above); ἐλαύνω = ἐλαννω. In the first stage of hyperthesis, the vowel is not only reflected, but also kept in its original place, as in Zend, where we find *upairi* (above), *bavaiti* = Skr. *bhavati* (he is), &c. In Ion. πουλύς = πολύς, and Ep. εἰνί = ἐνί, πλαίσιον (a square) = πλαθιον (from R. πλατ, whence comes πλατύς), αἰφνίδιος = ἀφνίδιος (compare ἄφνω), we have this stage of hyperthesis. When the original spirants y and v come after ν and ρ, they are generally vocalized and thrown back. Thus μέλαινα = μελανya; κείρω = κερyω; φθείρω = φθερyω; ἀμείνων = ἀμενyονς; γούνατος = γόνϝατος ; ἀμαυρός = ἀμαρϝος ; ταῦρος = ταρϝος, Gallic *tarvos;* νεῦρον = νερϝον, L. *nervus;* γαῦρος (proud) = γαρϝος, Skr. *garva* (pride) ; Ion. οὖλος (for ὅλος) = ὁλϝος = Skr. *sarvas* (all), L. *salvus, sollus;* παῦρος = παρϝος, L. *parvus;* κρίνω (ῑ) = κρινγω, Æol. κρίννω ; πλύνω (ῡ) = πλυνγω ; ι + ι becoming ῑ, and νι, υ. In one case y after λ is vocalized and thrown back, ὀφείλω = ὀφελγω, Hom. ὀφέλλω. We have traces of the older hyperthesis in κρείσσων = κρειτγων for κρετγους, New Ion. κρέσσων ; μείζων = μειγγων for μεγ-γους, New Ion. μέζων ; μᾶλλον = μαιλγον, θᾶσσον = θαιχγον, where ᾰ becomes ᾱ, on account of the loss of ι. In κρείσσων, μείζων, and θᾶσσον, we find hyperthesis of y over mutes. We find ι thrown back also in the following cases when a mute precedes: γυναικ- = γυνακι- = I. E. *ganaki;* αἴξ (a goat), stem αἰγ- = ἀγι-, Skr. *ag'á* (a goat) ; ἐξαίφνης = ἐξαπίνης ; κραιπνός = κραπινος, R. καρπ, compare καρπάλιμος ; δεῖπνον = δεπινον or δαπινον L. *dapinare;* ῥοῖβδος = ῥοβδγος (Hesychius has the form ῥυβδεῖ) ; αἰχμή = ἀκιμη, R. ἀκ, compare ἀκίς (a point); αἴγλη (light) = ἀγιλη, R. ἀγ, compare Skr. *agnis* (fire) = L. *ignis,* the termination being the same as that of στρόβιλος ; αἴκλοι (Hesych. αἱ γωνίαι τοῦ βέλους) = ἀκιλοι, R. ἀκ, as in ἀκίς ; κραιπάλη = κραπιαλη, R. κραπ as in κραιπνος ; Ep. πείκω (I comb) from πεκγω beside πέκω.

§. 51. We frequently find a vowel prefixed to many Greek words, which is absent in the corresponding words in the cognate languages. This phenomenon was called by the old grammarians πρόσθεσις. Curtius points out that this prosthetic vowel is generally found before double consonants, nasals, λ, ρ, and ϝ, seldom before explosives, and never before single π, τ, and φ. Thus we have ἀσκαίρω (I skip) = σκαίρω ; ἀσταφίς (a raisin) = σταφίς ; ἄσταχυς (an ear of corn) = στάχυς ; ἀστήρ beside στεροπή, and·L. *stella;* Lesb. Æol. ἄσφε, ἄσφι = σφέ, σφί ; ἀσπαίρω (I pant) = σπαίρω ; ἀσπάλαξ (a mole) = σπάλαξ ; ἀσφάραγος (the throat), beside σφάραγος (noise); ἐξατράπης from Persian *kshatrapâvan* (ruling the kingdom) beside the form ζατράπης given by Hesychius; ἐψία (play)=ψία; ἐχθές=χθές; ἰκτίς (a weasel)=κτίς; ὀκρυόεις, beside κρύος; ἀκροάομαι beside Skr. *s'ru* (to hear); ὀφρύς=Skr. *bhrûs* (eyebrow). In some cases one of the two consonants falls out after the prosthetic vowel, as in ὄνομα, Ion. οὔνομα for ὀγνομα, L. *nomen* for *gnomen*; ὀλισθάνω for ὀγλισθανω, R. γλιτ; ἠπανία (want), beside σπάνις; ἐρωέω (I flow), beside Skr. *sru* (to flow); ὀδυσσάμενος (hating), R. ὀδυς for ὀδϝις, beside Skr. *dvish* (to hate). We have ἐννέα beside L. *novem*; ἀνήρ beside L. *Nero*; ἐνεγκεῖν beside Sl. *nesti* (to bear); ἐμέ = με; ὀμιχέω beside L. *mingo*; ἀμέλγω beside L. *mulgeo*; ἀμάω beside E. *mow*; ἐλαχύς beside Skr. *laghu*; Ὄλυμπος from R. λαμπ; ἐλαύνω from R. λα; ἔρεβος beside Skr. *rag'as* (darkness); ἐρετμός beside L. *remus*; ἐρυθρός beside L. *ruber*; ἐϝείκοσι = ϝείκοσι; ἐϝίργειν = ϝέργειν; ἐϝέδνα = ϝέδνα; ἐϝέρση = ϝέρση (dew). We have in the case of the explosives, ὀδούς beside L. *dens*; ὀδάξ (mordicus) beside δάκνω; ἐθέλω = θέλω; ὀβελός beside βέλος; ἀγανός (noble) beside γαῦρος (proud). The opinion that these prosthetic vowels are fragments of prepositions does not appear to rest on any sufficient ground, for the apokope of dissyllabic prepositions is limited to the Æolic and Epic dialect, and the preposition ἐν never loses its final consonant.* Another explanation has been suggested to account for the vowels prefixed to λ, μ, ν, ρ, ς. It is this, that, as we pronounce *l*, *el*, *m*, *em*, &c., so these letters were predisposed to the adoption of prosthetic vowels. In a similar way it is possible to account for the origin of ἠνεμόεις, Πειρίθυος, οὐλόμενος from ἀνεμόεις, Περίθυος, ὀλόμενος, by supposing them to have passed through the stages ἀ'νεμοεις, Πε'ριθοος, ὀ'λομενος; unless the lengthening is due to the exigencies of the metre. We find in Æolic the form ἔδοντες for ὀδόντες,† and consequently some writers derive ὀδούς from the

---

* Curtius, "Grundzüge," p. 655.

† Schleicher considers ἔδυντες to be the participle of ἔδω, poetically used for ὀδόντες.

R. ἰδ (to eat); but this is extremely unlikely, as the initial vowel does not appear in any of the sister languages. It is much more probable that o is a prosthetic vowel, as we find ἀδαγμός (a sting), ἀδαξέω and ὀδάξω (I bite, sting), beside δάκνω. Ὀφρύς has been treated by some as equivalent to ὀφ+φρυς=eye+brow, ὀφ appearing in ὀφ-θαλμός. The initial vowels in ὀμφαλός and ὄνυξ are not prosthetic, for the corresponding Latin terms are *umbilicus* and *unguis*, and the Latin language is not inclined to prosthesis. From a comparison of the Skr. *nábhi* (navel) and *nakha* (a nail), it is likely that the original forms of the corresponding roots were *nâbh* and *nagh*, from which in Græco-Italic times were developed the roots *ânbh* and *angh*. Prosthetic vowels are of common occurrence in the Romance languages. Thus we have in French, *épée* for *espée*, from L. *spada*, *échelle* for *eschelle*, from L. *scala*, *établir* for *establir*, from L. *stabilire*, *espérer* from L. *sperare*, *escabeau* from L. *scabellum* *estame* from L. *stamen*; in Spanish, *estar* = L. *stare*; in Italian, *aringa* from G. *ring*, whence E. *harangue*. This tendency of the Romance languages to prefix initial vowels appears to have already begun in the fourth century, for on inscriptions of that date we find such forms as *istatuam*, *ispirito*, *Isticho* = *Sticho*. In Welsh, *y* is prefixed to words borrowed from the Latin which begin with *s* followed by another consonant, as in *ysgol*, *yspryd*, *ysgwyd* from L. *schola*, *spiritus*, *scutum*.

§. 52. The insertion* of a vowel is of frequent occurrence in Greek, and is called ἀνάπτυξις. This insertion occurs before or after λ, ρ, and the nasals, and, according to Curtius, arises from the tone, perceptibly heard in these sonants, upon which fact also rest the frequent metathesis of these sounds, and the possibility of *r* and *l* being treated as vowels in some languages. The vowels that are inserted are generally *a* and

---

* Consult Curtius, "Grundzüge," p. 656; and Walter, in "K. Z.," vol. x., p. 428, *seq.*, vol. xii. p. 375, *seq.*, p. 401, *seq.*, on Vocaleinschiebung in Griechischen.

ε, less frequently ο and ι, and very seldom υ. We find a vowel inserted before or after λ, in the following cases: ὠλένη, L. *ulna*; χάλαζα, L. *grando*; καλύπτω = κρύπτω; ἀλώπηξ, St. Faλωπεκ, L. *vulpes* (?); ἀλεγεινός beside ἄλγος; ἀλέξω and ἀρήγω beside ἀρκέω, ἄλκη, L. *arceo*, Skr. *raksh* (to protect); ἀλικίνος (δυνατός, Hesych.) = ἄλκιμος; δολιχός = Skr. *dirghas* (long); ἠλακάτη (spindle) beside ἄρκυς (a net); ἤλυθον = ἦλθον (?); θάλασσα for ταραχγα from R. τραχ (according to Walter, however, for θλατ-γα, connected with L. *fret-um*); κολεκάνος (long and thin), κολοσσός (a great statue), O. L. *cracentes* (graciles), L. *gracilis*; μόλυβδος, L. *plumbum*; μαλακός beside βλάξ (weak); πέλαγος beside πλήσσω, R. πλαγ (to strike), not connected with πλάξ (a plain), as πέλαγος denotes the sea in its dangerous aspect; πέλεθρον = πλέθρον. In the case of ρ we have the following examples: ταράσσω = ταραχγω, R. τραχ, whence the perfect τέτρηχα; ὀρέγω, ὀρόγυια = ὀργυιά ὀριγνάομαι (I stretch), R. ὀργ, Skr. *arg* (to acquire), L. *rego*; Æol. φέρενα = φερνή; ἐρωδιός (a heron) L. *ardea*; χεράς (gravel), St: χεραδ, E. *grit*; θόρυβος beside θρῦλος (noise); ὄροβος (vetches) and ἐρέβινθος (pulse), L. *ervum*; ἀράχνη (the 'spinner') beside ἄρκυς; Makedon. δάρυλλος for δρῦς; ἀραβύλαι (Hesych.) = ἀρβύλαι (a kind of shoes); ταριχεύω (I embalm), τάριχος (a mummy, dried or salted fish), beside ταρχύω (I bury solemnly), perhaps connected with R. τερς (to dry), Skr. *tarsh* (to thirst), L. *torreo* for *tors-eo*. In the case of the nasals we have as examples, κονίς, pl. κονίδες (eggs of lice, nits), from R. *knid*, as appears from A. S. *hnit*, Lith. *glindas*, L. *lendes*; ὄνυξ, Sl. *onuch* from R. *angh*; πινυτός (wise) from R. πνυ, whence πνέω, πεπνυμένος; σκηνίπτω = σκνίπτω (I pinch); ἄφενος beside ἀφνειός; τέμαχος (a slice), beside τμήγω (I cut), from R. τμαγ (?); Τόμαρος = Τμᾶρος (a mountain in Thesprotia); Τυμῶλος = Τμῶλος (a mountain in Lydia). In other languages also we find vowels similarly inserted. Thus, in Zend *e* is in certain cases inserted between two consonants; and *r* when followed by a consonant, or when final, becomes *re*, as *dademahi* (we give) = Skr. *dadmasi*, *dadares'a* (1 sing. perf.) = Skr. *dadars'a* = δέδορκα, *dátare* (voc. sing.) from St. *dátar*. In O. H. G. we have *puruc* = Goth. *baurgs*, *farah* = L. *porcus*, *araweiz* = L. *ervum*. In Latin, we have *Æsculapius* = 'Ασκληπιός, *Procina* = Πρόκνη, *Alcumena* = 'Αλκμήνη, *sumus* from *esumus* = I. E. *asmas*. In Oscan a vowel is frequently inserted, as *Alafaternom* = L. *Alfaternorum*, *aragetud* = L. *argento*, *sakarater* = L. *sacratur*.

§. 53. The Gutturals.

K = I. E. *k* : καλός, καλλύνω (I make clean), Skr. *kalya* (healthy), E. *heal*, *hale;* κάρυον (a nut), Skr. *karaka* (cocoa nut), L. *carina* (a shell, keel); καρκίνος (a crab), Skr. *karka* (a crab), L. *cancer;* κείω, κέαζω, R. ске or ска, Skr. *k'há* (to divide), L. *descisco*, *scio;* λύκος = Skr. *vṛkas* (a wolf); δείκνυμι, R. дик, Skr. *dis'* (to show), L. *dico;* δέκα = Skr. and Z. *das'an* (ten), L. *decem;* ἕκατον for ἑν-κατον, Skr. *s'atam* (an hundred), L. *centum*.

Γ = I. E. *g* : γῆρυς, Skr. *gar* (to call), L. *garrio;* ἐγείρω, Skr. *gar* (to awake); στέγω, Skr. *sthag* (to cover), L. *tego;* ἀγρός = Skr. *ag'ras* (a level plain), L. *ager;* ἀργής (bright), ἄργυρος, ἀργῖλος (white clay), Skr. *arg'una* (bright), *rag'ata* (silver), L. *arguo* (I make clear), *argentum*. Γ is found for an I. E. *k* in ἀρήγω from R. арк ; τήγανον (a frying pan) from τήκω ; μίσγω, R. миг, beside Skr. *mis'ra* (mixed), L. *misceo;* λύγη (gloom) beside R. люк (λευκός, &c.); πηγός (firm), πήγνυμι, beside L. *pac-iscor*, Skr. *pas'* (to bind); ἅρπαξ, St. ἁρπαγ = L. *rapax*, St. *rapac;* κραυγή, beside Skr. *krôs'a* (a cry); ἐφράγην beside φράσσω = φρακ-yω = L. *farcio;* μαγεύς (one who kneads) beside μάσσω = μακyω, L. *macerare;* πληγή beside πλήσσω = πληκyω, Lith. *plàkti* (to beat). We find a tenuis weakened to a media in It. *luogo*, from L. *locum*, It. *padre* from L. *patrem*, Fr. *abeille* from L. *apiculam*, &c. Γ is lost in αἶα = γαῖα, ὄρος = Skr. *giri* (a mountain), Bœot. ἰών

= ἐγών, Tarentine ὄλίος = ὀλίγος, Φιαλία = Φιγαλία (an Arcadian city). In the following cases, in which γ corresponds to a Sanskrit *h* or *gh*, either each root existed in two forms, one with *g*, and another with *gh*, in the Indo-European, or else the I. E. form had *g* only, from which by aspiration *gh* was developed in Sanskrit, and this *gh* became *h*: γένυς = Skr. *hanus* (the chin), L. *gena*, Goth. *kinnus* ; γε, Skr. *ha*, Ved. *gha*, Goth. *k* in *mi-k*, O. H. G. *h* in *unsi-h* ; μέγας, μεγάλος = Goth. *mikils*, Skr. *mahat* (great), L. *magnus* ; ἐγών = Skr. *aham*, Goth. *ik*. In these cases the Gothic *k* points back to an I. E. *g*. In the following examples γ = I. E. *gh*; ἐγγύς, Skr. *aṅhu* (narrow), Goth. *aggvus* (narrow), the original *gh* being still retained in ἄγχι ; θυγάτηρ = Skr. *duhitâ* ; and perhaps in λαγώς (a hare) beside Skr. *laṅgh* (to jump).

Χ = I. E. *gh*: δολιχός = Skr. *dîrghas* (long) ; ἐλαχύς = Skr. *laghus* (light) ; στείχω, Skr. *stigh* (to ascend), Goth. *steiga* (I go up) ; χρίω, χρῖσμα, Skr. *ghar* (to sprinkle), *gharsh* (to rub), *ghṛta* (clarified butter) ; χοῖρος, Skr. *ghṛshti* (a pig), O. N. *gris* (a little pig). Χ, θ, and φ, frequently represent an I. E. *k*, *t*, and *p*, as we shall see in §. 63, on Aspiration.

The spiritus asper represents a Græco-Italic initial *y*, *v*, and *s*. It is = *y* in ἧπαρ, Skr. *yakṛt*, L. *jecur* ; ὥρα, Z. *yâre* (a year), E. *year* ; ὅς = Skr. *yas* (who). It is = *v*[*] in ἕσπερος, L. *vesper* ; ἕννυμι = Fεσ-νυμι, Skr. *vas* (to clothe). It is = *s* in ὁ, ἡ, = Skr. *sa* (he), *sâ* (she), O. L. acc. *sum*, *sam* ; ἁ in ἅ-παξ = *sa* in Skr. *sa-kṛt* (once), L. *simplex* ; ἑ = L. *se* ; ῥέω, R. ῥυ for σρυ, Skr. *sru* (to flow) ; ῥοφέω, L. *sorbeo*. In εἰπόμην (for ἐσεπομην, R. σεπ), εἰστήκειν (for ἐσεστηκειν, R. στᾱ), the initial aspirate perhaps arose from the σ lost in the second syllable. Sometimes the original initial σ is retained beside the younger aspirate, as in σῦς = ὗς, Ἑλλοί = Σελλοί. The spiritus asper

---

[*] Similarly in Spanish we have *hijo* = L. *filius*, *heno* = L. *fenum*, *herir* = L. *ferire*, *hacer* = L. *facere*.

is preserved between two vowels in ταώς = L. *pavo*, and in Laconian ἐποιεέ for ἐπόιησε. In ῥίν beside Skr. *ghrana* (the nose), the sp. asp. represents *gh*. In Attic an initial sp. asp. is frequently added where it does not exist in the other dialects. Hence the Athenians were called δασυντικοί in opposition to the Æolians, who were called ψιλωτικοί, from their aversion to this sound. Thus we have ἵππος beside Lesb. ἵππιος, Tarent. ἵκκος, Sikil. ἰπνή (ἐφιππίς), and the common forms Λεύκιππος, Γλαύκιππος, L. *equus* = Skr. *as'vas* : ἥλιος = Ep. ἠέλιος; ἡμεῖς = Æol. ἄμμες, Skr. *asmân*; ἡγεῖσθαι beside ἄγω; ἑώς = Ep. ἠώς, Æol. αὔως. We also find the Heraklean ὀκτώ, ἐννέα, perhaps from the analogy of ἕξ, ἑπτά. Initial υ in Attic always is aspirated, as in ὑπό, Skr. *upa* (near); ὑπέρ, Skr. *upari* (above); ὕδωρ, Skr. *udan* (water); ὕστερος = Skr. *uttaras* (later). Similarly we find *h* prefixed in L. *humerus* for *umerus*, *humor* for *umor*, Span. *hedrar* = L. *iterare*, Fr. *haut* = L. *altus*.

The spiritus asper was frequently changed into the lenis, as in Ep. ἦδος beside ἡδύς; Ep. οὖλος beside ὅλος; ἔδαφος and οὖδας beside ὁδός, R. ἑδ = Skr. *sad* (to go); ἄω (I satiate) only found in inf. pres. ἄμεναι and ἄδδην beside ἄδην, and L. *satis*, *satur*; Ἐρινύς = Skr. *Saranyûs*; εἴρω (I join), beside σειρά, ὅρμος, and L. *sero*; ἐτεός = Skr. *satyas* (true); ὀπός beside L. *sucus*; ὀρός beside L. *serum*; ἁ (in ἄλοχος &c.), for ἁ = Skr. *sa*; ἤθω = σήθω (I sift); ἰδίω (I sweat); beside ἱδρώς; ἴδιος beside ἑ = σϜε; ὄφρα from pronominal stem ὁ = Skr. *ya*. In Ionic we also see a tendency to weaken the spiritus asper in the fact that after elision a preceding tenuis was not aspirated by a following aspirate, as in ἀπ' οὗ, κάτοδος. In Æolic the initial aspirate was kept, according to Ahrens, whenever it represented an original *s* or *y*, except in ὔμμες beside Skr. *yushman*, and κατιδρύσει beside L. *sedeo*, Goth. *sita* (I sit), but it was lost whenever it had arisen from any other cause. Thus we find the aspirate kept in ἅγνος beside Skr. *yag'* (venerari), ὁδός in ἔφοδος beside Skr. *sad* (to go), &c. ; and it is absent in ἄμμες beside ἡμεῖς and Skr. *asmán*, ἶρος = ἱερός, ἰπέρ = ὑπέρ, ἴψος = ὕψος, &c. This view of the case does not appear to be exactly correct; for we find in Alkæus καθύπερθεν, πρώτισθ᾽ ὑπό, where the aspiration before υ is retained, though it is not original, as we see from the Skr. forms *upari* and *upa;* and moreover in ἇδυς = Skr. *svadus*, and Ὑῤῤαδήῳ (Alk. 73), beside L. *spurius*, the aspiration is lost, though the words originally began with *sv*. This tendency of the Æolic to ψίλωσις refutes the old-fashioned idea that Latin was closely connected with it, for the sibilant is retained in Latin, from which the aspiration in Greek was developed. The spiritus asper is entirely lost in Modern Greek.

§. 54. The Dentals.

T = I. E. *t*: ἀντί, Skr. *anti* (before) ; πέτομαι, R. πετ, Skr. *pat* (to fly) ; στένω, R. στεν, Skr. *stan* (to groan) ; στόρνυμι. Skr. *star* (to strew) ; τείνω, R. τεν or ταν, Skr. *tan* (to stretch) ; &c.

T = I. E. *kv*: τίς = L. *quis* = Osc. *pis*, Skr. *kim* (quid), Z. *k'isk'a* (quisquis), Osc. *pitpit* = L. *quidquid;* τέ = L. *que*, Skr. *k'a*, Goth. *h* in *nih* = L. *neque;* πέντε = L. *quinque*, Æol. πέμπε; ἄλλοτε = Dor. ἄλλοκα; ταῶς = L. *pavo*. T appears to correspond to *k* in τίω (I honour), τίνω (I punish), Skr. *k'i* (to distribute), Z. *k'i* (to punish), and in ἀκιναγμός = τίναγμος (κίνησις). Here *k* became *t*, through the stages *ky* and *ty*. In Latin, *c* and *t* are frequently interchanged before *i* as in *patricius = patritius, Mucius = Mutius*.

Δ = I. E. *d*: δαμάω, R. δαμ, Skr. *dam* (to tame), L. *domare*, Goth. *ga-tamjan* (δαμᾶν), O. H. G. *zamón* (to tame); δρῦς = Skr. *drus*, Goth. *triu* (tree) ; ἔδω, R. ἐδ, Skr. *ad* (to eat), L. *edo*, Goth. *ita* (I eat) ; ἕζομαι, R. ἐδ, Skr. *sad* (to sit), L. *sedeo*, Goth. *sita* (I sit) ; &c.

Δ = I. E. *t*: δάπις (a carpet), beside τάπης and ταπίς; Ἄρτεμις, Ἀρτέμιδ-ος, beside Dor. Ἀρτάμιτος, whence Ἀρταμίτιος (name of a Spartan month), and 'Αρταμίτιον ; θέμις, θέμιδ-ος beside θέμιτος, in Pindar; ἕβδομος from ἕπτα ; ὄγδοος from ὄκτω ; νέποδες (= ἀπόγονοι in Alexandrian Poets), beside L. *nepotes*.

Δ = I. E. *dh* in πύνδαξ (the bottom) beside πυθμήν, Skr. *budhna* (the bottom), I. E. *bhudh* being the root; and perhaps in ἀλδαίνω (I increase) beside ἀλθαίνω (I heal) and Skr. *ardh* (to increase).

Δ = I. E. *g*: δελφύς (the womb) = Skr. *garbhas* (the womb); Lakon. διφοῦρα = γέφυρα; Δημήτηρ = Γη-μήτηρ. Conversely we find γλυκύς for δλυκυς, L. *dulcis*, and γνόφος for and beside δνόφος. We also find δ for β in Dor. ὀδελός = ὀβελός, and Kret. ὀδολκαί = ὀβολοί.

Θ = I. E. *dh*: ἄνθος, Skr. *andhas* (plant), L. *ador*; θῆσθαι (Hom. to milk), θῆλυς, R. θα, θη, Skr. *dhâ* (to drink), *dhênu* (a cow), L. *filius, femina, felare* (to suck) ; θρασύς, Skr. *dharsh* (to dare), Goth. *ga-daursan* (θαρρεῖν) ; θυγάτηρ, I. E. *dhughatar*, Skr. *duhitar*, Goth. *dauhtar*; θύρα, Skr. *dhvâra* (door) L. *fores*, Goth. *daur* (door); &c.

Θ = I. E. *gh* in θερμός, R. θερ, Skr. *gharma* (heat), L. *formus* (hot), *fornax, forceps*, Goth. *varmjan* (θάλπειν). We find θ and χ interchanged in ὄρνιθος = Bœot. ὄρνιχος, Mod. Gr. Λιθαδό-νησα = Λιχάδες, and ἤρχα beside ἦλθον, unless it be derived from ἔρχομαι. This change is not easily accounted for: it has been suggested that θ developed a hard aspirate after it, before which it afterwards fell out, and that this aspirate afterwards developed χ before it, and then fell out. This explanation is, however, very improbable. We also find θ interchanged with φ in Kret. ὄθρυς (a mountain) = ὀφρύς (brow of a hill), ὀθρυόεν (κρημνῶδες), 'Οθρυάδας (superciliosus) ; θύλλα (κλάδους ἢ φύλλα ἢ ἑορτὴ 'Αφροδίτης, Hesych.) = φύλλα; and perhaps in θυλλίς, θαλλίς, θύλακος, all meaning a *bag*, if these words are connected with Goth. *balgs* (a bag).

Ρ = I. E. *r*: εὐρύς = Skr. *urus* (wide), from I. E. *varus* ;

οὐρανός = Skr. *Varunas* (the god of the water); ὄρος, Skr. *giri* (a mountain), Ch. Sl. *gora* (a mountain); ὄρνυμι, R. ὀρ, Skr. *ar* (to move), L. *orior;* ῥέω, R. ῥυ, σρυ, Skr. *sru* (to flow); σῦριγξ, Skr. *svar* (to sound), &c.

P is lost in ποτί = προτί, πρός. Προτί became πορτί, which is found in the Kretan dialect, and then ποτί: similarly we have φρέατος, ὕδατος, σκατός for φρεαρτος, ὑδαρτος, σκαρτος, L. *pedo* = πέρδω, &c. Leo Meyer asserts that ρ is lost in πετάννυμι beside Skr. *prath* (to extend), and φέγγος beside Skr. *bhrâg* (to shine): but πετάννυμι is connected with L. *pateo, pando*, O. H. G. *fadam* (filum), E. *fathom,* and *prath* is found in πλατύς; *bhrâg* is connected with φλέγω, L. *fulgeo, flagro,* Goth. *bairhts* (δῆλος), and, according to Curtius, φέγγος (for φεγγϜος) is related to φάϜος (Æol. φαῦος, Pamphyl. φάβος), exactly as βένθος is to βάθος.

The Laconians frequently changed σ, especially when final, into ρ: thus they used ἀκκόρ, πίσορ, σιόρ, ἀβώρ, πόρ, βίωρ, μιργάβωρ, &c. for ἀσκός, πίθος, θεός, ἠώς, ποῦς, ἴσως, μισγήως, &c. The only other example of the same change in any other Doric dialect is the Kret. τεύρ (σοῦ) for τέος. This change is also found in a few cases in the Æolic dialects of Elis and Eretria. In no case does σ appear to have been changed into ρ, when it comes between two vowels: thus we find in the Elean treaty τοῖρ Ϝαληῖοις, but τοῖς Ἠρ Ϝαψοις.

Initial ρ is always aspirated, except in Ῥάριον πεδίον and ῥάρος (a child untimely born).

Λ = I. E. *r*: ἅλλομαι, R. ἀλ, Skr. *sar* (to go); ἅλς, Skr. *sara* (salt); βούλομαι, Skr. and Z. *var* (to choose); ὅλος = Skr. *sarvas* (all), O. L. *sollus* (all), &c.

Λ = I. E. *l*: see §. 21.

Λ represents an older ν in λίτρον beside νίτρον, from Heb. *neter;* πλεύμων beside πνεύμων; σκολόπαξ (a large bird, of snipe kind), beside G. *schnepfe,* E. *snipe;* and perhaps in ἄλλος = Skr. *anyas* (alius). Conversely the Dorians often changed λ before τ and θ into ν, as in βέντιστος, φίντατος, ἦνθεν, &c.

We find *n* and *l* interchanged in other languages, as in Skr. *skandha* (shoulder), Med. L. *spalda*, E. *shoulder*; Skr. *kanyâ* (a girl), Ir. *caile* (a woman); κονίδες (eggs of lice, nits), L. *lendes*, Lith. *glindas*; It. *Bologna* = *Bononia*, *veleno* = L. *venenum*; Prov. *namela* (a blade) = L. *lamella*.

Λ is vocalized in Kret. αὐκάν, αὖμα, αὐγεῖν, &c., for ἀλκάν, ἄλμη, ἀλγεῖν, &c., as in E. *talk*, *calm*, and Umbr. *muta*, *vutu* for *multa*, *vultum*.

Σ = I. E. *s* : R. ἐς, εἰμί (Æol. ἔμμι) = ἐσμι = Skr. *asmi* (I am), ἐστί = Skr. *asti* (he is), L. *sum*, *est*, Lith. *esmi*, *esti*, Goth. *im*, *ist*; R. ἐς from Fες, ἔννυμι for ἐς-νυμι, ἐσθής, Skr. *vas* (to clothe), L. *vestis*; R. ἧς, ἧσται = Skr. *âstê*; ἶσος, Skr. *vishu* (æque); R. συ, κασσύω (from κατά and σύω), Skr. *siv* (to sow), L. *suo*, Goth. *siu-ja* (ἐπιρράπτω).

Σ is generally omitted between two vowels, as in μένους for μενεσος = Skr. *manasas* (gen. sing.); φέρῃ for φερεσαι; Fιός (poison), = Skr. and Z. *vishas* (poison), L. *virus*; &c. Σ in these cases probably first became the spiritus asper, and then fell out. Σ is, however, frequently retained, especially when it represents an original *t*, as in φησί, Dor. φατί; ἐνιαύσιος, Dor. ἐνιαύτιος, from ἐνιαυτός; πλούσιος, Dor. πλούτιος, from πλοῦτος; πλησίος beside ἄπλητος, Dor. πλατίος; διακόσιοι, Dor. διακάτιοι; εἴκοσι, Dor. Fείκατι; πέρυσι, Dor. πέρυτι, Skr. *parut*; ἔπεσον, Dor. ἔπετον, from πίπτω = πι-πετω; Ποσειδῶν, Dor. Ποτειδάν.

The Laconians generally changed θ into σ: in the Lysistrata of Aristophanes we find such forms as σέλει, σέτω, ἀγασός, σιός (θεός), Ἀσάνα, &c., and yet in other cases, without any apparent reason, θ is retained, as in θείκελοι, &c.; in Thucydides, in the Lakonian decree (v. 77), we find τῶ σιῶ σύματος for τοῦ θεοῦ θύματος, &c. In every case they used σ for θ, except where the law of euphony would be violated by the change; as in θίασος, on account of the following σ; ἔσθος, not ἔσσος; ἄθροος not ἄσρυος, as no Greek used the conjunction of σρ, &c. This change did not set in till late;

for we find that it was unknown to the Spartan Colonists who founded Tarentum and Heraklea. The Dorians once possessed another sibilant, which they called San, and of which traces are found in the double σ in such Dorian forms as Ἀρισστόδαμος.

N = I. E. *n*: R. ἄν, ἄνεμος, Skr. *an* (to breathe), *anila* (wind), L. *animus, anus*; ἀνήρ, Skr. *nara* (a man), Sabin. *nero* (brave); ἐννέα, Skr. and Z. *navan* (nine); R. μεν, μαν, μένος, μῆνις, Μέντωρ, μνήμη, Skr. and Z. *man* (to think), L. *maneo, memini, moneo*, Goth. *muns* (νόημα), O. H. G. *minna* (love); ναῦς = Skr. *náus* (a ship); L. *navis*, &c.

N = I. E. *m*: ἔφερον = Skr. *abharam*; ποδῶν = Skr. *padám*, L. *pedum*; ἐφέρετον = *abharatam*; τόν = Skr. *tam*, L. *istum*; τάων (τῶν) = Skr. *tásám*, L. *istarum*; and similar terminations. Curtius also compares ἡνία (the reins), with Skr. *yam* (to bind); R. θαν, ἔθανον, with Skr. *dham* (to blow); βαίνω = βαν-ϳω, with Skr. *gam*; κύανος (dark blue steel), with Skr. *s'yáma* (dark); χθών with χαμάι, L. *humus*; χιών with Skr. *him* (frost), *hima* (snow), L. *hiems*. These are, however, doubtful cases; and it is quite possible that ν may have originally been part of the pronominal suffix *na*, as is certainly the case with βαίνω, the root of which is βα = Skr. *gá* (to go).

§. 55. The Labials.

Π = I. E. *p*: ἀπό, Skr. *apa* (away) Z. *apa* (from) L. *ab*; ἐπί, Skr. *api* (to), Z. *aipi* (after); ἑπτά = Skr. *saptan*, Z. *haptan*; R. λιπ, λίπα (oil), Skr. *lip* (to anoint), &c.

Whenever π corresponds to a Skr. *k, k', s'*, either the original sound must have been *kv*, or, if *k* was the original sound, it must have passed through the stage *kv* in becoming π. Thus we have ἵππος = Skr. *as'vas*, L. *equus*, O. S. *chu*; R. ἐπ, ἔπομαι, Skr. *sak'* (to follow), L. *sequor*; R. λιπ, λείπω, Skr. *rik'* (to leave), L. *linquo*; πεντε, Skr. *pañk'an*, L. *quinque*; R. πεπ, πίπτω, Skr. *pak'* (to cook), L. *coquo*; πού, πῶς, Ion. κοῦ, κῶς,

Skr. *ka* (who), *kva* (where), L. *quis*, Goth. *hvas* (who); in all which cases the I. E. forms had *kv*, where the Greek has π. Σπ and σκ are interchanged in some cases; thus we have σπάλαξ (a mole) = σκάλοψ, σπάλαθρον (a poker) = σκάλευθρον; similarly we have σπινθήρ beside L. *scintilla*, Goth. *skeinan*; σκῦλον, L. *spolia*; R. σκεπ, σκέπτομαι, L. *specio*; R. σφαλ, σφάλλω; Skr. *sphal* and *skhal* (to totter). Σπ and στ are also interchanged : στάδιον, Æol. σπάδιον, L. *spatium*; Æol. σπόλα for στολή; similarly we have σπεύδω beside L. *studeo* and στροῦθος beside Goth. *sparva*, E. *sparrow*.

Π appears to represent an I. E. *bh* in the two following cases : R. πι, πω, πίνω, Æol. πώνω, Skr. *pî, pâ, pibâmi* (I drink), where we find a trace of the I. E. *bh* in *b*, L. *potus, bibo*, E. *beer*; πυός (beestings), Skr. *piyusha* (beestings), O. H. G. *biost*, N. H. G. *biest*, E. *beestings*.

B = I. E. *b*: see §. 22.

B = I. E. *bh* : βρέμβος (ἔμβρυον, Hesych.) beside βρέφος; θάμβος which is related to Hom. τάφος as βένθος to βάθος; φέβομαι for φεβιομαι, a reduplication of R. φι = Skr. *bhî, bibhêmi* (I fear); βρεχμός (the top of the head), A. S. *bregen* (the brain), which Grassman connects with φράσσω (R. φραγ) = Goth. *bairga* (R. *barg*), just as Goth. *hvairnei* (the skull), is derived from a root signifying *to cover;* βρέμω, Skr. *bhram* (to whirl),* L. *fremo*, O. N. *brim* (the surge), φόρμιγξ may be derived from this root, as βρέμεσθαι is used of the lyre in Pindar (Nem. xi. 7); θρόμβος (a clot of blood), beside τρέφω (to curdle), τροφαλίς (fresh cheese); κόρυμβος (the top), beside κορυφή; κράμβος (dry) beside κάρφω (to dry); κύμβος (a cup) = Skr. *kumbhas* (a jug) ; ὄμβρος beside Skr. *ambhas* (water); στέμβω, στιβαρός beside ἀστεμφής (unmoved), στῖφος, Skr. *stambh* (to prop); στρόμβος (a whirlwind, a top), beside στρέφω; βλύω = φλύω (to bubble); λαμβάνω, R. λαβ,

---

* Max Muller (ii. p. 217), opposes this view, and connects Skr. *bhram* with Gr. φρίμασσειν.

beside εἴ-ληφ-α, Skr. *labh* (to seize). In addition to these examples, Grassman (" K. Z.," vol. xii., pp. 91, 93), adduces ὄβριμος beside Skr. *ambhṛna* (powerful), βασκαίνω beside L. *fascino*, and βάζω (I speak), beside φήμη, R. φη, Skr. *bhâ*, but ὄβριμος is rather connected with R. βρι, βρίθω, and the other two cases are extremely doubtful.

B = I. E. *v*: βούλομαι, Skr. *var* (to choose), L. *volo;* βλάστη (a shoot), Skr. *vardh* (to grow). Similarly we find Lakon. βέργον, βιδεῖν, βείκατι for Ϝέργον, Ϝιδεῖν, Ϝείκοσι ; here, however, β may have been pronounced as F.

B = I. E. *p*: ἁβρός (luxurious), beside ἁπαλός (tender), perhaps connected with L. *sapor;* Ἀμβρακία beside the older Ἀμπρακία, π becoming β on account of the preceding μ, just as in Modern Greek μπ is written for the sound of the old β ; ἴαμβος beside ἰάπτω ; καλύβη (a hut), beside καλύπτω, L. *clupeus;* καρβατίνη (a shoe) = καρπατίνη ; κέβλη and κεβάλη (the head), κυβιστάω (I jump headlong), beside Skr. *kapâla* (the skull), κεφαλή, and κύπρος (κεφάλαιον ἀριθμοῦ); κεκλεβώς (found on an inscription of Andania) = κεκλοφώς, from R. κλεπ ; κομβακένεται (κόμπους λέγει, Hesych).) and κρέμβαλον (a clapper) beside L. *crepare*, owe their βς to the influence of μ ; λεβηρίς (a skin) and λοβός (a pod) beside λέπω ; στίλβω beside στιλπνός (glittering), perhaps connected with στεροπή, ἀστράπτω ; στοιβή (stuffing) beside στύπος, Skr. *stupâ* (a heap), L. *stipa, stupa* ; ὕβρις from ὑπέρ ; βατεῖν and βικρός were used at Delphi for πατεῖν and πικρός ; βόσκω is connected with L. *pasco* by Leo Meyer, but this comparison is very doubtful, as there are no analogous cases save the last-mentioned Delphic forms. In the Kret. ἀβλοπές for ἀβλαβές, π appears to represent an older β ; but Curtius suggests that π may be original, and that the root is not βλαβ, but βλαπ for μλαπ, a causative formed from μλα = Skr. *mlâ* (to fade), which is the root of μαλακός, βλάξ.

Whenever β corresponds to a Skr. *g* or *g'*, either the original sound was *gv*, or, if *g* was the original sound, it must have passed through the stage gv in becoming β. Thus we have R. βa, Skr. *gâ* (to go), *agâm* = ἔβην, Lat. *betere, venio*, Osc. *ben* (to come), Goth. *quiman* (to come); R. βαλ, βάλλω, Skr. *gal* (to drop), O. H. G. *quillu*, (scaturio); βαρύς = Skr. *gurus* = Goth. *kaurs*; βία, Skr. *g'i* (to conquer); βίος, Skr. *g'iv* (to live), L. *vivo*, E. *quick*; βοή, γόος, Skr. *gu* (to sound), L. *boere, bovare*; R. βορ, βορά, Skr. *gar* (to devour), L. *vorare*; βοῦς = Skr. *gâus*; Bœot. βανά = γυνή; πρέσβυς = Kret. πρεῖγυς, Dor. πρέσγυς, from πρες (L. *pris* in *pris-cus, pristinus*) = πάρος = Skr. *puras* (before), and R. γυ = γα, γεν, from which also comes Πελασγοί (the ancients); ἔρεβος beside Skr. *rag'as* (darkness), Goth. *riquis* (darkness); τάρβος beside Skr. *targ'* (to threaten). When β represents an older gv we occasionally find instead of it the dialectic variety ζ, as in Arkad. ἐπιζαρεῖν = ἐπιβαρεῖν, Arkad. ζέρεθρον = βάραθρον, from same root as βορά, Skr. *gar* (to devour), L. *vorare*; Arkad. ζέλλω = βάλλω; Hom. πεφυζότες = πεφυγϝοτες. We find β for δ in Thess. Βωδών = Δωδώνη for ΔϜωδωνη from R. διϝ, Skr. *div* (to shine), whence come Ζεύς, δῖος, δῆλος, L. *divus*, as L. *bis* and *bonus* arise from *duis* and *duonus*; Æol. βελφίς = δελφίς, connected with Skr. *grah* for *grabh* (concipere), Skr. *garbhas* (nom. sing. masc. a child), Z. *garewa* (fœtus), Gr. βρέφος, δελφύς, δολφός (ἡ μήτρα, Hesych.), δελφίς thus meaning "the fish with the belly;"* Æol. Βελφοί = Δελφοί, from last root, and perhaps so called from its position in a deep ravine;† Æol. σάμβαλον = σάνδαλον, borrowed from Pers. *sandal* (a shoe);‡ Æol. βλῆρ = δέλεαρ, connected with δόλος, L. *dolus*, O. N. *tál* (fraud). We have also Dor. ὀδελός = ὀβελός, where δ and β represent an original gv, if this word belong to the same root as βέλος, βελόνη, βάλλω, Skr. *gal* (to fall).

* Or δελφίς may be the "voracious fish," as Skr. *grah* means "to seize."
† Curtius, "Grundzüge," p. 420.   ‡ Ibid. p. 425.

Φ = I. E. *bh*: R. φερ, φέρω, Skr. *bhar* (to bear), L. *fero*, Goth. *baira* (φέρω); φράτηρ (member of a φρατρία), Skr. *bhrātā* (nom. sing. brother), L. *frater*, Goth. *brôthar*; R. φυ, φύω, Skr. *bhû* (to be), L. *fui*; R. φαρ, φάρος (a plough), φάραγξ (a ravine), Z. *bar* (to bore), L. *forare*. In νίφα (acc. snow), φ represents an I. E. *ghv*, L. *ningu-it*, *nix*, St. *niv* for *nigv*. We find φ and χ interchanged in φλιαρός beside χλιαρός (Hesych.), Æol. αὔφην = αὐχήν, δάφνη = Thess. δαύχνη, where χ is perhaps original, if the root be Skr. *dah* for *dagh* (to burn).* Similarly in Latin we find *f* = I. E. *gh* in *fri-are* = χρί -ειν, &c.

Φ sometimes takes the place of θ, especially in the Æolic dialect; thus we have Æol. φρόνος = θρόνος in ποικιλόφρον' (Sappho I. 1)†; Æol. φήρ = θήρ; Æol. φοίνα = θυίνη (a feast); φαρυμός (bold, Hesych.), beside θρασύς with ρ for ρρ, ρς; φλάω, φλίβω beside θλάω, θλίβω (I crush) ; κόφινος beside Skr. *kathina* (vas fictile). Similarly L. *f* = I. E. *dh*, in L. *fera*, Gr. θήρ, L. *fumus* = Skr. *dhûmas* (smoke); L. *famulus*, Skr. *dhâman* (a house), Gr. τίθημι, R. θε, Skr. *dhâ* (to place). Grassmann suggests that in such cases the initial sound originally was *dhv;* but, though this in some cases may be true, it is very unlikely that it is so in all. We can explain the interchange of *f* and *dh* much more easily; for we know that if, in pronouncing *dh* or *th*, we move the lower lip very slightly towards the upper teeth, we change them into *f*.

Φ = I. E. *p* in some cases : κεφαλή, Skr. *kapála* (cranium) ; βλέφαρον from βλέπω. In τύφω, R. τυφ for θυφ (to smoke), beside Skr. *dhûp* (suffire), *dhûpayâmi*, and στέφω, R. στεφ, Skr. *sthapâyâmi* (I place), φ has arisen from an older *p*, which was employed to form causatives from the roots *dhû* (to move), and *sthâ* (to stand.)

M = I. E. *m*: ἅμα, Skr. *samâ* (together), L. *simul;* R. ἐμ, ἐμίω, Skr. *vam* (to vomit), L. *vomo;* ἡμι-, ἥμισυς, Skr. *sâmi*-,

---

* See Max Muller, vol. ii., p. 502.
† Ahrens " De Dial. Æol.," pp. 42, 256.

COMPARATIVE GRAMMAR. 83

L. *semi-*; ἠρέμα, Skr. *ram* (to rejoice), Goth. *rimis* (peace); με, Skr. and Z. *ma*, L. *me*; μέσσος = Skr. *madhyas* = L. *medius*. We find μ used for π in Kret. ἄμακις = ἅπαξ; Lak. δολομάν = δόλοπα (a spy), Lac. Μερσεφόνα = Περσεφόνα; and μ for β in Lak. ἄμυσσος = ἄβυσσος, and Lak. ἀμάκιον = ἄβαξ.

§. 56. THE SPIRANT Y.

Although the Greek alphabet contained no special sign for the palatal spirant, traces of its presence are found even more extensively than of that of the Digamma. Y must have existed in Græco-Italic times, and even in Greek till after the separation of the dialects from each other. In Homer we find traces of *y* in the frequent lengthening of short syllables before ὥς (= γως), as ὄρνιθες ὥς, πέλεκυς ὥς, &c. Y is both a spirant and a semivowel, and hence is easily vocalized.

Y = ι: ἰδίω = Skr. *svidyâmi* (sudo); ε(σ)ίην = Skr. (*a*)-*syâm* = L. (*e*)*siem*; -οιο (gen. sing. term. of o-declension) = Skr. -*asya*, as in ἵπποιο = Skr. *as'vasya*; -σιομες (first plural of Doric future) = Skr. -*syâmas*, as in Dor. πραξίομες, φυλαξίομες, beside Skr. *tótsyâmas*, &c.; -ιων (term. of comparative) = I. E. -*yans*, Skr. -*îyans*, as in ἡδίων = Skr. *svâdîyans*, &c.; πάτριος = Skr. *pitryas*, &c.; φθείρω = φθερψω, &c. According to Curtius, we find initial ι for *y* only in proper names like Ἰάονες = *Yavanas*,* and in ἰέναι beside Skr. *yâ*.

Y = ε: in the Doric future ι is kept only before o-sounds, as in πραξίω, πραξίομες, &c.; but before e-sounds it becomes ε, as in ἐργαξῆται; in milder Doric ι always becomes ε, as in πραξῶ, πραξοῦμες, &c.; Ion. τέψ, τέοισι = Lesb. τίψ, τίοισι, from τι + ο; Argive ὤβεα (eggs) = ὠϜya, I. E. *âvyam*, according to Benfey, being a neuter adjective, meaning, "what comes from a bird," from I. E. *avi-* (a bird); Δεύννσος = Διόνυσος; ἠνορίη beside ἀνηνορίη; Βορέης for Βοργας (whence

* Curtius is wrong here, for *Yavanas* is a borrowed word. Ἰάονες, however, may be equivalent to Skr. *yuvânas*.

Βορρᾶς, by assimilation), which is a spondee in Iliad I. 5, Ψ 195; στερεός, Att. στερρός, for στεργος, feminine στεῖρα for στεργα; κενεός, Æol. κέννος, Ep. κεινός, for κενγος = Skr. s'ûnyas (empty) = I. E. kvanyas; ἐτεός = Skr. satyas (true); εἰνάτερες beside L. *janitrices*, ya becoming εε, and this again ει; εὖτε = ἰοτε for γοτε; δοκέω, γαμέω, &c., for δοκυω, γαμυω, &c.* In such forms as πόλεως, ε does not stand for y, but πόλεως = πόλεος for πολεγος, εγ being the guna of ι. Curtius considers that ε in δωρεά, συκέα, κρανέα, &c., beside δωριά (Hesych.), συκία, κρανία, &c., represents εγ, and not y; these words being originally collectives in -yá; δωρεά, from an older δωρεια, means, therefore, "a collection of gifts;" συκέα, "a collection of figs;" and hence "the fig tree" itself, &c. Similarly τέλεος = τέλειος for τελεσγος, γενεά = γενεια for γενεσγα. In Modern Greek we sometimes find the old ε represented by y; and even in ancient times ε before vowels must have had a peculiar pronunciation, since we find θεοί, νέα, &c., frequently treated as monosyllables. The Modern Greeks also frequently represent the y of other languages by ε, as Βέασα = Skr. *Vyása* (Ἰνδικαὶ μεταφράσεις of Gulanus).

Y = υ in κύανος (a dark blue substance) = Skr. *syámas* (dark), υ here being equivalent to *w*.

Y = Spiritus asper: ἧπαρ, Skr. *yakṛt* (liver); L. *jecur*; ὑμεῖς, Skr. *yushmat* (abl. pl.); ὥρα, Z. *yáre* (a year); ὑσμίνη, R. ὑθ = Skr. *yudh* (to fight); ἅγιος = Skr. *yag'yas* (to be honoured by sacrifice).

Y has disappeared in Æol. ὕμμες; fut. term. -σω = Dor. σίω, from I. E. -*syámi*; term. s. -έω, -άω, -όω, as τελέω for τελεσγω, φορέω = Skr. *bharayâmi*, &c.; gen. term. ου for οο = οιο = οσιο = Skr. *asya*, as in ἵππου = ἵπποιο, &c.; πλέον beside πλεῖον; Æol. πάλαος, ἀλάθεα, λαχύην, beside παλαιός, ἀλήθεια, λαχοίην; Ep. ὠκέα = ὠκεῖα; κάω = καίω, &c.

Y = γ: ἄγουρος = ἄωρος, ἄγουρον being read by Aristo-

---

* Consult Curtius, "Grundzüge," p. 538; and "Tempora und Modi," pp. 92, 93.

phanes in place of ἄκουρον in Od. η 64; Kyprian θέαγον (sulphur) = Ion. θεήιον; Kyprian ἀπόγεμε (ἄφελκε, Hesych.) and ὕγγεμος (συλλαβή, Hesych.) from root γαμ = Skr. *yam* (to take), L. *em-o;* whence comes γέντο. In Bœot. ἰών = ἐγιών, Tarent. ὀλίος = ὀλίγος, σίαλος (fat) beside σιγαλόεις (shining, Φιαλία = Φιγαλία, γ appears to have been lost from its approximating to the sound of *y*. In L. *spargo* = σπείρω for σπεργω, *g* = *y*. In Modern Greek γ (pronounced *y*) has arisen from and beside the old ι, as in χωργά = χωριά, μυῖγα = μυῖα, κλαίγω = κλαίω, αὐγόν (an egg) = I. E. *âvyam*. Curtius remarks that the Doric future term. -ξω of verbs in -ζω, as δικάζω, Dor. fut. δικαξῶ, is a proof that the old *y* was not far removed from the gutturals.

Y = ζ : ζεά (spelt), Skr. *yava* (barley) ; R. ζες, ζέω, ἔζεσμαι (to gush, boil), Skr. *yas* (to strive), *niryas* (to perspire) ; ζημία, ζητρός (a hangman); Skr. *yam* (to restrain) ; ζητέω, Skr. *yat* (to strive), which is connected with *yâ* (to go) ; ζίζυφον, a tree, the fruit of which is called *jujubæ;* ζυγόν = Skr. *yugam*, L. *jugum*; ζωμός (soup), Skr. *yusha* (pease porridge), L. *jus;* ζώνη, ζώννυμι, ζούσθω (= ζωννύσθω, Heysch.), Skr. *yu* (to bind) ; in the verbal terminations -αζω, -ιζω, beside Skr. -*ayâmi*, which became in Greek either -αζω, or, by the falling out of *y*, -αω, -οω, -εω, -ω. In these cases the original *y* produced *d* before it, and this *dy* became *dz* and then *z*. We find a similar phenomenon in other languages; thus we have Ital. *diacere, diacinto, maggiore*, from L. *jacere, hyacinthus, major;* Middle Lat. *madius*, from L. *majus;* Mod. Gr. διάκι, from οἰάκιον (the tiller); Goth. *daddja* (lacto) = O. H. G. *tâju*, Skr. *dhayâmi;* Goth. *tvaddjê*, for *tvajê*, gen. of *tvai;* Goth. *iddja* (I went) = Skr. *iyâya*, Gr. ἦια. This assumption by *y* of a parasitic *d* is similar to that by *v* of a parasitic *g*, in Ital. *guastar*, from L. *vastare*, &c. When *y* had assumed this parasitic *d*, it frequently became δι instead of ζ, as in the suffix -διος, in διχθάδιος, ῥηΐδιος, &c., and the Æolic patronymics in -αδιος, from A-stems, as Ὑῤῥάδιος,

Τινάδιος. The corresponding patronymics in Skr. end in -*éyas* (nom. sing. masc.), *dâsêyas* (the son of a slave), from *dâsa* (a slave); and in Latin in -*ejus*, *plebejus*, *Pompejus*, &c. The termination of ἴδιος (Dor. Ϝίδιος) is explained in the same way by Curtius; the root is ἰ for σϜε, Skr. *sva*, L. *se*, whence we have ἴδιος through the steps σϜεγος, σϜεδγος, σϜεδιος, Ϝεδιος, whence finally ἴδιος. Such patronymic forms, as Τύρραιος (Ahrens, "De Dial. Æol.," p. 158), are related to Ὑρράδιος, as the verbal term, -αω to -αζω. As *y* becomes ε in some cases, so δι becomes δε, as in the term -δεος, Att. δυῦς, ἀδελφίδεος, Att. ἀδελφιδοῦς. We frequently find *y*, after it has produced before it the parasitic δ, vanishing and δ alone remaining; Bœot. δυγόν = ζυγόν; Bœot. δωμός = ζωμός; Dor. δατίν = ζητεῖν; χθές = χδες (by assimilation) = χδγες = χγες = I. E. *ghyas*, whence Skr. *hyas*, L. *heri, hes-ternus*; ῥοῖβδος (a rushing noise) = ῥοιϜδγος = ῥοιϜγος (from ῥοϜγος by umlaut), connected by Curtius either with L. *rumor*, or with R. ῥυ (to flow), Ῥοῖζος, another form of ῥοῖβδος, is from ῥοιδγος. Curtius connects δή with L. *jam*, Goth. *ju* (already); he treats δή as an instrumental, and *jam* as a locative of the same pronominal root *ja*. Beside Hom. ἀμέρδω (I rob), Pindar has ἀμείρω, both being from ἀμεργω, R. μερ. Ἔχιδνα is perhaps for ἐχινδα by metathesis, which is for ἐχινγα, a feminine form of ἔχις; this feminine termination -νγα is found directly in πότνια, as -ινα by umlaut in δέσποινα, θέαινα, λύκαινα, which correspond to the Latin forms *gallina*, *regina*, *Diana* for *Deana*, and this again for *Deaina*, *Deania*, and as -ννα by assimilation in the Æolic forms Κόριννα, βασίλιννα. Μόλυβδος is for μολυβγος, which is related to the older form μόλυβυς, as χρυσίον to χρυσός. Ῥάβδος is for ῥαβδγος = ῥαπδγος = ῥαπγος, which is related to ῥάπις, as δάκρυον to δακρυ. Λάβδακος is for ΛαϜιακος from Λάϊος (popular) from λαϜός (the people).*

---

* For additional examples consult Curtius, "Grundzüge," p. 559, *seq.*, to whom I am chiefly indebted for the materials of this and the following section.

§. 57. The Digamma.

The sound of F was very nearly the same as that of the E. *w*. Dionysius of Halikarnassus defines it as ου συλλαβὴ ἐνὶ στοιχείῳ γραφομένη. It is both a spirant and a semivowel; and, as a semivowel, is easily vocalized.

F = υ : We have six cases where initial F becomes υ : ὐάλη (a worm, Hesych.) ὐάλεται (it breeds worms, Hesych.), from R. FεΛ (to twist), whence εὐλή (a worm), ἔλ-μινς ; Ὑέλη (Herod. I., 167), the Italian town commonly called Elea or Velia ; ὔεσις (στολή Πάφιοι), ὐεστάκα (clothing), perhaps from a nom. ὐεσταξ, from R. Fες (to clothe), L. *vestis* ; ὐιή (the vine), υἰόν (the wild vine), connected with L. *viere, vitis*, with which Curtius also connects οἶνος and L. *vinum* ; ὐίλη (a host, Hesych.), beside Lacon. βείλη = ἴλη (a host), from R. FεΛ, Skr. *var* (to surround) ; ὑρειγαλέον (a cleft), beside Hom. ῥωγαλέον The change of F into υ is very common in the middle of words : κύων = Skr. *s'vá* (a dog) ; κυέω (I am pregnant), Skr. *s'vayámi* (I swell) ; εἰλύω, L. *volvo* ; βίδυοι (or βίδεοι, certain Spartan magistrates), meaning συνίστορες, μάρτυρες, from R. Fιδ, and suffix –Fo, –Fa = Skr. –*va*, and L. –*vo*, –*va*, βίδυος (Att. ἰδύος or ἰδυῖος). When F is vocalized, it is frequently thrown back into the preceding syllable, as in ταῦρος through ταυρFος, from ταρFος = Gall. *tarvos;* Ion. οὖλος = ὅλος from ὀλFος = Skr. *sarvas* (all) ; γουνός, γούνα from γονFος, γονFα, gen. sing. and nom. pl. of γόνυ ; δουρός from δορFος, gen. sing. of δόρυ ; οὐλαί (Att. ὀλαί, L. *mola*), from ὀλFαι, as the Syracusan word ὀλβαχόϊον (a bread basket) proves. In the Lesbian-Æolic F between two vowels became υ, and thus formed a diphthong with the preceding vowel, as in αὔως (Lak. ἀβώρ), φαῦος (Pamph. φάβος) (Ahrens, "De Dial. Æol.," p. 36, *seq.*).

F = o: δοάν in Alkman = δήν from δFην = διFαν, acc. of St. διFα (a day) ; δοάσσατο (it seemed) from R. διF, Skr. *div* (to shine), for δFασσατο; ζόασον = σβέσον (Hesych.), F becoming in the one case o, and in the other β, the root being σFες = I. E. *svas*, connected with G. *sausen* (to whistle), and O. S. *svistu* (sibilus), not connected with Skr. *s'vas* (to breathe), which is = I. E. *kvas*, L. *queri*, R. *ques*, E. *whistle, wheeze*, the F is entirely lost in ζέιννυμεν = σβέννυμεν (Hesych.); δοιοί (two) for δFιοι from St. δFι, δίς, L. *bis*; κοάξ (the croaking of frogs) = G. *quak*, E. *quack*; κοΐζειν (to squeak like a young pig) from κοί, G. *quiek*, E. *squeak*; Ὄαξος (the Kretan town Ἄξος) the inhabitants of which are called Fάξιοι upon coins, and the district is called Οὐαξίς by Apollonius Rhodius, where οι (= u^i) very nearly has the sound of υ; Οἰάνθη, or Οἰάνθεια (a Lokrian town), called in Plutarch Ὑάνθεια, from Fι-ανθη (violet blossoms); Ὀϊλεύς = Ἰλεύς, from Fίλη (a host); ὁρόδαμνος (a sprout) = ῥάδαμνος, beside Æol. βρίσδα = Fριδια, ῥίζα; Οἴτυλος (a Laconian town), also called Βείτυλος (Βίτουλα by Ptolemy) from Fιτυλος; Ὀλισσήν (a Kretan town), called by the later Kretans Βλισσήν; οἰσύα, οἶσος (osier), beside ἴτυς, Æol. βίτυς for Fιτυς, L. *vieo, vimen*. The Sicilian river Ἄνις was sometimes called Ὤανις, where ω represents F. This change of F into o is similar to that of y into ε; for, as y became first ι and then ε, so F became first υ and then o. In O. H. G. we find o for v, as in *snéo* = Goth. *snairs*. It is not probable that F ever became ι; for then it must have passed through the three stages, u, u^i, i, which is not likely; and in nearly all the cases adduced in proof of this change, ι is susceptible of another explanation. Thus in ὤϊον = L. *orum*, F was present along with ι, as is proved by the Argive ὤβιον, from ὤFιον; πλείειν = πλεFγειν, while πλέειν = πλεFειν, *ya* being a common verbal suffix; ἀδελφειός = ἀδελφεFιος from St. αδελφεF = αδελφυ and suffix *ya*; ιαρείον (πρόβατον, βοῦς, Hesych.) is from ἱερός, Dor. ἱαρός, and not from St. Fαρυ (a sheep), &c.

After a prosthetic vowel F vanishes, as in Kret. ἄερσα,

Hom. ἱέρση = ἕρση (dew), Skr. *varsha* (rain); ἄλοξ (a furrow), Hom. αὖλαξ, Dor. ὦλαξ for ἀϝλαξ, from R. ϝελκ (to drag); ἄεθλον (a prize), for ἀϝεθλον, beside L. *vas*, St. *vad* (Leo Meyer, however, connects this with L. *avere, avidus*, and treats θλο as a suffix, the same as τρο); ἐείκοσι = ἐϝείκοσι; Hom. ἔεδνα = ἕδνα from R. σϝαδ, whence ἡδύς, &c., Skr. *svad* (to please), *svâdu* (sweet) = ἡδύ, &c.

ϝ = spir. asp.: ἕσπερος, L. *vesper;* ἕννυμι for ἑσνυμι, R. ϝες, L. *vestire;* ἵστωρ from R. ϝιδ; ὄφις, for ὀπίς = ὀπϝις; ʽΕνετοί = Veneti; ʽΕστία beside *Vesta*. We find a similar change in Fr. *hors* = L. *foras*, in Sp. *haba, harina, heno, hijo, herir* = L. *faba, farina, fœnum, filius, ferire*.

ϝ = β : βούλομαι, R. βολ = Skr. *var* (to choose), L. *volo;* ἴβυξ (the name of an ὄρνειον κρακτικόν), beside ἰυγή (shrieking), St. ἰϝυγ ; ὄροβος beside L. *ervum ;* ὄλβος beside ὁλοός = L. *salvus*, &c. We find this change frequently in the dialects: in Lesbian we find β for ϝ before ρ, as in βρόδον, βρίσδα, Βραδάμανθυς, &c.; in Lak. we have βείκατι = εἴκοσι, βεκάς = ἑκάς, ἀβήρ = ἀήρ, ὠβά beside ὀγή (κώμη) and οὐαί (φυλαί); &c. We find a similar change in L. *ferbui* for *fervui, bubile* for *bovile;* and in G. *Schwalbe, Farbe, Erbse*, &c., from O. H. G. *swalawâ, farawâ, araweiz*, &c.

ϝ = μ : ἀμνός = ἀϝινος beside ὄϊς = Skr. *avis*, Lith. *avinas* (mutton); ἀμνός, therefore, is equivalent in meaning to *ovilis*, and then easily comes to mean *lamb;* μαλλός (shaggy hair) beside L. *villus, vellus*, from same root as οὖλος (crisp), ἔριον (wool), Skr. *urâ* (a sheep), *ûrṇa* (wool); E. *wool;* μελδόμενος (ἐπιθυμῶν, Hesych.) beside ἔλδομαι and ἐέλδομαι (ἐπιθυμῶ) from R. ϝελδ, as is proved by the last form with the prosthetic ε; μολπίς = ἐλπίς from R. ϝελπ, whence ἔολπα, ἐέλπετο ; ἀμφήν = Æol. αὐφήν = αὐχήν (the neck). Conversely we find *v* in place of *m* in Lith. *vidùi* = μέσσοι, Ch. Sl. *crŭvĭ* (a worm) = Skr. *krmis, prŭvy* = L. *primus*, Skr. *vayam* (we), Goth. *veis* (we), beside Skr. *mám* (me), &c.

The change of ϝ into γ is very doubtful: we find ἀγάτημαι (βέβλαμμαι) from ἀϝατα = ἄτη, Pindaric αὐάτα; φέγγος for φενϝος which is related to φάος, Æol. φαῦος, Pamphyl. φάβος, as βένθος to βάθος, and πένθος to πάθος. The other cases in which this change is said to occur are words of very uncertain origin.

We find φ = ϝ in σφε = Skr. *sva*, and σφύγγος beside Goth. *svamms* (a sponge), E. *swim*; ρ = ϝ in Kret. τρί, δεδροικώς, for τϝε, δεδϝοικως;. π is said to be = ϝ in Πάξος found in Skylax for Ὄαξος, but the reading is doubtful; in Kret. πόλχος = ὄχλος, but these words may be of different origin, the root of πόλχος, perhaps, being πελ found in πολύς, L. *populus*; Lac. ἀμπέσαι = ἀμφίεσαι, which Ahrens derives from αμ - ϝεσαι, ἀμ being for ἀμφί: Curtius, however, considers the π to be due to the influence of the φ of ἀμφί; Lac. ἀπέλλα = ἀϝελλα, according to Ahrens, from ἀ = ἁ (together) and R. ϝελ found in εἴλειν (to press), ἀολλής (crowded together); but, as we have the forms ἀπείλλω, Æol. ἀπέλλω (ἀποκλείω, Hesych.), it is possible that the π may be due to the preposition ἀπό, and not to the ϝ. Ἀπειλή (threatening) may be from this root, and mean literally "shutting out," "excommunication."

The existence of ϝ is in many cases shown by its effects on a preceding consonant, as in πύσος (Ion. κόσος) for κϝοσος, or on a following vowel, as in ὄχος for ϝεχος, Dor. τέτορες for τετϝαρες, Æol. ὄρανος = Skr. *Varunas*, beside οὐρανός, Æol. ὤρανος, Dor. ὠρανός, ϝ becoming ο, and υο then ου, Æol. and Dor. ω. This effect of ϝ or *v* on a following vowel is found also in κοδράντης = L. *quadrans*, L. *socer* Skr. *s'vas'uras*, L. *socrus* = Skr. *s'vas'rûs*, L. *soror*, beside Skr. *svâsar* (sister),&c.; and in the pronunciation of *a* in E. *water, what*, &c.

§. 58. Assimilation.

I. When two consonants come together, the first is often made the same as the second. Thus νν = σν in ἕννυμι = Fεσ-νυμι, R. Fες; ζώννυμι = ζωσ-νυμι, Skr. *yu* (to bind); Æol. φάεννος = φαεσνος from φάος, St. φαες, found in φαεσφόρος; Æol. ὄρεννος = ὀρεσνος, from ὄρος, St. ὀρες found in ὀρεσκῷος; ἐρέβεννος = ἐρέβεσνος, from ἔρεβος, St. ἐρεβες, found in ἐρέβεσφι; ἔννεον (they swam, Il. xxi. 11) = ἐσνεον, R. νυ for σνυ, Skr. *snu* (to flow). Νν = τν in καννεύσαν (Od. xv. 464) = κατ-νεύσαν. Μμ = νμ in καμμονίη = κατ-μονιη; κάμμορος (in Od., but never in Il.) = κατ-μορος. Μμ = σμ in Æol. ἔμμι = ἐσμι; Æol. ἔμμενος, ἔμμα = ἐσ-μενος, ἐσ-μα, R. Fες; Æol. χρίμμα = χρίσμα; Lesb. ἄμμες, ὕμμες, beside Skr. *asman, yushman*; φιλομμειδής = φιλο-σμειδης, Skr. *smi* (to laugh), E. *smile*. Μμ = γμ in Dor. πούμμα (ἡ τῆς χειρὸς πυγμή, Hesych.). Μμ = βμ, πμ, φμ, in κομμός (a striking) from R. κοπ (as L. *summus* = *sup-mus*), τέτριμμαι from R. τριβ, γράμμα from R. γραφ, &c. Λλ = πλ in Lak. ἀλλανής (safe) = ἀπλανής. Λλ = νλ in συλλέγειν = συν-λεγειν, &c. Λλ = τλ in καλλιπέειν (Od. xvi. 296) = κατ-λιπεειν. Τπ = μπ in Bœot. ἔππασις = ἔμπασις (ἔγκτησις); Γλυππία (the name of a Lakonian village) = Γλυμπία; Λάππα (the name of a town in Krete) = Λάμπα. Ππ = τπ in κάππεσον = κατ-πεσον. Ββ = πβ in ὑββάλλειν (Il. xix. 80) = ὑπ-βαλλειν. Ββ = τβ in κάββαλε = κατ-βαλε. Δδ = τδ in κὰδ δέ = κὰτ δέ. Γγ = τγ in κὰγ γόνυ = κάτ γόνυ. Κκ = τκ in κὰκ κορυφήν = κὰτ κ. and κὰκ κεφαλῆς = κὰτ κ. Κκ = σκ in Lak. ἀκκύρ = ἀσκύρ, διδάκκει = διδάσκει (in Decr. in Timoth.), Lak. (?) κακκός (ὁ μικρὸς δάκτυλος, Hesych.) = κασκός. Ττ = στ in Bœot. ἴττω, ἔττε, ἔττια, ἔττασαν = ἴστω, ἔστε, ἐστία, ἔστησαν; Lak. βεττόν (a garment) beside βεστόν = ἐστόν; Lak. κίττορ = κίστος; Lak. ἄττασι for ἄνσταθι = ἀνάστηθι. Ττ = δτ in Tar. Ἄφραττος (ἡ Ἑκάτη παρὰ Ταραντίνοις) = ἀφραδτος. Ττ = κτ in Λύττος (a Kretan town) beside Λύκτος. Ρρ = σρ in ἔρρεον = ἐσρεον, περίρρυτος = περισρυτος, beside ἀμφίρυτος, χειμάρροος, καλλίρροος beside καλλίροος, all from R. ῥυ for σρυ = Skr. *sru* (to flow). Ρρ = νρ in ἀγάρροος from ἄγαν and R. ῥυ; συρρεῖν = συν-ρειν, &c. Ρρ = τρ in καρρέζουσα (Il. v. 424) = κατ-ρεζουσα. Ρρ = Fρ in ἔρριψε = ἐFριψε; ἀντίρροπος from R. Fρεπ; πρόρριζος from Fρίζα, with which root may be connected περιρρηδής (headlong); ἄρρηκτος, Æol. αὔρηκτος from R. Fραγ, L. *frango*; &c. Σς = νς in συσσίτιον = συνσίτιον, and other compounds of συν, except when ζ or σ followed by a consonant come after, in which cases ν is dropped, as in σύζυγος, σύστημα. The ν in ἐν is always kept, and the ν in πᾶν and πάλιν is either kept or assimilated to the following σ. Σσ = δς in Hom. πυσσί = ποδ-σι. Σς = κς in δισσός, τρισσός beside διξός, τριξύς, ξ becoming σσ through the steps χς, ἡς. This is Ebel's view, who compares L. *nisu s* = *nixus*. Ch. Sl. *desinu* (dexter), Ir. *des* (dexter), Ir. *ass* and *ess* = L. *ex* beside *echtar* (extra), Umb. *testru* = L. *dextro*, &c. Curtius considers δισσός to have arisen from δFιτγος = Skr. *dvitiyas* for *dvityas*.

II. When two consonants come together, the second is often made the *same* as the first. This is very common in Æolic, especially when a liquid is followed by F, y, or σ. Thus νν = νσ in Æol. μῆννος (a month) beside L. *mensis*; Æol. ἐγγένvατο, κτέννυσι = ἐγενσατο, κτενσαι; ἔννεπε = ἐνσεπε, L. *insece*. Nν = νF in Æol. γόννυς = γουννός from γονFος. Nν = νy in Æol. κτέννω = κτείνω from κτενyω; Æol. κρίννω = κρίνω from κρινyω; Æol. κέννος = Skr. *s'únyas* (empty), Ion. κεινός, κενεός, Att. κενός. Μμ = μσ in ἐνέμματο = ἐνεμσατο. Λλ = λν in ὄλλυμι = ὀλνυμι, as E. *ell* = *eln*, L. *ulna*, and E. *full* = *fuln*, Skr. *pûrṇa* (full), L. *plenus*. Λλ = λσ in Æol. ἔστελλα = ἐστελσα. Λλ = λF in πολλή = πολFη from πολύ; κυλλός (crooked) = κυλFος L. *curvus*. Λλ = λy in ἄλλος = ἀλyος, L. *alius*; φύλλον = φυλyον, L. *folium*; μᾶλλον = μαλιον; ἄλλομαι = ἀλyομαι, L. *salio*; κάλλος, καλλύνω, Dor. καλλά (καλῶς), beside Skr. *kalya* (sound); στέλλω = στελyω; Hom. ὀφέλλω = ὀφείλω from ὀφελyω. Ππ = πμ and φμ in Æol.

ὄππατα, ἄλιππα for ὄμματα, ἄλειμμα from the roots ὀπ and ἀλιφ. Δδ = δy in the Bœotic forms μᾶδδα = μᾶζα = μαδya for μαγ-ya; σφάδδω = σφαςyω for σφαγyω; σαλπίδδω = σαλπιδyω for σαλπιγyω; ῥέδδω = ῥέζω, Att. ἔρδω = ῥεδyω for Fρεγ–yω, R. Fρεγ and Fεργ; the same change is found in Lakonic, as is proved by the examples in the Lysistrata, γυμνάδδομαι (82) μυσίδδω for μυθίζω (94), ποτόδδει for προσόζει (206), &c. When δy is initial, we sometimes find it represented by δ instead of δδ, as in Bœot. Δεύς = Ζεύς, Δάν = Ζήν, δυγόν = ζυγόν; Lak. δωμός = ζωμός; δα- = ζα- from διά in δαφοινός, δάσκιος. Κκ = κρ in Bœot. μικκός = μικρός. Κκ = κF in Æol. ἵκκος = L. equus; γλυκκόν (γλυκύ, Hesych.) = γλυκFον; πελεκκᾶν = πελεκFαν from πέλεκυς. Ττ = τς in καττύειν = κατσυειν. Ττ = τF in τέτταρες = τετFαρες. Ττ = τy in the Attic forms, μέλιττα = μελιτya; κρείττων = κρειτyων; περιττός = περιτyος; νεοττός = νεοτyος. Ρρ = ρσ in ἄρρην = ἄρσην, ἄρριχος (a basket) = ἄρσιχος, θάρρος = θάρσος, πόρρω = πορσω beside πρόσω, ὄρρος perhaps from ὀρσος, πυρρός = πυρσός, Att. χέρρος (dry land) = χέρσος, Att. κόρρη = κόρση. Ρρ = ρν in μύρρα = σμύρνα. Ρρ = ρy in the Æolic forms φθέρρω = φθερyω, πέρρυχος = περίοχος, περρέχειν = περιέχειν, περρ ἀπάλω (in Theokr. 29, 25) for περὶ ἀπάλω, Πέρραμος = Πρίαμος, μέτερρος = μέτριος, &c. Σσ = σF in Hom. πόδεσσι = ποδεσFι from St. ποδε for ποδ (in later Greek this σF becomes σ, as in πόλεσι, &c., which, however, does not fall out, as it represents the old σσ); Æol. ἴσσος = FισFος, ἴσυς, Skr. *vishu* (æque); traces of the initial F being found in Hom. εἴση and Lak. βίωρ = ἴσως. Σς = σy in ἔσσομαι = ἐσyομαι; νίσσομαι = νισyομαι from R. νες, found in νέομαι, νόστος, Νέστωρ, Skr. *nas* (to come); πτίσσω = πτίσyω, L. *pinso*, Skr. *pish* (to pound).

III. When two consonants come together, the first is generally made *like* the second. Thus, when labials or gutturals precede mute dentals, they must be of the same order as the following dental; hence the only combinations allowed are κτ, πτ, γδ, βδ, χθ, φθ, as in λεκτός for λεγτος, R. λεγ, γραπτός for γραφτος, and γράβδην for γραφδην, R. γραφ, λεχθῆναι for λεγθηναι, R. λεγ, τυφθῆναι for τυπθηναι, R. τυπ. Before σ, γ and χ become κ, and β and φ become π, as in ἄξω, R. αγ, τρίψω, R. τριβ, γράψω, R. γραφ. Before μ a guttural becomes γ, and a dental becomes σ, as in διωγμός from διώκω, βέβρεγμαι from βρέχω, ἤνυσμαι from ἀνύτω, πέπεισμαι from πείθω, ἴσμεν beside οἶδα; sometimes this change does not occur, as in ἀκμή, δραχμή, ῥυθμός, ἀριθμός, ἀτμός, and in compounds with preposition ἐκ, also in the Ionic forms ὀδμή = Att. ὀσμή, ἴδμεν = Att. ἴσμεν, κεκορυθμένος = Att. κεκορυσμένος, ἴκμενος (favourable), ἀκαχμένος from R. ακ (to sharpen), ἀϋτμή (breath). N becomes μ before labials, and nasal γ before gutturals, as in ἔμπειρος from ἐν, πεῖρα, συγκαλέω from σύν, καλέω, &c. Labials become μ before ν, as in σεμνός from R. σεβ, σέβομαι; but we find ὕπνος beside L. *somnus*. T frequently becomes σ before υ and ι, as in σύ = Dor. τύ, suffix -συνη for -τυνη, φησί = Dor. φατί, φάσις = Hom. φάτις, πλούσιος from πλοῦτος, εἴκοσι = Dor. Fίκατι, φέρουσι = Dor. φέροντι, &c.

IV. When two consonants come together, the second is often made *like* the first. Thus initial δy becomes *dz*, written ζ, as in Ζεύς = Skr. *dyâus*, Osk. ΔιουFει (dat.), O. L. *Diovis*; ζα = διά in Hom. ζάθεος, ζάκοτος, &c., also in the Æolic forms ζαβάλλειν, ζὰ νυκτός, Ζόννυξος = Διόνυσος, &c. Medial δy very frequently becomes ζ, as in ἕζομαι, R. ἑδ; ὄζω, R. ὀδ; σχίζω, R. σχιδ; χίζω, R. χεδ; τράπεζα for τετραπεδya, compare L. *acupedius*; χάλαζα from St. χαλαδ, I. E. *ghrâd*, Skr. *hrâduni* (bad weather), L. *grando*; ῥίζα = Fριδya, πεζός = πεδyος; Æol. κάρζα = καρδία; -ζος in χθιζός and πρωΐζος, from R. διF, whence come δίαλος, δέελος, δῆλος, &c.; ἀρίζηλος = ἀριδηλος from R. διF.

V. Mutual approximation of two united consonants to each other. Thus γy becomes ζ through the step δy in ῥέζω = ῥεγyω beside ἔργον; μείζων = μεγyων; ἄζομαι = ἀγyομαι beside ἅγιος; Hom. ὑπολίζων = ὑπολιγyων; μᾶζα beside μάγειρος; φύζα = φυγya, R. φυγ; ζάω = γyαω, I. E. *ĝîv*, Skr.

g'iv (to live), beside δίαιτα = γγαιτα ; κλάζω beside κλαγγή ; ρέζω (I dye) beside ρηγεύς (a dyer) ; and some other verbs in -ζω. Z = βy in λάζομαι beside R. λαβ, ἔλαβον. In νίζω beside χέρ–νιβ-ος, νίπτω for νιβτω, ζ may represent γy, as the Skr. *nig'* (to wash), proves that the root once contained γ. Σσ = τy in λίσσομαι, R. λιτ ; μέλισσα from St. μελιτ ; Κρῆσσα = Κρητyα ; ἐρέσσω = ἐρετyω beside ἐρετμός ; κρείσσων = κρειτyων beside κράτιστος ; νῆσσα = νητyα, L. *anas*. Σσ = θy in Hom. μέσσος = Skr. *madhyas* ; βάσσων = βυθυων beside βαθύς ; κορύσσω = κορυθyω beside κεκόρυθμαι. Σσ = κy in ἥσσων = ἥκyων beside ἥκιστος ; Θρῆσσα = Θρηκyα ; μαλάσσω = μαλακyω beside μαλακός ; ὄσσε (the eyes) = ὄκyε beside Bœot. ὄκταλλος (the eye), and ὄκκος (the eye, Hesych.); ὄσσα (a voice) = ὄκyα, L. *vox;* ἐνίσσω (I attack, = ἐνίπτω) = ἐνικyω, L. *ico*. Σσ = χy in ἐλάσσων = ἐλαχyων beside ἐλαχύς ; βράσσων = βραχyων beside βραχύς, βρόσσυνος βραχυτέρου, Hesych. (Ahrens, " De Dial. Dor.," p. 505). Σσ = βy in φάσσα (the ring dove) = φαβyα, beside φάψ (a smaller species of ring dove). Σσ = πy in κόσσος (a slap in the face) κοπyος from R. κοπ. Σσ = δy in Æol. πέσσον = πεδίον ; Æol. ἴσσος = ἴδιος ; Tar. φράσσω = φράζω from R. φραδ (whence ἀριφραδής, πέφραδον), which Curtius deduces from an older form πρατ = L. *pret* in *interpretari*, beside Lith. *prat* (to understand), Goth. *fraths* (understanding). Σσ = γy in πήσσω = πηγyω beside πήγνυμι ; φράσσω = φραγyω beside ἐφράγην ; ῥήσσω = ρηγyω beside ῥήγνυμι ; ἄσσω = ἀγyω beside ἄγνυμι ; φρύσσω (I parch) = φρυγyω beside φρύγω ; πλήσσω = πληγyω beside ἐπλάγην ; ὀρύσσω = ὀρυγyω (beside ὀρυγή) or ὀρυχyω ; μάσσω = μαγyω beside μαγεύς (a baker) ; τάσσω = ταγyω beside ταγύς (a ruler) ; and perhaps in a few other cases. In all those, however, which are enumerated here, with the exception of ἄσσω (which does not appear till after Augustus), φρύσσω, and τάσσω, older forms of the roots occur with κ instead of γ, so that in these cases σσ may represent κy, and not γy.

§. 59. Dissimilation.

Mute dentals before mute dentals become σ, as in ἀνυστός = ἄνυττος from ἀνύτω; ᾀστέον = ᾀδτεον from ᾅδω; πεισθῆναι = πειθθῆναι from πείθω. The ending θι of the 2 sing. imperative, first aorist passive, becomes τι when an aspirate occurs in the preceding syllable, as σώθητι beside κλῦθι: we find, however, φαθί or φάθι from φημί. We have also ἐτύθην = ἐθυθην, from R. θυ and ἐτέθην = ἐθεθην from R. θε; yet we find ἐφυφή (the woof) from R. ὑφ. When two consonants begin a root, the first is only kept in reduplicated syllables; hence aspirates are reduplicated by the corresponding tenues. Thus we have γέγραφα = γρεγραφα, κίχρημι = χριχρημι, ἵστημι = σιστημι = στιστημι, πέφυκα = φεφυκα: similarly in Sanskrit we have *babhûva* = πέφυκα, *dadrâma* = δέδρομα.* Roots which originally began with one aspirate, and ended with another, replaced the first aspirate by the corresponding tenuis. Thus we have πῆχυς (the arm) = φηχυς = I. E. *bhâghus* = Skr. *bâhus* (the arm), beside O. N. *bógr*, O. H. G. *buoc*; πυθμήν beside βυθμήν, Hesych. (the bottom) = φυθμην, Skr. *budhna* (the bottom) = I. E. *bhudhna*, beside O. H. G. *bodam*, L. *fundus*; &c.† We see the effects of Dissimilation in other languages as in L. *Parilia* beside *Palilia* from *Pales*, L. *meridies* from *medidies*, L. *popularis* for *populalis* beside *regalis*, &c.; It. *veleno* = L. *venenum*; E. *cinnamon* for *cinnamom*, &c.

---

* Curtius has pointed out that Sanskrit, Greek, and Latin had not, before their separation from each other, already fixed their peculiar laws of reduplication, from the different ways in which they treat groups of consonants of which the first is a sibilant. Thus we have the Latin *steti* = *stesti*, *spopondi* = *spospondi*, while conversely the Sanskrit has only kept the sibilant in the second syllable, as *tishtâmi* (I stand). We find some traces of this latter kind of reduplication in Greek and Latin, as in *quisquiliæ* = κοσκυλμάτια (parings of leather) beside σκύλλειν (to flay) and κασκαλιζειν (to tickle) beside σκάλλειν (to stir up). A third form of reduplication is found in L. *sisto* = *stisto*, as ἵστημι = στιστημι.

† For other examples consult Grassmann in K. Z., vol. xvi., p. 114.

§. 60. The Rejection of a Consonant.

Dentals, when standing before σ, are generally dropped without compensation, as in ἄνυσις = ἀνυτσις, ἤσομαι = ἡδσομαι, κόρῦσι = κορυθσι, δαίμοσι = δαιμονσι. N also disappears before ζ, as in σύζυγος = συνζυγος. N in ἐν is never lost; ν in πᾶν and πάλιν is either kept, or assimilated to the following σ; ν in συν is dropped before ζ and σ with a consonant following, but before a single σ it is assimilated, as in συσσίτιον. In some cases the loss of ν is compensated for by lengthening the preceding vowel, as in μέλᾱς = μελανς, τάλας = ταλανς, &c. Ντ, νθ, νδ, are also omitted before σ, but are nearly always compensated for, as τιθείς = τιθεντς, πείσομαι = πενθσομαι, σπείσω = σπενδσω. N is also sometimes omitted between two vowels, as in μείζους = μείζονες. K is lost in συλάω from σκῦλον (plunder), as in Skr. *savyas* (left) = σκαιός, L. *scævus*; σύν = ξύν; Kypr. σοάλα = ξυήλη (a carpenter's plane), from ξύω. Π is lost in Dor. ἄσεκτος (ἀγαθὸς παρὰ ʽΡίνθωνι Ταραντίνῳ) = ἄψεκτος from ψέγω; σίττακος = ψίττακος (a parrot); Ion. σώχειν = ψώχειν (to scrape); ἄμμος = ψάμμος through σαμμος. T is lost in κέρως = κέρατος, from St. κερατ (a horn); φέρει = φερετι, &c. The rejection of y and F has been already noticed; we may add that F is lost in σομφός (spongy), beside Goth. *svamms* (a sponge); σόβη (a horse's tail), beside O. N. *svipa* (a tail); σιγή beside G. *schweigen* (silence); σίδηρος beside Skr. *svidita* (molten); σάλος (swell of the sea) beside E. *swell*; Σείριος, σέλας beside Skr. *svar* (heaven), Z. *hvare* (the sun). Σ, as we have already seen, is generally rejected between two vowels; also between two consonants, as in γεγράφθαι = γεγραφσθαι, τέτυφθε = τετυφσθε, &c.; also before another σ, as in γλυκέσι = γλυκεσσι for γλυκεσFι, &c. Initial σ is always lost before ν, as in νίφα beside Z. *s'nizh* (to snow), Goth. *snaivs* (snow); νεῦρον, L. *nervus* beside O. H. G. *snuor* (laqueus); νέω (I swim) = σνεFω, Hom. ἔννεον = ἐσνεον, νεῦσις (swimming), beside Skr. *snu* (to

H

flow); νάω (I flow) = σναϝω, Æol. ναύω, beside Skr. *snu* (to flow), and not *snû* (to flow) as the Æolic form shows; νυός (daughter-in-law) = σνυσος, beside Skr. *snushâ*, and L. *nurus*. It is sometimes lost before μ, as in μειδιάω beside φιλομμειδής, Skr. *smi* (to smile), E. *smile;* μέλδω (I melt), E. *smelt;* μέρμερος (care-laden), L. *memor*, beside Skr. *smar* (to remember); μύδος (damp, foulness), Skr. *mid* (to be clammy), Goth. *bismeitan* (ἐπιχρίειν), O. H. G. *smiz* (nævus), and E. *smut*. Σ is lost before κ in κάρφος (a twig) = σκάριφος; κίμψαντες (ἐρείσαντες, Hesych.), beside σκίμπτειν (to prop), L. *scipio* (staff); κνίψ (a small insect) = σκνίψ; καρθμοί (κινήσεις, Hesych.), beside σκαίρειν (to hop); κάπετος (a grave) = σκάπετος, beside σκάπτειν (to dig); κίδνασθαι = σκίδνασθαι (to be scattered); σκῦτος (skin) = κύτος, Skr. *sku* (to cover). Σ is lost before π in πένομαι (I work, am poor), from R. σπεν, beside σπάνις (want), G. *spinnen* (to spin, to do); πίνος (dirt), beside σπῖλος (stain); and before φ in φηλός (deceitful), beside σφάλλω. Σ is lost before τ in ταῦρος Goth. *stiur** (bull); τέγος = στέγος, Skr. *sthagâmi* = στέγω, L. *tego*, Lith. *stogas* (roof), O. N. *thek* (roof), O. H. G. *dakju* (I cover); Τυδεύς, from R. τυδ = Skr. *tud* (to strike), L. *tundo, tudes* (a hammer), beside Goth. *stauta* (I strike); τύπτω beside στυπάζει (ὠθεῖ, Hesych.), O. H. G. *stumbalón* (obtundere); τυρβάζειν = στυρβάζειν (to trouble), G. *sturm, stürzen* (to rush).

§. 61. The Insertion of a Consonant.

The groups νρ, μρ, μλ, become νδρ, μβρ, μβλ: thus ἀνδρός = ἀνρος; μεσημβρία = μεσημρια; μέμβλωκα = μεμλωκη, and βλώσκω = μβλωσκω for μλωσκω, beside μολεῖν (to go); βροτός = μβροτος (found in ἄμβροτος) for μροτος = Skr. *martas* (mortal); γαμβρός = γαμρος, L. *gener;* βλίττω (I take the

---

* The Vedic *sthúras* (nom. sing. masc.) is an adj. meaning *strong;* it never means a *bull*.

honey) = μβλιττω for μλιτγω from μέλι; βλάξ (lazy), beside μαλακός; ἤμβροτον = ἤμαρτον. In these cases β and δ were inserted to facilitate the pronunciation; consult §. 30. N is inserted in the root syllable of the present tenses of many verbs, as in λαγχάνω, μανθάνω, &c., beside λαχεῖν, μαθεῖν, &c. This ν was originally the sign of the present tense, and is found in its full form νυ in δείκνυμι, &c. Similarly we have Skr. *s'aknômi* (I can), *s'aknumas* (we can), from R. *s'ak, yuñg'anti*) they bind), from R. *yug'*, &c., and in L. *jungunt* from R. *jug*, *tundo*, from R. *tud*, &c. Y frequently assumed before it the sound of δ, which when initial became ζ, and when preceded by a tenuis became τ, while the *y* was dropped. Thus ζεύγνυμι = δyευγνυμι = Skr. *yunag'mi* (I join), L. *jungo*, &c.; similarly in Italian we have *giacere* for *diacere* = L. *jacere, giocondo* for *diocondo* = L. *jucundus*, &c.; consult §. 56. We have χαλέπτω* from χαλεπός, through the steps χαλεπδyω, χαλεπyω; similarly we may derive τύπτω from R. τυπ, κλέπτω from R. κλεπ, &c. In βλάπτω from R. βλαβ we might expect βδ in place of πτ; but, as the verbs in -πτω were so numerous, this case was assimilated to the others; unless, indeed, the root be βλαπ, found in Kret. ἀβλόπες = ἀβλαβές. Νίπτω from R. νιβ, Skr. *nig'* does not occur till very late. Perhaps we may in this way explain the forms πτόλις, πτόλεμος, &c.; πτόλις = πyολις; πτόλεμος = πyολεμος; πτίσσω beside Skr. *pish* (to pound), L. *pinso;* πτέρνα (the heel), beside Skr. *pârshni* (the heel); πτύω beside Goth. *speiva* (I spit), L. *spuo;* κτείνω beside καίνω; πταίω (I make to fall), beside παίω (I strike); βδέω = βyεω beside L. *visium* (βδέσμα), Lith. *bezdù* (βδέω); χθές = I. E. *ghyas*, whence Skr. *hyas* (yesterday), L. *heri;* χθαμαλός beside χαμαί.

---

* Lottner considers τ in these cases to be the sign of a presential form, lost in Skr. but kept in Gr., Lat., and Lith.

§. 62. Aspiration.

Although most of the Greek aspirates represent the I. E. soft aspirates, yet under certain circumstances we find an aspirate developed from an original tenuis, after the Greek had separated from the other cognate languages. The two chief conditions for this development of an aspirate from the corresponding tenuis are, firstly, the influence of a preceding σ; and, secondly, that of a following λ, μ, ν, or ρ. In the following cases we find the aspirate due to the influence of a preceding σ: σχίζω, Skr. *khid* (to cut), L. *scindo*, Goth. *skaida* (I separate); Att. σχελίς = σκελίς (the ham); ἀσφάλαξ = ἀσπάλαξ (mole); Att. σφυρίς = σπυρίς (basket); Att. σφονδύλη = σπονδύλη (insect), &c. This influence of σ is very common in Attic. Σ sometimes was dropped after it had aspirated the following consonant, as in τρύχω (I wear out) = τρύσκω (Hesych.); νήχω = σνησκω; γλίχομαι (I long for), beside γλίσχρος (sticky); πτωχός, beside πτωσκάζω (I crouch); ἔρχομαι = ἐρσκομαι, &c. Λ, μ, ν, ρ aspirate the preceding consonants in ἀνδράχλη (a coal pan), from St. ἀνθρακ (coal); ναυσθλόω (I carry by sea) = ναυστολέω; suffix -θλο (θέμε-θλον) = -θρο, -τρο; σιφλός (crippled) = σιπαλός; αἰχμή = ἀκμή; ἰωχμός (pursuit), beside ἰωκή; λαχμός (kicking) beside λακτισμός; λύχνος from R. λυκ; ἐξαίφνης = ἐξαπίνης; βληχρός (sluggish), beside βλάξ; suffix -θρο (κλεῖθρον) = -τρο (ἄροτρον), &c.; τέφρα (ashes), beside Skr. *tap* (to be warm) L. *tepidus*; θρίναξ (a three-pronged fork) = τρίναξ; φροίμιον from older προοίμιον, &c. Sometimes the same effect is due to a preceding nasal, as in ἔγχος beside ἄκων; ῥέγχω = ῥέγκω (I snore); σπινθήρ (spark), beside L. *scintilla;* ὀμφή (voice) from R. Fεπ; Bœot. ἔχωνθι = ἔχουσι, from ἔχοντι, &c. We have also a few isolated examples where a Greek aspirate represents an older tenuis, without being influenced by λ, μ, ν, ρ or σ, as in ταχύς = Skr. *takus* (quick); ἐννύχιος from St. νυκ; ἀλείφω beside λίπος (fat), Skr. *lip* (to anoint); κεφαλή beside κεβάλη (Hesych.), Skr. *kapâla* (skull); κεκαφηώς (gasping), beside καπύω (I gasp), and a few other cases.

§. 63. Final Consonants.

N, ρ, and ς are the only consonants allowed to end a word. The only exceptions to this rule are ἐκ (from ἐξ), οὐκ (from οὐκι), and the interjections ὤόπ, ὄπ, ἰόφ. A final τ and δ are dropped, or τ is changed into ς, as in τό = Skr. *tad*; ἔφυ = Skr. *abhut*; ἔφερον = Skr. *abharant*; τέρας for τερατ, &c. Final θ becomes ς, as in δός for δοθ from δοθι, θίς for θεθι, σχές for σχεθι. Δ is lost in παῖ, voc. of παῖς, St. παιδ; also κ in γύναι, voc. of γύνη, St. γυναικ; also κτ in ἄνα, voc. of ἄναξ, St. ἀνακτ, &c. When several consonants, the last of which is ς, come together, only one is generally retained, and the preceding vowel is lengthened in compensation, as in φέρων = φεροντς; ποιμήν = ποιμενς; εὐμενής = εὐμενες; σκώρ = σκαρτς; γίγᾶς = γιγαντς; μέλᾶς = μελανς; τετυφώς = τετυφοτς; τιθείς = τιθεντς; διδούς = διδοντς, &c. We sometimes find, as final sounds, the combinations γξ, ρξ, ψ, as in φόρμιγξ, λάρυγξ, σάρξ, δόρξ, (gazelle), ὄψ, ὤψ, ἄψ, &c. We have λς in the single case ἅλς; ρς in Æol. forms, as μάκαρς; νς only in ἕλμινς (worm), πείρινς (wicker basket), but more frequently in the Argive and Kretan dialects, as Τίρυνς, ἐνς = εἰς, τόνς = τούς, ἀγρόνς = ἀγρούς, &c. Final μ is dropped or changed into ν, as in πόσιν = Skr. *patim*; νέον = Skr. *navam*; ἔφερον (1 sing.) = Skr. *abharam*; δέκα = L. *decem*; πατέρα = L. *patrem*; ἔδειξα = Skr. *adiksham*; φέρω = Skr. *bharâmi*. The ν ἐφελκυστικόν in ἔφερεν = Skr. *abharat*, ποσσίν, &c., is peculiar to the Greek language. Schleicher is wrong in treating ν in φέρομεν (1 pl.) &c., as this ν; for the Dor. φέρομες and the common φέρομεν both point back to an older φερομενς.

CHAPTER VI.

THE LATIN ALPHABET.

§ 64. TABULAR VIEW OF THE SOUNDS.

MUTES.		SEMIVOWELS.			VOWELS.
unasp. surd. son.		*Spirants.* surd. son.	*Nasals.* son.	*r & l-sounds.* son.	
Gutt. c, q g		h	n		a, ā } e, ē
Pal.		j			i, ī }
Cer.				(r, l)?	} o, ō
Dent. t d		s	n	r, l	
Lab. p b		f v	m		u, ū)

The Romans borrowed their alphabet from the Dorians of Cumæ, omitting the three aspirates, θ, φ, χ, as they did not possess the corresponding sounds. Their alphabet consisted, therefore, of the following letters, in the given order: a, b, c, d, e, f, z, h, i, k, l, m, n, o, p, q, r, s, t, v, x. Z is still found in a fragment of the Carmen Saliare; but it was soon lost, and was not employed again by the Romans till it was reintroduced in Cicero's time to represent Gr. ζ in borrowed words, at which period also Υ was introduced, as well as the custom of marking the Greek aspirates, θ, φ, χ, by *th, ph, ch.* Q is the Doric Koppa. X appears at the end of the alphabet, because it was not introduced as early as the other letters, *cs* or *gs* being used for it. It must have been adopted, however, before the archonship of Eukleides, for after his time the Greeks used the sign Ξ. The oldest document in which X is found is the Senatus Consultum de Baccanalibus. Some time after the introduction of the Doric Alphabet at Rome the distinction between the guttural tenuis and media was lost there, as well as in Etruria and Umbria, and C and K repre-

sented the same sound.* Thus on the Columna Rostrata
c = *g* in such forms as *leciones, pucnandod,* &c. This force of
c was still retained in the abbreviations *C.* and *Cn.* for *Gaius*
and *Gnæus.* *K* at last was only used in certain cases, as when
the words *Kæso, Kalendæ, Kalumnia, Kaput,* were marked by
the first letter merely. After *k* had thus been almost lost,
the Romans felt that a distinction should be made between
the guttural tenuis and media ; and, to represent the latter, *G*
was introduced by Sp. Carvilius, a freedman of Sp. Carvilius Ruga, and was placed by him between *f* and *h,* in the
place of the old *z*. The Emperor Claudius attempted to introduce three new signs—the inverted Digamma ⅃ for *v,* Antisigma Ɔ for *bs* or *ps,* and the sign of the Greek spiritus asper
⊦ for *ü*. This attempt, however, failed, for after his death
these signs at once were given up. The sounds of the Latin
language are not so far removed as those of the Greek from
those of the Indo-European ; for, while Greek has changed *u*
into *ü,* altered the three aspirates from mediæ to tenues, lost
y entirely, *v* nearly entirely, and nearly always lost or changed *s*
into the spiritus asper before vowels, Latin, on the other hand,
has kept the pure *u, y, v, s,* although *y* and *v* sometimes disappear, and *s* between two vowels becomes *r,* but represents the
three original aspirates by *f,* or when medial by *b,* and also
the I. E. *gh* by *h*. The vowel-system is, however, very far
removed from the I. E.; for the distinctions of guṇa and vṛddhi
have been almost lost; the effects of assimilation and dissimilation are very great; nearly all the old diphthongs have disappeared in classical Latin and Umbrian, and non-original
lengthenings and shortenings of vowels continually occur.
The old diphthongs are found in old Latin and Oscan, but
these have been handed down in too fragmentary a state to be
of much assistance. The substitution of monophthongs for

* This is Corssen's view, but it appears to be only a theory invented
to account for the fact that the third letter of the Latin Alphabet has a
k-sound.

diphthongs is easily explained, from the assimilation of one sound to the other, *ei* becoming *ī*, &c.; or from the mutual approximation of both to each other, *ai* becoming *æ*, &c.

§ 65. Pronunciation of the Vowels.

A had in classical Latin the full clear sound of the Italian *a*. Long and short *e* had each two different sounds: *ĕ* in *intĕr, patĕr,* &c., sounded like *e* in E. *father;* *ĕ* in *tempestatĭbus, merĕto,* &c., had an *i*-sound,* and was supplanted by *i* in the language of the educated classes, but finally returned to *e* in the language of the common people; *ē* had an *œ*-sound, as we see from the O. L. forms *quēstores, Victoriē,* &c., and the ordinary forms *fēcundus, fēnum,* &c.; *ē* had an *ī*-sound, which was anciently written *ei*, and which Quintilian notices (I. 4, 18, "in here neque *e* plane neque *i* auditur"). Short *i* had a thin *i*-sound; but in vulgar Latin in early times it was generally pronounced *e*, to which sound it also returned in the later Empire. The Oscan had an *i*-sound, for which they used the sign ⊦, and which was probably the same as the Fr. *é fermé.* Long *i* had a thin *i*-sound, and a broad *e*-sound, which was written *ei*. In Latin there also existed a sound between *i* and *u*, equivalent to the Gr. *υ*, for which Claudius introduced the sign ⊦. This sound was generally found before labials, as in *maxŭmus, volŭmus,* &c. It approached nearer to *u* than to *i*, inasmuch as the oldest inscriptions generally present *u*. The Claudian ⊦ is only found on inscriptions, in place of Gr. *υ*, as in *Aegṷti, Cḷenus,* &c., except once for Gr. *ι*, in *b⊦b (liotheca)*, and once in L. *gṷbernator*, on account of its relationship to Gr. κυβερνήτης. This sound generally became *i* in Italian, as *massimo*, &c.; yet we find it kept as *u* in It. *documento* and *monumento*. *O* had a clear sound in *colo, honestus,* &c., and an obscure one in termination –*os*, later –*us, plostrum,* &c. The L. *u* is a true *u*, and not the same as the Gr. *υ*; for the Greeks

* Of course I mean the Italian, and not the English *i*.

generally transcribed it by ου, as in Καρβούλων, Νουμᾶς, &c., and in some few cases by ο and υ, as in Ποπλικόλας, Φαυστύλος, &c. This proves that the L. *u* was equivalent to neither Gr. ο nor υ, but that it lay between these sounds. That the Gr. υ had not the same sound as the L. *u* is also shown by the fact, that on inscriptions before the time of Augustus Gr. υ is represented by L. *i*, as in *Stigio* for Στυγίῳ, and *Sisipus* for Σίσυφος, and that they naturalized Gr. Υ in their transcription of Greek words. In later Latin also Gr. υ was pronounced as *i*; thus we have *simbolo, gimnasio,* &c., whence come It. *simbolo, ginnasio,* &c.

§. 66. PRONUNCIATION OF THE SEMIVOWELS.

H is a soft spirant, though traces of a hard *h* are found in *vexi* and *traxi* from *veho* and *traho*. It seems to be hard before *t*, in the Umbrian forms *ahtu* beside L. *acto*, *rehte* = L. *recte*, *screihtor* = L. *scripti*, beside Osc. *scriftas* = L. *scriptæ*, &c., though even in these it may scarcely have been heard in pronunciation; for we find Umb. *subator* = L. *subacti*, and *ā* is represented in Umb. by *aha*, or *ah*. In Latin *h* had a very weak sound between two vowels, for we find *vemens* = *vehemens*, *Ala* = *Ahala*, *prendo* = *prehendo*, &c. Initial *h* in early times seems scarcely to have been pronounced; for we find, in the Senatus Consultum de Baccanalibus *abuisse* for *habuisse*, and *harenam* for *arenam*. It at last entirely disappeared about the end of the fourth Century A. D. Final *h* is found only in *ah!* and *vah!*

J, when initial in simple words, or in the second part of compounds, had the sound of the E. *y*. Hence we see that it is often lost in the latter case, as in *abicit, obicit, eicit, coicit*, &c. When it occurred between two vowels in simple words, *j* had a sound much nearer a vowel, and was frequently written II. This sound is also sometimes lost, as in *plous* (Sc. de Bac.) for *ploius*. It finally became z^2 (p. 13), as in

Fr. *jeune, juge, joint,* It. *giovane, giogo, giunto,* from L. *juvenem, jugum, junctum*. This change had already appeared in late Latin; for on a very late inscription *congiunta* is found for *conjuncta; cujus* is also found written κοζου, and *Jesu Zesu*, where *z* is *z³*.

S, when initial, or when medial, before and after any consonant, except after *n*, was always sharp. Initial *s* only occurs before consonants in the groups *sp, sc, st,* and consequently must have been sharp. Initial *s* before a vowel was also sharp, for it has this sound in the Romance languages. When medial, it was also sharp before and after other consonants, as is proved by the forms *nupsi, lapsus,* &c. It generally vanishes before *m, n, l,* and *d,* as in *Camena* for *Casmena, cena* (Umb. *çesna*), *corpulentus, idem,* &c., while in a few cases it becomes *r,* as in *carmen,* &c. On account of its sharp sound, *s* was lost before *f,* as in *fallo* beside σφάλλω, &c. Between two vowels *s* was soft, as in the Romance languages; consequently in this position it generally became *r,* as in the termination of the gen. pl. *-arum* = Osc. *-azum* = Skr. *-âsâm* (so Goth. *-izô* led to O. H. G. *-iro,* &c.), *generis* = I. E. *gunasas,* &c. *S* between two vowels was lost in *spei* for *spesi,* as we see from the old nom. pl. *speres* for *speses*. *S* had this soft sound after *n,* as in *consul, censor,* &c., beside *cosol, cesor,* &c. So we find μηζες on an inscription for *menses,* and in Umb. *menzaru* = L. *mensarum*. Final *s* had in old Latin a very faint sound, as we see from its loss in such nominatives singular, as *vigil,* &c., in the nominatives plural of the *a*- and *o*- stems, in the verbal forms of 2 sing. *delectare, loquerere,* &c., beside *delectaris, loquereris,* &c., and in the adverbs *mage, pote,* for *magis, potis*. On inscriptions of the time of the Punic Wars, we find the *s* of the nom. sing. of the *o*-stems sometimes not written, and on inscriptions of the later Empire we find the same *s* also omitted. Cicero calls the omission of a final *s* before an initial consonant *subrusticum,* which is a proof that in his time this *s* had a very faint sound in the language of the common people. Z, as we have already pointed out, was lost in early times, and *s* was employed to represent it, when initial, and *ss*, when medial, as in *sona, Saguntum, badisso, malacisso,* &c.; hence, to the old Romans, the Gr. ζ must have had a sound like a sharp sibilant. In the later Empire *z* must have had a sound between *d* and a sibilant; for we find such forms as *zabolus, zaconus,* &c., for *diabolus, diaconus,* &c. In old Umbrian *z* had perhaps, two sounds—a hard one, as in *pihaz* for *pihats* = L. *piatus*; and a soft one, as in *menzaru* = L. *mensarum.* In Oscan perhaps also, *z* had two sounds: it was soft in the gen. pl. term *-azum* = L. *-arum*, in *censazet* for *censasent* (censebunt), and it was hard in *húrz* for *hurts* = L. *hortus,* &c. In the pronunciation of *x* the sibilant predominated, for we also find it written *xs* from the time of the Gracchi; hence we find it represented by *s* in *sescenti, Sestius,* &c. This *s* has also disappeared before *d, n, m, v,* in *sedecim, seni, semestris, sevir.* In later Latin *x* and *s* were pronounced alike; for we find *visit, bisit,* and *bissit* for *vixit, coius* for *conjux,* &c., and conversely *xancto* for *sancto, milex* for *miles,* &c. In Italian *x* has become *s* or *ss*, as in *straneo, esempio, vissi, sasso,* from L. *extraneum, exemplum, vixi, saxum.* Similarly in Greek we find ξ interchanged with σ or σσ, as in δισσός = διξός.

F is a peculiar Italian spirant, the symbol of which the Romans borrowed from the Æolic F, while the Etruscans, Umbrians, and Oscans used for it the symbol 8. From its standing beside the digamma in such forms as *frango,* Gr. Fρήγνυμι, *frigus,* Gr. Fρῖγος, &c., it is supposed *f* and F had the same sound, but this is absurd; for it might similarly be argued that *f* and φ had the same sound, from the parallel forms *fama* = φήμη, *fero* = φέρω, &c. Now, though the Greeks used φ for *f*, as in Φάβιος = *Fabius,* &c., we know that their sounds were perfectly distinct from the fact that Cicero ridiculed a Greek witness for his mispronunciation of Fundanius.* Raumer accordingly considers φ to have been equivalent at a certain period to *bhv*; otherwise, he says, no one could say φ in trying to say *f*. Priscian asserts that the only difference between φ and *f* is, that the latter is pronounced *non fixis labris;* thus there would be produced a strong aspiration. This agrees with Quintilian's description of the sound, that it was formed *inter discrimina dentium*. The labial element in *f* was very weak; for we find *confero*, *infero*, Umb. *anferener*, and not *comfero*, &c.

V, when initial, or when medial after a consonant, had the same sound as the E. *v*; but when medial between two vowels, it had the sound of E. *w*; and consequently in this latter position frequently vanished, as in *boum*, *petii*, *Gnæus* for *Gnævus*, &c. This loss of *v* became very common under the Empire, when we meet *Faonius* for *Favonius*, *Flaus* for *Flavus*, &c. *V* in the perfect of the *a*-conjugation was omitted by the common people, as *laborait* for *laboravit*, &c., which is identical with the Italian form of the perfect, as in It. *lavorai*, *amai*, &c. In Greek *v* was represented by ου or β, as in Οὐάρρων beside Βάρρων, &c., and once on an inscription by ουβ in Μηουβιανος for *Mevianus*. This shows that Latin *v* had a sound between ου and β.

Initial *n* had the strong sound of E. *n*, as is shown by the fact that it never in this position interchanges with any other sound within the limits of the Latin language. When medial, it was also strong between two vowels, as we see from its being frequently doubled, as in *Porsenna*, beside *Porsena*, &c. It was also strong before dental mutes. *N* (*adulterinum*) had a guttural sound before *c*, *q*, and *g*. Final *n* had the sound of French nasal *n*, as we see from its vanish-

* "Nam contra Græci aspirare solent, ut pro Fundanio Cicero testem qui primam ejus literam dicere non posset, irridet." Quint. "Ins. Or.," I., 4, 14.

ing in nominatives singular in -*on*, as *ordo, homo*, &c.,* and in *ceteroqui, alioqui*, and also from the fact that in the old dramatists it sometimes did not make position with a following consonant. Medial *n* was also weak† before *s, j, v, f*.

M had the sound of E. *m*. When final, it was very weak, and frequently disappeared. In compounds of *circum* and *com* it always was lost before a vowel, except in *comitium*. Final *m* was sometimes pronounced as *n* before *n, d, t*, as in *cun nobis* ("Cic. Orat.," 45, 145) for *cum nobis, an terminum* for *am* (= ambi) *terminum* (Orig. Macrob., Sat. I., 14), &c., and before an initial guttural sometimes as *n adulterinum*. On inscriptions of the times of the Punic Wars, final *m* of case term. s is sometimes written, and sometimes not; but after the time of the Sen. Cons. de Bac. it was nearly always written. In the first century A. D. final *m* was scarcely pronounced in vulgar Latin, and was at last entirely lost.

L had a strong sound when it ended a word or syllable, or when it had another consonant before it in the same syllable, as in *sol, silva, clarus*. It had a weaker sound when it began a word or syllable, as in *lectum, talis*; and it was weaker still when it succeeded another *l*, as in *ille*. *L* was probably strong in such words as *lac, latus* (for *tlatus*), *lis* (for *stlis*), &c., where a preceding consonant has been lost. On account of *l* having this strong sound when following a mute, it was frequently separated from this mute by a vowel, as in

---

* I have here assumed that in the Græco-Italic period these nominatives ended in -*on*. This assumption is supported by the fact that we find corresponding nominatives in Greek ending in -ων; but, notwithstanding this, the existence of such nominatives is still very doubtful. As regards *ceteroqui* and *alioqui*, they may have originally ended in *i*, as other locatives, *domi*, &c.

† Priscian asserts that *n* was weak when it came after *m*, as in *damnum, columna, autumnus, scamnum, alumnus*, &c., but this is very unlikely; for the corresponding Italian words *danno, colonna, autunno, scanno, alunno*, &c., show that *n* here was at least a stronger sound than *m*, otherwise it could not have assimilated to itself the preceding *m*.

dulcis beside γλυκύς, *pulmo*** beside πνεύμων, *scalpo* beside γλάφω, *sculpo* beside γλύφω. This *l* had a *u*-sound inherent in it, hence *periclum* became *periculum*, &c. In French this *u*-sound overpowered *l*, as in *chevaux* from *caballos*, *cheveux* from *capillos*, &c. *L*, beginning a syllable, was easily interchanged with *r*, as in *ruralis*, *floralis*, beside *solaris*, &c. *Ll* was pronounced nearly as *l*, as we see from the fact that *ll* and *l* are frequently interchanged on inscriptions and in manuscripts.

R was a dental sound, formed by the vibration of the tip of the tongue, as is shown by its being interchanged with *d* and *s*.

§. 67. Pronunciation of the Mutes.

C was originally pronounced in all positions as E. *k*. That it was = *k* before *e* and *i*, is shown by inscriptions, where we find *Æcetiæ* for *Æquitiæ*, *dekem* for *decem*, and by its being interchanged with *q*, *g*, and *ch*, in *quercetum* beside *Querquetulanus*, *vicies* beside *viginti*, *pulcer* beside *pulcher*. *C*, however, finally became a surd palatal spirant before *e* and *i*, as in Italian. Traces of this change are found in the interchange of *ci* and *ti*, in the suffix *–icius* or *–itius*, where the Skr. *–ika* shows that the former is original, as in *concio* beside *contio*, where the latter is original, as being contracted from *conventio*, &c.

It appears that *c* before *i* and *e* was still pronounced as *k* in the sixth and seventh centuries, A. D.; for we then find δεκιμ for *decem*, φεκιτ for *fecit*, κρουκες for *cruces*, &c. Besides Gothic *k*, was used for L. *c* as in *aikeits*, *lukarn*, &c., beside L. *acetum*, *lucerna*, &c. Now, if *c* at this period had become the palatal spirant, neither Gr. κ nor Goth. *k* would have been used for it.†

---

* *Pulmo* is not borrowed from the Gr. πνεύμων; for, if it were, its genitive sing. would be *pulminis* (= πνεύμονος), and not *pulmōnis*.

† Consult, however, "Gesammelte sprachwissenschaftliche Schriften," by Rudolph von Raumer, p. 93.

In Umbrian we find c weakened not only to the pal. spir. ç, for which the Umbrians employed the peculiar symbol d, but also to the dent. spir., as in Volscian: thus we have çesna = L. cena, iseçetes = L. insectis, desenduf = L. duodecim, pase = L. pace, façia = Volsc. fasia = L. faciat, &c.

Qu was perhaps nearly equivalent in sound to the E. qu, but the u assumed various shades of pronunciation according to the vowel that followed: thus before a and o it was a pure u, before æ, e, and i, it was u^i, and it finally coalesced with a following u, so that at last cu supplanted the older quu. In early times quu was frequently written qu, for on inscriptions we find such forms as qum, pequniam, &c. During the Empire qu was also written q before other vowels than u, as in qintæ, qa, qe, &c. The Umbrian and Oscan expressed qu in words borrowed from the Latin by kv, as Umb. kvestur, Osc. kvaisstur for L. quæstor. In later Umbrian q is used without u, as in New Umb. dequrier = Old Umb. tekuries = L. decuriis, New Umb. peiqu = L. pico. In Greek qu is expressed by κου and κο, and qui generally by κυ, as Gr. υ = u^i: thus we have such forms as Κούαδοι, Κουιρῖνος, Κόϊντος, Κόαδοι, Κυρῖνος, &c.

G was pronounced as E. g. In Latin an older k was frequently replaced by g, while conversely in Old Umbrian g was hardened into k, at least in writing, if not in pronunciation, as in antakres beside L. integris, vestikatu beside L. vestigium, &c.

T was pronounced as E. t. When medial, it had a sharp sound, for it was frequently doubled on inscriptions, and in manuscripts, where we find such forms as Attilia beside Atilius, quattuor beside quatuor, &c. Final t was very weak; for we find it changed into d in quid, quod, id,* &c., and in the old termination of abl. sing., as pucnandod, altod, marid (Col. Rostr.); and it was so weak, that it was sometimes entirely lost

* In these cases d was perhaps the original sound; for final t in E. what, it, &c., points back to a Skr., Gr., and L. d.

in old Latin, as in *dede, dedro*, &c. In classical Latin *t* was restored, except in 3 pl. perf. as *censuere*, &c., but in later Latin it was again lost. In Umbrian, final *t* in the 3 sing. of the verb was lost, as in *habe* = L. *habet, portaia* = L. *portet*, &c.; and also in the 3 pl., as in *benuso* = L. *venerunt*, &c. In Volscian *t* in 3 sing. was lost, as in *fasia* = L. *faciat*.

D was pronounced as E. *d*. Final *d* is sometimes interchanged with *t*, as in the forms *aput, at*, for *apud, ad*, found on inscriptions.

P was pronounced as E. *p*. Final *p* was weakened to *b*, after the falling away of a vowel, as in *ab* = Skr. *apa, sub* = Skr. *upa, ob* = Umb. *up*, but the original *p* was restored before *s* and *t*. Final *p* was also aspirated in old Latin, for we find *af* (Sen. Cons. de Tiburt.) for *ab*. Plautus, however, retains final *p* in *volup* for *volupe*.

B was pronounced as E. *b*. *B* could not have had the sound of *v* in early times; for we find *Burrus* for Πύῤῥος, *Boblicola* an old form of *Poplicola, hapeat* beside *abuisse*, &c. In the later Empire, however, *b* was sounded as *v*, as we find on inscriptions such forms as *devitum* for *debitum, verva* for *verba, acerva* for *acerba, bixit* for *vixit, laborabit* and *laborait* for *laboravit*, &c.

§. 68. The Vowels.

An original *a* is lost in *sum* for *esum* = Skr. *asmi, gigno* for *gigeno* from I. E. *gan, patris* = I. E. *pataras*, &c.

A = I. E. *a*, especially before *c* and *g*; *acus*, Skr. *as'* (to be sharp); *ago* = Skr. *ag'âmi; lacrima*, Skr. *as'ru* (a tear); *ab* = Skr. *apa* (from); *animus, anus*, Skr. *anila* (wind); &c. In Umbrian and Oscan an original *a* is retained more frequently than in Latin, as in O. U and O. O. *anter* = L. *inter, Anterstataí** (dat. sing.) = L. *Interstitæ* (the name of a goddess), N. O. *amprufid* = L. *improbe*.

---

* The vowel *í* was perhaps equivalent to the Fr. *é fermé*. It is written *i* on the Bantine Table, but in the National Oscan Alphabet its sign is ᛗ.

E. = I. E. *a* : *equus* = Skr. *as'vas* (a horse) ; *decem* = Skr. *das'an* (ten) ; *ferentem* = Skr. *bharantam* (acc. sing.), &c. This *e* has in some cases passed through *o* : *verto* = O. L. *vorto*, Skr. *vart* (to turn) ; *vester* = O. L. *voster*, Skr. *vas* (vos), &c. In Umbrian and Oscan *e* = I. E. *a* : N. U. *desen* = Skr. *das'an* ; N. U. *petur* = L. *quatuor*; O. O. *set* (sunt) = Skr. *santi*; O. O. *mefiai* (dat. sing.) = L. *mediæ*, Skr. *madhya* (medius), &c. Short *e* was developed in some cases in Græco-Italic times, as we see from a comparison of *fero, decem, sex, ego*, &c., with φέρω, δέκα, ἔξ, ἐγώ, &c. In other cases, however, *a* existed then, from which in after times *e* was developed in one language, while *a* was kept in the other, as in *maneo* beside μένω, *egenus* beside ἀχήν (needy), *anguis* = ἔχις, *centum* = ἕκατον, &c. Long *e* was also developed in Græco-Italic times, as in *semi-* = ἡμι -, *her* = χήρ (hedgehog), *siem* = εἴην, &c.

I = I. E. *a* : *ignis* = Skr. *agnis* (fire) ; *quinque* = Skr. *pañk'an* (five); *inter* = Skr. *antar* (within), &c. So also in Umbrian and Oscan, as in N. U. *dirsans* (3 pl. pres. conj.) from *dirs*, O. U. *ter*,* for *did*, a reduplicated form of *da* ; O. O. *ist* = Skr. *asti* (est), &c. *A*, in becoming *i*, passed through an *e*-stage, as we see from *assideo* beside *sedeo*, Skr. *sad* (to sit) ; *nominis*, gen. of *nomen* = I. E. *gnâman* ; *artificis*, gen. of *artifex*, from *facio*, &c. *I* in some cases may represent an older *o*, as in *levis* = λεῖος, *-lis* (in *similis*, &c.) = -λος (in ὑμαλός, &c.) *-aris* (in *popularis*, &c.) = -ηρος (in λυπηρός, &c.), *imber* beside ὄμβρος, *ille* beside *ollus*, *illico* beside *locus*, *inquilinus* beside *incolo*, &c.

O = I. E. *a* : *vomo*, Skr. *vam* (to vomit) ; *vōs* = Skr. *vas* (ye) ; *ovis* = Skr. *avis* (a sheep); *morior*, Skr. *mar* (to die), &c. *So* represents *sva* in *somnus* = Skr. *svapnas* (sleep) ; *soror*, Skr. *svasâr* (sister) ; *sonus* = Skr. *svanas* (sound) ; *socer* = Skr.

---

* *R*, represented in the Old Umbrian Alphabet by q, and in the New Umbrian by rs, marks a peculiar change of *d*, and was probably a strong hissing *r*.

s'vas'uras (father in-law); *socrus* = Skr. *s'vas'rûs* (mother-in-law). In Old Latin *o* is kept, where in later Latin *u* is found, before *s* and *m*, in the terminations *-tos* (nom. sing. masc.) and *-tom* (acc. sing. masc. and neut.), in neuters in *-os*, as *genos* = Skr. *g'anas*, and *Venos* (fem.), in dat. pl. term. — *bos* = Skr. *bhyas*. In New Umbrian, ŏ̄ = I. E. ă. This N. U. ŏ is represented in Old Umbrian by ū̆, and is consequently a return to that older stage through which the Old Umbrian ū̆ must have passed, just as the old *o* has been restored in Italian. Thus we have O. U. *puplum*, N. U. *poplom* = L. *populum*, from I. E. and Skr. *par* (to fill); N. U. *ortom* = L. *ortum*; O. U. *nŭmen*, N. U. *nōmen* = L. *nōmen*; N. U. *erom* (infinitive of verb *es*, to be), an accusative of an *o*-stem; N. U. *aferom* (ambiferre), &c. In Oscan, ŏ̄ = I. E. ă: O. O. *pŭtŭrŭs** (nom. pl.) = I. E. *kvataras* =•Gr. πότεροι, L. *utri*; O. O. *pŭd*, N. O. *pot* = L. *quod* = I. E. *kvad*; O. O. *vĭu̇* = L. *via* (but *a* is kept in acc. *vĭam*, *via*, = L. *viam*, *pam* = L. *quam*, &c.); in O. O. abl. sing. *sakaraklŭd* (sacello), although the usual term is *-ād*. This ŏ̄ = I. E. *ā* was developed in some cases in Græco-Italic times, as in *sollus* = ὅλος; *pro-* = προ-; *odor* beside ὄζειν; *ferō* = φέρω; *duō* (*duŏ*, however, is more usual) = δύω; *ambō* = ἄμφω. In many other cases, however, *a* existed then, as we see from the fact that the original *a* is kept in one of these languages, and *o* in the other, or it becomes *e* in one language, and *o* in the other: thus we have *o* beside *a* in *domare*, beside δαμᾶν, *arduus* beside ὀρθός, *dare* beside διδόναι, *cornus* beside κράνον, *lancea* beside λόγχη, &c., and *e* beside *o* in *novus* = νέϝος = Skr. *navas* (new), *vomo* beside ἐμέω, Skr. *vam* (to vomit), *vox* beside ἔπος, Skr. *vak'* (voice), &c.

U = I. E. *a*, which had previously passed through *o*: *genus* = O. L. *genos* = Skr. *g'anas*, Gr. γένος; *opus* = Skr. *apas* (work); *ferunt* = O. L. *feront* = Gr. φέροντι = Skr. *bharanti* (they bear); *navibus* from *navibos* = Skr. *nāubhyas*; *datus* = Gr. δοτός;

---

* *Ŭ*, in the Oscan Alphabet represented by **V̇**, was pronounced as Latin *o*.

quum = O. L. *quom* = I. E. *kvam*, &c. In Umbrian *ŭ* = I. E. *ă*; O. U. *puplum* = *populum*; N. U. *dupursus* (δίποσι) = Skr. *dvipadbhyas* (bipedibus); O. U. and N. U. *vinŭ* = *vino* = O. L. *veinōd* = I. E. *vaināt*; N. U. *kvēstŭr* = O. L. *quaistōr*. In Oscan *ŭ* = I. E. *ă*: *-ŭd* (term. of abl. sing.) = I. E. *-āt*, as in O. O. *aragetud* = L. *argento*; N. O. *kenstŭr* = L. *censōr*; *-um*, the termination of the infinitive, which was an old acc. of an *o*-stem, and therefore was = I. E. *-am*, as in *deicum* (dicere), *ezum* [esse, U. *erom*], *moltaum* (moltare), &c. Traces of this infinitive are found in Latin, in *venum-ire* and *venum-dare*. It is possible that this *u* may have been developed in Græco-Italic times, but such Græco-Italic examples are rare; perhaps λύκος = *lupus*, from I. E. *varkas*, is one. *U* = I. E. *a* in some cases passed through the *uⁱ-stage*, and became *i*; this *uⁱ*-sound was represented by ⊢ by Claudius. Thus we have *optimus* = O. L. *optumus*; *mancupium* (in Plautus) = *mancipium*; *occupare* beside *incipere* from *capio*, &c.

I = I. E. *i*: *imus* = ἴμεν = Skr. *imas* (we go); *scindo*, σχίζω, Skr. *k'hinadmi* (I split); *linquo*, λείπω, Skr. *rik'* (to leave); *quid* = τί, Skr. *kim* (what); *ovis* = ὄις = Skr. *avis* (a sheep), &c.

E = I. E. *i*: *index*, *indicis*, from R. *dic* = Skr. *dis'* (to point out); *ignem* = Skr. *agnim* (fire); *navem* beside *navim*; *mare* for *mari*, as is shown by *maria*; *navebos* (Col. Rostr.) *tempestatebus* (t. Scipion, B. f.) from the stems *navi-* *tempestati-*. In these cases *e* is younger than *i*, whereas in the cases where *i* = I. E. *a*, *i* must have passed through an older *e*-stage.

U = I. E. *u*: *cluo* = κλύω, Skr. *s'ru* (to hear); *jugum* = ζυγόν = Skr. *yugam* (par); *rumpo* = Skr. *lumpâmi* (I break); *uro* for *uso*, Skr. *ush* (to burn); *tundo, tutudi*, Skr. *tudâmi* (I strike); *supér* = ὑπέρ, Skr. *upari* (over), &c. Long *u* sometimes appears to arise from a non-original lengthening of an older *ŭ*, as in *tū*, Skr. *tvam* (thou), Gr. τύ, Goth. *thu*, and perhaps in *sūs* = ὗς, *mūs* = μῦς, &c. *U* = I. E. *u* also in Umbrian and

Oscan; O. U. *fuia* (sit) = Skr. *bhúyát*, and *fuiu* (esto) from R. *fu* = Skr. *bhu* (to be); N. U. *rufrēr* (nom. pl.) = L. *rubri*, Skr. *rudhira* (blood), N. O. *fuid* (opt. perf.) and *fust* (3 sing. fut.) from R. *fu*.

O = I. E. *u*, only in *fore* from R. *fu*.

I = I. E. *u*: *libet* beside *lubet*, Skr. *lubh* (to desire); *cliens* from *cluo*; *lacrima* = *lacruma*, Skr. *as'ru* (a tear); *tibi*, Skr. *tubhyam* (to thee); *manibus* for *manubus*; *fructifer*, *arcitenens*, *corniger*, &c., for *fructufer*, *arcutenens*, *cornuger*, &c. So also in Umbrian we find O. U. *sim* (acc. sing.), *sif* (acc. pl.) from a stem *si* (a pig), L. *sus*; O. U. and N. U. *mani* (abl. sing.) = L. *manu*; O. U. *tiu*, N. U. *tiom*, *tio* (acc. sing) = Skr. *tvam*.

§. 69. GUNA AND VRDDHI.

The I. E. *a* is represented in Latin by *e, o, a*; its guna is *o, ē, ā*, as in Greek; its vrddhi is perhaps *ō* and *ū*. The guna of *i* was in O. L. *ei*, later *ī* and *ē*, and *ai*, later *ae*; its vrddhi was in O. L. *oi*, later *oe, ū, ī*. The guna of *u* was in O. L. *eu*, and later *au, ō*; its vrddhi was in O. L. *ou*, later *ū*. In Latin *eu*, the old guna of *u*, was supplanted by the vrddhi *ou*, while conversely in Greek the vrddhi ου was supplanted by the guna ευ. In the following table* the O. L. diphthongs are placed in brackets.

Primitive Vowels	*e, o, a,*	*i*	*u*
Guna	*o, ē, ā,*	(*ei*) *ī ē*, (*ai*) *ae*	(*eu*), *au ō*
Vrddhi	*ō ū*	(*oi*) *œ ū, ī*	(*ou*) *ū*

* In this table I have followed Schleicher, except that in some cases I consider *ī* to be a vrddhi of *i*. Many of the examples given by him to illustrate this table are very doubtful. Indeed, it is almost impossible to separate from each other the spheres of guna and vrddhi in Latin, on account of the almost universal reduction of the old diphthongs to monophthongs. This is also the case with Umbrian. In Old Latin and Oscan these diphthongs have been kept, but then here we labour under a want of materials.

$\bar{A}$ is the guna of a in the following examples: *pāx, pācis* beside *pācisci; lāterna* beside *lăteo; vāgina* beside *văco; suffrāgium* beside *frăgor*, from R. *frag* (to break); *sāgire, sāgus* beside *săgax; lābi* beside *lăbare; amb-āges* beside *ăgo, ambigere; frāter*, Skr. *bhrātar*, from R. *bhăr*, &c. The feminine of the *a*-stems also ended in $\bar{a}$ originally; *novā* = Gr. νέFā = Skr. *navâ* (new); *coctā* = Gr. πεπτή = I. E. *kvaktâ*, &c. So in Umbrian $\bar{a}$ (written *aha, ah*) is guna of $\breve{a}$, as in O. U. *frātrum*, N. U. *frātrom* (fratrum), &c. So also in Oscan, as in *Staatiis* = L. *Stătius*, beside *stătus*, from R. *stă*.

$\bar{E}$ is guna of $\breve{e}$: *tēgula* beside *tĕgo; lēx, lēgis, collēga* beside *lĕgo; rēx, rēgis* beside *rĕgo: sēdes* beside *sĕdeo; sēmen* beside *sătus* from R. *să;* and perhaps a few other cases. $\bar{I}$ may be guna of $\breve{e}$ in *sīca* beside *sĕco*.

$\bar{O}$ is guna of $\breve{e}$: *procus* beside *precor; fors, fordus* (pregnant) beside *fero; toga* beside *tĕgo*, Skr. *sthagāmi* (I cover); *moneo* beside *mens, memini*, Skr. *man* (to think); *noceo* beside *nĕco*, Gr. νέκυς, Skr. *nas'* (to kill); *modus* beside *mederi;* also before two consonants in *pondus* beside *pendere, extorris* beside *terra*, &c. $\bar{O}$ is guna of a in *portio* beside *pars, scobina* beside *scăbo*, &c.

$\bar{U}$ is considered by Schleicher to be the vrddhi of a, especially when an original a in a root is represented by o: *persōna* beside *sŏnus*, Skr. *svan* (to sound); *vōmer* beside *vŏmo*, Skr. *vam* (to vomit); *sōpio* beside *sŏpor*, Skr. *svap* (to sleep); *sōdes* beside *sŏdalis; vōx, vōcis* beside *vŏco; ōcior* beside Gr. ὠκύς = Skr. *ás'us* (quick), from R. *as'* (to be sharp); *dōnum, dōs, dōtis* beside *dătus* from R. *dă; gnōtus* = Gr. γνωτός, *gnōmen* beside *nŏta, cognitus; datōrem* = Gr. δοτῆρα = Skr. *dátāram*, &c. $\bar{U}$ is found beside $\bar{o}$ in *-tūrus* beside *-tōr* (*datūrus* beside *dator*, &c.); term. of gen. pl. *-um, -rum*, for *-ūm, -rūm* = Skr. *-âm, sâm*. In Umbrian we find O. U. $\bar{u}$, N. U. $\bar{o}$, as vrddhi of a: O. U. *nūmen*, N. U. *nōmen* = L. *nōmen;* term. of gen. pl. O. U. *-ūm*, N. U. *-ōm*, as in O. U. *frātrūm*, N. U. *frātrōm;* N. U. *kvēstūr* = O. L. *quaistŏr*, &c. In Oscan $\bar{u}$ is vrddhi of *a* in N. O. *kenstūr* = L. *censor*; O. O. *Fluusai* = L. *Flōræ* from R. *fla*.

(*Ei*), *ī, ē* is the guṇa of *i* in the following examples: *dīvus* (*deivæ, deivinam*, &c., are found on inscriptions) from R. *div* (to shine); *dīco*, O. L. *deico*, beside *causidīcus* from R. *dic* = Skr. *dis'* (to point out); *īdus*, O. L. *eidus* (the days of full moon, and therefore the brightest days), beside Skr. *idh* (to burn); *is, it, itur* (from *eo*, I go), beside *eis, eit, eitur*; *difeidens, confīdo* beside *perfīdus*; *leibertinus* beside *lībido*, &c. In Oscan we find O. O. *ei̇̀*, N. O. *ei* as guṇa of *i* in N. O. *deicum* (infin.) from R. *dic*; N. O. *deivaum** (infin. to swear), O. O. *dei̇̀vai* (dat. sing.) beside L. *dīvus* from R. *div*.

(*Ai*), *ae* is the guṇa of *i* in *aidilis, aedes, aestas* (for *ædtas*) beside Skr. *idh* (to burn), Gr. αἴθω, αἴθηρ; *aevom*, O. L. *aivom*, from R. *i* (to go); *aemulus* beside *imitari*; *mæstus* beside *miser*; and perhaps a few other cases. In Oscan we find *ai̇̀* as guṇa of *i* in O. O. *ai̇̀dilis* = L. *ædiles*, and in Umbrian *ē̇*, as in O. U. *kvḗstur* = O. O. *kvai̇̀stur* = O. L. *quaistor*.

(*Oi*), *œ, ū* is the vṛddhi of *i*, as in *fœdus* beside *fīdes*; O. L. *læbesum* (= liberum) beside *lībet*;† *oitile, oetier, ūtier*; *loidos, loedos, lūdus*; *moiros, moeros, mūrus*; *ploirume, ploera, plures*; *coiravit, coeravit, cūravit*; *moinicipium, comoinem* (Sc. de Bacc.), *inmœnis, comūnis*; *oinvorsei* (Sc. de Bacc.), *œnus, ūnus*, &c. In Oscan we find O. O. *ui̇̀*, N. O. *oi*, as vṛddhi of *i*, as in O. O. *mui̇̀niks* (nom. sing. masc.) beside O. L. *comoinem*; *ui̇̀ttiuf* beside *oitile, ūtier*.

I appears to be the vṛddhi of *ĭ* in a few cases: *mītis* for

---

* As *deivaum* in Oscan means 'to swear,' from St. *deiva* (a god), so in Lettic we find the infin. *devatees*, also meaning 'to swear,' from St. *deeva* (a god), *devs* (nom. sing.) = L. *divus*.

† The roots *lib* and *fid* are the only two roots in Latin that appear as well in their simple as in their guṇa- and vṛddhi-forms: thus we have R. *lib, libet, leibertinus, loebesum*; R. *fid, fides, difeidens, foidus*.

moitis, O. Ir. *moith* and *moeth* (tender); *vīnum** for *voinum*, beside Gr. οἶνος; *vīcus* for *voicus*, beside Gr. οἶκος. Schleicher considers *vinum* and *vicus* to be examples of guṇa and not vṛddhi; but it is better to suppose that the vṛddhi-forms existed in Græco-Italic times. In Sanskrit the guṇa-forms occur, *vés'as* = οἶκος and *véna* (pleasant).

Eu, the old guṇa of *u*, is found only in the proper name *Leucesius* (Carm. Saliar.), beside *lūcerna* from R. *luc*. In some other words *eu* is found, where it is not a guṇa; thus we have *neuter* for *ne-uter*, *neutiquam* for *ne-utiquam*, *neu* for *neve*, *seu* for *seve*, *ceu*, *heu*, *eheu*, in which cases *eu* is not the guṇa of *u*. The vṛddhi *ou* has in other cases been substituted for *eu*, as in *dūco*, O. L. *douco;* *ūro* for *ouso*, and this again for *euso* = Gr. εὕω = Skr. *óshámi* (1 burn), from R. *ush* = I. E. *us* ; *jūs*, O. L. *jous*, is for *jovos*, and this again is for *jevos*, which is formed by guṇa from R. *ju* (to join), as κλέϝος is formed from R. κλυ and Skr. *s'ravas* (nom. sing. neut.) from R. *s'ru;* *jūs* (sauce) is also formed in the same way from R. *ju*, which is found in Gr. ζύμη (leaven), and Sl. *jucha* (sauce); *pūs* = *povos* = *pevos* beside Skr. *púy* (to be foul), Z. *pû* (to stink); *pluont* = *plovont* = *plevont* = Gr. πλέϝοντί, whence πλέουσι, from R. *plu*; *fluont* = *flovont* = *flevont*, from R. *flu*, and similar present forms; *trūdo* = *troudo* = *treudo*, beside *trŭdis*, &c. In Oscan also the vṛddhi of *u* appears to have taken the place of the guṇa, as in O. O. *tuvtiks* (urbanus), N. O. *touto* (a city) from R. *tu* = Skr. *tu* (valere).

Au may be the guṇa of *u* in *raudus* (unpolished brass), from R. *rud* (to be red) = Gr. ῥυθ.

Curtius and Schleicher consider also that *aurora* and *augeo* are cases of *au* as guṇa of *u*: *aurora* and Gr. αὔως pointing

---

* The connexion of *véna* (pleasant), an adjective applied in Sanskrit to the drink *Soma*, with οἶνος is very doubtful. I have already connected the latter with the root *vi* (to bind), whence came υἰή (the vine), and L. *vieo*, *vitis*. Others treat οἶνος as a borrowed word, and connect it with Heb. *yain*, Æthiop. *wain*, (wine).

back to a Græco-It. *ausōs*, from R. *us* = Skr. *ush* (to burn), this root appearing in its guna-form in the European languages as O. N. *austur* (oriens), Lith. *auszrà* (morning), while it appears in its simple form in Sanskrit and Zend as Skr. *ushásá* (morning), *ushá* (early), Z. *usha* (morning); *augeo* beside Gr. αὔξω, Lith. *áugu* (I grow), from R. *ug*. I have already (p. 65) pointed out that these words are susceptible of a different explanation. *Au* frequently becomes *o*, by passing through the step *ao*, which is found in *Aorelius*, which occurs on an old inscription. Thus we have *rōdus* for *raudus*, *cōda* for *cauda*, &c. *Au* frequently arises from *av*, as in *cautus* from *caveo*, *fautor* from *faveo*, &c.

(*Ou*), *ū* is the vṛddhi of *u*, as in O. L. *Loucina*, *loumen*, *Loucetios* from R. *luc*; *rūfus* from R. *rudh*, &c. In *poublicos*, *ou* appears to be the vṛddhi of an *u* that represents an original *a*. In Umbrian, O. U. *ū*, N. U. *ō* is also the vṛddhi of *u*, as in N. U. *rōfu* = L. *rūfos*, &c. (*Ou*) *ū* in Latin arises also from the rejection of the spirant *j*, and from the vocalization of *v*, as in *cuncti* = *cojuncti*, *plous* for *plojus*, *noundinum* (Sc. de Bacc.) for *novendinum*, *nountios* for *noviventios*, &c.

§ 70. Assimilation of the Vowels.

One vowel is often assimilated to a preceding one, as in *luteolus* from St. *luteu-*, *vinolentus* from St. *vinu-*, beside *hortulus*, *truculentus*; *tristities* beside *tristitia*; *siem* = Skr. *syâm*; *-iens* (in *totiens*, &c.) beside Skr. *-iyâns*; *o* being nearer than *u* to *i* and *e*, and *e* being nearer than *a* to *i*.

One vowel is assimilated to a following one, as in *exilium* beside *exul*; *nihil*, *nisi*, *nimis*, *nimirum* beside *ne*, *nefas*; *familia* beside *famulus*; *bene* beside *bonus*; *illecebræ* beside *illicio*; *soboles* for *suboles*; *socors* for *secors*; *queam* beside *quire*; O. L. *filea* = *filia*; *mihi*, *tibi* beside *me*, *te*, U. *mehe*, *tefe*; *nausea* = Gr. ναυσία; &c.

Vowels are frequently influenced by neighbouring consonunts. Thus the labials and *l* prefer *u*, as in *Hecuba* = Ἑκάβη; *occupo, aucupium,* beside *capio; contubernium* beside *taberna;* O. L. *pocolom* becomes *poculum; epistula* = ἐπιστολή; *monumentum* beside *monimentum; puls* beside πόλτος; *sepultus* from *sepelio; insulsus* from *salsus,* &c. *R* frequently prefers *e* before it, as in *operis, cineris,* beside *nominis; camera* from καμάρα, &c. In some cases *r* takes before it *o,* where otherwise we should have expected *u,* as in *ancora* = ἄγκυρα; *foris* beside θύρα; *fore* from R. *fu; corporis,* gen. sing. of *corpus; por* (in *Marcipor*) = *puer.* The dental *n* prefers *i* in *cecini* from R. *can; machina* from μηχανή; *nominis, hominis,* &c. Final *n,* however, changed this *i* into *e,* as in *cornicen, nomen,* &c.

§. 71. Dissimilation of the Vowels.

The Latin language does not allow one vowel to be followed by the same without the intervention of a consonant, but always changes the first or second of these vowels into another, as *i* into *e,* and *u* into *o.* Thus we have *pietas, ebrietas, societas,* for *piitas,* &c., beside *levitas, caritas; arietis, parietis,* for *ariitis,* &c., beside *militis; alienus, Avienus,* &c., beside *peregrinus,* &c.; *hietare* beside *clamitare; variegare* beside *levigare; laniena* beside *carnificina; meio* for *miio,* and this for *migjo,* beside *mingo,* Gr. ὀμίχω; *peior* for *piior; ei, eis, dei,* &c., are older and more classical forms that *ii, iis, dii,* &c., which were also sometimes written ī*s,* dī, &c.; *petiei, ostiei, Juliei, vicis,* &c., beside the later forms, *petii, ostii, Julii, viis,* &c. Up to the period of Augustus we never find *uu* or *vu,* but always *uo* and *vo,* as in *equos, servos, novom, æquom, vulpes, volt,* &c.

§. 72. Vowels lengthened in Compensation.

When a consonant is lost, the preceding vowel is frequently lengthened in compensation; or, if two vowels are thus brought together, they are contracted into one. Thus we have in the first case *pēs* for *peds* ; *aries* for *ariets* ; *pŏno* for *posno*, R. *pos*, found in *pos-ui* ; comp. term. *-iŏr*, *-ioris* = I. E. *-yans*, *-yansas* ; acc. pl. term. *-ōs* = I. E. *-ans*, &c. In many cases, however, this vowel is again shortened, as in *pedĕs* for *pedēs* = *pedĕts*, *patĕr* = Gr. πατήρ, for *patĕrs*, &c. Again, we find contraction in *fēci* for *fĕfĭci*, R. *fac* ; *frēgi* = *frĕfrĕgi*, R. *frag* ; *fōdi* for *fŏfŏdi*, R. *fod* ; *mōvi* for *mŏmŏvi*, R. *mov* ; *fāvi* for *făfăvi*, R. *fav*, &c. Similarly we have *nēmo* for *neemo* = *ne-homo* ; *vemens* = *vehemens* ; *amō* = *amao*, and other verbs of the first conjugation, &c.

§. 73. Weakening of the Vowels.

Vowels are generally weakened in words whose weight is increased either by *reduplication*, or by *composition*, or by being formed from other stems by means of *suffixes*. Thus *a* becomes *e*, as in *fallo, fefelli; parco, peperci ; barba, imberbis; farcio, refercio ; factus, perfectus*, &c.

A becomes *i*, as in *tango, contingo ; capio, accipio ; fateor, confiteor ; manus, eminus ; nam, enim ; pater, Jupiter ; cano, cecini*, &c. This *i* of course passed through the stage *e*, and *e* is still kept in cases where *i* might have been expected, as in *peperi (pario), tubicen (cano)*, where the retention of *e* is due to *r* and final *n*.

A becomes *u*, as in *capio, occupo ; datus* = I. E. *datas*, Gr. δοτύς ; *taberna, contubernium*, &c. This *u* passed through the stage *o* ; thus L. *datus*, and Gr. δοτός, point back to a Græco-Italic *datos*.

Ā becomes *ē*, as in *hălo, anhēlo*.

E becomes *i*, as in *lego, colligo ; emo, redimo ; teneo, retineo*, &c. In reduplicated syllables *e* is unchanged, as in *tetendi, pependi*. *Ē* becomes *ī*, as in *lēnis, delīnire ; tēla, subtīlis* ; it becomes *ĕ* in the reduplicated perfect *pĕpĕdi*.

Ae becomes *ī*, as in *aequus, iniquus ; caedo, cecīdi*, &c.

Au becomes *ō* and *ū*, as in *fauces, suffōco ; plaudo, explōdo ; causa, accūso ; claudo, inclūdo*, &c.

Long vowels and diphthongs are even weakened to short vowels, as in *agnĭtus, cognĭtus,* beside *nŏtus ; dejĕro, pejĕro,* beside *jūro,* O. L. *jouro.*

O and *u* are also weakened to *i,* as in *duritas* from St. *duro– ; corni-ger* from St. *cornu,* &c. In reduplicated syllables, however, *o* and *u* remain generally unchanged, as in *poposci, spopondi, totondi, momordi, pupugi, tutudi, cucurri.* In Old Latin these forms were sometimes lightened, as we find O. L. *spespondi, peposci, memordi, tetuli, pepugi, cecurri.*

In Umbrian and Oscan the original vowel is not weakened, as in Latin, in compounds, &c. Thus we have O. U. *arkani* from R. *kan* (canere), and *ar* (ad) ; N. U. *procanurent* from same root as last; O. U. *arhabas* = L. *adhibeas ;* N. U. *Jupater* = L. *Jupiter ;* O. O. *Anterstatŭ* = L. *Interstita ;* O. O. *anter* = L. *inter;* N. O. *amprufid* = L. *improbe ;* N. O. *fefacid* (3 sing. opt. perf.), *fefacust* (3 sing. fut. exacti) from *fefac,* a reduplicated form of R. *fac.* If *hipid* (3 sing. opt. perf.), *pruhipust* (3 sing. fut. ex.) be from the same root as L. *habeo,* we have here a case of *a* being weakened to *i,* in Oscan ; *hip* being for *hihip,* and this for *hihap,* and therefore having been *hīp* originally.

§. 74. Shortening of the Vowels.

Vowels in unaccented final syllables are very generally shortened in Latin, and hence a a few examples will suffice. The final *a* of the feminine *a*-stems was long in Indo-European, and is still long in Sanskrit. In Old Latin it was also long, but in classical Latin it has been shortened. Final *a* in *triginta,* &c., was once long, but in the later poets it is short. Final *e* of the ablative of the *i*-stems was also long, as representing an I. E. *ait* or *aid ; patrē* is still found in *Gnaivŏd patré prognátus, fŏrtis vír sapiénsque* (tit. Scip. Barb.). We find *cavĕ, jubĕ* beside *cavē, jubē ; mihĭ, tibĭ* for *mihei, tibei ; duŏ, ambŏ, octŏ, egŏ,* beside Gr. δύω, ἄμφω, ὀκτώ, ἐγώ ; *homŏ,* &c., for *homō ;* final *o* of the first pers. sing. pres. and fut. active is either long or short, representing an I. E. *a*, as - *ŏ* (in *ago*, Gr. ἄγω) = –*ā* = -*ámi*, &c.

Vowels are shortened always before final *t*, as in *amăt* for *amāt*, &c. : traces of the original *ā* are still found in the Poets, as in Plautus, Terence, &c. The same is the case with the verbal terminations –*et*, *it*, and *is*. We find also *matĕr* for *matēr*, Gr. ματήρ ; *prætŏr* for *prætōr*, &c.

Medial vowels are also frequently shortened, as in *docĕo* for *docēo* ; *audĭo* for *audīo* ; *rĕi* for *rēi* ; *spĕi* for *spēi* ; *dĕus* for *dēus*, and this for *deivos* ; *Dĭana* for *Dīana* ; *unĭus* beside *unīus* ; &c.

§. 75. Total Loss of the Vowels.

Final *e* is lost in the imperatives *dic*, *duc*, *fac*, *fer*, *inger* (Catull. 27, 2) ; in *hic*, *hæc*, *hoc* for *hice*, &c.; in voc. *fili* for *filie*, &c. ; in imper. *audi* for *audie*, &c.; in *amor* (1 sing. pres. pass.) for *amose ;* &c.

Final *i* is lost in *est* = Gr. ἐστί ; *ferit* = Skr. *bharati*; *ferunt* = Skr. *bharanti* (*tremonti* is still found in Carm. Saliar.; *feris* = Skr. *bharasi*, &c. *I* is lost in *pulvinar* beside *pulvinare* for *pulvinari*, and similar nouns in –*ar* = –*ari* ; *piper* = Gr. πέπερι ; *facul*, *difficul*, *simul* = *facile*, &c., for *facili*, &c.; *tot* = Skr. *tati*; *quot* = Skr. *kati* ; *ut* beside *uti*, U. *ote*, O. *auti* ; *ob* = Gr. ἐπί = Skr. *abhi* (ad) ; *ad* = Skr. *adhi* (super, ad), &c.

Final *o* is lost in *ab* = Gr. ἀπό = Skr. *apa* (ab) ; *sub* = Gr. ὑπό = Skr. *upa* (ad) ; for, as the *o*-stems in Greek and Latin correspond to the *a*-stems in Sanskrit, the Græco-Italic forms of *ab* and *sub* must have ended in *o*.

Medial vowels are lost before either vowels or consonants: thus before a vowel *i* is lost in *minus* for *minius*, *semanimus* for *semi-animus ;* *e* is lost in *nullus* for *ne-ullus*, *nusquam* for *ne-usquam ;* *o* is lost in *unŏculos* for *uno - oculus*.

Medial *a* is lost before a consonant in *palma* = Gr. παλάμη through *paluma ;* *cypressus* = Gr. κυπάρισσος through *cuperes*-

sus; cervos = Gr. κεραϝός (horned); *domui** for *domāvi*, and similar perfects, *a* being first weakened to *i*, and then this *i* falling out, &c.

Medial *e* is lost between *b* and *r* in the suffixes *-bra, -bris, -brum*, from R. *fer* = Skr. *bhar;* between *p* and *r* in *capri, supra* beside *supera* (in Lucr.), *infra* beside *infera*, &c.; between *t* and *r* in *intra, contra, dextra* beside *dextera* (*-tra* being the comparative suffix, Skr. *-tara*, Gr. *-τερο*, Osc. *-toro*, U. *-tro); patris* for *pateris; habui* for *habēvi*, and similar perfects, *ē* having first passed through *i*, as in *habitum ; repperi* for *repeperi ; rettuli* for *retetuli*, &c.

Medial *i* is lost in *caldus* = *calidus* (warm); *soldus* = *solidus ; valde* = *valide ; cante* (Carm. Saliar.) = *canite ; nauta* = *navita ; calx* = Gr. χαλίξ ; term. *-mnus* (in *alumnus, vertumnus*) = *-minus* (in *terminus, amamini*) = Gr. -μενος = Skr. *-mānas ; fertis* = *feritis, fert*† = *ferit, volt* = *volit*, and similar verbal forms; *dixti* for *dixisti*, &c. Under the later Empire we find such forms as *fect, vixt, expensavt*, &c. *I* is often lost in the *i*-stems: thus we have *primas* for O. L. *primatis ; sors* beside *sortis ; plebs* for *plebis*, whence *plebes ; scobs* beside *scobis*, &c. In consequence of this loss of *i*, the consonantal and the *i*-stems coincide in the form of nom. sing. Medial *i*, is lost before a consonant sometimes in Umbrian and Oscan, as in U. *nōmnē* = L. *nomini*, &c.; O. *cevs* = *civis;* U. *fus* = O. *fust* = L. *fuerit ;* U. *habus* = O. *hipust* = L. *habuerit ;* U. *convortust* = L. *converterit*, &c. Comparing U. *habus*, O. *hipust* with L. *habessit*, we see that the Umbrian and Oscan forms have lost two *i*s, the *i* of the perfect, and the conjunctive mark *i*. The perfect *-vi* has completely disappeared in L. *habessit ;* and the only trace of it is found in the sharp *s*, written *ss*, while *habuerint* stands nearest to the original form *habe-visint*.

---

* In Latin the accent was originally placed as far back as possible. Consult Appendix B.

† *Fert* may be the older form, as we find Ved. *bharti* (fert).

In nouns of the *o*-stem, *o* or *u* (= I. E. *a*), is frequently lost before *s* of the nom. sing. Thus we have *puer* for *puers* = *puerus*; *vir* for *virs* = *virus*; *famul* (Enn. Ann.) beside *famulus*; *damnas* for *damnats* beside *damnatus*; *Sallustis, Clodis*, &c. (on inscriptions), for *Sallustius*, &c. Similarly we have O. U. *pihaz* = L. *piatus*; O. U. *katel* = L. *catulus*; N. U. *termnas* = L. *terminatus*; N. U. *tertis* = *tertius, tertim* = *tertium*, just as in Old Latin *alis, alid*, = *alius, aliud*. We have also O. O. *tŭrtiks* = L. *tuticus*, *Pŭmpaiians* = L. *Pompeianus, hŭrz* = L. *hortus, Heirennis* = L. *Herennius*, &c.; N. O. *Bantins* = L. *Bantinus*.

Medial *u* is also lost in *stella* for *sterula*; *ampulla* for *amporula* from *ampora*; *corolla* for *coronula* from *corona*; *misellus* for *miserulus*; *lapillus* for *lapidulus* from St. *lapid*; *vinclum* beside *vinculum*, &c. Similarly we have in Umbrian *Treblaneir* = L. *Trebulanis, vesclir* = L. *vasculis, pihaclu* = L. *piaculum*, &c., unless these be the original forms.

In Gothic we find *i* and *u* frequently omitted before a final *s*; thus we have *vulfs* (nom. sing. wolf) = Skr. *vṛkas*, and similar nominatives; *brōthrs* (gen. sing.) = I. E. *bhrátras*, *namins* (gen. sing.) = L. *nominis*, &c.

§. 76. INSERTION OF A VOWEL.

We find a vowel inserted in the following cases: *drachuma* (Plaut.) = δραχμή, *sumus* for *esumus* = Skr. *smas, volumus* for *volmus, Tecumessa* = *Tecmessa, Hercules, Æsculapius, Patricoles*, where the neighbourhood of *l* or *m* determines the inserted vowel to be *u* or *o*; *techina* (Plaut.) = τέχνη, *Procina, Ariadine*, &c., where the inserted vowel is *i*, on account of the neighbouring *n*; *umerus* = Græc.-It. *omsos* beside Gr. ὦμος, and Skr. *amsa* (the shoulder), *ruber* for *rubros* = Gr. ἐρυθρός = Skr. *rudhira* (blood, also with an inserted *i*), *gener* for *genros* = Gr. γαμβρός, *caper* = Gr. κάπρος, &c., in all which forms *r* determines the inserted vowel to be *e*. *l* is inserted in *moriturus* beside *mortuus, oriturus* beside *ortus*, &c. Similarly in Oscan we find between a liquid and a following consonant the vowel of the preceding syllable inserted, as in *aragetud* (abl. sing.) = L. *argento, teremniis* = L. *terminus*, &c., just as in O. H. G. *puruc* for *purc*, Goth. *baurgs, waram* for *warm*, Goth. *varms*; and between a liquid and a preceding consonant the vowel of the following syllable is inserted, as in *puturămpid* gen. pl., utrorumque), *puturuspid* (nom. pl. mas. utrique), *putereipid* (loc. sing. masc.

§. 77. The Gutturals.

C and *q* = I. E *k*: *acus, acer, acupedius, ocior*, Skr. *as'ri* (the edge of a sword), *ás'u* (quick), Z. *aku* (a point) Gr. ἀκωκή, ἄκρις (a mountain-top), ὄκρις (a point), ὠκύς; *calo*, Gr. καλέω, E. *halloo; cella, celo, domi-cilium*, Skr. *s'álá* (a house), Gr. καλιά (a hut), E. *hell, hole; cedo*, Gr. ἐκεκήδει (ὑπεκεχωρήκει, Hesych.), κεκάδοντο (Il. 15, 574), a redupl. aor. 2 of χάζομαι from R. χαδ = σχαδ = I. E. *skad; castus*, Skr. *s'udh* (to purify), Gr. καθαρός, Ch. Sl. *cistŭ* (clean); *cor*, Skr. *hrd* (heart), Gr. καρδία; *cerebrum, crista* (in capite stans), Skr. *s'iras* (head), Gr. κάρα, κρανίον; *carpo*, Gr. καρπός, E. *harvest; civis* = Osc. *kevs*, Skr. *s'i* (to lie), Gr. κεῖμαι, Goth. *haims* (κώμη), *heiva* (domus), &c.

Qu = I. E. *kv*: *quinque* = I. E. *kvankvan*, whence Skr. *pañk'an* (five), Gr. πέντε, Æol. πέμπε, Ir. *coic*, W. *pump; quod* = I. E. *kvad* or *kvat*, whence Skr. *kat*, Gr. ποῦ, Ion. κοῦ, E. *what*, &c. In a few cases in Latin *k* may have had *u* developed after it, as in *quies* beside Skr. *s'i* (to lie), *squalor* beside Skr. *kála* (black), and Gr. κελαινός, &c.; but in nearly all the cases where this development of *u* is supposed to have taken place, it is much more probable that *kv* had originally existed in Indo-European. In Old Umbrian we find *k*, and in New Umbrian *c* and *q* = I. E. *k*, except in the pronouns and numerals where *p* takes the place of I. E. *kv*: O. U. *kapres* = L. *capri;* N. U. *pequo* = L. *pecua*, &c. This *k* is weakened to *ç* and *s* before *e* and *i*,* as in N. U. *curnaçe* (abl. sing. of a noun corresponding to L. *cornix*) beside N. U. *curnaco* (acc. sing.); N. U. *paçe* and *pase* = L. *pace*, &c. In Old Oscan *k*, and in New Oscan *c* = I. E. *k*, except that *p* = I. E. *kv* in the same cases as in Umbrian : O. O. *líkitud* = *licitud* = L. *liceto*; O. O. *sakaraklúd* (abl. sing.) beside L. *sacellum*, &c. *C* = I. E. *g* in N. O. *acum* (inf.) beside L. *ago*. In Old Umbrian, as has been already remarked, *k* represents L. *g*.

G = I. E. *g*: *ago*, *igitur* for *agitur*, Skr. *ag'âmi* (I go), Gr. ἄγω, O. N. *aka* (ago); *genus*,† *gigno* (*g*)*natura*, Skr. *g'an* (to be born), *g'anitâ* (nom. sing. of St. *g'anitar*) = L. *genitor*, Gr. γένος, γίγνομαι, γείνομαι for γενγομαι, Goth. *keinan* (to germinate), O. H. G. *chind* (offspring) ; *grus*, γέρανος, E. *crane*; *gnosco*, (*g*)*notus*, *gnarus*, (*g*)*narrare*, O. L. *gnarigare*, Skr. *g'nâ* (to know), Gr. γιγνώσκω, γνωτός, O. H. G. *knâu* (I know), Goth. *kann* (I know), *kunths* (γνωστός) whence E. *uncouth*; *urgeo*, Skr. *varg'* (arcere), Gr. εἴργω, Λυκόοργος, Goth. *vrika* (διώκω), A. S. *vringan* (stringere), E. *wring*, *wrong*; *genu* = Skr. *g'ânu*, Gr. γόνυ, E. *knee*, &c. In New Umbrian and Oscan, *g* = I. E. *g*.

G = I. E. *k* in a few words : *digitus*, Gr. δάκτυλος, Goth. *taihō* (toe) ; *viginti* beside *vicies*, Skr. *viṅśati*, Gr. εἴκοσι, Bœot. Ϝίκατι ; *triginta*, Gr. τριάκοντα ; *gracilis* beside O. L. *cracentes* (graciles), Skr. *krś'a* (thin), Gr. κολεκάνος (long, lank), κολοσ-

---

* *K* is retained in O. U. *akeruniamem*, N. U. *acersoniem*, O. U. *kebu* (cibo), and a few other cases; also in nominal stems of the *o*-declension that end in *-ko*, as N. U. *Naharce* (dat.), *Tesenocir*, (abl. pl.), except that we find O. U. *pupriçe* beside *puprike* (publico), and *pupriçes* beside *puprikes* (publici). We find *ç* sometimes before *l*, as in O. U. *tiçlu*, *ereçlu*, &c. Was this the beginning of that change which we see in Italian *chiamare* = L. *clamare*, *chiaro* = L. *clarus*, *occhio* = L. *oculus*, *piano* = L. *planus*, *piangere* = L. *plangere*, &c. ? *K* is also found unaltered before *l* in O. U. *ehvelklu*, *fiklas*, &c.

† There probably existed, in I. E. times, as a side form of R. *gan*, *gvan*, as we find Gr. γυνή, Bœot. βανά for γϝανα, Goth. *gvêns* (θῆλυς), E. *quean*, *queen*, and perhaps L. *venter* for *gventer*.

σός for κολοκγος; *gubernator* beside Gr. κυβερνήτης; *Agrigentum** from Gr. 'Ακράγας; *negotium* = *necotium*; *pingo*, Skr. *pis'* (to adorn), *pés'alas* = Gr. ποικίλος; *ungulus, angulus* beside *uncus, ancus* (qui aduncum brachium habet), Skr. *añkas* (nom. sing. masc. the part above the hip), *añkus'a* (stimulus quo elephanti impelluntur), Gr. ὄγκος (a curve), ἀγκάλη (the bent arm), ἀγκών; *cygnus* = Gr. κύκνος; *gurgulio* = *curculio*; *ilignus* from St. *ilec*; *salignus* from St. *salic*, Gr. ἑλίκη (the willow, in Arkadia); *dignus* connected by Curtius with *decet, decus*, Skr. *das'as* (glory), Gr. δοκέω, but by others with Skr. *dis'* (to point out), Gr. δείκνυμι; *larignus* from St. *laric*; *langula* (a little dish), from St. *lanc*; *pango, pignus*, beside *paciscor, pax*, Skr. and Z. *pas'* (to bind), Gr. πηγός (fast), πήγνυμι, πάσσαλος = πακγαλος, Goth. *fahan* (to seize), *fagrs* (εὔθετος); *gloria* from St. *clovos-* = *clevos-* = Gr. κλέϝος- = Skr. *s'ravas-* (glory) from *s'ru* = Gr. κλυ; *gummi* = Gr. κόμμι; *gobius* = κωβιός; and a few other cases.† In all these cases where *k* is softened to *g*, it either begins a syllable or is in close proximity to *l, m, n,* or *r*.

G = I. E. *gh* : *fugio*, I. E. *bhugh*, Skr. *bhug'* (flectere) Gr. φεύγω, Goth. *biuga* (κάμπτω); *rigo*, Gr. βρέχω, Goth. *rign* (rain); *unguis*, Skr. *nakha* (a nail), Gr. ὄνυξ, from St. ὀνυχ; *fingo, figura*, I. E. *dhigh*, Skr. *dih* (to smear), *dêha* (the body), Gr. θιγγάνω, Goth. *deiga* (πλάσσω), O. H. G. *teig* (dough); *ango, angustus*, Skr. *añhu* (close), Gr. ἄγχω, ἄχος, Goth. *aggvus* (close); *lingo, ligurio*, Skr. *lih* and *rih* (to lick), Gr. λείχω, Goth. *bilaigôn* (ἐπιλείχειν); *mingo, mejo*, Skr. *mih* (mingere), Gr. ὀμιχέω; *grando, suggrunda* (eaves), Skr. *hrâdunî* (bad weather), *hrâdinî* (lightning), Gr. χάλαζα for χαλαδγα, Ch. Sl. *gradŭ* (hail); *gratus*, O. and U. root *her* (to wish), Skr.

---

* *Agrigentum* is the accusative of 'Ακράγας, and therefore must have been introduced at a time when the intercourse between Rome and Sicily was carried on without the use of writing.

† Consult Corssen über Aussprache, Vokalismus und Betonung der Lateinischen Sprache, p. 39, seq.

haryâmi (I love), Gr. χάρις, χαίρω, Goth. *faihu-gairns* (greedy of money); &c. In no case does an initial I. E. *gh* become L. *g*, except when succeeded by *r*, as in *gratus*, &c., and perhaps by *l*, if Grassman be correct in deducing initial *g* in *glisco, glaber*, and *glubo*, from an I. E. *gh*. In two cases *fr* appears to represent an I. E. *ghr*: *frio, frico*, Skr. *ghar* (to sprinkle), *gharsh* (to rub), Gr. χρίω; *fragro* a reduplicated form of R. *gra* = Skr. *ghrâ* (odorari).

Schleicher considers that in some cases *u* was developed after *g*, generally when a nasal, and sometimes when *r* preceded, as in *langueo* beside Skr. *lañg'â* (a whore), Gr. λαγαρός (slack), λάγνος (lustful), and *urgueo* beside *urgeo*, Skr. *varg'* (to exclude), so that *gu* = I. E. *g* or *gh*, and afterwards through assimilation of *g* to *v*, *v* alone remained, as in *nivis* for *nigvis* from *nix*. Now this development of *u* after *g* is extremely doubtful. In many cases *gu* most probably existed in Indo-European times, in others *u* is merely a suffix, while in others it seems to be inserted from a false analogy. Thus *u* was a suffix, to which afterwards a secondary suffix *i* was added, in *pinguis* beside Gr. παχύς, *brevis* for *bregvis*, beside Gr. βραχύς, *levis* for *legvis*, beside Gr. ἐλαχύς = Skr. *laghus* (light), &c. In the following cases we infer the existence of an I. E. *gu* or *ghu* from the related words: *voro* for *gvoro*, I. E. *gvar*, whence *gar* (to devour), Gr. βορά; *vivus* for *gvigvus*, a reduplication of I. E. *gvi* whence Skr. *g'îv* (to live), Gr. βίος, E. *quick*. Again *u* may have arisen from a false analogy in *ninguit* beside *ningit* and *nivis* for *nigvis*, gen. sing. of *nix*, from I. E. *snigh*, whence Gr. νίφα, ἀγάννιφος for ἀγασνιφος, Lith. *snigti* (to snow), Goth. *snaivs* (snow); *urgueo* = *urgeo*; *anguis* beside Skr. *ahis* (nom. sing. masc., a serpent), Gr. ἔχις, ἔγχελυς, Lith *angis* (a snake).

H = I.E. *gh*: *hospes, hostis*, O. L. *fostis*, Ch. Sl. *gostĭ* (guest), Goth. *gasts* for *gastis* (a guest), Lith. *gaspadà* (hospitium); *hĕrus, hĕres*, O. L. *hir* (the hand), Skr. *har* (to seize), Gr. χείρ; *heri, hes-ternus*, Skr. *hyas* (yesterday), Gr. χθές, O. H. G. *gester* (yesterday); *hirundo*, Gr. χελιδών; *hiems, hibernus*, Skr.

hima (snow), Gr. χιών, χειμών; helus, helvus,* Skr. hari (green), Gr. χλόη, O. H. G. grōni (green); haruspex, hariolus, hira and hilla (entrails), Skr. hirá (entrails), Gr. χολάδες, χορδή; hortus = Gr. χόρτος; haedus, Gr. γοῖτα (Hesych. οἷς), Mod. Gr. γίδα, Goth. gaits (a goat); humus, Gr. χαμαί (a locative from χαμα = I. E. ghamá); homo (connected with humus), O. L. hemōnes (nom. pl.), Goth. guma from St. guman, whence -gam in G. Bräutigam (bridegroom); hio, Gr. χαίνω, χάος, χειά (a hole), O. N. gîn (I gape); prehendo for praehendo, hedera, praeda, perhaps for praehida, hasta, Skr. hasta (the hand) (?), Gr. χανδάνω, E. get; veho, Skr. vah (to carry), Gr. ὄχυς from R. Feχ, Goth. vigs (via); traho, perhaps connected with Skr. drâgh (adniti) and dhrâgh (posse), E. drag, which presuppose an I. E. dhragh. In the two last cases we have traces of the guttural in the perfects vexi and traxi for vegsi and tragsi. Gh passed through f in becoming h, as we see from the Old Latin forms folus, fostis, fordus, &c., for holus, hostis, hordus, &c. Similarly in Spanish, h represents L. f, as in hijo = filius, hablar = fabulari, hierro = ferrum.

H = I. E. gh in Oscan and Umbrian, as O. herest, U. heriest (volet) beside Skr. haryâmi (amo), and Gr. χαίρω.

H = I. E. bh in mihi, U. mehe, Skr. mahyam, beside tibi, Skr. tubhyam, and in horda beside forda (pregnant), from R. fer = Skr. bhar. Schleicher suggests that amavi for amafui, &c., passed through the stage amahvi, &c., and that the dat. pl. of the a-stems in -îs for -ais passed through the stage -ihis = I. E. -abhyams, but these cases are extremely doubtful. Grassman considers that h = bh in herctum or horctum. Festus tells us that horctum or forctum meant bonum; and Grassmann considering that it meant originally "what is heaped up," connects it with Skr. bhrs'am (multum, valde), with

---

* Grassmann is mistaken in connecting L. gilvus with this root, for an initial I. E. gh followed by a vowel never becomes g in Latin, but always h through O. L. f. Lottner agrees with Grassmann, and connects L. germen also with the same root.

which he also connects L. *farcio, frequens*. Curtius, on the other hand derives *herctum, hercisco*, from a root *her* lengthened by *k*, connected with Skr. *har* (to take), Gr. χείρ, χέρης, L. *hir, hĕrus*.

H appears to represent an I. E. *k* in *hic*, from St. *hi-* = Goth. *hi-* = I. E. *ki-*, and in *habeo* = Goth. *haba* (I have). *Hic* (for *hice*) may be a reduplicated form of *ki-*, the original *k* perhaps appearing in the second syllable; compare *citra*, which may come from this root. Schleicher treats R. *hab* in *habeo* as a side form of R. *cap* in *capio*, and compares O. *hipust* (habuerit) and *hafiest* (habebit). He considers that *p* is weakened to *b* in *habeo*, just as in *bibo*, which he deduces from an I. E. *pipâmi;* this latter comparison is, however, extremely doubtful, as it is much more likely that the I. E. root began with *bh*, of which we still find a trace in Skr. *pibâmi*. *H* = I. E. *k* in Skr. *hṛd* (heart) beside Gr. καρδία, E. *heart*.

H in Umbrian and Oscan not only corresponds to L. *h*, as in O. O. *hurz* = L. *hortus*, &c., but it also takes the place of *c* and *p* before *t*, as in O. U. *scrēhto* = L. *scriptum*, *rehte* = L. *recte*, *subahtu* for *subactu*, and this again for *subagtu* = L. *subigito*, O. O. *ehtrad* = L. *extra*, *saahtim* = L. *sanctum*, N. O. *Ohtavis* = L. *Octavius*, &c. The long vowels in Umbrian are written, *aha* or *ah*, &c.

Corssen considers that *h* has sprung from *y* in L. *ahenus*, beside Skr. *ayas* (iron); in *Mahestinus* (found on inscriptions) = *Majestinus;* and in O. U. *pihaz*, N. U. *pihos* = L. *piatus*, Volscian *pihom* = L. *pium*,* beside Skr. *priya* (carus). *Hora* is borrowed from Gr. ὥρα, which is connected with Z. *yâre* (year), E. *year*. If Pott is correct in treating *hornus* as = *ho-jornus*, as *biga* = *bijuga*, we find in it the original Latin form corresponding to Z. *yâre*, and E. *year*. *Hercules* (O. *Hercklo-*) is also

---

* L. *pius* has been also connected with Skr. *piy* (conviciari in dial. vēd.), Goth. *fijan* (to hate), E. *fiend;* L. *piare* is then explained to mean " to reconcile an enemy."

borrowed from Gr. Ἡρακλῆς; it has nothing to do with a Latin verb *hercere*, which cannot be = Gr. ἕρκειν, for Greek spiritus asper = I. E. *s*; Mommsen erroneously connects the Greek and Latin verbs, and considers Hercules to be a Ζεὺς ἑρκεῖος.

An inorganic *h* is added to *humerus* for *umerus*, Gr. ὦμος = Skr. *aṅsas* (nom. sing. masc.), Goth. *amsa*, all of which forms point back to an I. E. *amsas*, whence came a Græco-It. *omsos* or *omesos*, of which latter form we find a trace in Gr. ἀμέσω (Hesych., the shoulder blades). Also *humor* = *umor*, connected by Curtius with Gr. ὑγρός Skr. *uksh* (humectare). Similarly we find *h* added in Sp. *hedrar* = L. *iterare*, Fr. *haut* = L. *altus*.

§. 78. The Palatal *J*.

J = I. E. *y*: *jecur*, Skr. *yakṛt*, and in the weak cases *yakan* (the liver), Gr. ἦπαρ from St. ἤπαρτ; *jugum*, Skr. *yugam* (par), Goth. *juk*, O. H. G. *joch*; *jus*, Skr. *yûsha* (pease soup), Gr. ζωμός (soup); *juvenis*, Skr. *yuvan* (young), E. *young*; *jam*, Goth. *ju* (now). Lith. *jau* (now); &c.

I. E. *y* is often vocalised in Latin: *medius* = Skr. *madhyas*; *siem* = Skr. *syâm*, Gr. εἴην from I. E. *asyâm*; &c.

§. 79. The Dentals.

T = I. E. *t*: *ante* (for *anted*, an ablative form found in *antidea*), Skr. *anti* (before), Gr. ἀντί; *stella* (for *sterula*), Skr. *staras* (the stars, in dial. Ved.), *târâ* (a star), Gr. ἀστήρ, τείρεα; *et*, *at*, in *at-avus*, Skr. *ati-* (ultra), Gr. ἔτι; *vetus*, Skr. *vatsara* (a year), Gr. ἔτος; *peto*, *penna*, O. L. *pesna* for *petna*, Skr. *pat* (to fly), Gr. πέτομαι; *sto*, Skr. *sthâ*, Gr. ἵστημι; *sterno*, *torus* for *storus*, Skr. *star* (sternere), Gr. στόρνυμι; *tendo*, *teneo*, *tenus*, Skr. *tan* (to stretch), Gr. τάνυμαι, τείνω, Goth. *thanya* (I extend): *tu*, Skr. *tvam* (thou), Z. *tûm* (thou), Dor. τύ, Bœot. τούν, Goth. *thu* (thou); *tuli*, O. L. *tulo*, *tetuli*, Skr. *tul* (to lift), Gr. τλῆναι, τελαμών, τάλας, Goth. *thula* (I endure);

termen, *in-tra-re*, *trans*, U. *traf* = L. *trans*, Skr. *tar* (to cross), Gr. τέρμα, E. *through*, &c.

St = I. E. *sk* in *stercus*, Skr. *s'akṛt** (stercus), Gr. σκώρ from St. σκαρτ, στεργάνος (Hesych. κοπρών), σπατίλη (excrement), A.S. *skearn* (dung); *sturnus*, Gr. ψάρ for σπαρ, ἀστραλός (Hesych. ὁ ψαρὸς ὑπὸ Θετταλῶν), A. S. *stearn*, Bohem. *skorec* (a starling), where Curtius believes *sk* to be original, *talpa* for *stalpa*, Gr. σπάλαξ, σκύλοψ (a mole); *talla* (caepae putamen) is, according to Curtius, for *stalla*, and comes from an I. E. R. *skal*, whence G. *schale* (husk, rind), &c.

St = I. E. *sp* in *studium*, Gr. σπουδή, E. *speed* ; *turgeo* for *sturgeo*, Gr. σπαργάω, σφριγάω (I swell, burst), perhaps connected with σφάραγος (a noise), Skr. *spurg'* (to make a noise); and perhaps one or two other doubtful cases.

T never = I. E. *dh* (except in the case of the initial group *tr*, as in *traho*). All the examples brought forward to prove the contrary can be easily explained without such a supposition. Thus, *rutilus* is for *rudtilus*, from R. *rud* = Skr. *rudh*, and -*tilus* is the same termination as is found in *futilis*, *mutilus*, &c.; *pati* and Gr. παθεῖν† are both independent formations from a root *pa*, *πα*, which bears the same relation to πεν (in πένομαι) and πον (in πονέω) as γα (in γεγαώς) does to γεν (in ἐγενόμην) and γον (in γέγονα) and τα (in τάνυμαι) to τεν (in τείνω); *putāre* is not connected with πυθέσθαι, for the latter comes from I. E. *bhudh*, whence Skr. *budh* (to know), and the former from L. *putus* (clean), beside Skr. *pû* (to clean), *putare* therefore signifying "to make clean" (compare *amputare*, *lanam putare*), and then "to make clear;" *pătĕre* and πυθέσθαι are independent formations from

---

* Bopp considers that *s'* in *s'akṛt* represents an original *k*, and connects it with Gr. κόπρος for κοκρος, L. *caco*, &c. Curtius connects κόπρος with καπύω, καπνός, &c. All the comparisons in this section and the succeeding one are extremely doubtful.

† Lottner and others, however, identify *t* in *lateo*, *patior*, with θ in λαθεῖν, παθεῖν, and consequently infer the existence of the hard aspirates in Indo-European.

R. *pŭ*, connected with Skr. *pûyé* (putresco), Z. *pû* (to stink), and Goth. *fuls* (foul); the connexion of *lateo* with λαθεῖν is not so easily explained as the last examples, for we find Skr. *rah* (to leave), and *rahas* (a secret, or secretly), which point back to an I. E. *radh*, but it is likely that *latere* is formed from a R. *la*, as *pûtere* is from R. *pû*.

D = I. E. *d*: *do*, *dăre*, Skr. *dâ* (to give), Gr. δίδωμι; *dexter*, Skr. *dakshiṇa* (dexter), Gr. δεξιός, Goth. *taihsvō* (δεξιά); *duo*, Skr. *dva*, Gr. δύω, Goth. *tvai*; *domus*, Gr. δόμος, A. S. *timber*; *suadeo*, *suavis* for *suadvis*, Skr. *svad* (to please), *svâdus* = Gr. ἡδύς; *sedeo*, Skr. *sad* (to sit), Gr. ἕζομαι for ἕδυομαι, &c.

D = I. E. *t* in *quadraginta* from *quatuor*.

D = I. E. *dh*: *medius* = Skr. *madhyas*, Gr. μίσσος for μεθyoς, Goth. *midjis* (medius); *aedes*, *aestus* for *aedtus*, Skr. *indh* (to burn), Gr. αἴθω, ἴθη (Hesych. εὐφροσύνη), perhaps Αἴτνη and Ἥφ-αιστος; *do* in *condo*, *credo*, *abdo* is connected with Skr. *dhâ* (to place) = Z. *dâ*, Gr. τίθημι; *vidua** = Skr. *vidhavá* from *vi-* (without), and *dhava* (vir); &c.

D may be = I. E. *y* in *tendo* = Gr. τείνω for τενyω, Goth. *thanja* (I stretch); in *fendo* = Gr. θείνω for θενyω; and perhaps in the part. term. *-endus* or *-undus* = I. E. *-anyas* = Skr. *-aniyas*. In Zend we find the corresponding termination *-énya* in *verezénya* (working), from R. *verez* = Gr. Ϝεργ. In Oscan *ny* perhaps became *nn*, as in O. O. *upsannam* = L. *operandam*: in Umbrian also *ny* became *nn* or *n*, as double consonants are generally not both written in Umbrian, as in N. U. *pihaner* = L. *piandi* (gen. sing.), &c.

D = Gr. λ and ρ in the two borrowed words, *adeps* and *caduceus*, from Gr. ἄλειφα and καρύκιον. We also find *d* for *l* in *Capitodium*, a side-form of *Capitolium*, for *Capitālium*, *ā* becoming *ō* as in *ignōro* beside *gnārus*, &c. *Cadamitas*, a side-form of *calamitas*, is generally supposed to be original, but it is much more likely that *calamitas* is the older form. *Calamitas* means "destruction of the *calami*;" thus we are

---

* It is better, however, to derive *vidua* from the R. *vid* (to separate).

told (Serv. Verg. Georg. I. 151), Robigo, genus est vitii, quo *culmi* pereunt, quod a rusticanis *calamitas* dicitur. *Calamitas* is formed from St. *calamo* by means of the suffix *-tat-*, just as *civitas* is from St. *civi*, &c. If on the other hand *d* is original in this word, we would first have to form from *cado*, from which it is derived, the St. *cadımo*, but as the Romans never kept *ă* before the suffix *-mo*, but always changed it into *u* or *i*, this supposed stem is foreign to the Latin, and most probably never existed. That *l* sometimes became *d* in vulgar Latin is shown by *vodeba* on an inscription at Pompeii for *volebam*.

D in Old Umbrian, when initial, was represented by *t*, and in New Umbrian by *d*; when medial or final it was in Old Umbrian changed into a sonant hissing sound, represented by **q** (*ṛ*), which in New Umbrian became *rs*. Thus we have N. U. *dur* = L. *duo*; N. U. *dupursus* (bipedibus) from *purs-* = L. *ped-*; O. U. *asam-aṛ* = L. *aram-ad* (ad aram); O. U. *aṛveitu* = L. *advehito*; N. U. *virseto* = L. *visus* from R. *vid*; O. U. *pere, piṛi*, N. U. *perse, pirsi* = L. *quid*, with the same *i* attached as is found in Gr. *-ι* (οὑτοσί) compare Lith. *-ai* (tas-aí); O. U. *teṛa*, N. U. *dersa* = *didat* (det), a reduplicated form of R. *da*, &c. We find *ṛ* for initial *d* in O. U. *ṛere* = L. *dedit* (3 sing. perf.) and *ṛunum* = L. *donum*, but these forms may be, as Schleicher suggests, only dialectic.

In Oscan *d* = L. *d*; it is also retained in some cases where *l* is found in Latin. Thus we have O. O. *púd*, N. O. *pod* = L. *quod*, O. O. *píd* = L. *quid*; N. O. *deicans* (3 pl conj. pres.) = L. *dicant*; O. O. *dedet* = L. *dedit*; O. O. *Akudunniad* = L. *Aquiloniā(d)*.

R = I. E. *r*: *aro*, Gr. ἀρόω, Goth. *arjan* (to plough); *orior*, Skr. *ar* (to move), *árta* = Gr. ὦρτο, Gr. ὄρνυμι; *rivus, Rumo,* (the old name of the Tiber), Skr. *sru* (to flow), Gr. ῥέω; *fero,* Skr. *bhar,* Gr. φέρω; *ruber*, Skr. *rudhiram* (nom. neut. blood); *-tor, -ter,* = Skr. *-tár -tar,* as *dator* = Skr. *dátá* for *dátárs, pater* = Skr. *pitá* for *patars*; *rēs* = Skr. *rás* (divitiae) from St. *rái*; &c.

R = I. E. d in *arbiter* for *ad-biter* and *arcesso*. In Old Latin r is frequently found for d, as in *arvenas* (Prisc. I. 45), for *advenas, arvorsum* (Sc. de Bacc.) for *advorsum, arfuisse* (Sc. de Bacc.) for *adfuisse*, &c. Even *apor* and *ar* were used for *apud* and *ad*. This is similar to the change of d into r in Old Umbrian.

The Latin language, however, afterwards recovered itself from this weakening of d to r, and restored d, except in *arcesso, arbiter*, and *meridies* where $r = d$ = I. E. dh as *medius* = Skr. *madhyas*. R in *mirus* is not developed from d, as is asserted by those who look upon r as belonging to the root, and compare it with Gr. μειδάω, but -*ro* is a suffix, found also in *clarus*, &c., and d does not belong to the root in μειδάω; these words are probably independent formations from the I. E. R. *smi* = Skr. *smi* (to laugh), whence also O. H. G. *smielen, smieren*, (to laugh), E. *smile*, Lett. *smeet* (to laugh).

R = an older n in *crepusculum*, *creperus* (dubius), beside Gr. κνέφας; *groma* borrowed from Gr. γνώμων. Leo Meyer also derives *germen* from R. *gen*, and *carmen* from R. *can;* but in both cases he is entirely wrong. Curtius connects *germen* with Skr. *garbha* (uterus, foetus), Z. *garewa* (foetus), Gr. δελφύς (uterus); βρέφος, from I. E. *grabh* (concipere), whence Skr. *grah* (capere); *germen* would therefore be for *gerbmen*. *Carmen* is for *casmen*, compare *Casmenae*. We find r representing an older n in Fr. *diacre* (= diaconus), *Londres, ordre* (= ordinem); Sp. *hombre* (= hominem), *fembra* (= femina), &c. Conversely in Wall. *suspina* = *suspirare* we find n for r. It is a mistake to identify the n- with the r- suffixes in ὕδωρ beside Skr. *udan* (water); in L. *jecur*, Gr. ἧπαρ, Skr. *yakṛt* beside Skr. *yakan* (from which the weak cases of *yakṛt* are formed), Lett. *aknis* (the liver); in Skr. *s'akṛt*, Gr. σκώρ, L. *stercus, stercor-is* beside Skr. *s'akan* (from which the weak cases of *s'akṛt* are formed), for we frequently find these suffixes coexisting in the same language, and sometimes in the same word: thus, we have Gr. ὕδνης (watery) beside ὕδωρ, the former word being formed from R. υδ by means of the suffix -να; in L. *jecinoris*, gen. sing. of *jecur*, we find both suffixes coexistent; and similarly we find both in A. S. *skearn* (dung) = σκώρ and A. S. *stearn* = L. *sturnus*.

L = I. E. *r*: *loquor*, Skr. *lap* (to speak), Gr. ἔλακον, Ch. Sl. *reku* (to speak); *linguo* Skr. *rik'* (to separate), Gr. λείπω; *luceo*, Skr. *ruk'* (to shine), Gr. λευκός, λύχνος; *sollus* = Skr. *sarvas* (all); *culter, cultus*, Skr. *kartari* (shears), Gr. κείρω; *plēnus* = Skr. *pūrṇas* (full); *lacero*, Gr. λάκος, ῥάκος, Æol. βράκος from R. Fρακ = Skr. *vras'k'* (scindere); *latus* for *platus* beside Skr. *prath* (extendere); *gallus* for *garlus* beside *garrio*, Skr. *gar* (to call), Gr. γῆρυς; *gula, gur-gul-io* beside *gurges*, (*g*)*voro*, Skr. *gar* (to swallow); *volo*, Skr. *var* (to choose); *vulgus*, Skr. *vargas* (nom. sing. masc. a multitude); *vellus*, Skr. *úrṇá* (wool), Gr. ἔριον, Ion. εἶρος, &c.

L = I. E. *l*: see § 21.

L = I. E. *d*: *lacrima*, O. L. *dacruma*, Gr. δάκρυ, Goth. *tagr*, O. H. G. *zahar*; *levir*, Skr. *dēvar* (husband's brother), Gr. δαήρ, A. S. *tācor*, O. H. G. *zeihhur*; *lingua*, O. L. *dingua*, Goth. *tuggō*, O. H. G *zunga*; *impelimenta* (in Festus) = *impedimenta*; *ol-facio*, *oleo* beside *odor*, Gr. ὄζω = ὀδyω, ὄδωδα; *lautia* (entertainment) beside *dautia*, which Aufrecht connects with Skr. *dûta* (nuntius); *Ulixes* = Ὀδυσσεύς; *lignum* connected by Bopp with *dah* (to burn), Gr. λιγνύς (thick smoke mixed with flame); but Curtius prefers to follow Jos. Scaliger in deriving it from *legere* (to gather), whence *legumen*, &c., *lignum* would then mean "a bundle of sticks;" *limpidus* connected by Bopp with Skr. *dip* (to shine), but by Curtius with Gr. λάμπω, Ὄλυμπος; *lacero* connected by Bopp with Skr. *daṅs'* (to bite), Gr. δάκνω, but much more probably from R. *lac* = Gr. Fρακ; *pol-lingo, lino* beside Skr. *dih* (to smear); *larva* (a mask) connected with Skr. *dars'* (to see), Gr. δέρκω; *laurus* for *daurus*, Skr. *druma* (a tree), *dâru* (wood), Gr. δρῦς, δόρυ; *-ilius* (in *Popi-*

lius, &c.) = *idius** (in *Popidius*, &c.); *delicare* beside *dedicare*, *-sul* (in *consul*, &c.) is generally connected with R. *sed*, whence *sĕdeo*, *sella* for *sedla*, *sēdes*, *solium*, but Mommsen connects it with *salire*, and Corrsen with Skr. *sar* (to go). In Oscan we find *d* kept between vowels, where in Latin *l* is found, as in O. O. *Akudunniad* = L. *Aquiloniā* (*d*), O. U. *Akerụniam–em*, N. U. *Acersoniam–e* (in Aquiloniam), the modern *Acedogna*.

L appears to represent an I. E. *n* in a few cases : *lendes* for *clendes* beside Gr. κονίδες (eggs of lice, nits), A. S. *hnit*, Lith. *glìndas*, for no word in Latin can begin with *cn* ; *pulmo* beside πνεύμων. For a similar change in other languages consult § 54. Although L. *alius*, Gr. ἄλλος, Goth. *alis* (ἄλλος) are generally connected with Skr. *anya* (another), it is more likely that there were originally two independent pronominal stems, *al* and *an* ; from the former of which came L. *alius*, &c.; and from the latter Skr. *anya*, Gr. ἔνιοι, Goth. *anthar* (ἄλλος), Ch. Sl. *inŭ* (alius). *Pulmo* and *lendes* appear therefore to be the only Latin words where *l* = I. E. *n*. The opposite change never occurs in Latin, though it does sometimes in Greek, as Dor. βέντιστος, &c., = βέλτιστος, &c., νάρναξ (Hesych. a chest) = λάρναξ.

S = I. E. *s* : *sum, est*, Skr. *asmi* (sum), *asti* (est), Gr. εἰμί, Æol. ἔμμι = ἐσμι, ἐστί, Goth. *im, ist*, Lith. *esmì, ésti*, Ch. Sl. *jesmĭ, jestĭ*; *uro, ustus* from R. *us* = Skr. *ush* (to burn), Gr. εὕω ; *septem* = Skr. *saptan*, Gr. ἑπτὰ ; *sto*, R. *sta* = Skr. *sthâ* (to stand), from I. E. *sto*; *-s* (term. of nom. sing.) = I. E. *-s*, as in *equus* = Skr. *as'vas* = Gr. ἵππος, &c. ; O. L. *sum*

---

* As we find O. U. *famerias, karitu, Pumperiaṣ* beside L. *familia, calare, Pompilia*, it hasbeen suggested (Die Umbrischen Sparchdenkmäler von S. Th. Aufrecht und A. Kirchhoff, p. 84) that the original forms of these words had *d* in place of *ṛ* and *l*, as O. U. *ṛ* = I. E. *d*. I cannot assent to this view as far as relates to *familia* and *calare*, for *familia* is from *famulus*, which is formed from a St. *fama*, as *humilis*, from St. *humo*, and *calare* is connected with Gr. καλέω, G. *hallen*. *R* was, perhaps, written for *r* by a mistake of the stone-cutter in these two cases.

(him), *sam* (her), Skr. *sa, sá* = Gr. ὁ, ἡ, &c. S is retained in Umbrian and Oscan, where it is found in the corresponding Latin words, and also in other cases where it is either lost or changed into *r* in Latin. Thus we have O. U. *tutas Ijuvinas* (gen. sing.) = L. *totæ Iguvinæ, kaprēs, katlēs* = L. *capri, catuli,* O. O. *pumpaiianeis* = *pompeiani*, N. O. *eituās* (gen. sing. pecuniæ). The *a*-stems in Oscan and Old Umbrian still retain the final *s* in the nom. pl.: O. O. *Núvlanús* = L. *Nolani*, N. O. *pas, scriftas* = L. *quæ, scriptæ*, O. U. *urtas* = L. *ortæ*. In New Umbrian this final *s* has generally become *r*; *screihtor* (nom. pl.) = L. *scripti, totcor* (nom. pl.) = L. *tutici, motar* (nom. pl.) = L. *multæ* (pœnæ), *totar* (gen. sing.) = L. *totæ*, *popler* (gen. sing.) = L. *populi*. In New Umbrian final *s* is still kept in the dat. and abl. pl. of the *i*-stems, as in *aveis* = L. *avibus*. In Old Umbrian and Old Oscan the change of final *s* into *r* had already begun in the passive voice, as O. U. *emantur* = R. *emantur*, O. O. *sakarater* = L. *sacratur*, &c. S is generally kept between two vowels in Oscan and Umbrian, as in U. *asa* = L. *ara*, O. O. *aasas* = L. *aræ*. In Oscan *s* became a sonant *s*, represented by *z*, between two vowels in certain cases, as in *-azum* (term. of gen. pl.) = L. *-arum* = I. E. *-ásám, censazet* for *censasent* (censebunt), &c. Final *ts* was represented by *z* in Old Umbrian and Old Oscan, and by *s* in New Umbrian, as O. U. *pihaz* = N. U. *pihos* = L. *piatus*, O. O. *hurz* = L. *hortus*, &c. In Umbrian an original *k* is generally weakened to a sibilant before *e* and *i*, as in *pase* = L. *pace*, *desenduf* = L. *duodecem, çesna* = L. *cena*, &c.

N = I. E. *n*: *in-* (neg. prefix), Skr. and Z. *an-, a-*, Gr. ἀν-, ἀ-, O. and U. *an-, a-*; *inter, indu*, Skr. *antar* (within), Gr. ἔνδον, ἔντερον, O. U. *anter*, N. U. *ander*; *mens, maneo*, Skr. and Z. *man* (to think), Gr. μένω, μένος; *navis*, Skr. *nâus* = Gr. ναῦς; *novus*, Skr. *navas* = Gr. νέϝος, O. O. *Núvla*; *ne, non*, Skr. and Z. *na* (not), Gr. νη- = Ved. *ná*; term. *no-* (in *plenus, somnus*, &c.) = Skr. *na-* (in *púrṇa*, &c.); term. *men* (in *nomen*, &c.) = Skr. *man* (in *náman*, &c.); &c.

N = I. E. *m* in a few cases : *nonus* for *novimus* from *novem*, as *decimus* from *decem*, &c. ; *gener* for *gemer* beside Gr. γαμ-βρός, although it may come directly from R. *gen* (to produce); *tenebræ* beside Skr. *tamisra* (darkness), O. S. *thim* (dim), O. H. G. *demar* (crepusculum), Ir. *temel* (dark). Some writers consider that *n* = *m* in *venio* beside Skr. *gam* (to go), *jànitrix* beside Skr. *g'âmâtar* and *yâmâtar* (gener), and *aeneus* = Skr. *ayasmayas* (ferreus), but these comparisons are extremely unlikely : consult §. 54.

§. 80. THE LABIALS.

P = I. E. *p* : *super*, Skr. *upari* (above), Gr. ὑπέρ, Goth. *ufar* (over) ; *plus, plerique*, Skr. *puru* (much), Gr. πολύς, Goth. *filu* (πολύς) ; *potis, potior, potens*, Skr. *pati* (a master), Gr. πόσις ; *pluit, pluvia*, Skr. *plu* (to swim), Gr. πλέω, πλύνω, O. H.G. *fliozan* (to flow) ; *pons*, Skr. *patha* (a way), Gr. πάτος, O. N. *fatt* (ibam) ; *per*, O. *perum* (outside), Skr. *parâ* (away, Z. *para* (outside), Gr. παρά, Goth. *fra-*; *porta, ex-per-ior*, Skr. *par* (to cross), Z. *par* (to bring over), Gr. πόρος, περάω, Goth. *faran* (to go); *serpo*, Skr. *sarp* (to creep), Gr. ἕρπω ; &c.

P perhaps represents an I. E. *bh* in *potus;* consult §. 55.

Sp in Latin has in no case been developed from an older *st*. *Spica* and *spiculum* are not connected with Gr. στάχυς, but rather with O. N. *spiot* (hasta), G. *spies* (a spear), *spitze* (a point); perhaps Gr. πικρός and ἐχεπευκής (pointed) belong to the same root. *Spatium* = Æol. σπάδιον is connected with Gr. σπάω, O. H. G. *spannan*, and Gr. στάδιον is a later form. *Spuo* is connected with Gr. πτύω, L. *pituita*, Goth. *spciva* (spuo), Lith. *spjauju* (spuo). We find σπ = an original στ in Æol. σπολά = στολή, κασπολέω = καταστελῶ, where στ is original, as we see from L. *praestolor*, O. H. G. *stellan* (to place), E. *stall*. We also find Goth. *sparva*, O. H. G. *sparo* beside Gr.

στροῦθος. We find *sp* beside Gr. σκ in *spolium* beside Gr. σκῦλον, where σκ is original. We also find *specio, specto* beside Gr. σκέπτομαι for σπεκτομαι from I. E. *spak*, whence Z. *s'pas'* (to behold), Skr. *pas'* (to see), E. *spy*.

In Umbrian and Oscan *p* = I. E. *kv* and L. *qu* in the pronouns and numerals and words derived from them, and perhaps, in some other cases. Thus we have O. U. and N. U. *pis* = L. *quis*, O. O. *pid*, N. O. *pod*, = L. *quod*, N. O. *pomtis* = *quinque*, N. U. *peturpursus* = L. *quadrupedibus*, N. U. *panta* = L. *quanta*, &c. Hence when we find *p* = I. E. *kv* in any Latin word, we may infer that that word is borrowed from either Umbrian, Oscan, or Sabine. Corssen* believes that *p* has been developed from an I. E. *kv* within the limits of the Latin language; but the examples by which he supports this view are either extremely doubtful or susceptible of another explanation. Curtius† also asserts that L. *p* has arisen from an Older *k* in *sapio, lupus, Epona, trepit*, and *sæpio*, comparing these words with *sucus*, Gr. λύκος, *equus, torqueo*, and Gr. σηκός. Now *sapio* has nothing to say to *sucus*, but is connected with O. H. G. *sab* (to understand), whence *antseffan* (Præt. *ant-suob*), and Gr. σοφός and σαφής, where φ represents an older π; *lupus* is most probably a Sabine word, but Schleicher connects it with Z. *urupis, raopis* (a kind of dog), and derives it from R. *rup* or *lup* (to tear); *saepio* does not agree with σηκός in the vowel of the root for Gr. η = I. E. *â* and L. *ae* = I. E. *ai*; *Epona* is a Keltic term; *trepit* (vertit) and Gr. τρέπω are, perhaps, formed from a root *tar* by the suffix *p*, and *torqueo* from same root by the addition of a different suffix. Corssen adds to these examples *popina, palumbus, opinari*, comparing them with *coquina, columba*, and Gr. ὄσσεσθαι for ὀκγεσθαι. Now *popina* and *palumbus* are most likely borrowed words, as we have beside them the genuine Latin form, *coquina* and *columba*, just as we have Osc. Πομπ-

---

* Kritische Nachträge zur Lateinischen formenlehre, p. 29.
† Grundzüge der Griechischen Etymologie, p. 408.

τιος = L. *Quinctius* beside L. *Pompejus* (borrowed from Oscan) and *Petrejus* from Osc. *petora* (four). The connexion of *opinari* with ὄσσεσθαι is very doubtful; Curtius assents to Crain's suggestion that an initial *kv* has been lost, and that it comes from the same root as Gr. καπύω, L. *vapor* for *kvapor*, Lith. *kvapas* (smoke). *Limpidus* is considered by Schleicher to be a dialectic form of *liquidus;* Bopp, however, connects the former with Skr. *dîp* (to shine), Gr. λάμπω, and the latter with Skr. *lî* (liquefacere). Curtius connects *liquēre, liquidus* with Skr. *rik'* (to separate), Z. *ric* (to leave, to pour out), L. *linquo*, &c.

B = I. E. *b* in *brevis* for *bregvis* beside Gr. βραχύς, and *labi* beside Skr. *lamb* (to fall), and a few imitative words: consult §. 22.

B = I. E. *gv*: *be-tere, ar-bi-ter, venio* for *gvenio*, N. U. *benust* = O. U. *benus* (3 sing. fut. ex.) from R. *ben* (to come), Skr. *gâ* (to go), Goth. *quiman* (to come); *bos*, Skr. *gâus* (nom. sing. bos), Gr. βοῦς, γαῖος (ὁ ἐργάτης βοῦς, Hesych.) O.H.G. *chuo* (cow); *bŏvare, re-boare*, Skr. *gu* (to sound), Gr. βοή, βοάω, γόος, γοάω, γόης; *super-bus*, Skr. *g'i* (to conquer), Gr. ὑπέρβιος, from I. E. *gvi*, whence, perhaps, also come Gr. Fίς, ἰσχύς, Lac. βίσχυς, L. *vis* for *gvis; bullio* connected by Bopp with Skr. *gval* (flammare).

B = I. E. *bh** (when medial): *amb-*, Skr. *abhi* (towards), Gr. ἀμφί, O.S. *umbi*, O. H. G. *umpi; ambo*, Skr. *ubhâu* (both), Gr. ἄμφω, Goth. *bai* (both); *nubes, nebula*, Skr. *nabhas* (aer, coelum), Gr. νέφος; *umbilicus*, Skr. *nâbhi* (the navel), Gr. ὀμφαλός; *orbus*, Gr. ὀρφανός; *labor*, Skr. *rabh* (desiderare), Gr. ἤλφον (I acquired), ἀλφηστής, Goth. *arbaiths* (toil); *-brum* (in *candelabrum*, &c.) from I. E. *bhar* = Skr. *bhar* (to carry); *imber*, Skr. *ambhas* (water), *abhra* (clouds), Gr. ὄμβρος; *-bus*

---

* Benary connects L. *ebur* with Skr. *ibha* (an elephant), from which he also derived Gr. ἐλ-έφας by prefixing the Semitic article. Others derive ἐλέφας from Heb. *eleph* (an ox), as, in Old Latin, the elephant was called *bos Lucas*.

(term. of dat. pl.) = Skr. *-bhyas; -bam, -bo* (in *amabam, amabo*, &c.) for *-fuam, -fuo* from I. E. *bhû* (to be); &c.

B is never = I. E. *bh* (when initial), except in *bibo*, respecting which consult §. 55. Bopp indeed connects *bacca* *
with Skr. *bhaksh* (to eat), and suggests that *bucca* comes from the same root, unless it belongs to Skr. *mukha* (the face)!
He also connects *brachium* with Skr. *bâhu* (the arm), Gr. πῆχυς, I. E. *bhâghu*. These examples are, however, so doubtful that we cannot conclude that L. *b* is ever = I. E. *bh*, except in *bibo*.

B = I. E. *dh* (when medial): *ruber, robigo*, Skr. *rudhira* (blood); *uber* for *ouber*, Skr. *ûdhas* (uber), Gr. οὖθαρ, O. H. G. *ûtar*, A. S. *ûder; uber* (rich) for *oiber*, Skr. *êdhatê* (he increases), from R. *idh; verbum*, U. *verfale* (= verbale), Goth. *vaurd* (a word), G. *wort*, Lith. *vàrdas* (a name); *barba*, G. *bart*, E. *beard; robur*, connected by some with Skr. *râdh* (perficere), but by Bopp with Skr. *ruh* (crescere) for *rudh*. Other examples of this change have been adduced, but in each case a better explanation of the L. *b* can be given: *liber* has nothing to say to Gr. ἐλεύθερός, for we find O. L. *loebesom* = *liberum*, which is connected with Skr. *lubh* (to desire), Gr. λίψ (ἐπιθυμία, Hesych.), λίπτομαι, Goth. *liubs* (loved), while the old derivation of ἐλεύθερος, παρὰ τὸ ἐλεύθειν ὅπου ἐρᾷ, is probably correct; *plebes* and Gr. πλῆθος are independent formations from the root *par* (to fill), and L. *b* is not Gr. θ here; *urbs* is not connected with Skr. *ardha*, for the latter meant originally *half*, and then it came to mean *side*, as G. *halbe* means both *half* and *side;* the term. *-brum* should

---

* Corssen (Kritische Nachträge zur Lat. Form. p. 33) connects *bacca* with Skr. *pak'* (coquere, maturescere), and considers *bacca*, therefore, to be for *pacca*. In no case, however, except in a few words borrowed from the Greek, does initial *b* in Latin represent an I. E. *p*; besides, Skr. *pak'* is connected with L. *coquo*, Gr. πίπτω, ἀρτο-κόπ-ος, Ch. Sl. *peka* (I cook), Lith. *kepù*, and all these forms seem to point back to an I. E. *kvakv*. *Bucca* is also connected by Corssen with Skr. *bukk* (latrare, loqui); this is explaining *obscurum per obscurius*.

not be identified with Gr. -θρον, for the latter was originally -τρον and the former belongs to Skr. *bhar* (to bear). *Libra* is, perhaps, borrowed from λίτρα (for τλίτρα beside τλάω, as L. *latus* for *tlatus*) through λιθρα, or else λίτρα is borrowed from *libra*, the term *-bra* being connected with Skr. *bhar* (to bear).

B is never = I. E. *gh*. The only example adduced in proof of this change is *bilis*, which is wrongly connected with Gr. χόλος, χολή (gall, anger), O. H. G. *galla* (gall). L. *fel, fell-is*, is the true Latin representative of χόλος.

B =. I. E. *dv* : *bini, bis*, Skr. *dva* (two), *dvis* (twice), Z. *dva* (two), *bi-* (two, in composition), Gr. δύο, δίς, δεύτερος by metathesis from *dvataras*, L. *duo, dis-*; *bi-* occurs several times in composition, as in *bivira* (noticed by Varro in the sense of *widow*), *bipes*, St. *biped* = Skr. *dvipad* (a man), *bīmus* = *bi-himus* (according to Aufrecht) from *bi-* and *himo-* = Z. *hima* (a year) connected with Skr. *hima* (snow), L. *hiems*, but = *bi-smus* (according to Bopp) from *bi-* and *smo-* connected with Skr. *samā* (a year) ; *bellum* = *duellum; Bellius* = *Duellius, bonus* beside *duonoro* (t. Scip. Barb. f.) = *bonorum*.

B = I. E. *m* in *blandus* for *mlandus*, a participial form of a R. *mlā*, the original form of which was probably *marl*, which is found in Skr. *mṛd* (exhilarare), Gr. μείλια (propitiatory gifts), E. *mil-d*. This is the only example of this change that has been adduced. It is better, however, to suppose that *blandus* came from *mlandus* through the step *mblandus*, as Gr. βροτύς = μβροτος = μροτος, than to suppose that *b* immediately represented *m*.

B (according to Bopp) represents Skr. *v* in *-ber (September*, &c.) beside Skr. *vāra* (time), and in *balneum* beside Skr. *bāḍ* (lavare). This latter comparison is certainly wrong, for *balneum* is borrowed from Gr. βαλανεῖον, which was derived from βάλανος (an acorn), on account of the similarity of their shapes, and the Skr. *bāḍ* is a very obscure word.

B = I. E. *p* (when final) : *ab*, Skr. *apa* (away), Gr. ἀπό,

L

Goth. *af*, O. H. G. *aba; ob* (which originally meant the same as *ad*, as in *obviam, obire, opportunus*), Skr. *api* (used as an adverb = *also*, and as a prefix = *after*, as in *apig'as* = ἐπίγονος), Gr. ἐπί, ἐπεί; *sub*, Skr. and Z. *upa* (to), Gr. ὑπό, Goth. *uf.* (sub), O. H. G. *oba* (super). *B* = Gr. π in some borrowed words, as *Burrus* = Πύῤῥος, *carbasus* = κάρπασος, *buxus* = πύξος *Buxentum* from Πυξοῦς.

F = I. E. *bh*: *fari, fatum, fax, facies, favilla*, Skr. *bhá* (to shine), *bhásh* (to speak), Gr. φημί, φαίνω, φάος; *forare*, Z. *bar* (to bore), Gr. φάρος (a plough), φάραγξ (a ravine), O. H. G. *poran* (to bore), E. *bore; fero, fordus, far*, Skr. *bhar* (to bear), Z. *bar* (to bear), Gr. φέρω, E. *bear; flare, flos*, Gr. ἐκφλαίνω (I flow out), φλα-σμός (bubbling, boasting), O. H. G. *blâan*, (to blow), *blatara* (pustule), *bluojan* (florere), Goth. *blōma* (bloom), *blōth* (blood); *fui*, Skr. *bhû* (to be), Gr. φύω, E. *be; fugio*, I. E. *bhugh*, Skr. *bhug'* (to bend), Gr. φεύγω, Goth. *biuga* (I bend); *fagus*, Gr. φηγός, E. *beech; fulgeo, fulvus*, Skr. *bhrâg'* (to shine), Gr. φλέγω, E. *bright; fremere, frētum, Frentani*, Skr. *bhram* (to whirl), Gr. βρέμω, βροντή, O. N. *brim* (the surge); *furvus*, and *fuscus*, perhaps for *fur-scus*, as *Tuscus* for *Turscus*, Skr. *babhru* (red, and the ichneumon), Gr. φρύνη (the toad, from its colour), E. *brown; findere*, Skr. *bhid* (to cleave), E. *bite*, &c. A medial *f* (= I. E. *bh*) between two vowels is only found in such compounds as *signifer*, &c.; and in *scrofa* (a sow), Gr. γρομφάς (a sow), so called from its *rooting*, connected with γράφω, γροφεῖς (ζωγράφοι, Hesych.), Goth. *graba* (I dig), L. *scrobs;* &c. In Oscan and Umbrian we not only find *f* = initial *f* in Latin, but also *f* = medial L. *b*: O. U. *tefe, ife* = L. *tibi, ibi;* O. U. *trifor* = L. *tribus;* O. U. *prufe* = L. *probe*, Skr. *prabháva* (excelsus) (?); O. O. *puf* = L. *ubi;* O. O. *sifei* = L. *sibi;* N. O. *amprufid* = L. *improbe*, &c.

F = I. E. *dh*: *of-fendo*, Gr. θείνω; *festus, feriae*, Gr. θίσσεσθαι (ἱκετεύειν, Hesych.), perhaps θεός for θεσ-ος, θέσφατος; *famulus*, Skr. *dhá* (to place), Gr. τίθημι; *femina, filius*

Skr. *dhê* (to drink), Gr. θῆσθαι (to milk) ; *fumus* = Skr. *dhûmas* (smoke), Gr. θυμός, &c. A medial *f* (= I. E. *dh*) between two vowels is only found in *rufus*, Gr. ἐρυθρός. In Oscan and Umbrian medial *f*, as well as initial *f*, = I. E. *dh*, as in O. U. *mefa* for *mefia*, O. U. *mefiai* = L. *mediae*, O. U. *verfale* = L. *verbale*, &c. This interchange between *f* and *dh* is easily explained ; consult §. 55. We frequently hear children saying *fum* for *thumb*, &c. ; also *fyrst* is a dialectic form of *thirst*.

F = I. E. *gh* : *formus*, (hot) *fornax*, Skr. *gharma* (warm), Gr. θερμός, E. *warm*; *frio*, *frico*, O. U. *frehtu* = L. *frictum*, Skr. *ghar* (to sprinkle), *gharsh* (to rub), Gr. χρίω ; *fons*, *futis* (vas aquarium), *fundo*, Gr. χέω for χεϝω, from R. χυ, Goth. *giuta* (I pour) ; O. L. *fostis** = *hostis* = Goth. *gasts* (a guest), Skr. *ghas* (to eat); O. L. *folus* = *holus*, *olus*, *helvus*, *flavus* (*flava* is applied to Ceres, as χλοή is to Demeter), Skr. *hari* (green), Gr. χλοή, E. *green:* O. L. *fariolus* = *hariolus*, *haruspex*, Skr. (Ved.) *hirâ* (entrails), L. *hira*, *hilla* (entrails), O. N. *garnir* (intestines) ; O. L. *fœdus* = *hœdus*, E. *goat;* *fra-gra-re* is said to be a re-duplicated form of an I. E. *ghrâ* = Skr. *ghrâ* (to smell), &c. In the same way *gh* is pronounced as *f* in E. *laugh*, *cough*, *tough*, &c.

F never represents an I. E. *p*, except when *s* originally preceded, as in *fallo* = Gr. σφάλλω, *fungus* = Gr. σφόγγος, *funda* beside σφενδόνη, *fides* (catgut) beside Gr. σφίδη (catgut). We hear children frequently saying *funge* for *spunge*, *foon* for *spoon*, &c. Aufrecht connects N. U. *frite* (ritu) with Skr. *prî* (to love), and ascribes *f* to the aspirating influence of the following *r*, as in Gr. τέφρα (ashes) beside Skr. *tap* (to burn), A. S. *thefian* (aestuare), G. *dampf* (steam). *Fluo* has nothing to do with Gr. πλέω from R. πλυ, but is probably connected with Gr. φλύω ; *pluit* is the true Latin representative

---

* As *f* in O. L. *fostis*, &c., became *h*, so L. *f* becomes *h* in Spanish, as *hijo* = *filius*, &c. Similarly in Irish initial *p* is lost, as in *athir* = L. *pater*, *lán* = *plenus*, &c. ; *p* in Irish probably became *ph*, then *h*, and finally disappeared.

of R. πλυ. In Oscan *t* aspirates a preceding *p*, as in N. O. *scriftas* = L. *scriptae* (nom. pl. fem.); in Umbrian this *f* became *h*, as in O. U. *screhto* = L. *scriptum*.

Medial *f* between vowels occurs in *scrofa*, *rufus*, compounds of R. *fer*, as *signifer*, *sifilus* beside *sibilus*, *Afer*, *vafer*, and *tofus*, and the derivatives of these words.

V = I. E. *v*: *aevum*, Skr. *êva* (course), Gr. αἰές, Goth. *aivs* (αἰών); *ventus*, Skr. *vâ* (to breathe), Gr. ἄω, ἀήρ, αὖρα, from R. aF, Goth. *vinds* (wind); *ver*, Skr. *vasanta* (ver), Gr. ἔαρ, Lith. *vasarà* (summer); *virus* = Skr. *vishas* (poison), Gr. ἰός; *vitex*, *vimen*, *vitta*, *vitis*, *vinum*, Skr. *vitikâ* (a band), *vêtra* (a reed), Gr. ἴτυς, E. *withe*; *ovis* = Skr. *avis* (a sheep), Gr. ὄϊς, Lith. *avis* (a sheep), E. *ewe*; *novus* = Skr. *navas* (new), Gr. νέος, Ch. Sl. *novŭ* (new); *venum*, *veneo*, *vendo*, Skr. *vasnas* (nom. sing. masc. prime cost), *vasnam* (nom. sing. neut. hire), Gr. ὦνος, Ch. Sl. *rĕniti* (to sell); *verna*, *vestibulum** (according to Bopp), Skr. *vas* (to dwell), Gr. ἄστυ; *Vesta*, Skr. *ush* (to burn) = I. E. *vas*, Gr. ἑστία; Bopp, however, connects *Vesta* and ἑστία with Skr. *vas* (to dwell), &c.

V is vocalised frequently in Latin : *quatuor*, Skr *k'atvâras*, Goth. *fidvōr*; *vacuos* for *vacvos*, *contiguos* for *contigvos*, *ingenuos* for *ingenvos*, &c., where term. -*uo* = -*vo*, as found in *alvos*, *arvom*, &c.; *sūdo* (according to Schleicher) for *suido*, as *senatus* for *senatuis*, Skr. *svid* (to sweat), Gr. ἰδίω.

V is retained in Old Latin, Old Umbrian, and Old Oscan, after *o*, *u*, and *u̇*, where, in later times, it disappeared, as O. L. *sovos* = *suus*, *flovont* = *fluunt*; O. U. *tuves* = N. U. *duir* = L. *duobus*, O. O. *sŭreis*, *sŭvad* = O. L. *sovi*, *sovad* = L. *sui*, *sua*, &c. In Old Oscan we find *v* retained before consonants, as in *tŭvt̯ĭks* = L. *tūticus* beside N. O. *toutad*, from St. *tuvta-* = O. U. *tuta-* (a city).

---

* Mommsen explains *vestibulum* as meaning dressing-room, from *vestis*, so called from the fact that the Romans only wore the tunic in the house, and put on the toga when they were going out.

M = I. E. m: *morior*, Skr. *mar* (to die), Gr. ἄ-μβρο-τος, from R. μορ, μαραίνω, Goth. *maurthr* (murder); *memor*, Skr. *smar* (to remember), Gr. μέριμνα, μάρτυρ, μέρμερα ἔργα; *mensis* = I. E. *mansas* = Skr. *mâsas* (a month), Z. *mâonha* (a month), Gr. μήν, Ion. μείς, μήνη, Æol. μῆννος for μηνσος; *me*, Skr. *mâm*, and *ma* (me), Gr. μέ, Goth. *mik* (me); *–m* (sign of acc. sing.) = Skr. *–m*, as *equum* = Skr. *aś'vam*; *–m* (in *sum*) = Skr. *–mi* = Gr. -μι, as *sum* = Skr. *asmi* = Gr. εἰμί; *mergo*, perhaps for *mesgo* connected by Bopp with Skr. *mag'g'* (mergi), Lith. *mazgóju* (lavo), &c.

M represents a Skr. *v*, according to Bopp, in *clamo* = Skr. *s'rávayâmi*, a causal of *s'ru* (to hear), and *mare* = Skr. *vâri* (water). In both these cases Bopp appears to be wrong, for *clâ-mo* is much more easily connected with Gr. καλέω, κλῆσις, L. *calare*, *nomen-clâ-tor*, than with Skr. *s'ru*, and *mare* probably meant originally *a desert*, connected with Skr. *maru*, (a desert), *mar* (to die), Ir. *muir*, E. *moor*, *mere*, Gr. Ἀμφί-μαρ-ος (a son of Poseidon). Other examples of this interchange of *v* and *m* have been brought forward, but all of them are even more doubtful than *clamo* and *mare*. Thus Bopp considers Gr. δρέμω = Skr. *dravâmi* from *dru* (to run), though it is much simpler to connect it directly with Skr. *dram* (to go).

M represents a Skr. *bh*, according to Bopp, in *maxilla* beside Skr. *bhaksh* (to eat), and *multus* beside Skr. *bhûri* (multus). These comparisons are just as doubtful as those between *v* and *m*. Curtius is inclined to assent to the opinion that *maxilla* is connected with Gr. μάσσω, μαγεύς (a baker), and, consequently, means the organ "quod cibos depsit ac subigit." Bopp had his own misgivings about the connexion of *multus* with *bhûri*, for he also suggests that it may be related to Skr. *puru* (multus). *Multus*, though apparently connected with Gr. μυρίος, has never yet been satisfactorily explained.* *M* is = *bh* in the Umbrian sing. loc. term.

* *Multus* may have originally meant " pounded," " ground into many small fragments;" and from this its ordinary meaning may have been de-

-mem; if this be = Skr. *-bhyam* (in *tubhyam*) or *-bhyâm*. Similarly in Lith. dual dat. *wilkam, -m* = Skr. *-bhyâm*.

§. 81. Assimilation.

1. When two consonants come together, the first is often made the *same* as the second. After *long* vowels only one of these double consonants could be heard in pronunciation, and consequently only one was written; it is therefore impossible to distinguish such cases from those where a consonant has disappeared with or without compensation. Schleicher reduces all the latter cases to those of assimilation, and considers that a consonant, before it vanished, was first assimilated to the following one. After *short* vowels the double consonants are generally written. *Cc* (*cq*) = *dc* in *accurro, quicquid, quicquam, iccirco*. *Cc* = *bc* in *succurro, occurro*. *Cc* perhaps = *gc* in *saccus* and *soccus** beside Skr. *sag* (to cover), and Gr. σάγη; *saccus* is however most likely borrowed. *Cc* = *sc* in *siccus* = Skr. *s'ushkas* (dry). *Gg* = *dg* in *aggero*. *J* = *jj* = *gj* in *major* = *mágjor* beside *magnus; ajo* = *agjo* beside *ad-ǎg-ium; mějo* for *mījo* = *mĭgjo* beside *mingo*, Gr. R. μιχ = Skr. *mih; pulějum* for *pulěgjum*. We find *j* = *dj, rj, sj, nsj* in *sējungo, pějero, dījudico, trājicio* respectively, &c. *Pejor* is connected by Benfey with Skr. *păpa* (bad), and if this view be correct, it must stand for *pepjor;* Bopp, however, connects it with Skr. *pîy* (conviciari), Goth. *fijan* (to hate), E. *fiend*. *Tt* = *dt* in *attraho*. *Tt* = *kt* in *littera* for *lictera*, beside Skr. *likh* (to write); Schweitzer con-

---

veloped. There existed, most probably, in Indo-European a root *mar* (to pound) from which were derived L. *mola*, E. *mill, meal*, Gr. μύλος, μύλη, &c.; for a full discussion of this root, consult Max Müller, Lectures II., p. 315, seq.

* Spiegel connects *soccus* with Z. *hakha* (the sole of the foot) connected with Skr. *sak'* (to follow, to cling to), whence Skr. *sakhi* (a friend) *sak'iva* (a friend) beside L. *sequor, socius*.

ncets this word with Skr. *lip* (oblinere), and therefore considers it to have arisen from *liptera;* but *pt* remains unchanged in Latin, as in *aptus, ruptus,* &c. In *Vitorius* (on an inscription belonging to times of First Punic War, and also on very late inscriptions), and the late forms *autor, Adauta* for *auctor, Adaucta, c* was probably first assimilated to *t,* and then fell out, just as in late Latin we find such forms as *otto, praefetto,* and in Italian *benedetto, maledetto. Autumnus* is also for *Auctumnus,* from *aug-eo ;* Corssen appears to be mistaken in connecting it with Gr. ἄω for ἄϝω, which is found only in infin. pres. ἄμεναι (to satiate). *T' = Tt = nt* in N. O. *set* = L. *sunt*. Similarly in Old Irish we find –*t* = –*nt* in the term. s of the 3 pl. of the verb, as –*at,* –*et* = L. –*unt,* –*etar* = L. –*untur ;* we also find *etar* = L. *inter, cét* = L. *centum*. *Dd* (and then *d*) = *sd* in *jūdex* for *jusdex,* īdem for īsdem, dīduco for dīsduco. *Ss* (and then *s*) = *cs* (*x*), as in *Sestius* = *Sextius ; praetestati* = *praetextati; frassinus* = *fraxinus ; trissāgo* (the herb germander) = *trixago* (Cels. 8. 3); *cossim* (on both the hips), from *coxa,* connected with Skr. *kukshi* (the belly), and Gr. κοχώνη for κοξώνη ; O. U. *esuk* for *cksuk ;* O. O. *meddeĭs* beside μεδδειξ. Similarly we have O. I. *dess, des* beside *dexter,* Ch. Sl. *desinŭ* (dexter) Skr. *dakshina* (dexter); O. I. *ass-, ess-* = L. *ex*. *Ss* = *ds* in *assuesco, assimulo, cessi* for *cedsi,* pĕs for pĕds, *esse* (to eat) for *edse*. *Ss* = *ts* in *possum* for *potsum, concussi* for *concutsi, fŏns* for *fonts,* &c. *Ss* = *ns* in Oscan acc. pl. *viass* = L. *vias* for *vians,* &c.; similarly in *o–* and *i–* stems the Oscan acc. pl. ends in –*uss* and –*ĭss*. We find *s* = *ss* = *ns* in *formōsus* for *formonsus,* the suffix of which is perhaps the same as Skr. –*vant;* also in *cosul, cesor, quoties,* &c. beside *consul, censor, quotiens,* &c. *Ss* = *rs* in *russum, sussum, retrossum,* beside *rursum, sursum, retrorsum,* also written *rūsum,* &c. ; *prossum* and *prosa* beside *prorsum ; dossuarius* (bearing a burden), from *dorsum ; possideo* from *porsideo*. *Ss* = *bs* in *jussi ;* = *ms* in *pressi ;* = *vs* in *lucassim, amasso,* &c. *Nn* = *dn* in *annuere, annare, annectere*. Benfey connects L. *annona* with Skr. *anna* (food) for *adna*, from R. *ad* (to eat), but it much more probably belongs to L. *annus*. *Nn=mn* in *annus* for *amnus*, whence comes *solemnis*, from *am = ambi* (round), meaning a ' complete revolution of the sun'; *Vitunnus* beside *Vitumnus*, *Neptūnus* beside *Neptumnus*, *Portūnus* beside *Portumnus*. *Nn = mn* in *conniti*. *Nn = sn* in *penna* for *pesna*, and this for *petna* from R. *pet* (to fly). *Rr = dr* in *arridere*; *= br* in *surripere*; *= nr* in *irrumpere*; *= mr* in *corripere*; &c. *Rr = cr* in *serra* from R. *seo* (to cut) and *= tr* in *parricida* for *patricida* (?). *Ll = dl* in *alligare*; *= nl* in *illinere*; *= ml* in *collocare*; *rl* in *intelligere, pellucere*; &c. *Ll = dl* also in *sella* for *sedla*; *lapillus* for *lapidlus*; *Aufellius* beside *Aufidus*, &c. *Ll = rl* in *gallus = garlus*, Skr. *gar* (to call), Gr. γῆρυς, Γηρυών, E. *call*; *olla = orula* from a R. *var* (to seethe), which is found in Gr. βράσσω and βράζω (I boil) from R. βρα = Fρα, Lith. *virti* (to boil), Ch. Sl. *vrěti* (fervere), O. H. G. *wāli* (heat); *puella = puerla* for *puerula*; *ampulla* beside *ampora*; *stella* beside ἀστήρ; *Tibullus* from *Tibur*, &c. *Ll = nl* in *asellus* beside *asinus*; *corolla* beside *corona*; *homullus* beside St. *homon-*; *Messalla* from *Messana*; *illico* (in Plautus *ilico*) = *in loco*. *Ll = cl* in *paullus* for *pauculus* (?). *Pp = dp* in *appello*; *= bp* in *oppono*. *Ff = bf* in *officium, suffoco*; *= df* in *afferre*; *cf* in *efferre*; *= sf* in *diffugere*. When a preceding consonant is assimilated to *v*, it disappears sometimes with and sometimes without compensation. Thus we have no compensation in *lĕvis* for *legvis*, Gr. ἐλαχύς; *brĕvis* for *bregvis*, Gr. βραχύς; *nivis* for *nigvis*, beside *nix* for *nigs*, *ninguo*: in *vīvere* and *connīvere*, on the other hand, we find compensation for the *v* thrown out. *Mm = pm* in *summus*; *= gm* in *flagma*; *= bm* in *summittere*; *= nm* in *immittere*, &c.

II. When two consonants come together, the second is often made the same as the first. *Tt* perhaps = *ty* in *mitto* for *mityo*. *Ss = st* in superl. term. *-issimus*, as in *longissimus*, *-is-* being the remains of the old compar. term *yans*; *os*, St. *ossi = osti*, Skr. *asthi* (a bone), Gr. ὀστέον; *censor = cens-tor = N. O. censtur, censum = N. O. censtum*. When *t* is preceded by *t* or *d*, the first dental generally becomes *s*, and then the second is assimilated to it, so that *dt* and *tt* become *ss*, or *s* after long vowels and consonants: thus we have *fessus* for *fettus*, beside *fatigo, adfatim; ēsum* for *edtum*, from *edo* (I eat), beside *est* (he eats) = *edit ; fossa = fodta, fodio ; missus = mittus, mitto; ūsus* and *ussus* (on inscriptions) = *uttus, uti ; clausus = claudtus claudo ; fissus = fidtus, findo ; versus = vert-tus, verto*, &c. So in Irish we find *ss* for *st* in borrowed words, as *fess* = L. *festum ;* also in words not borrowed the same law holds as in Latin; thus we find *fiss* (scientia) for *fidtis*, from R. *fid* = I. E. *vid* (to know), &c. In Oscan *tt* is kept, and does not become *ss* as in Latin: we find O. O. *uittiuf* beside L. *ūsus* from *uti*. *Nn* = *nd*: *dispennite hominem divorsum et distennite* (Miles Gloriosus, 1407), *for dispendite, distendite; grunnio* for *grundio*, E. *grunt ;* O. O. *upsannam* = L. *operandam ;* N. U. *pihanēr* = L. *piandi* (gen. sing.); N. U. *panupei* = L. *quandoque ;* but when *nd* in Umbrian represents an older *nt*, it does not become *nn*. *Rr* = *ry* in *curro*, Skr. *k'ar* (to go), O. H. G. *horsc* (quick), E. *horse*. *Rr* = *rs* : *torreo* for *torseo* beside *tostus* for *torstus*, Skr. *tarsh* (to thirst), Gr. τέρσομαι ; *terra* (dry land) for *tersa* from same root as last; *ferrem* for *fersem; porro* for *porso*, Gr. πρόσω; *far* for *fars-* and this perhaps for *fart-*, compare Skr. *bhṛti* (nourishment) from *bhar* (to bear), N. U. *farsio* = L. *farreum ; terreo = terseo*, Skr. *tras* (to tremble), Gr. τρέω from R. τρες, ἔτερσεν (ἐφόβησεν, Hesych.), Hom. τρέσσα (1. aor.); *erro = erso*, Goth. *airzjan* (to wander); *verres* (a boar) = *verses* beside Skr. *varsh* (to sprinkle), *vṛsha* (a bull); *garrio** = *garsio* beside Lith. *gàrsas* (the voice); *horreo = horseo*, Skr. *hṛsh* (horrere). *Rr* = *rt* in *pulcerrimus, celerrimus;* here *rt* probably passed through the stage *rs*. *Ll* perhaps = *lk* in *follis* (a bag) be-

---

* Leo Meyer suggests that *garrio* is for *garnio*, from which latter he explains *gannio* (I yelp). Bopp considers *garrio* to be for *gargio*, beside Skr. *garg'* (clamare), but this is most improbable.

side Gr. θύλακος (a bag), θυλλίς (a bag), Goth. *balgs*. *Ll* = *ly* in *pello, fallo, percello, tollo*; *cella* for *celia* beside L. *celo, domicilium*, Skr. *khala* (a threshing-floor), *s'álá* (a house) Gr. καλιά (a hut), unless *cella* be for *celula*; *procella* for *procelia*, beside Skr. *kal* (to impell), Gr. κέλης, βουκόλος (a cow-herd), L. *cello, celox, celer*; O. *allo* (nom. sing. fem.) = L. *alia*, Gr. ἄλλος, O. H. G. *alles* (otherwise). *Ll* = *lt* in super term. *-illimus* = *-iltimus*, as *facillimus*, &c.; *fel, fell-is* (gen. sing.) = *feltis* (?); *mel, mell-is* (gen. sing.) for *melt-is* = Gr. μέλιτ-ος, μελίσσα = μελιτyα, Goth. *milith* (honey). Bopp wrongly considers *mellis* to be for *melvis*, connecting it with Skr. *madhu* (honey). *Lt* in becoming *ll* probably passed through the stage *ls*, as *pulsus* is for *pultus*. *Ll* = *ld* in *Pollux* = Gr. Πολυδεύκης, and, according to Bopp, in *malleus* for *maldeus*, beside Skr. *mard* (to pound). *Ll* = *ls* in *vellem* = *velsem, velle* = *velse*; *collum* = *colsum*, G. *hals* (the neck). *Ll* = *ln* in *vellus villus* beside Skr. *úrṇa* (wool), Lith. *vìlna* (wool), Ch. Sl. *vlăna* (wool), Goth. *vulla* (wool); *collis* (according to Curtius) = *colnis* beside Gr. κολωνός, Lith. *kálnas* (height), A. S. *holm* (a hill). *Ll* = *lv* in *pallor, pallidus* beside O. H. G. *falo, falwer*, G. *falb*, Lith. *pàlvas*, (pale), Ch. Sl. *plavă* (white);* *pellis* = *pelvis*, beside *pulvinar*, G. *fell* (a hide), Gr. πέλλα (a hide), *vallis* perhaps for *valvis*, Gr. ἕλος, Ἐλέα, Ἥλις; *sollus* (*solliferreus, solli-citus, soll-ers*) = Skr. *sarvas*, (omnis), Gr. ὅλος, Ion. οὖλος = ολϜος; *mollis* = *molvis*, beside Gr. μῶλυς (sluggish). *Pp* = *pt* in *quippe, ipsippe* (ipsi neque alii, Fest. p. 105), beside *mepte, mihipte* (Cato pro 'mihi ipsi,' Fest. p. 152, 154.), *vopte* (vos ipsi, Fest. p. 379): *-pte* = *-pote*, (compare *ut-pote*), *-potis*.

III. When two consonants come together, the first is generally made *like* the second, or affected by it in some way,

---

* Gr. πιλλός (dusky) is for πιλγος, compare πολιός (grey), πιλιδνός, πιλιός, πιλός, Skr. *palita* (grey). Now, if *ll* (in *pallor*) = *lv*, we have a trace of a more intimate connexion between Latin, Lith. O. H. G. &c., than between Lat. and Gr.

the second consonant still remaining unchanged. Thus, sonant consonants become surd before surd consonants: *actus* = *agtus*, R. *ag* ; *scriptus* = *scribtus*, R. *scrib*, connected perhaps with Gr. γράφω; *ructo* = *rugto*, beside L. *erugo*, Gr. ἐρεύγω; *fictor, fictilis* beside L. *fingo, figura*, Skr. *dih* (to smear), Gr. ἔ-θιγ-ον; *luctus* beside L. *lugeo*, Skr. *rug'* (vexare), Gr. λυγρός ; *mulctus* beside L. *mulgeo*, Skr. *marg'* (mulcere), Gr. ἀμέλγω ; *vectus* beside *veho*, Skr. *vah* (vehere), Gr. ὄχος ; *lectus, lectica* beside Gr. λέχος, Goth. *liga* (I lie down); &c. There are some apparent exceptions to this rule : thus, we find *absens, subter, obtego, obtineo*,* &c., where *b* is still retained; but these words were pronounced as *apsens*, &c., for Quintilian (I. 7, 7) writes " cum dico obtinuit secundam *b* litteram ratio poscit, aures magis audiunt *p*," and consequently we find them frequently written according to the pronunciation, as *apsens, optineo*, &c., on inscriptions and in manuscripts. Before *r* and *l* surds frequently become sonants, as *publicus* = O. L. *poplicos* ; *negligo* from *nec* and *lego* ; *quadrupes* and *quadraginta* beside *quatriduo*, from *quatuor;* O. U. *abruf* = L. *apros.* We also find surds becoming sonants before other sonants, as in *segmentum* from *seco* ; *salignus* from St. *salic* ; *dignus* from R. *dic* ; *ilignus* from St. *ilec* ; *cygnus* = Gr. κύκνος. M before gutturals becomes guttural *n*, and before dentals, dental *n*, as in *anceps* = *ambiceps* ; *concors* = *comcors* ; *nunquam* = *numquam* ; *contero* = *comtero* ; *tandem* = *tamdem* ; &c. Initial gutturals and dentals influence a preceding *m*, as in *con quo* = *com quo* (on late inscriptions) ; *an terminum* = *am t.* = *ambi t.*; &c. *N* before labials becomes *m*, as in *impleo*, &c. Labial mutes before *n* become *m*, as *somnus* = *sopnus*, beside L. *sopio*, Skr. *svapnas* = Gr. ὕπνος ; *Samnium* = *Sabnium*, beside *Sabini* ; *scamnum* beside *scabellum*. In Old Latin *t* before *n* became *s*,

---

* The junction of two mutes is sometimes avoided by inserting *s*, as in *abstineo, abscondo, ostendo* for *obstendo, asporto* for *adsporto.*

as in *pesna* (*penna*) = *petna, resmus* (*rēmus*) beside Gr. ἐρετμός. In these cases *t* became *th* through the aspirating influence of the nasal, and then *th* became *s*. This aspirating influence of a nasal upon a preceding surd mute is very common in Greek. O. L. *cesna* (*cena*) is perhaps = *cedna* beside Skr. *khad* (to eat), *khádana* (food). *Tr* appears also in some cases to have become *br*, through the steps *tr, thr, dhr, br*, the dental being aspirated by the following *r*: *consobrinus*, from *con* and *sostor* = I. E. *svastár* (sister), passed through the stages *consostorinus, consostrinus, consosthrinus, consosdhrinus*, and then *dh* became *b*, as in *ruber*, &c.: *salubris* passed through stages *saluttris* (from St. *salut*), *salustris, salusthris, salusdhris, salūdhris*, compare *palustris* from St. *palud; muliebris* = *muliestris*, through a similar series of steps; *tenebrae** = *tenesthrae* = *tenestrae*, perhaps from an I. E. *tamastra*, whence Skr. *tamisra*, beside Skr. *tamas* (darkness), Z. *temanh* (darkness), Lith. *tamsà* (darkness), O. H. G. *demar* (crepusculum), O. S. *thim* (dim), Ir. *teim* and *temel* (dark), W. *tywyll* (dark).

T exercised an aspirating influence upon the preceding tenuis in Umbrian and Oscan: thus in Umbrian *ct* and *pt* became *ht*, as O. U. *scrēhto* = L. *scriptum*, O. U. *rehte* = L. *recte*, O. U. *subahtu* for *subactu* = L. *subigito*: in Oscan *pt* became *ft* and *ct, ht*, as N. O. *scriftas* = L. *scriptae*, N. O. *Ohtavis* = L. *Octavius*, O. O. *ehtrad* = L. *extra*, O. O. *saahtúm* = L. *sanctum*. This aspirating force of *t* upon a preceding tenuis manifested itself also in late Latin, as in *jachtivus*. Such Italian forms, as *oggetto, otto, perfetto, ottare, ottuso*, &c., from L. *objectus, octo, perfectus, optare, obtusus*, &c., most probably passed through the intermediate forms *objechtus, ochto, per-*

---

* Consult Ebel, K. Z. XVI. 77, seq.; Ascoli, K. Z. XVI. 196, seq.; Bopp, Skr. Gl. under *tamas*, who considers that *tenebra* is for *tembræ*, *b* being inserted for euphony (as in ἀμβροσία) in *temræ* beside Skr. *timira* (obscuritas) and *tamisra*.

fechtus, *oftare*, *oftusus*, &c. In Irish* *c* and *p* before *t* become *ch*, as *ocht* = L. *octo*, *recht* (lex) for *rect*, *lacht* (milk) for *lact*, *secht* = L. *septem*, *necht* = L. *neptis*, &c. In Welsh this *ch* has disappeared, and we find W. *wyth* (eight) = Ir. *ochto*, W. *noith* = Ir. *nocht* (night), W. *reith* = Ir. *recht* (lex), W. *taith* = Ir. *techt* (iter), &c., the palatal vowel (*i*) making its appearance on account of the palatalization of the original guttural. A change similar to this last is found in E. *night*, *might*, *eight* beside G. *nacht*, *macht*, *acht*; and in the Romance languages as Port. *oito*, Prov. *oit*, Fr. *huit* from L. *octo*; Port. *noite*, Prov. *noit*, Fr. *nuit* from L. *noctem*; Port. *feito*, Fr. *fait* from L. *factom*.

In Gothic we find a mute before a dental changed into the corresponding spirant, after which the dental always is or becomes *t*: *sauhts* (sickness) for *sukthis* beside *siuks* (sick); *mahts* (might) for *magthis* from R. *mag*; *ga-skafts* (creation) beside *ga-skap-jan*; *fra-gifts* (lending) beside *giban* (to give. *H* in these Gothic forms, *sauhts*, *nahts* (night) = Lith. *naktis*, *raihts* = L. *rectus*, &c., was very guttural; and the corresponding *gh* in English once had a strong guttural sound, as it still has in lowland Scotch, as in *eneugh* (enough), *sheugh* (a ditch), which are pronounced as *enŭch*, *shŭch* would be in English, or in the notation of the general alphabet as $\iota n \breve{u} \chi^2$, $s^3 \breve{u} \chi^2$. The guttural spirant prefers as neighbouring vowels, *o* and *u*, and hence in Portuguese we find *auto* from L. *actom*, *Outubro* (October), *doutor* (doctor), &c.: compare the English pronunciation of *enough*, *laugh*, *thought*. We can account for the remarkable substitution of *pt* in Wallachian for L. *ct* from this

---

* Aspiration is of common occurrence in the Keltic languages. In Welsh *r* and *l* aspirate a succeeding consonant as in *march* (a horse) = Ir. *marc*. In Irish *c*, *t* and *p* are aspirated between two vowels, as *ech* (a horse) for *ecu*, and this for *ecus* = L. *equos*, O. S. *ehu*, &c. Similarly initial *p* disappeared, as in *athir* = L. *pater*, *iasc* = *piscis*, *lán* = L. *plenus*, &c.; *p* here passed through the stages *ph*, *f*, *h*, and then vanished as in L. *faedus* = *haedus* = *aedus*, &c.

aspirating force of *t*. *Ct* passed through the stages *cht, ght, ft* in becoming *pt*, and in a few cases remained at the *ft* stage. Thus we have *doftor* = L. *doctor, leftice* = L. *lectica*, where *ct* becomes *ft* and *copt* = L. *coctus, fript* = L. *frictus, pept* = L. *pectus*, &c., where *ct* advances to *pt*.

In Modern Greek we also see the aspirating force of *t* in ὀχτώ (eight), κλέφτης from κλέπτης, χτένι from κτένιον.

IV. When two consonants come together, the second is sometimes made *like* the first, or affected by it in some way. Thus *t* often become *s* after *r, l, c* and the nasals: *noxa* for *nocta* from *noceo*; *fixus* for *figtus* from *figo*; *maximus* for *magtimus*; beside *actus* from *ago*; *fictus* from *fingo*; &c.; *sparsus* for *spargtus* from *spargo* beside *tortus* for *torctus* and *sartus*; *pulsus* for *pultus* from *pello*; *perculsus* for *percultus* from *percello*; *excelsus* for *exceltus* from *excello*; &c., beside *sepultus* from *sepelio*; *mansum* for *mantum* from *maneo*; *tensus* and *tentus* from *tendo*; &c. When the group *nt* belongs to the same element of a word it is unchanged as in *ferunt, amantem*, &c. *T* after *p* is unchanged except in *lapsus* for *laptus* from R. *lab*. In Sanskrit we also frequently find *ksh* (= *ks*) representing an older *kt*, as *takshá* (a carpenter = Gr. τέκτων, *nakshatra* (a star) from *nakta* (night); consult §. 38.

V. Mutual influence of two consonants upon and approximation to each other, both consonants being changed. Thus *suggillatio* comes from *sub* and *cilium*: it is a translation of ὑπώπιον (a blow under the eyes), whence was derived ὑπωπιάζειν (to beat black and blue, to mortify), *Appulus* for *Akvulus* (as ἵππος from ἰκϝος) from *aqua* connected with Skr. *ápas* (nom. pl. water), Goth. *ahva*, A. S. *ewe*. This root is found in Μεσσ-άπ-ιοι (the people between to two seas, compare such formations as Μεσοποταμία, Μεθύδριον, *Interamna*), γῆ 'Απία (the Peloponnesus, now called *Morea* from Sl. *more* = L. *mare*), ἐξ ἀπίης γαίης (from the land across the sea), and perhaps the Volscian town *Apiola*.

§. 82. DISSIMILATION.

A dental before a following *t* becomes *s*: thus we have *equester* for *equet-ter* from St. *equet*; *pedester* for *pedetter* from St. *pedet*; *claustrum* from R. *claud*; *est* (he eats) beside *edit* (in Plautus and Lucilius), &c. We find a similar change in Zend, Greek, Irish, Slavic, Lithuanian and Gothic, but not in Sanskrit. Thus in Skr. we have *atti* (he eats) from R. *ad*, &c., while in Zend* we find *bas'ta* (part. praet. pass.) from *band* (to bind), &c.: for Greek examples consult §. 59: in Irish we have *rofestar* (he knows) for *rofedtar* from R. *vid*, *estar* (he eats) from R. *ed*: in Slavic we have *daste* (2 pl. pres.) for *dadte* = I. E. *dadatasi* from R. *da* (to give), *dasti* (he gives) for *dadti* = I. E. *dadati*, &c.: in Lithuanian we have *sė́s-czas* (sitting) for *sed-tjas* beside *sėdė́ti* (to sit), *mèsti* (to throw) beside *metù* (I throw), &c.: in Gothic we have *vaist* (thou knewest) for *vaitt* beside *vait* (he knew), &c.

The termination *-alis* is used for *-aris* when the stem to which it is added does not contain *l* in the syllable preceding this termination; thus we have *mortalis* beside *popularis*, &c. Similarly we find *caeruleus* for *caeluleus* from *coelum* and *Parilia* from *Pales*. When two consonants, the same or similar, follow each other, only separated by a vowel, this vowel is thrown out, and only one of the consonants retained: thus we have *veneficus* for *venenificus*; *semestris* for *semimestris*; *semodius* for *semimodius*; *stipendium* for *stipipendium*; *nutrix* for *nutritrix* from *nutrire*; *consuetudo* for *consuetitudo*; *aestas* for *aestitas* from *aestus*; *antestari* for *antetestari*, &c.† Similarly in Greek we have τράπεζα for τετραπεζα; τέτραχμον for τετραδραχμον; ἀμφορεύς for ἀμφιφορευς; κελαινεφής for κελαινονεφης; &c.

---

* Consult Schleicher, Compendium, &c., pp. 203, 235, 289, 308, 321, 335.

† Consult Leo Meyer, Comp. Gram. I. 281.

The following words may also be cases of dissimilation: *dulcis* for *gulcis* beside Gr. γλυκύς, the gutt. *g* becoming *d* on account of the next syllable beginning with gutt. *c*; in *tenebrae* beside Skr. *tamisra* and *mihi* beside *tibi* = Skr. *tubhyam*, *m* may have been changed into *n* in the first case and *bh* into *h* in the second, to prevent two labials immediately following each other; in a few words *v*, when followed or preceded by *o* or *u*, became *b** as in *ferbui* for *fervui* and *bubile* for *bovile*; *proximus* for *propsimus* beside *prope*; *tamen* is for *tamem*, and it bears the same relation to *tam* that *item* does to *ita*.

§. 83. Change of *S* into *R*.

S, when it comes between two vowels, or between a vowel and a sonant consonant, or when final after a vowel, generally becomes *r*. Thus we have *gero* for *geso* beside *ges-si*; *uro* beside *us-si*; *eram* from R. *es* (to be); *queri* beside *questus*, R. *ques* = Skr. *s'vas* (to sigh); *auris* for *ausis* beside *aus-culto*, Gr. οὖς Hom. οὔατα (pl.); *haurio* beside *haus-tus*; *dirimo* and *diribeo* for *disimo* and *dishibeo*; *heri* beside *hes-ternus*; *sero*, for *seso*, a reduplication of R. *sa* (to sow); *nurus*, Skr. *snushá* (a daughter-in-law); *virus*, Skr. *visha* (poison); *soror*, Skr. *svasár*; *haereo* beside *haesito*; *aurora*, Skr. *ushas* (the dawn); *maero* beside *maestus*; *generis* = Gr. γένεος = Græco-It. *genesos*; *ovis*, *maris*, *muris*, *Liguris*, &c., from *os*, *mas*, *mus*, *Ligus*, &c., beside *masculus*, *musculus* (a little mouse), *Ligusticus*, &c.; *–rum* (term. of gen. pl.) for *–sum* as (*is-*) *tarum* = Skr. *tásán*; *veternus* for *vetesnus* from *vetus*; *diurnus*, *hodiernus* beside *Diespiter*; *jurgo* beside *jus*, *justus*; *carmen* beside *Casmenae*, connected with Skr. *s'ans* to praise); &c. Final *s* becomes *r*

---

* Curtius compares to this change the substitution of β in Greek for a Græco-It. *r*, as in βούλομαι beside L. *volo*, &c. Consult his Grundzüge der Gr. Etym., p. 516.

in those cases where a vowel originally followed it, and perhaps in some other cases from the influence of analogy: *amor* (I am loved) is for *amose*, &c.; *amatur* (he is loved) is for *amatise*, &c.;* *major* is for *majōs*, *r* probably arising from the influence of the oblique cases, beside *majus*, &c.; similarly we have *honor* for *honos*, &c. *S* is often retained, as in *vesica*, *casa*, *vasa* (pl. of *vas*), *pusillus*, *cāsus* = *cassus* for *cadtus*, and whenever *s* represents *ss*, *quaeso* beside *quaero*, *nasus* beside *nares*, *miser* beside *maereo*, *posui*, *nisi*, and compounds with *de* as *desino*, &c. In Old Latin we find such forms as *Lases* for *Lares*, *fasena* = *harena*, *Fusius*, *esit* = *erit*, &c. L. Papirius Crassus (Consul B. C. 366) changed his name from *Papisius* to *Papirius*; from this we see that the substitution of *r* for *s* had already shown itself early in the fourth century B. C. In Umbrian and Oscan *s* is often retained between two vowels: O. U. *asa* = O. L. *asa* (*ara*), O. O. *aasas*, *aasai* = O. L. *asas*, *asai* (*aras*, *arae*). We find, however, O. U. *eru*, N. U. *erom* as the infin. of R. *es* (to be). In Oscan the term. of gen. pl. becomes -*azum* and in Umbrian -*aru* = L. -*arum* I. E. -*âsâm*.

§ 84. THE REJECTION OF A CONSONANT.

The rejection of one of two medial consonants belongs perhaps properly to the province of assimilation, as has been already pointed out in § 81. The vanishing of a consonant between two vowels is also treated by Schleicher as a kind of assimilation; when a surd in this position vanishes, it must

---

* This is the ordinary account given of the origin of the Latin passive, but there are several objections to it which render it somewhat doubtful. In the first place, the form of the second pers. pl. (*amamini*, &c.) is evidently a participle in -*menus* = Gr. -μενος = Skr. -*mânas*, and if in the 1st and 3rd pers. pl. final *r* represents the reflexive pronouns, how can we account for the 2nd pers. being formed so differently from them? In the second place, the passive in Irish ended in *r*, which never represented an older *s*; e. g. Ir. *bertar* = L. *feruntur*, Ir. *berthar* = L. *fertur*, &c.

have first become a sonant. The disappearance of initial consonants is quite a distinct phenomenon, and cannot be ascribed to the influence of assimilation.

Initial *c* has very rarely vanished; it may have done so in the following examples:—*ubi, unde, uter, ut* beside *ali-cubi, ali-cunde,* from I. E. St. *kva* (who), whence Skr. *kas* (who) = L. *quis* = Goth. *hvas,* Skr. *kataras* = Gr. πότερος (Ion. κότερος) = L. *uter,* E. *whether; ut* = *quod:* Weber however connects *ubi, uti,* &c., with a pronominal stem that is found in Skr. *u* (utrum), *uta* (vel, aut), but the preceding view is far more probable. Curtius connects Gr. νεύω, L. *nuo, co-niveo (co-nixi), nīco, nictus, nictor* with Goth. *hneiva* (I bend), O. H. G. *hnīga* (I bend), and accordingly assumes that the original root was *knu* from which by gunation we form *knav,* whence we have Goth. *hniv;* the form *co-niveo* points back also to an initial guttural, for, if the root began with *n,* we would have found *con-niveo :* he supposes also that we find the lost κ in κνώσσω (I nod, slumber) = κνωκyω from κνωκ (as πτώσσω from πτωκ) = κνοακ = κνοϝ–ακ. *Ludus,* O. L. *loidos,* may be connected with Skr. *krīd* (to play). *Libum* may be for *klibum* beside Gr. κριβάνη, Goth. *hlaifs,* E. *loaf,* &c. Jurmann derives *lustrum* (for *clustrum* = *cludtrum*) from *klud,* a secondary form of R. *klu* whence O. L. *cluere,* ('cluere antiqui purgare dicebant.' Plin. xxv. 29, 36), *cloaca,* Gr. κλύζω (I wash), Goth. *hlutrs* (pure), O. H. G. *hlūtar.* Corssen derives *luscinia* from *cluos* or *clovos* (= Skr. *s'ravas* and Gr. κλεος) and *cano,* explaining the name accordingly as "the sweet songstress;" others derive it from *luscus,** and explain it as meaning "the twilight songstress." *K* was similarly lost in Gr. λάξ for κλαξ beside L. *calx,* E. *heel. Vapor* and *vappa* are for *cvapor* and *cvappa* beside καπύω (I breathe out), κάπος (ψυχή, πνεῦμα, Hesych.), καπνός, &c., Lith. *kvápas* (breath) : Crain connects

---

* *Luscus* properly means "*blind of an eye,*" hence "*dimsighted,*" and *luscum* never means "*twilight,*" consequently the proper translation of the word would be "the dimsighted songstress."

opinor with this root, but Corssen prefers to connect it with Gr. ὄσσομαι for ὀκγομαι. *Vermis* is for *kvermis* = Skr. *kṛmis* (a worm) according to Corssen, but Curtius considers that Skr. *kṛmis* (nom. sing.) Lith. *kĭrmis* (a worm), Ch. Sl. *crĭvĭ* (a worm) are quite unconnected with *vermis*, Gr. ἕλμινς, Goth. *vaurms*, which belong to I. E. root *var* (to roll), whence Gr. ἐλύω, ἴλλω, L. *volvo*, &c.

Medial *c* is lost before a vowel in *sirpea*, *sirpicus* beside *scirpus*, *scirpeus*, O. H. G. *scilaf* (sedge); *sipo*, *dis-sipo* beside Skr. *kship* (to throw) for *skip*, G. *schupfen* (to push); *sarmentum*, *sarpio* for *scarmentum*, *scarpio* beside O. H. G. *scarf*, G. *scharf* (sharp), from a root *scar + p*, *scar* being found in Gr. κείρω, ξυρόν, E. *sheers*, *plough-share*, &c. Medial *c* is lost before *t* in *Sestius* beside *Sextius*, *mistus* beside *mixtus*; *sescenti* for *sexcenti*; *mulsus* for *mulctus* from *mulceo*; *fartus* for *farctus*; *sartus* for *sarctus*; *Quintius* = *Quinctius*; *ultor* for *ulctor* beside *ulcisci*; *tortus* for *torctus* from *torqueo*; *vito* for *vic(i)to* beside Skr. *vik'* (to separate), Gr. εἴκω from R. Fικ; *in-vitus** for *in-vic(i)tus* beside Skr. *vas'* (to desire), Gr. ἑκών from R. Fεκ; *in-vito* for *in-vic(i)to* beside Skr. *vak'* (to speak), Gr. ἔπος, L. *voco*. *C* is lost before *d* in *quindecim* for *quincdecim*; *sedecim* for *sexdecim*. *C* is lost before *s* in *torsi* for *torcsi*; *sarsi* for *sarcsi*; *disco* for *dicsco* beside *didici*; *ursus* for *urcsus*, Skr. *ṛksha* (a bear), Gr. ἄρκτος; *parsimonia* for *parcsimonia*; *musca* for *mucsca*† beside Skr. *makshikâ* (a fly), Z. *makshi*, Gr. μυῖα for μυσια, O. H. G. *mucca* (culex), A. S. *micge*. *C* is lost before *n* in *quernus* for *quercnus*; *vānus* for *văcnus* beside *vă-*

---

* Benfey connects *invitus* and *invito* with Skr. *vî* (to desire), and Corssen (Kritische Nachträge zur Lateinischen Formenlehre, p. 52, seq.) supports the same view. Corssen connects *vito* with Skr. *vî* (to throw), whence a participial stem *vita-* may be formed meaning "removed, placed at a distance," beside which he also places O. H. G. *wit* (far off), G. *weit*, the *t* of suffix, Skr *ta-*, L. *to-*, being unchanged in German, an exception to Grimm's law.

† Perhaps *musca* has merely arisen from *mucsa* by transposition.

cuus; dĕni, for *dĕcni; pĭnus* for *pĭcnus* beside *pĭc-is; quini* for *quincni; lūna* for *lūcna* from R. *luc* = Skr. *ruk'* (to shine); *sēni* for *sexni; ex* becomes *e–* in *enarro, enato; pānis* for *păcnis*, according to Bopp, beside Skr. *pak'* (to bake), but according to Curtius connected with Skr. *pâ* (sustentare), L. *pa-bulum, pa-scor, pas-tor, Pă-les, pe-nus* (omne quo vescimur, Cic.), *pe-nates, penes*, Lith. *pénas* (fodder), *pénŭ* (pasco), &c. *C* is lost before *l* in *āla* for *ac-la* beside *axilla*, Gr. ἀκχός (the shoulder), O. H. G. *ahsala* (the shoulder); *tela* for *texla* beside *texo; culina* for *cuclina* beside *coquo, coquina*. *C* is lost before *v* in *sevir* for *sexvir; coniveo* for *conicveo* beside *conixi, nico, nictus; obliviscor* perhaps for *oblicviscor* beside *linquo*, but Corssen prefers to connect it with the same root as *līvor, lividus*, comparing Horace's expression *lividas obliviones. C* is lost before *m* in *tormentum* for *torcmentum* from *torqueo; semestris* for *sexmestris; lūmen* for *lūcmen* from R. *luc; pomum* for *pocmum* (lit. "what is ripe") beside Skr. *pak'* (coquere), but, according to Curtius, for *povmum* (lit. "what has grown") from an I. E. root *pu* (to grow), whence Skr. *pu-mâns* (a man), *pu-tra* (a son), Gr. ποία for ποϜια, πῶλος for ποϜλος, παῖς and πάϊς for παϜ-ιδς, L. *pa-pav-er, præ-pu-tium; ōmen* for *ocmen* beside Gr. ὄσσομαι for ὀκγομαι, Goth. *ahman* (spirit), *amnis* for *acmenis* from I. E. R. *ak* or *akv* (to be quick) whence *aqua*, &c., but Bopp connects it directly with Vedic *apnas* (aqua); *temo* for *texmo*, beside Skr. *taksh* (to form, to cut), Gr. τίκ-τω, τέχ-νη, τεύχ-ω, O. H. G. *dehsa* (an axe).

Initial *g* was lost before *n* in *nosco, notus, nomen, narro* beside *co-gnosco, co-gnomen*, O. L. *gnarigo* (narro), *gnarus* from I. E. *gna* (to know), whence Skr. *g'nâ*, Gr. ἔ-γνων, O. H. G. *knău* (I know), &c.; *norma* (= Gr. γνώμων in meaning), is for *gnorima* from last root, according to Benfey; *natus* beside *cognatus, nitor, nixus* beside *gnitor, gnixus*, O. H. G. *hnegenti* (nitens), *ana-hnekenti* (innitentes), Goth. *ana-hnaiv-jan* (to place upon something). *G* was lost before *l* in *lucuns* from Gr. γλυκυῦς; *lact-* beside Gr. γάλακτ-; and according to

Bopp, in *lassus* for *glassus* beside Skr. *glásnu* (weary). *G* is lost before *v* in *venio, vădum, vādo* from I. E. *gva* (to go), when Skr. *gá* (to go), Gr. βαίνω, ἔβην from R. βα, Goth. *quiman* (to come); *voro* from I. E. *gvar*, whence Skr. *gar* (to devour), Gr. βορά; *vivus, vita, victus* beside Skr. *g'ĭv* (to live), Gr. βίος, Goth. *qvius* (living), E. *quick;* *volo* beside Skr. *gal* (to fall), Gr. βάλλω (as Skr. *pat* means both *to fly* and *to fall*); *venter* perhaps for *gventer*, from R.'*gen* = I. E. *gvan*, but connected by Curtius and Benfey with Skr. *g'athara* (venter), Gr. γαστήρ, Goth. *quithus* (the belly), *laus-quithr-s* (inanem ventrem habens); *vescor*, according to Bopp, for *gvescor* beside Skr. *ghas* (to eat), to which he also joins Gr. γαστήρ; Bopp connects *vasto* with Skr. *g'as* (laedere), Goth. *fra-qvistja* (deleo), considering the original form to have been *gvasto;* he also connects *vigilo* for *gvigilo* with the Skr. *g'âgar* (vigilare), O. H. G. *wachar* (vigil). These comparisons of Bopp are, however, extremely doubtful: as to *vigil*, Curtius is probably correct in connecting it with L. *vigeo, vegeo*.

Medial *g* is lost before a following *j*, after having been assimilated to it, and then the preceding vowel, if short, is lengthened in compensation: thus we have *mējo* for *mĭgjo, mājor* for *măgjor*, &c. *G* is lost before *t* in *indultus* for *indulgtus*, *sparsus* = *spartus* for *spargtus, mulsus* for *mulgtus, tersus* for *tergtus*, &c. *G* is lost before *s* in *fulsi, ursi, versi, indulsi, tersi*, &c., from *fulgeo*, &c.; *compesco* for *compegsco*, from R. *pag* (or *pak*) beside *pignus, pango, pac-iscor, pax*, Skr. *pag'-ra* (firm), Gr. πήγνυμι, &c. *G* is lost before *l* in *stīlus* for *stiglus* beside Gr. στίζω, L. *distinguo;* *pālus* for *paglus* from the root *pag*, and perhaps in *fīlum* (a string) for *figlum* beside *figo*. *G* is lost before *v* in *vivus* for *gvigvus;* *brĕvis* for *bregvis*, Gr. βραχύς; *lĕvis* for *legvis*, Gr. ἐλαχύς; *nivis* for *nigvis* beside *ninguo, nix;* *malo* for *mavolo* from *magevolo; malva* beside Gr. μαλάχη; *uveo, uvidus* for *ugveo, ugvidus* from I. E. *ug* whence Skr. *uksh* (conspergere, humectare) = *ug* + *s*, Gr. ὑγ-ρός, &c.;

fruor for *frugvor* beside *frugi** (useful), *fruges*, Skr. *bhug'* (edere, frui), Goth. *brukjan*, O. H. G. *prūchan*, *brūchan*, G. *brauchen* (to use), E. *brook*; *torvus* for *torgvus* beside Skr. *targ'* (to threaten), Gr. ταργαίνω (ταράσσω), τάρβος, perhaps τραχύς, A. S. *threagan* (to chide), O. H. G. *drawa* for *drahwa*, G. *drohen* (to menace); *fulvus* for *fulgvus* beside *fulgeo*, *flagro*, &c.; *lues* for *lugves*, if it be connected with Skr. *rug'* (vexare), Gr. λυγρός, λοιγός, L. *lugeo*, *luctus*, &c.; *faveo* and *foveo* are for *fagveo* and *fogveo*, according to Corssen, who connects them with Skr. *bhag'* (colere, amare, coquere?), which he supposes to have originally meant "to heat." Curtius connects *faveo* with Skr. *bhâ* (to shine), *bhâsh* (to speak), Gr. φά-τις, φη-μί, φαίνω, φά-ος, L. *fa-ma, fa-ri, fa-teor, fa-cies, fav-illa*, &c. G is lost before *m* in *fulmen* for *fulgmen*, *flāmen* for *flagmen* beside Skr. *bhrâg'* (to shine), Gr. φλέγω, φλόξ, L. *flagro*, *fulgeo*, *fulvus* (for *fulgvus*), &c.; *frumentum* beside *fruges*; *rumino* for *rugmino* beside Gr. ἐρυγή (a vomiting), L. *ructo, erūgo*, used by Ennius in the line *contempsit fontes quibu' sese erugit aquae vis*; *stimulus* for *stigmulus* beside Skr. *tig'* (to be sharp), Z. *tighri* (an arrow), Gr. στίζω, στίγμα, L. *distinguo, instigo*; *umor, umecto* for *ugmor, ugmecta* from I. E. *ug*, whence Skr. *uksh*, Gr. ὑγρός; *fames*, according to Bopp, for *fagmes* beside Skr. *bhaksh* (to eat), Gr. ἔ-φαγ-ον, L. *faba* (for *fagva*?), but Curtius rejects this account of *fames* on the ground that a nominal suffix cannot signify *desire*; *exāmen* from *exago*; *contamino* beside *tango*, R. *tag*.

Initial *h* is lost in *olus* = *holus* = *folus*; *aedus* = *haedus* = *faedus*; *ircus* = *hircus* = *fircus*; *er* = *her* (a hedgehog) = Gr.

---

* *Frugi* meant *utilis*; Qui *frugi homines* χρήσιμους appellant, id est tantummodo utiles; at illud est latius (Cic. Tusc. III. 8, 16). Ulfilas translates Gr. ὠφέλιμος, εὔχρηστος by Goth. *bruks*. In the expression *homo frugi, frugi* can be only a genitive like *nihili, nauci, flocci, pensi*, &c., but whether it be the gen. of a noun in *-um* or *-ium* cannot be decided. Consult Corssen, Nachträge, &c., p. 83.

χήρ (a hedgehog); *anser* beside Skr. *hansa* (a goose), Gr. χήν, O. H. G. *gans*; *arvina* (lard) beside Skr. (Ved.) *hirá* (intestines), Gr. χολάδες, χύλιξ, χορδή, L. *haru-spex, har-iolus, hira* (entrails), *hilla* for *hirula*; &c.* *H* is lost before *l* in *lūtum* whence *lūteus* (yellow), *hlū* being = χλω in Gr. χλω-ρός (yellow); the root of this word was probably an I. E. *ghar* (to shine) whence on one side came Skr. *hiraṇa, hiraṇya* (gold), Z. *zaranu, zaranya* (gold), Gr. χρυσός, χρυσίον, Goth. *gulth*, Ch. Sl. *zlato*, and on another, Skr. *hari* (green, yellow), Z. *zairi* (yellow), Gr. χλόη, χλόος, χλωρός, L. *helus, holus, flavus, helvus*, O. H. G. *gröni, cröni* (green), Ch. Sl. *zelije* (olera), Lith. *zeliù* (viresco), Ir. *glas* (green) : Bopp connects *viridis* with Skr. *harit*, supposing that *gviridis* was the original form, but all the forms in the cognate languages point back to a root *ghar* and not *ghvar*.

Medial *h* is lost in *mi* = *mihi*; *nemo* for *nehemo*; *nil* = *nihil*; *vemens* = *vehemens*; *Ala* = *Ahala*; *cors* = *cohors*; *debeo* = *dehibeo*; *praebeo* = *praehibeo*; *aenum* = *ahenum*; *pius* beside Volsc. *pihom* (pium), U. *pihaclu* (piaculum); *via, vea* for *veha* from *veho*; *prendo* = *prehendo* for *praehendo, praeda* for *prae-hid-a*, both from R. *hed* = I. E. *ghad* whence Skr. *hasta* (manus) for *had-ta* (?), Gr. χανδάνω, ἔ-χαδ-ον, L. *hasta* for *had-ta, hĕd-era* (the "clinging" shrub), Goth. *bi-git-an* (to find), E. *get*; *bīmus* for *bihimus†* (so *trīmus, quadrīmus*, &c.) beside Skr. *hima* (snow) Z. *hima* (a year), *zima* (winter), Gr. χειμών, χιών, L. *hiems*, Ch. Sl. *zima* (hiems); *lana* perhaps for *lahna* = Gr. λάχνη; *aranea* for *arahnea* beside Gr. ἀράχνη from I. E. *ark* (to spin) whence Gr. ἄρκυς, ἀρκάνη (a thread, seam), ἠλακάτη; *velum* for *vehlum* beside *vexillum* from *veho*.

Initial *j* is lost in *uxor* beside *conjux* from *jungo*. Some connect *uxor*‡ with Skr. *vas'* (to wish for), *vas'á* (a woman), Gr.

* Consult Corssen über Aussprache, Vokalismus und Betonung der Lateinischen Sprache, p. 49.

† *Bimus* may be for *bi-amnus*, c. f. *sol-emnis*.

‡ *Uxor* has also been connected with Skr. *uksh* (to sprinkle), whence Skr. *ukshan* (a bull).

ἑκών. Pott has suggested two explanations of the word, both equally wrong, (1) *uxor* = "she who is carried off" from *vah* (to carry) and suffix *-tor*, but a passive sense never coexists with this suffix, (2) *uxor* = "ducta femina" from Skr. *vah* + *strî* (a woman).

Medial *j* (*y*) is lost in *domo* for *domayo* = Skr. *damayâmi*, *amo* for *amayo*, &c. ; *doceo* for *doceyo*, &c.; *audio* for *audiyo*, &c. ; *doceam, doceyam*, &c. ; *audiam* = *audiyam*, &c. ; *ferreus* = *ferreyus, aureus* = *aureyus*, &c. ; *liga, quadriga* for *bijuga, quadrijuga* ; *cuncti* for *cojuncti* ; *hornus* for *hoyornus, yor*— corresponding to Z. *yâre* (a year), Gr. ὥρα, E. *year* ; *minor* for *minyor, minus* for *minyus*, the comparative terminations *-ior, -ius* being = I. E. *-yâns, -yas*, Skr. *-iyâns, -iyas*; O. L. *plous* (plus) for *ployus, pleores* (plures, Carm. Arv.) for *pleyores*; *pris-* (in *pris-tinus, pris-cus*) = *prius* for *proyos*; *ero* for *esyo* beside Gr. ἔσσομαι = ἐσγομαι; *obex* for *objex* ; *abicio* = *abjicio*; *-bus* (term. of dat. pl.) = Skr. *-bhyas*.

Initial *t* is lost in *lātus* for *tlatus* beside *tollo*, O. L. *tulo*, &c.

Medial *t* is lost in *ac* for ˈ*atc* = *atque* ; *misi* for *mitsi* from *mitto* ; *lens* for *lents* = *lentis*, *mens* for *ments* = *mentis, sors* for *sorts* = *sortis*, &c. ; *primas* = O. L. *primatis, optimas* = O. L. *optimatis, Samnis* = O. L. *Samnitis, Tiburs* = O. L. *Tiburtis*, &c.; *miles* for *milets*, beside *milit-em* ; *quartus* for *quat*(*u*)*rtus*.

Initial *d* is lost in *Juppiter, Jovis*, U. *Jupater* beside O. L. *Diovis*, O. ΔιουFει (dat.), &c. ; *viginti* for *dviginti*.

Medial *d* is lost in *hoc* for *hodc; corculum* for *cordculum ; pēs* for *pĕds ; suāsi* for *suādsi ; frons* = *frondis ; concors* = *concordis ; glans* for *glands ; māno* for *madno* beside Gr. μαδάω (madeo), L. *măd-idus*, &c. ; *mercenarius* for *mercednarius; finis* for *fidnis* beside *findo* from R. *fid* = Skr. *bhid* (findere), E. *bite ; scalae* for *scadlae* beside *scando*, Skr. *skand* (scandere) ; *suāvis* for *suādvis*, Gr. ἡδύς, &c.; *squāma* for *squădma* from I. E. *skad* (to cover) beside Skr. *k'had* (tegere), *k'hadman* (occultatio, alienae formae assumptio), perhaps *sku* (tegere), Gr. σκοτός, σκιά, σκηνή, Goth. *skildus* (a shield), *skalja* (tegula), Ir. *scath*

(shade), &c.; *caementum* beside *caedo*; *ramentum* beside *rado*.
The prefixes *sĕd-* (*sed-itio*), *rĕd-* (*red-eo, red-igo, redi-vivus*),*
prōd- (*prōd-esse, prōd-eo, prōd-igus*) lose their final *d* before a
consonant, as in *sēgrego, sējugo, sēduco, sēvoco, rēducor, rēpono,
rēmoveo, prōduco, prōmitto*, &c.

Initial *s* is lost in *cutis* for *scutis* beside Skr. *sku* (to cover),
Gr. σκῦτος, κύτος, L. *ob-scu-rus, scu-tum*, Lith. *skurà* (skin),
A. S. *hūd* (a hide); *caveo, cautus* from R. *skav* beside Skr.
kavi (wise, a poet), Gr. θυο-σκόο-ς, κόεω, κοννέω (I perceive)
= κοϝνεω, κοᾷ (ἀκούει, Hesych.), ἀκούω for ἀ-κοϝ-ω, ἔ-κο-μεν
(ᾐσθομεθα, Hesych.), Goth. *us-skav-jan* (to be cautious), *skaus*
(cautious), *skauns* (beautiful), O. H. G. *scawōn* (to look), G.
schauen, schōn; *caedo* for *scaedo* beside Skr. *k'hid* (to tear, cut)
Z. *sk'id* (to tear asunder), Gr. σκίζω, σκίδη, σχινδαλμός (a
splinter), L. *scindo*, Goth. *skaida* (I separate), O. H. G. *sceit*
(discissio), O. N. *skīd* (lignum fissum); *cena* for *cesna* = *ced-na*
for *sced-na* from I. E. *skad* (to eat, lit. to cut, cleave) whence
Skr. *khâd* (to eat); *cedo* may be also connected with last root
beside Gr. ἐκεκήδει (ὑπεχώρει, Hesych.), κεκαδῆσαι (βλάψαι,
Hesych.), κῆδος, &c., the idea of *cutting asunder* being closely
connected with that of *separation*, and then with that of *sorrow*; *capis* (a vessel) from St. *capid* = O. U. *kapir̩, capulum*
(the hilt of a sword, a bier), *capedo, capisterium*, &c., if Froehde,
Corssen,† and others be correct in connecting these words
with Gr. σκαφίς, σκάφη (a basin, skiff), σκάπτω, κάπετος (a
trench), Ch. Sl. *kopati* (fodere), Lith. *kápas* (a grave), Goth.
skip (a ship), *ga-skap-jan* (to make), G. *schoppen* (a scoop),
schaufel (a shovel), &c.; but it is much preferable to connect
capis, &c., with L. *capio, capax*, Gr. κώπη whence was borrowed
L. *cupa*, Goth. *hafja* (I lift), M. H. G. *haft* (vinculum), E.
heave, haft, &c.; *tego, tegula*, &c., for *stego*, &c., beside Skr.
sthag (to cover), Gr. στέγω, στέγος, τέγος, L. *istega* (a cover)

---

* *Re-div-ivus* is explained by some as meaning "*shining again*," from
R. *div*.

† Consult Corssen's Nachträge, &c., p. 293, and K. Z. xiii. 452.

for *instega*, Lith. *stogas* (a roof), O. N. *thek* (a roof), O. H. G. *dakju* (I cover), E. *thatch, deck; tundo, tudes* (a hammer), &c., for *stundo*, &c., beside Skr. *tud* (to strike), Gr. Τυδεύς, Goth. *stauta* (I strike), O. H. G. *stōzu ; torus* for *storus* beside Skr. *star* (sternere), Gr. στόρνυμι, στρατός, &c., L. *sterno, stramen,* &c., Goth. *strauja* (στρώννυμι), O. H. G. *strāo* (straw), Ch. Sl. *strēti* (extendere); Corssen supposes that initial *s* is also lost in *littera, linea, limus, lino* beside O. H. G. *slim*, G. *schleim* (slime) ; *nurus* for *snurus*, beside Skr. *snushā*, Gr. νυός, O. H. G. *snur*, A. S. *snor*, Ch. Sl. *snochā ; na-re, na-ta-re, nā-sus* for *sna-re*, &c., beside Skr. *snā* (lavare), Gr. νῆσος, Νάξος; *nix* for *snix* beside Z. *s'nizh* (to snow), Gr. ἀγάννιφος for ἀγασνιφος, Goth. *snaivs* (snow), Lith. *snìgti* (to snow), Ch. Sl. *snĕgŭ* (snow); *nutrix* beside Skr. *snu* (to flow), according to Corssen who explains it to mean "the person who makes to flow," viz. "milk," as *stator* signifies "the person who causes to stand;" *repo* for *srepo* beside L. *serpo*, Skr. *sarpa* (a serpent); *rete* for *srete* from *sero* beside Skr. *sarit* (a thread), Gr. σείρα, εἴρω, ἕρμα, Lith. *seris* (a thread); *rivus, Rumo* (an old name of the Tiber), *rumen* (the udder), *Rumina* beside Skr. *sru* (to flow), Gr. ῥό-ος, ῥεῦ-μα, ῥυ-θ-μός, &c., O. H. G. *stroum* (a stream), Lith. *sravju* (I flow) ; *palea* (chaff), *pulvis, pollen* from I. E. R. *spar* (to move quickly), when Skr. *sphurāmi* (vibror), *palāla* (straw), Z. *s'par* (to go), Gr. σπαίρω, ἀσπαίρω, σπείρω, σπαράσσω, πα-σπάλ-η (fine meal) = παι-πάλ-η, πα-λύνω, πάλλω, πάλη (pollen), &c., O. H. G. *sprua* (chaff), *spor* (vestigium), *sporōn* (calcitrare), *spurnan* (offendere), E. *spurn*, L. *sperno*, Lith. *spìrti* (to push), &c. ; *pituita* for *spituita* beside *spuo, spu-tum* from I. E. *spyu* beside Skr. *shṭiv* (spuere), πτύω for σπγυω, ψύττ-ω, πυτ-ίζω for πτυ-πτι-ζω, a frequentative form, Goth. *speiva* (spuo), O. H. G. *spīuvan, spīhan* (to spit), Lith. *spiáu-ju* (I spit), &c.; *fallo, fides, funda, fungus* beside Gr. σφάλλω, σφίδη, σφενδόνη, σφόγγος; *memor* for *sme-smor* beside Skr. *smar* (to remember), *smara* (love), Gr. μέρ-μηρ-α, μέρ-ι-μνα, μάρτυρ, &c. *St* is lost before *l* in *lātus* = O. L. *stlā-*

tus beside *sterno*, &c.; *lis* for *stlis* beside O. H. G. *strīt*, G. *streit* (a fight); *locus* for *stlocus* beside Skr. *sthala* (a place), from *sthal*, a secondary root formed from *sthâ*: Bopp, however, connects *locus* with Skr. *lôka* (mundus), Lith. *laukas* (campus).

Medial *s* is lost between two vowels in *viola* for *visola* beside Skr. *visha* (poison), Gr. ἰός, ἰον, L. *virus*, Benfey remarks, "poison is connected with blue, cf. *visha-pushpa* (the blue lotus), and Siva's neck growing blue, by swallowing the poison churned out of the sea;" *Cerealis* for *Ceresalis* beside *Ceres, Cereris; Ramnes, Tities, Luceres* for *Ramneses, Titieses Lucereses; spei* for *spesi* beside *speres* (nom. pl. in Ennius); *ver* for *veser* beside Skr. *vas-anta* (ver), Gr. ἔαρ for Fεσαρ, Lith. *vas-ara* (summer), Ch. Sl. *ves-na* (ver), O. N. *vār* (ver); *vīs* perhaps for *visis* beside *vires, virium*; *diēs* perhaps for *diesis* beside *diur-nus, Dies-piter, ho-dier-nus*, Skr. *divas-a* (day), *Divas-pati* (the lord of day, i. e. Indra); *nūbēs* perhaps for *nubēsis* beside Skr. *nabhas* (nom. neut.), Gr. νέφος, νέφε(σ)-ος, Lith. *débesis* (nubes); *sēdēs* perhaps for *sēdesis* beside Skr. *sadas* (nom. neut.) = Gr. ἕδος; and perhaps some other cases like *nubes* and *sedes*. Medial *s* is lost before consonants in the following cases :—*digredior* for *disgredior; dijudico* for *disjudico; trājicio* for *transjicio; diduco* for *disduco; trāduco, trādo* beside *transduco, transdo; īdem* for *isdem; judex* for *jusdex; nīdus* for *nisdus*, E. *nest; prīdie, prīdem* for *prisdie, prisdem; audio* perhaps for *ausdio* beside *aus-culto, aur-is*, Gr. οὖς, Lith. *ausìs* (the ear); *cena* for *cesna; pono* for *posno* beside *pos-ui; aeneus* for *aesneus; satin* for *satisne; audin* for *audisne; pōne* (behind) for *posne; ānus* for *asnus* beside Skr. *âsana* (a seat), *âste* = Gr. ἧσται, &c.; *pēnis* for *pesnis* beside Skr. *pasas* (penis), Gr. πέος, πόσθη; *fanum* for *fasnum* = O. *fūsnu* beside *fes-tus, fer-iae*, Gr. θεσ-σάμενοι, &c.; *canus* for *casnus*, but Bopp considers that the original form of the root was *skan* whence Skr. *kan* (splendere), Goth. *skeina* (I shine); *vēnum* for *vesnum* beside Skr. *vasna* (price); *corpulentus* for *corpuslentus; quālus* (a basket), beside *quasillus* ; *diligo* for *disligo* ; *tenebrae* for *tenesbrae; dimitto* for *dismitto* ; *rēmus* for *resmus* = *retmus*, Gr. ἐρετμός; *Cămena* for *Casmena* beside *carmen*, Skr. *s'ás* (to say, teach), *s'áns* (to praise), with which Benfey connects *censeo, cano, concinn-us*,* but the two latter words belong to Skr. *kvan* (sonare) ; *pomoerium* for *pos-moerium* ; *dumus* beside *dusmus* (incultus, dumosus), *densus*, Gr. δασύς, δαυλός for δασυλος, Ἐπί-δαυρος for Ἐπιδασυ-ρος, Δαυλίς for Δασυλις. The words *ex* and *sex*, as we have already seen, become *e-* and *se-* in composition, except before *c*, *t*, *p* ; thus we have *egero*, *educo*, *sedecim*, &c., but *extendo*, *expello*, &c.

Medial *n* is lost before *gn* in *ignavus*, *ignarus*, *ignoro*, *cognatus*, *cognatus*, &c. ; *signum* is connected by Ebel with Skr. *sañg'na* (sign, name), and therefore stands for *singnum*, *sin-* being found also in *sin-guli*, *sin-cerus*, *simplex* and *-gnu-m* being from R. *gnō* = Skr. *g'ná* (to know). The preposition *con* (= *com*) frequently loses its final *n* before *h*, *j*, *v*, and *s* in composition; thus we find *cohibeo*, *coicio*, *cojunx*, *coventio*, *cosol*, &c. *N* is lost before *s* in *istega* for *instega* (deck), *isculponeae* from *insculpo*, *intresecus* beside *intrinsecus*. In Umbrian we likewise find *kuveitu* = L. *convehito*. *kuvertu* = L. *convertito*, *covortust* = L. *converterit*, &c.

Medial *r* is lost in *rubigo* for *rubrigo* from *ruber; pejero* for *perjero; sempiternus* from *semper* ; *pēdo, podex* beside Skr. *pard*, Gr. πέρδω ; *sūsum* = *sursum*, &c. ; *tostus* for *torstus* from *torreo* ; *fuscus* for *furscus* beside *fur-vus; formosus* for *formonsus; retrōsum* beside *retrorsum; Tuscus* for *Turscus* = *Etruscus*, beside O. U. *Turskum*, N. U. *Tuscom: Etru-s-cus*† being formed from U. *etru-* (alter) as *pri-s-cus* from *pri* = *prae*, *-s* being the remains of the comparative termination *-ius*, *Etrusci* therefore meant *exteri* "the strangers" in Umbrian.

---

* Lottner connects *con-cin-nus* with *cin-cin-nus*, in which case the root must have meant "to connect, to twist."

† Consult Corssen, Über Aussprache, &c , vol. i., p. 92, and his Kritische Nachträge, &c., p. 177.

Medial *l* appears to be lost in *cingere* = *clingere* (Fest. 56) beside O. H. G. *hring* (a ring).

Initial *p* is perhaps lost before *r* in *red* beside Skr. *prati*, Gr. προτί. It is lost before *l* in *lien* beside Skr. *plihan* (lien), Gr. σπλήν, σπλάγχνον; *laetus* for *plaitus* beside Skr. *prî* (to love, to rejoice); *lanx* beside Gr. πλάξ, L. *planca* (a plate), *plānus* for *placnus* (?), O. H. G. *flah*; *lātus*, *Latium* beside Skr. *prath* (to extend), *pṛthu* (broad), Gr. πλατύς, πλάτος, L. *planta* (sole of the foot), *plānus* for *platnus* (?), *plautus* for *plotus*, (planis pedibus, Fest. 239); *later* (a tile), which is perhaps connected with last root; *linter* or *lunter* beside Gr. πλυντήρ from R. πλυ whence πλέω. The connexion of *lavo* with R. πλυ is very doubtful; it is better to connect it directly with Gr. R. λυ whence λῦμα, λουτρόν, &c. Pott also connects *livor*, *lividus*, with Gr. μόλυβος, μόλιβος, L. *plumbum*, O. H. G. *pli*, Lett. *alwa*; but this too is very doubtful.

Medial *b* is lost in *sus* = *subs* in *suscipio*, *sustuli*, *susque*, *surgo* for *susrigo*; *surpio* beside *subripio*; *oportet* for *obportet*, beside *pars*, *portio*; *operio* for *obperio* beside *a-perio*; *opimus* for *obpimus* beside Skr. *pyâi* (crescere), *pîvara* (crassus), Gr. πίων, πιαρός, πιμέλη.

Initial *f* is perhaps lost in *rĭgeo*, *rĭgor*, *rĭgidus* beside Gr. ῥῖγος for φριγος, &c., L. *frīgeo*, *frīgus*, *frīgidus*.

Medial *f* is lost, according to Corssen, in *illim*, *istim*, &c., for *illo-fim*, *isto-fim*, &c., -*fim* being = Skr. -*bhyam*.

Initial *v* is lost in *olla* (a pot), for *vorula* from I. E. *var* (to boil), whence Gr. βράσσω, βράζω (I boil), O. H. G. *walm* (fervor), Ch. Sl. *vrěti* (fervere), Lith. *vìrti* (to boil), &c.; *odi* beside Skr. *vadh* (to strike), Gr. ὠθέω; *orno* beside Skr. *varṇa* (colour). In these cases *a* becomes *o* on account of the preceding *v*. Initial *v* is also lost in *rigo* beside Gr. βρέχω, Goth. *rign* (βροχή) from I. E. *vragh*; *repente*, *repens*, *repentinus* beside Gr. ῥέπω for Fρεπω, ἀντί-ρροπος, &c., Lith *virpiu*, (I totter), *radix* beside Gr. ῥίζα, Lesb. βρίσδα, Goth. *vaurts* (a root),

O. H. G. *wurzala*, *wurza*; *ros* perhaps for *vros* beside Skr. *varsh* (pluere), Gr. ἔρση for Ϝερση; *laqueus* beside Gr. βρόχος, Goth. *vruggō* (a noose); *lacer, lacus, lacinia* beside Skr. *vras'k'* (to tear), Gr. ῥάκος, λάκος, λακίς (a rent), Æol. βράκος (= ῥάκος) which points back to a root Ϝρακ, Benfey connects Gr. ἕλκος, L. *ulcus*, with this root; *lacio* beside Gr. ἕλκω from R. Ϝελκ, Lith. *velkù* (I pull), with which Corssen connects *laqueus*; *lupus*,* Sabine *irpus*, beside Skr. *vrkas* (nom. sing. masc.), Gr. λύκος, Goth. *vulfs*, Ch. Sl. *vlŭkŭ*, Lith. *vìlkas*, connected by some with Skr. *vras'k'* (to tear), and by others with an I. E *vrak*, whence Gr. ἕλκω; *lana* perhaps for *vlana* beside Skr. *var* (to cover), *ûrṇa* (wool), *urubhra* (a ram, lit. the woolbearer), Gr. εἶρος, ἔριον, οὖλος (woolly), ἄρνες (lambs), βαρνίον (ἀρνίον Hesych.), βάριχοι (ἄρνες Hesych.), L. *vellus, villus,* Goth. *vulla* (wool), Lith. *vìlna* (wool), Ch. Sl. *vlŭna* (wool).

Medial *v* is often lost between vowels as in *suus* = O. L. *sovos* = Gr. ἱός; *tuus* for *tovos* = Gr. τεός; *momentum* for *movimentum*; *ploro* for *plovero* from R. *plu*, according to Corssen; *domui, habui,* &c., for *domavi, habevi,* &c.; *mox* for *movox* from *moveo*; *Mars* for *Mavors*; *nuntius* for *noviventius*; *praes* for *praeves*, the plural of which, *praevides*, is found in Thorian law, from *prae* and *vas*; *junior* for *juvenior*; *rursum* for *revorsum*; *nosse* = *novisse*, &c.; *amaram* = *amaveram*; &c.; *audisti* = *audivisti*, &c.; *nolo* for *nevolo*; &c. *V* is lost after *c* in *canis* beside Skr. *s'van* (a dog), Gr. κύων; *cano* beside Skr. *kvan* (to sound): and after *s* in *si* (= O. *svai*), *se, sibi, sed* from St. *sva; somnus* = Skr. *svapnas*, Gr. ὕπνος; *soror* = Skr. *svasā*, Goth. *svistar; sodalis* from a lost stem *sodā* beside Skr. *svadhā*

* Some separate L. *lupus* from Gr. λύκος, and connect it with Z. *urup-is, raop-is* (a species of dog), from root *rup* or *lup* (to tear). The Sabine *irpus* bears a great resemblance to the Zend words. It is not clear whether this group of words is connected in any way with Gr. ἀ-λώπ-ηξ, Lith. *lápė* (a fox), *lapùkas* (a young fox).

(the will, properly "one's own action" from *sva* and *dhâ*),*
Gr. ἦθος, ἔθος from R. σϝεθ, the form ἐυέθωκα (εἴωκα Hesych.)
proving that the root originally contained F, L. *suesco*, Goth.
sidus (ἦθος), G. *sitte* (custom); *sonus* beside Skr. *svan* (to
sound); *socer* = Skr. *s'vas'uras*, Gr. ἑκυρός; *socrus* = Skr.
s'vás'rûs ; *sermo* perhaps for *svermo* beside Skr. *svar* (to sound),
Gr. σῦριγξ, L. *susurrus*, *absurdus* (compare *absonus*) ; *serenus*,
sol beside Skr. *svar* (heaven), Z. *hvarĕ* (sol), Gr. Σείριος, σέλας, σελήνη.

Initial *m* is lost in *imago* and *imitor* for *mimago* and *mimi-
tor* beside Skr. *mâ* (to measure), *mimatê* (imitantur), Gr. μέ-
τρον, μι-μέ-ομαι, μί-μη-σις, μῖ-μο-ς.

Corssen connects *imitor* and *imago* with a Latin root *ic* =
I. E. *ak*, whence G. *ah-men*, L. *aequus*, and considers their
original forms to have been *icmitor*, *icmago*.

§. 85. The Insertion of a Consonant.

P is inserted between *m* and a following dental, as in *hiemps*,
emptus, *sumpsi*, *sumptus*, *contempsi*, *contemptus*, &c. *S* is inserted in *mon-s-trum* (from same root as *maneo*, *moneo*, *mens*,
&c., and *-trum*), *lu-s-trum* (from same root as *luo*, *di-luv-ium*,
lav-o, &c., and *-trum*), *abstineo*, *ostendo* for *obstendo*, *sustineo*
for *substineo*.

§. 86. Final Consonants.

The combinations *rs*, *ls*, *ns*, are in general never allowed
to end a word, except when they represent *rts*, *lts*, *nts* ; thus
we have *ferens*, *amans*, &c., for *ferents*, *amants*, &c., *puls* for
pults, &c., but *puer* for *puer(u)s*, *vir* for *vir(u)s*, *quatuor* for
quatuor(e)s, *vigil* for *vigil(i)s*, *novōs* (acc. pl.) for *novons* and
similar accusatives, *sāl* for *sāls*. We have, however, *fers* for
feris.

---

* This is Curtius' explanation, who translates *dhâ* by G. *thun*, E. *do* ;
Kuhn explains *sradhâ* to mean "selbstsetzung" from *dhâ* (to place)
= Gr. θε in τίθημι.

Double consonants are never allowed to end a word: thus we have *os* (*oss-is*) for *oss-* = *ost-*; *fel* (*fell-is*) for *fell-* = *felt-*; *novŏs* for *novoss* = *novons*, *novas* for *novass* = *novans*, &c., while in Old Oscan the acc. pl. still ends in *-ss*, as *viass* = L. *vias*, &c.; *damnas* for *damnass* = *damnat(u)s*, compare O. U. *pihaz*, N. U. *pihos* = L. *piatus*, O. U. *taçez*, N. U. *taçes* = L. *tacetus*, O. O. *hŭrz* = L. *hortus*, &c.

Two mutes are not allowed to end a word: thus we have *lac* for *lact* (*lact-is*).

Final *t* was frequently lost: thus we find in Old Latin *dede* (dedit), *dedro* (dederunt), &c.; in Classical Latin the double form of the 3 pl. perf. *fecere* and *fecerunt*, &c.; in late Latin such forms as *vixse* (vixit), *quiesce* (quiescit), *fecerun* (fecerunt), &c. In Umbrian such forms are common: thus we find *habe* (habet), *façia* (faciat), *fuia* (fuat), *portaia* (portet), *benus* (venerit), *convortus* beside *convortust* (converterit), *benuso* (venerunt), &c. In Oscan *t* is retained, as in *fust* (fuerit), *fefacust* (O. L. faxit), *hipust* (O. L. habessit), &c.

Final *d* was also frequently lost: thus in abl. sing. we find *patre* (t. Scip. Barb.) beside *Gnaivod* and in Classical Latin this abl. -*d* was universally lost, while it was retained in Oscan, as in *suvad* (suā), *ehtrad* (extra), *toutad* (civitate), *castrid* (castro), &c. Similarly *d* was lost in the imperatives *esto*, *agito*, &c., beside Osc. *estud*, *actud*, &c.

In Old Latin *s* was frequently lost after a vowel, as in *Tetio*, *Albanio*, &c., for *Tetios*, *Albanios*, &c.; *Corneli* for *Cornelis*, and this again for *Cornelios*, &c.; in Classical Latin we also find *mage* beside *magis*, *pote* beside *potis*, *laudare* beside *laudaris*, &c. Final *s* was also lost in the nom. pl. of the *o-* stems, and in the gen. sing. of the *a-* stems, as in *hi* = O. L. *heis*, *magistri* = O. L. *magistreis*, *familiae* = *familias*, &c. In Oscan and Umbrian *s* (N. U. *r*) is retained in these cases, as in O. U. *urtas* (ortae), *tutas* (totae), N. U. *screihtor* (scripti), *totcor* (tutici), *totar* (totae), *motar* (multae, poenae), O. O. *Núvlanús* (Nolani), N. O. *pas* (quae), *scriftas* (scriptae), &c.

Final *n* was sometimes omitted as in *ceteroqui, alioqui* for *ceteroquin, alioquin,* and in nominatives in *-o* as *virgo, caligo,* &c.

Final *m* in Old Latin was frequently omitted as in the conjunctive forms *attinge, dice,* &c., for *attingam, dicam,* &c.; also in the following examples from the Epitaphs of the Scipios *Taurasia* (acc. sing.), *Samnio* (acc. sing.), *oino* (unum), *duonoro* (bonorum), *urbe* (urbem), &c.; in Classical Latin *m* before a vowel in verse was elided.

CHAPTER VII.

Roots and Stems.

§. 87. The root* of a word is that portion of it that remains when everything *formative* and *accidental* has been removed from it. Thus the root of L. *pater*, Gr. πατήρ, Skr. *pitá* (nom. sing.) is *pa* = Skr. *pâ* (to support), L. *-ter*, Gr. -τηρ, Skr. *-tar* being the same suffix that appears in L. *mater*, &c.; the root of *elementum* is *el*, *e* being a connecting vowel and *-mentu-m* the same suffix that appears in *rudi-mentu-m*; the root of ἐτίθετο is θε, ἐ being the augment signifying past time, τι the reduplication signifying duration, and το the sign of the 3rd pers. sing.; similarly the root of ἐγίγνετο for ἐγιγενετο is γεν; the root of ζεύγνυμι is ζυγ for νυ and μι are *formative* elements, the first signifying present time, and the second the first pers. sing., while ευ is the *guṇa* of υ, and ε is consequently merely an accidental element;† similarly the root of λέλοιπα is λιπ. In the above remarks I have used the word root in its ordinary signification as representing that portion of the

---

* Max Müller (Lectures, &c., II., p. 81) calls "root or radical whatever, in the words of any language or family of languages, cannot be reduced to a simpler or a more original form." The Indian Grammarians called a root *dhátu* from *dhá* (to nourish); *dhátu* means *any primary or elementary substance*, and consequently shows that these grammarians looked upon roots as the *primary elements, the constituent parts* of words. We generally translate roots by the infinitive, as this gives the most abstract idea of the word. The Indian Grammarians, however, represent them by abstract substantives in the Locative, as *gam* (to go) by *gatáu* (in going); Bopp's Skr. Gram., p. 69.

† Consult Curtius, Grundzüge, &c., p. 49 seq., and Bopp's Comparative Grammar, vol. I., p. 197.

word which contains the fundamental idea; but properly speaking, every Indo-European word consists of *two* or *more* roots: thus Skr. *asmi* (I am) = Gr. εἰμί consists of the two roots *as* (to be) and *mi* = *ma* (I); Skr. *bharâmi* (I bear) = Gr. φέρω, consists of the three roots *bhar* (to bear), *as* (to be)* and *mi* (I); Skr. *bharati* (he bears) = Gr. φέρει for φερετι consists of the three roots *bhar*, *a* (a demonstrative root) and *ti* (the pronoun of 3rd pers. sing.); Gr. ὄψ = L. *vox* = I. E. *vaks* when Skr. *vâk* (nom. sing.) comes from the two roots *vak* (to speak) = Skr. *vach* and *sa* (a demonstrative root), &c. In the earliest period of the I. E. language, long before any separation of the dialects occurred, roots existed as *independent* words, exactly as in Chinese at the present day; thus the words, just discussed, probably existed then as *as ma, bhar as ma, bhar a ta, vak sa*. There never was a period, however, in the history of Sanskrit, Greek, Latin, or any other I. E. language, after their separation from the parent stock and from each other, when roots existed as actual words. No exception to this statement is formed by such imperatives as *dic, fac*, &c., for these are merely shortened forms of *dice, face*, &c., nor by such vocatives as *vâk* from St. *vâk* (voice) from R. *vak*, for a vocative is not properly a word, but rather an interjection, nor by words which in the process of time appear only as roots on account of the loss of their terminations.

§. 88. All Indo-European roots are monosyllabic, and this is the only law to which they are subject. We consequently find as roots the following combinations of vowels and consonants:—

I. (Spiritus lenis +) Vowel: I. E. *i* (to go) = Skr., Z., Gr., L., Goth., Lith., Ch. Sl. *i* (to go), as Skr. *êmi* (I go) = Gr. εἶμι = Lith. *eimì*, L. *eo*, Skr. *imas* (we go) = Gr. ἴμεν, L. *īmus* (the ī of which seems to point to a root ī); Skr. *u* (to sound)

---

* I assume here that *bharâmi* is for *bhar-as-mi* (to bear am I, i. e. I bear): the second syllable may, however, be the only demonstrative root *a* lengthened to *â*.

is given by the grammarians ; L. *u* is found in *ind-u-ere*, *ex-u-ere*.

II. Cons.+vowel : I. E. *da* (to give), Skr., Z. *dâ* (to give), Skr. *dadâmi* = Gr. δίδωμι, Skr. *dâtâ* (nom. sing. from St. *dâtar*) = Z. *dâta* (from St. *dâtur*) = Gr. δοτήρ or δωτήρ = L. *dâtor*, L. *dăre*, *dŏnum*, &c.; I. E. *pa* (to guard), Skr. *pâ* (id.), *pati-s* (nom. sing., a master), *patnî* (a mistress), Gr. πόσις, δεσ-πό-της, πότνια, δέσποινα, L. *com-po-(t)s*, *po-t-is*, &c.; I. E. *dha* (to place), Skr. *dhâ* (id.), Z. *dâ* (id.), Gr. θέ-μα, τί-θη-μι = Skr. *dadhâmi*, &c.; I. E. *ki* (to lie), Skr. *s'î* (id.), *s'êtê* = Gr. κεῖται, L. *civis* (= Osc. *cevs*), *quiesco*, &c.

III. Vowel + cons.: I. E. *ak* (to be sharp, quick), Skr. *as'-ri* (point of a sword), *âs'-us* = Gr. ὠκύς, *as'-vas* = L. *eq-uus*, Gr. ἄκ-ρος, ἄκ-ων, L. *ac-er*, *ac-u-o*, *âc-er*, *ōc-ior*; I. E. *ap* (to obtain), Skr. *âp* (id.), L. *ad-ip-iscor*, *aptus* = Skr. *âptas* ; I. E. *ad* (to eat), Skr. *ad* (id.), Gr. ἔδ-ω, L. *ed-o*; I. E. *as* (to be), Skr. *asmi* = Gr. εἰμί (Æol. ἔμμι) = L. *(e)sum*, &c.

IV. Cons. + vowel + cons. : I. E. *bhugh* (to fly, bend), Skr. *bhug'* (to bend), *bhôga* (a snake), Gr. φεύγω, φυγή, φύζα = φυδya for φυγya, L. *fugio*, &c.; I. E. *lip* (to smear), Skr. *lip* (id.), Gr. λίπ-α (fat), ἀ-λείφ-ω, &c.; I. E. *pak* (to bind), Skr. and Z. *pas'* (id.), Gr. πάγ-ος, πάσσαλος = πακyαλος, L. *pax*, *pig-nus*, *compesco* = *com-pec-sco*, &c.; I. E. *bhudh* (to know), Skr. *budh* (id.), Z. *bud* (id.), Gr. πυνθ-άνομαι, &c.

V. Cons. + cons. + vowel : I. E. *kru* (to hear), Skr. *s'ru* (id.), Gr. κλύ-ω, L. *clu-o*, *cli-ens;* I. E. *plu* (to swim), Skr. *plu* (id.), Gr. πλέ-ω, πλεύ-σομαι, πλό-ο-ς, L. *plu-it*, &c.; I. E. *pri* (to love), Skr. *prî* (id.), Z. *frî* (id.), Gr. πρᾶος for πραy-ο-ς, πραΰς for πραy-υ-ς ; I. E. *sta* (to stand), Skr. *sthâ* (id.), Z. *s'tâ* (id.), Gr. στά-σις, L. *stă-tus ;* I. E. *gva* (to go), Skr. *g'i-gâ-mi* (I go), Gr. βαίνω for βα-νyω, L. *ar-bi-ter*.

VI. Vowel + cons. + cons. : Skr. *ard* (to kill), Gr. ἄρδ-ις (point of an arrow) ; I. E. *ard* (to water) ; Skr. *ârd-ra* (wet), Gr. ἄρδ-ω (*I* water); I. E. *argh*, Skr. *arh* (to be worthy), Z. *areg'* (id.), Gr. ἄρχ-ω, ὄρχ-αμος ; I. E. *arg* (to shine), Skr. *arg'-una* (white), Gr. ἀργ-ής (white), ἄργ-υρος, ἄργ-ιλος, L.

argentum, arg-u-o (I make clear); I. E. *ark* (to shine), Skr. *ark'* (id.), *arka* (the sun), Ir. *earc* (id.); I. E. *ardh* (to grow), Skr. *ardh* (id.), Gr. ἀλδ-αίνω, Ir. *alt* (nursing), according to Bopp.

VII. Cons. + cons. + vowel + cons.: I. E. *stigh* (to ascend), Skr. *stigh* (id.), Gr. στείχ-ω, στοῖ-χος, στίχος, Goth. *steiga* (I go up), O. H. G. *stega* (semita), Ch. Sl. *stĭza* (id.); I. E. *stag* (to cover), Skr. *sthag* (id.), Gr. στέγ-ω, στέγ-η, τέγ-η, I. *i-steg-a* (a deck) for *in-steg-a, teg-o*, O. N. *thek* (a roof), O. H. G. *dak-ju* (I cover); I. E. *bhrag* (to shine), Skr. *bhrâg'* (id.), Gr. φλέγ-ω, φλόξ, L. *fulg-eo, flag-ro, flam-ma*; I. E. *stan* (to sound), Skr. *stan* (id.), Gr. στένω, L. *ton-o, ton-itru*, O. N. *styn-ja* (I groan), O. H. G. *stun-ōd* (a sigh), E. *stun*.

VIII. Cons. + vowel + cons. + cons.: I. E. *varg*, Skr. *varg'* (to exclude), Gr. εἴργ-νυ-μι, εἴργ-ω from R. Ϝεργ, L. *urg-eo*, Goth. *vrik-a* (I pursue); I. E. *marg*, Skr. *marg'* (to wipe, rub), Gr. ἀμέλγ-ω (I milk), ὀμόργ-νυ-μι (I wipe), L. *mulg-eo*, O. H. G. *milch-u*. Benfey connects with this root Gr. γλάγος (for μλαγος), γάλα, L. *mulier, margo, lac* (for *mlac*); I. E. *tars* (to dry), Skr. *tarsh* (to be thirsty), Z. *tarsh-na* (thirst), Gr τέρσ-ομαι, L. *torr-eo, tŏs-tus, terr-a*, Goth. *thaurs-ja* (I thirst).

IX. Cons. + cons. + vowel + cons. + cons.: I. E. *skand* (to move quickly?), Skr. *skand* (to ascend), Gr. σκάνδ-αλον, L. *scand-o, de-scend-o*, Lith. *skènd-u* (I sink); I. E. *stambh*, Skr *stambh* (to prop up), Gr. στέμφ-υλον (pressed olives), ἀ-στεμφ-ής (firm), O. H. G. *stamphōn* (to stamp), A. S. *stemn* (mandatum); I. E. *sparg* (to move quickly), Skr. *sparh* (to desire), Z. *s'parez* (to strive), Gr. σπέρχ-ομαι (I hasten), σπερχ-νός (hasty), σπέργ-δην (ἐρρωμένως, Hesych.); I. E. *spardh*, Skr. *spardh* (to contend with), Goth. *spaurds* (στάδιον), O. H. G. *spurt*, A. S. *spyrd*, E. *spurt*.

§. 89. It is very doubtful whether any roots began or ended with three consonants in Indo-European. When such roots appear in any of the Indo-European languages, either one of the consonants is not original, and merely a late addition to the root, or else the phenomenon arises from transposition. In the following cases the conjunction of the three initial consonants may be original: Gr. στράγξ (a drop), στραγγ-εύω (I twist), στρογγ-ύλος, στραγγ-α-λίζω (I strangle), L. *string-o*, *strang-ulo*, O. H. G. *strangi* (strong), from a root *strang* or *strag*, signifying "to penetrate, to press," yet the original form of this root may have been *starg*, whence Gr. ταργάναι (πλοκαί, Hesych.), τεταργανωμέναι (ἐμπεπλεγμέναι, Hesych.), σαργάνη (a basket), with the loss of τ as in Ir. *sreang-aim* (stringo), *sreang* (a string); L. *scrof-a* (a sow), *scribo*, *scrob-s*, Gr. γρομφ-άς (an old sow), γράφω may point to an I. E. root *skrabh* ; L. *scruta* (trash), whence *scrutor* beside Gr. γρύτη (trash) ; Gr. σκνιπ-ός (stingy) beside γνίφων (id.), &c.

§. 90. Roots of the form cons. + *a* + cons. or *a* + cons. are frequently found in the form [cons. + cons. + *a*] or [cons. + *a*] : I. E. *mar* (to die) = *mra* (id.), Skr. *mryati* (he dies), *marta-s* (nom. sing. dead), Gr. βρoτός for μρο-τος, L. *morior*; I. E. *dhar* (to bear) = *dhra*, Skr. *dhar* (id.), Gr. θρᾶ-νος (a seat), θρό-νος, θρῆ-νυς (a stool), L. *frē-tus*, *frē-num*, *fir-mus*; I. E. *dhar* (to sound) = *dhra*, Skr. *dhárá* (vox), Gr. θρέ-ομαι, θρύ-ος, θρῆ-νος, θόρ-υ-βος, Goth. *drunjus* (a noise), E. *drone* ; I. E. *man* (to think) = *mna*, Skr. *man* (id.), Gr. μέ-μον-α, μέν-ος, μαν-ία, μνά-ο-μαι, μνή-μη, L. *me-min-i*, *mon-eo* ; I. E. *gan* (to know) = *gna*, Skr. *gñá* (to know), Gr. γνω-τός, L. *gno-sco*, Goth. *kann* (I know) ; Gr. θαν beside θνη, ἔ-θαν-ον, θάν-ατος, θνη-τός, θνή-σκω, perhaps connected with Skr. *dhmá* (to blow), and consequently θαν would have meant originally "to blow," hence "to breathe," and then "to expire," &c.

§. 91. According to the Indian Grammarians no Sanskrit verbal root ended in *á*, and they write such roots either with *á*, or with the addition of a suffix, such as *n*, *y* (*i*), *v* (*u*); consequently we find in place of *da* (to give), *s'a* (to sharpen), *g'a* (to be born), *hra* (to call), &c., the assumed forms *dá*, *s'ó* (for *sau*), *g'an*, *hvé* (for *hvai*), &c. The only roots that they write with *á* are pronominal roots, such as *ta*, *sa*, &c. We see, however, at once that this is merely an arbitrary custom, for we find numerous verbal roots in Sanscrit ending in *á* : *khyá* (to speak) is the original root, and not *khyâ*, as we see from *akhyăt; gă* (to go) is found in *gă-tas* (nom. sing. part. praet. pass.), *gă-hi* (2 sing. imperat.), *ga-kkhati* (he goes), Gr. βέ-βα-μεν; *dă* (to give), *dadmas* (we give) for *dadamas*, Gr. δί-δο-μεν, L. *dă-mus*; *dha* (to place), *dadhmas* (we place) for *dadhamas*, Gr. τί-θε-μεν, θέ-σις, θε-τός = Ved. *dhi-tas* = Skr. *hitas*; *sthă* (to stand), *ti-shtha-ti* (he stands), *sthi-tas* = Gr. στă-τός, L. *stă-tus*; *ma* (to measure), *mi-ti* (measuring), *mi-ta* (measured), Gr. μέ-τρον; *pă* (to drink), *pibăti* (he drinks), Gr. πό-σις; *pă* (to protect), *pătis* (a master) = Gr. πό-σις, δεσ-πό-της, Skr. *pi-tar*, Gr. πă-τήρ; *mă* (to think), *mati* (mind), *mătas* (nom. sing. perf. pass. part.) = μᾰτος (in αὐτό-μᾰτος), Gr. μέ-μα-μεν, μα-ίομαι (I seek), μά-την, μά-ταιος (not real, only imagined, according to Benfey); *ta* (to stretch), *tătas* (nom. sing. pass. part.) = Gr. τᾰτός, τέ-τᾰ-μαι; *ha* (to kill), *hăti* (a striking), *hatas* (nom sing. perf. pass. part.) = Gr. φατός (in Ἀρείφατος, μυλήφα-τος), πέ-φᾰ-μαι, &c. These roots are written by the Sanskrit grammarians under the forms *khyâ, gâ, dâ, dhâ, sthâ, mâ, pâ, pâ, man, tan, han*; but the grammatical forms above adduced prove that they also ended with *ă* in Sanskrit. In Greek and Latin we frequently find roots ending with *ă*, which corresponds to Sanskrit roots ending with *â* or *an*; thus we find Gr. γέ-γᾰ-μεν from R. γα beside Skr. *g'an* (to produce, to grow); Gr. φᾰ-λός (bright), φά-τις from R. φα beside Skr. *bhâ* (to shine); L. *rătus* from R. *ra* beside Skr. *râ* (to give), compare Ved. *râtam astu* with L. *ratum esto* and *reor*, &c.

§. 92. Neither in Sanskrit nor in Greek do any roots occur of the form, aspirated mute + vowel + aspirated mute; except a few dialectic forms in the former language, and the forms* ἐ-θάφ-θην, τε-θάφ-θαι, τε-θάφ-θω, τε-θάφ-αται, τε-

---

* Bopp (Vergleichende Grammatik., vol. i., p. 182, §. 104*) accounts for these forms (except τεθάφαται, which he confesses his inability to explain), partly from the inclination shown by the Greeks for the combination φθ, and partly from the fact that φ in these cases was felt to belong to the root, and was therefore allowed to show itself again contrary to the usual custom.

θράφ-θαι, ἐ-θρέφ-θην, in the latter. In Indo-European, however, roots of this form were common, as is shown by the cognate languages; consult §. 31. But Sanskrit and Greek were opposed to such a combination, and always omitted the aspiration of one aspirated mute. This disinclination of Sanskrit and Greek to the proximity of two aspirates, is shown by the fact that when aspirates occur in two groups of consonants belonging to the same roots, and merely separated by a vowel, one of these aspirates, generally the first, loses its aspiration.* Thus in Sanskrit and Greek aspirates are reduplicated generally by the corresponding unaspirated consonants, but this law did not hold in Indo-European, as we see from the Latin *fefelli*, and the Oscan *fufans, fefacust*, &c., in which, though *f* be not a true aspirate, it represents an original Indo-European aspirate. Originally the whole root was repeated in reduplicated syllables, as we see in Sanskrit intensive forms,† such as *daridrâ*‡ (to be poor) from *drâ* (to run) beside Gr. δι-δρά-σκω, ἔδραν, *daridrs'* or *daridrs'* or *dardrs* from *dars'* (to see) = Gr. δερκ, *k'rikar*, or *k'arikar*, or *k'arkar*, from *kar* (to make), &c., and in such Greek forms as παμ-φαίνω for φαν-φαν-yω, μέρ-μηρ-α (care) and μέρ-μερ-ος (care-laden) from R. μερ = Skr. *smar* (to remember), μαρ-μαίρ-ω (I shine) from R. μαρ whence μάρ-μαρ-ος (stone, marble, lit. "what glistens"); Κίρ-κυρ-α (lit. Round town) from same root as κίρ-κ-ος (a ring), κύ-κλ-ος, L. *circus*, &c.

---

* This does not happen when the aspirates belong to different roots or different suffixes, or when one belongs to a root and another to a suffix, or when more than one vowel intervenes between the groups of consonants, except in a few cases, such as ἐκε-χειρία from ἔχω and χείρ τηλεθάω from R. θαλ for θαλθα-ω, an irregular reduplicated form like φέρ-β-ω from R. φερ = Skr. *bhar* and φί-β-ομαι for φι-βι-ομαι from R. φι = *bhi* (to fear), &c.

† Consult Bopp's Sanskrit Grammar, p. 343 seq., and Grassmann in K. Z., vol. xii., p. 111.

‡ Lottner considers *daridrâ* to be a reduplicated form of I. E. *dar* (to tear).

Although in Greek we generally find no combinations such as aspirated mute + vowel + aspirated mute, we frequently find such as spiritus asper + vowel + aspirated mute or ῥ + vowel + aspirated mute; thus we find ἀφ-ή (a fastening, lightning) from ἅπ-τω; ὑφ-ή (a web) from R. ὑφ = I. E. vabh whence Skr. *ûrna-vâ-bhas* (nom. sing. a spider, lit. a weaver of wool); ἠθ-μός* (a strainer) from ἤθω = σήθω (I sift); ἐφ·θός from ἕψω beside ὄψον, ὀπ-τός, the initial aspirate perhaps compensating for π (as in ἵπταμαι = πίπταμαι from I. E. *pat*), if the root be πεπ, whence πεπ-τός, πέπ-ων, &c.; ὕθ-λος (idle talk), from R. ὑδ, whence ὕδωρ, or from same root as Skr. *vad* (to speak); ῥοφ-έω (I swallow), ῥυφ-άνω (id.) beside L. *sorbeo*, Lith. *srebiù* (I swallow); ῥιφ-ή (a throwing) beside ῥίπ-τω, &c. In these cases the spiritus asper either is inorganic, and did not exist in Indo-European, or represents a lost consonant, generally *s*, and the same may be said of the aspiration of ῥ; in no case does either aspiration seem to represent an original aspirated mute.

§. 93. In Sanskrit we find several combinations of more than one syllable classified as roots, but such forms are not *true* roots. They arise either from the reduplication of true roots, as *g'âgar* (to wake) from I. E. *gar* whence Gr. ἐγείρω† for γεγείρω, *k'a-kâs* (to shine) from *kâs* (id.), &c.; or from the union of prepositions with true roots, as *avadhîr* (to despise) from *ava* (de, ab) and *dhîr*, which Bopp connects with *dhî* (the mind), *sangrâm* (to fight) from *sam* (Gr. σύν, L. *cum*) and *kram* (to go), unless it be a denominative formed from *sangrâma* (a fight), &c.; or from nouns, as *kumâr* (to play) from *kumâra* (a boy), &c.

§. 94. Roots in general may be divided into the two great

* This word is generally written ἠθμός, the spiritus asper becoming the lenis on account of the following θ as in ἔχω. On Sigeian Inscription it is written ἠθμός.

† Some consider initial ε here to be merely *prosthetic*, while Pott derives it from ἐκ. The view taken above is, however, much more plausible.

classes, *verbal* (called also *qualitative* or *predicative*), and *pronominal* (called also *demonstrative*). The first class is composed of verbs and nouns, of which the former stand in a closer connexion with the root than the latter. *Originally* there was no difference between verb and noun, the root *da*, for example, signifying the *giver*, the *thing given*, the *act of giving*, &c. The second class consists of all the pronouns, most prepositions, conjunctions, and particles, which are generally derived from pronominal roots, and perhaps a few other words. In this class the root and the stem are identical, and the roots express some relation to the speaker, while those of the first class express a *state* or *action*.

§. 95. The chief pronominal roots in Indo-European were*
kva (who) whence Skr. *ku-tas* (whence), *ka-s* (who), *ka-d* (what) *ki-m* (what), Gr. τίς, πότερος, Ion. κότερος, πῶς, Ion. κῶς, τέ, κα-ί (an old locative), κέν (κέ, Dor. κάν) = Skr. *kam*, L. *quis, quae, quid*, &c.; *ga* or *gha* (perhaps derived from *kva* or *ka*), whence Skr. *ha* = Ved. *gha* or *ghá* (indeed), Gr. οὐ-χί, γέ; *ya* (who) whence Skr. *ya-s, yá, ya-d* = Gr. ὅς, ἥ, ὅ, L. *jam*; *i* (he, she, it) when Skr. *i-yam, id-am, i-ha* (here) for *idha*, Gr. ἵ, -ί (in οὑτοσί, &c.), L. *is, ea, id, i-terum, i-pse*, &c.; *ta* (this) Skr. *tam, tâm, tad* = Gr. τόν, τήν, τό, Gr. οὗ-τος, αὐ-τός, L. *is-te, is-ta, is-tud, tum, tam, ipse* (for *i-p-te*), *i-ta, i-tem*, &c.; *da* (perhaps derived from *ta*), Skr. *ka-dâ* (when), Gr. πο-δα-πός, οὑτι-δα-νός, ὅ-δε, δόμον-δε (homewards), L. *quam-do, qui-dam, in-de, un-de, qui-dem*, &c.; *dha* (closely connected with *da*), Skr. *a-dhas* (below), *adhara-s* (= L. *inferu-s*), *i-ha* (here) for *i-dha*, Gr. ἔν-θα, πό-θι, αὖ-θις (Ion. αὖ-τις), ἔν-θεν, L. *u-bi* and *i-bi*, according to Leo Meyer for *cu-dhi* and *i-dhi*; *sa* (he), Skr. *sa, sá* = Gr. ὁ, ἡ, Skr. *sa-krt* (once), Gr. ἅ-παξ, ἁ-πλοῦς, O. L. *sum, sam, sos, sas* (acc. sing. and pl., masc. and fem.), &c.; *na, an, ana*, Skr. *nas* (us), *na* (not, lest; like, Vedic), *ana-yâ* (instr. sing., through her), *an-tara-s* (alius), *an-ya-s* (alius), Gr. νώ, νίν, νή, νῦν, ναί, ἄν, ἐν, ἀνά, L. *nos, ne, num*,

---

* Leo Meyer, Vergleichende Grammatik, &c., vol. i., p. 323, seq.

nam,* *in*, &c.; *pa*, Skr. *a-pa* (away), *pa-rá* (away), Gr. ἀ-πό, πε-ρί, πα-ρά, π-ρό, L. *ab, p-ro, pe-r,*† &c.; *bha* (which is, perhaps, connected with *pa;* there does not appear to be any trace of a stem *ba*), Skr. *-bhis* (term of instr. pl.), *-bhyas* (term. of dat. and abl. pl.), *-bhyâm* (term. of instr., dat. and abl. dual), Gr. ἄμ-φω = Skr. *u-bha* (both) = L. *ambo*, βίη-φι, ναῦ-φιν, L. *ti-bi, mi-hi, no-bis*, &c.; *va*,‡ Skr. *va-yam* (we), which Bopp considers to be a weakened form of *ma-yam*, but E. *we*, Goth. *veis*, G. *wir*, establish the originality of the initial *v*, Skr. *vas* (ye, acc. pl.) and *vâm* (ye two, acc. dual), Gr. αὖ, αὐ-τός, οὖν (?), αὐ-τάρ, L. *ne-ve, vos, tu* = *t-va* (Skr. *tvam*, thou), &c.; *ma*, Skr. *mâm* and *mâ* (me, acc. sing.), *ma-yâ* (instr. sing.), Gr. μί, μά, μή (= Skr. *mâ*, not), μίν, L. *me, ego-me-t*, &c.

§. 96. No verbal root can by itself form a word. It becomes a word by the addition of a pronominal root; thus from the Latin verbal roots *reg* (to rule), *luc* (to shine), we form the *words rex* (*reg-s*) and *lux* (*luc + s*) by the addition of the pronominal root *sa*.

§. 97. Verbal and pronominal roots frequently agree in form : thus *i* is a verbal root meaning ' *to go*,' and a pronominal root meaning '*he*'; similarly *ta* (to stretch) and *ta* (this), *ka* (to be sharp) and *ka* (who), unless *kva* be the original form of this pronominal root, as is probable. In consequence of this agreement, some writers have derived the pronominal from the verbal roots: thus Schleicher (Compendium, §. 265, p. 642, 2nd Ed.), writes: " I take *ma* (I) to be identical with the verbal root *ma* (to measure, think); this root also signifies '*homo*' (compare Skr. *ma-nu-*, Goth. *ma-n-*), who was described as

---

* *Nam* is derived by some writers from I. E. *nâman* (a name).

† L. *per, pro*, Gr. παρά, &c., may, however, be all connected with I. E. root *par* (to penetrate, cross, &c.).

‡ *Va* originally meant "*is, ea, id.*" We have Old Persian *ava* (iste) from same root. Initial *t* was probably lost before Skr. *vas* and *vâm;* compare Skr. *tvam* (thou) = *t + va + m* for *ta + va + m*.

'*the thinker;*' what could '*I*' have been originally save '*man*'? The abstract conception of the '*I*' cannot certainly be attributed to the oldest stage of the Indo-European (ursprache)." Bopp adduces as an argument against the deduction of pronominal roots from verbal, his supposition, that no verbal root ends in *ă*, whilst pronominal roots for the most part end in this vowel. We have, however, already seen that many verbal roots do actually end in *ă*, so that this argument of Bopp is valueless. The Indian grammarians derive all words, without exception, from verbal roots, either existing or invented by them for this purpose; thus, *ta* (this, he) they derive from *tan* (to stretch), *ya* (who) from *yag* (to worship), *yadi* (when) from *yat* (to make an effort), &c. Such derivations are of course preposterous; but these grammarians are not the only persons who offend in this way.

The connexion between verbal and pronominal roots is is still unknown, and likely to remain so, for we have no materials on which to base our reasonings. A few sentences of Indo-European, as it was spoken when the Indo-Europeans first began to exist as a distinct race, would probably clear up the difficulty.

Even if verbal and pronominal roots were originally identical, they must have been distinguished from each other in very early times, in fact, before the origin of any grammatical forms whatsoever, for these forms presuppose the distinction. "First," writes Curtius (zur Chronologie der Indogermanischen Sprachforschung, p. 205), "through this duality light and shade come into language, first through this it becomes possible to arrange words beside each other so as to express a meaning, the necessary condition of all further development."

§. 98. Verbal roots are twofold, *primary* and *secondary*. The primary consists (1) of a single short vowel, as *ĭ* (to go); or (2) of a consonant + a short vowel, as *dă* (to give), *dhă* (to place), *pă* (to drink), *kĭ* (to lie); or (3) of a short vowel + a consonant, as ăd (to eat), ăk (to be sharp), ăs (to be), ĭdh (to burn); or (4) of a consonant + a short vowel + a consonant, as dăr (to tear), bhăr (to bear), dĭv (to shine), păt (to fall, fly); or (5) of two consonants + a short vowel, as stă (to stand).

The last division (5) of these roots is very small, and perhaps belongs to the *secondary* class.

Secondary roots are formed from *primary* by the addition of a new sound, or sounds, called by Curtius the *root determinative*. The object of this addition is to express a modification of the meaning of the primary root. Thus from I. E. *yu* (to bind, to mix dough, &c.), came I. E. *yug* (to unite *intentionally*, to yoke horses), and I. E. *yudh* (to unite for the purpose of fighting); from I. E. *gan* (to produce), came *gnâ* (for *ganâ* or *gna* + *a*) to express the idea of "*knowing how to produce*;" similarly from I. E. *man* (to think), came *mnâ* (to remember); &c.

§. 99. A complete list of the primary and secondary roots of Indo-European does not fall within the scope of the present work. It will be sufficient here to give a few examples of the chief *root-determinatives*.

K (root-determinative). Primary root, I. E. *tar* or *tra* (to move), whence Skr. *tarala* (tremulous), *tara* (a passage), *-tara* (term. of comparative) = Gr. -τερο = L. *-ter* (in *dex-ter*), *-tra* (in *con-tra*), *ter-minus* ; secondary root, Skr. *tark* (to suppose, lit., to turn in one's mind), *tarku* (a spindle), Gr. ἀ-τρεκ-ής, ἄ-τρακ-τος (a spindle), L. *torqu-eo*, *torc-ular*, *torqu-es*. Pr. root, I. E. *pat* whence Skr. *pat* (to fall, fly), *pat-ra* (a wing), Gr. κατα-πτή-την, πίπτω for πι-πετ-ω, πέτ-ομαι, πτε-ρόν,, πτῶ-σις, L. *pet-o*, *penna* = O. L. *pesna* for *pet-na* ; sec. root, Gr. πτᾰκ, ἔ-πτακ-ον, πτήσσω for πτηκ-γω, πτώξ, πτώσσω for πτωκ--γω. Pr. root, I. E. *gva* (to go), whence Skr. *gâ* or *ga* (to go), Gr. βα ; sec. root βακ, Gr. βάκ-τρον, L. *bac-ulum*. Pr. root, Gr. ὀλ (to destroy), ὄλ-λυμι for ὀλ-νυ-μι ; sec. root, ὀλεκ, ὀλέκ-οντο. Pr. root, I. E. *var* (? to draw) whence Skr. *var* (to choose), L. *vel-lo* for *vel-yo* ; sec. root, Gr. Fελκ, εἷλκον =

εϝελκον. In English we similarly find roots lengthened by *k*, as *hark, talk, pluck*, beside *hear, tell, pull*.

G (root-det.). Pr. root, *yu* (to bind; sec. root, Skr. *yug-a* (a yoke, pair), Gr. ζυγ-όν, L. *jug-um*.

Kh for *sk* (root-det.) = Skr. *k'h* = Gr. χ. Pr. root, *gva* (to go) = Skr. *ga;* sec. root, Skr. *gak'h-ati* (he goes) = Gr. βάσκ-ει. Pr. root, *ar* (to move); sec. root, Gr. ἔρχ-ομαι = ἐρσκ-ομαι probably. Σκ here is perhaps the remains of a root = I. E. *sak* to (follow) whence L. *sequ-or*, &c.

T (root-det.). Pr. root, Skr. *dyu* = *div* (to shine); sec. root, Skr. *dyut* (id.). Pr. root, I. E. *av* (to blow), whence Gr. αὔ-ω, ἄ-ημι ; sec. root, Skr. *ât-man* (breath), Gr. ἀϋτ-μήν, ἀτ-μός, ἄετ-μον (πνεῦμα, Hesych). From the sec. root, Skr. *tup* (to strike) = Gr. τυπ comes another sec. root, Gr. τύπ-τ-ω. Similarly from Gr. θαπ or ταφ, comes a sec. root, θάπ-τ-ω.* It is doubtful whether ταφ or θαπ be a primary or a secondary root; if it be = Skr. *tap* (to burn) beside Gr. τέφ-ρα, L. *tep-eo*, A. S. *thef-ian* (aestuare), it is a primary root and originally meant "*to burn*" (sc. the dead). On the other hand, if it be formed from *dha* (to place) = Skr. *dhâ*, by the root-determinative *p*, it is a secondary root, θαπ (ταφ) : *dhap* : : θυπ (τυφ) : Skr. *dhûp* (to fumigate).

D (root-det.). Pr. root, I. E. *ska* (to cleave) whence Gr. R. κε (= σκε), κε-ίω, κε-άζω, καιάδας, Skr. *k'hâ, k'hyâmi* (abscindo), L. *de-sci-sco, sci-o;* sec. root, Skr. *skhad* (to cut), Gr. σκίδ-αννυμι, L. *scindo*. Pr. root, I. E. *ma* (to measure), whence Gr. μέ-τρον, &c.; sec. root, Gr. μέδ-ιμνος, μέδ-οντες, L. *modius, mod-eror, mod-us*. Pr. root, I. E. *ru* (to sound) : sec. root, Skr. *rud* (to weep), L. *rud-o*.

Dh (root-det.). Pr. root, I. E. *yu* (to join); sec. root, Skr. *yudh* (to fight, manus conserere), Z. *yud* (to fight), Gr. ὑσ-μίνη for ὑθ-μίνη. Pr. root, I. E. *pa* (to suffer) ; sec. root, Gr. ἔ-παθ-ον, L. *patior* being formed from same root by means of a different suffix (*t*), unless Gr. θ and L. *t* represent an I. E.

---

* These forms are perhaps only *presential* bases.

th, as is supposed by those who believe in the existence of the hard aspirates in Indo-European. Pr. root, I. E. *dar* (to sleep) whence Skr. *drâ* (id.), L. *dor-mi-o ;* sec. root, Gr. ἔ-δραθ-ον, δαρθ-άνω. Pr. root, I. E. *pu* (to stink), whence Skr. *pûy* (id.), Z. *pû* (id.), Gr. πύ-ον, L. *pus, pu-t-eo*, Goth. *fu-ls* (foul); sec. root, Gr. πύθ-ω. This root-determinative is of frequent occurrence in Greek ;* thus we have such forms as νή-θ-ω from R. νε (νέ-ω), σή-θ-ω from R. σα (σά-ω), φλεγ-έ-θ-ω, πρή-θ-ω from R. πρα = I. E. *par*, whence Ch. Sl. *pal-iti* (to burn), ἰσ-θίω from R. ἰδ, βρί-θ-ω, ἔ-σχε-θ-ον, εἴργ-α-θ-ον, ἄχ-θ-ομαι beside ἄχ-ος, &c. θ is frequently added to secondary roots in ν: thus from πεν = πα + ν we have πέ-πονθ-α and πένθ-ος; from I. E. *man* (to think) = *ma* (to measure) + *n*, whence Gr. μῆν-ις, μέν-ος, L. *mens*, &c., we have Gr. μανθ-άνω, μενθ-ῆραι (φροντίδες, Hesych.). Βένθ-ος which is related to βάθ-ος as πένθ-ος is to πάθ-ος, is derived from R. βεν = βα + ν from βα (to go), unless indeed in both these cases (πένθ-ος and βένθ-ος), the forms παθ and βαθ are the older, and πενθ and βενθ formed from them by the insertion of ν. Βάθ-ος, βαθ-ύς, βυθ-ός perhaps come from a root βαθ (to dive into) = Skr. *gâh* (id.) = I. E. *gva* + *dh* from *gva* (to go).

S (root-det.). Pr. root, I. E. *ark* or *rak* (to preserve), whence Gr. ἄλκ-η, ἀρκ-έω, L. *arc-eo, arc-a ;* sec. root, Skr. *raksh* (to defend) = *rak* + *s*, Gr. ἀ-λέξ-ω. Pr. root, I. E. *tar* or *tra* (to move); sec. root, Skr. *tras* (to tremble), Z. *tares'* (id.), Gr. τρέω for τρεσ-ω, Hom. Aor. τρέσσα, τρηρός, perhaps for τρεσ-ρος, L. *terr-eo* for *ters-eo, tris-tis* (?). Pr. root, I. E. *dak* (to bite), whence Skr. *dans'* (id.), Gr. δάκ-νω, δάκ-ος (a bite, beast), Goth. *tah-ja* (I tear) ; sec. root, Gr. ὀ-δάξ-ω. Pr. root, I. E. *vag* (to increase), whence Skr. *ug-ra* (strong), *ôg'-as* (power), Z. *vaz* (to strengthen), Gr. ὑγ-ι-ής, L. *veg-eo, vig-eo, aug-eo*, Goth. *auka* (I increase) ; sec. root, Skr. *vaksh* (to grow), = *vak* + *s*, Gr. αὔξ-ω, ἀέξω = ἀ-ϝεξ-ω, Goth. *vahs-jan*, E. *wax*.

* Curtius, Grundzüge, &c., p. 62.

Pr. root, I. E. *dak* (to take), whence Ion. δέκ-ομαι, δάκ-τυλος; sec. root, Skr. *daksh-a* (clever), *daksh-ina* (right), Gr. δέξ-ιος, L. *dex-ter*, Goth. *taihs-vō* (δεξιά).

N (root-det.). Pr. root, I. E. *gva* (to go), whence Skr. *gâ* (id.), Z. *gâ* (id.), Gr. ἔ-βη-ν, βα-τός, L. *ar-bi-ter;* sec. root, βαίνω = βαν - γω, O. *ben-ust* (= L. *ven-erit*). Pr. root, I. E. *ga* (to be born, to produce), whence Gr. γέ-γα-α; sec. root, Skr. *g'an* (to bring forth), Gr. γέν-ος, L. *gen-us*. Pr. root, I. E. *bha* (to shine), whence Skr. *bhâ* (id.), Gr. φά-τις, L. *fa-teor;* sec. root, φαίνω = φαν-γω. Pr. root, I. E. *ta* (to stretch), whence Gr. τά·νυ-ται = Skr. *ta-nu-té*; sec. root, Gr. τείνω = τεν-γω.

R or *L* (root-det.). Pr. root, I. E. *ma* (to measure), whence Skr. *mâ* (id.), Gr. μέ-τρον; sec. root, Gr. μέρ-ος, μοῖρ-α, μείρ-ομαι = μερ-γομαι, L. *mĕr-eo, mer-ces, mer-x*. Pr. root, I. E. *sta* (to stand); sec. root, Skr. *sthal* (to stand firmly), *sthal-a* (firm ground), Gr. στέλλω = στελ-γω, L. *prae-stol-or, stul-tus, stol-idus*, O. H. G. *stel-lan* (to place). Pr. root, I. E. *sta* (to stand); sec. root, Skr. *sthir-a* (fast), *star-î* (vacca sterilis), Gr. στερ-ρός, στεῖρα = στερ-γα, Goth. *stairo* (στεῖρα), M. H. G. *star* (rigidus).

P (root-det.). Pr. root, I. E. *tar* or *tra* (to move); sec. root, Skr. (Ved.) *trp-ra* (hastening), *trap* (to be embarrassed), Gr. εὐ-τράπ-ελος, τρέπ-ω, Ion. τράπ-ω,* L. *trep-idus, turp-is* (according to Benfey). This I. E. root *tra* was weakened to *tru*, whence Gr. τρύ-χω (I rub away), τρύ-σκω (id. Hesych.), τρύ-ω (id.), τρῦ-μα (a hole); sec. root, Gr. τρύπ-ανον, τρυπ-άω. Pr. root, I. E. *dhu* (to move), whence Skr. *dhû* (to move, to blow), *dhû-ma-s* (smoke) = Gr. θυ-μό-ς = L. *fu-mu-s*, Z. *dun-man* (mist), Gr. θύ-ελλα, θύ-ος, L. *sub-fi-o*, O. H. G. *tunst* (storm), O. N. *dust* (dust), Lith. *du-mas* (mind); sec. root, Skr. *dhûp* (to fumigate), Gr. τυφ-ών (a whirlwind), τύφ-ω (I

---

* In these Greek works, however, π may represent an older *kv*, as we find in Latin *torqu-eo*, *torc-ulum*.

smoke), τῦφ-ος (mist). Pr. root, I. E. *da* (to cut), whence Skr. *dâ* (id.), Gr. δα-ίω, δα-ίς, δα-σμός, δαι-τυ-μών; sec. root, Gr. δάπ-τω, δαπ-άνη, δεῖπ-νον.

B (root-det.). Pr. root *tri* weakened from I E. *tra* (to move); sec. root, Gr. τρίβ-ω, L. *trib-ula*.

Bh (root-det.). Pr. root, I. E. *sta* (to stand); sec. root, Skr. *stambh* (to make firm), Gr. ἀ-στεμφ-ής (unshaken), στέμβ-ω (I shake by stamping), A. S. *stemn* (stem) = *stabh* + *na*. Pr. root, I. E. *va* (to twine round), whence Skr. *va-yámi* (I weave), Gr. ἤ-τριον (the warp), L *vimen;* sec. root, Skr. *úrna-vábh-a* (a spider, lit. a spinner of wool, Gr. ὑφ-ή, ὑφ-αίνω, ὑφ-ήφ-ασμαι.

V (root-det.). Pr. root, I. E. *sta* (to stand); sec. root, Skr. *sthâv-ara* (fixed), Z. *s'tavra* (strong), Gr. σταυ-ρός, στεῦ-το, Goth. *stiviti* (ὑπομονή). Pr. root, I. E. *bha* (to shine); sec. root, Gr. φά-ος for φαϜ-ος, Æol. φαῦ-ος, πι-φαύ-σκω, Pamph. φάβ-ος (= φαϜ-ος), L. *fav-eo, fav-illa, fau-stus.*

M (root-det.). Pr. root, I. E. *tra* (to move); sec. root, Gr. τρέμ-ω, L. *trem-o, trem-ulus*. Pr. root, I. E. *gva* (to go); sec. root, Skr. *gam* (to go), Z. *gam* (id.), Goth. *quim-an* (to come). Pr. root, I. E. *da* (to bind), whence Skr. (Ved.) *dâ* (id.), Gr. δί-δη-μι, δε-τός, δέ-ω; sec. root, Skr. *dam* (to tame), Gr. δαμ-άω, δμώ-ς, δάμ-αρ, L. *dom-o*, E. *tame*.

§. 98. The primary roots were chronologically older than the secondary. Some writers support the opposite, and believe that the so-called primary forms were obtained by generalization from the so-called secondary. They suppose that they were originally special terms, for different cognate ideas, e. g. for *yoking horses* (*yug*), *coming together for the purpose of fighting* (*yudh*), &c., and that from these roots was developed the general idea of *uniting for any purpose* (*yu*). This opinion is extremely unlikely; it is far more probable that the simplest form of the root was the oldest, as expressing the fundamental idea of all the secondary roots.

The oldest form of an I. E. root was perhaps either (1) *a*

\+ any consonant ; or (2) any consonant + *a*. Thus the most primitive roots were *ka*, *ak*, *da*, *ad*, &c. The origin of such roots is wrapped in impenetrable obscurity, for we have no remains of any I. E. language in its radical stage to supply us with materials on which we might found our investigations. We may theorize as much as we like, but that is all that we can do. It is puerile to dogmatize.*

§. 99. The origin of the root-determinatives is as obscure as that of the primary roots themselves. Various theories have indeed been invented to account for them ; but although a few of them may be explained by these theories, the vast majority of them are still as dark as ever. Thus it has been suggested that secondary roots arise from nominal stems, e. g. I. E. *gan* (to produce), from a nom. stem *gana* derived from R. *ga* + nom. suffix *na* ; but in the first place, on this theory, primitive verbs would be confounded with denominative, and in the second, very few of the usual root-determinatives ever appear as nominal suffixes, e. g. *p* is a common root-det., but never occurs as a nominal suffix. Again we are told that secondary roots are compounded of two primary verbal ones ; thus I. E. *yudh* (to fight), is derived from *yu* (to join), and *dha* (to place), and consequently meant originally "to make to join," I. E. *kalp* (to make), is from *kar* (to make) + *pa* (to do), &c. Thirdly, secondary roots are said to consist of a primary verbal root + a pronominal root ; e. g. the root determinatives, *k*, *t*, *m*, are identified with the pronominal roots *ka*, *ta*, *ma* : this is, however, the merest guess-work, and sheds no light at all on the subject.

We must, therefore, *for the present* be content to be ignorant of the origin of these secondary roots, but we need not

---

* Here is a specimen of dogmatism with respect to one theory of the origin of roots. "The onomatopoeic theory goes very smoothly as long as it deals with cackling hens and quacking ducks; but round that poultry yard there is a dead wall, and we soon find that it is behind that wall that language really begins."—Max Müller, Lectures II. p. 91.

give up all hope of being ever able to account for them, for it is quite possible that at some future period, when the non-Indo-European languages shall have been thoroughly studied and their connexion with the Indo-European family discovered, these root-determinatives may be easily explained.

§. 100. STEMS.

The stem of a noun or verb is that portion of the word that remains after the case-endings or personal endings have been removed. The first class of stems is called *nominal*, and the second *verbal*. Thus the nominal stems of Skr. *dêvas* (nom. sing. a god), *as'vasya* (gen. sing. a horse), Gr. ἵππος, ἵππου, L. *divus, equus*, &c., are Skr. *dêva, as'va*, Gr. ἱππο, L. *divo, equo*, &c. The verbal stems of Skr. *imas* (we go) = Gr. ἴμεν, Skr. *bharati* (he bears) = Gr. φέρει, L. *imus*, are Skr. *i̯*, = Gr. *i̯*, Skr. *bhara* = Gr. φερε, and L. *i̯*.

Stems may be of three kinds: (1) they may consist of the root alone, its vowel being sometimes affected by guṇa or vṛddhi; (2) of the root + a pronominal suffix, the vowel of the root being affected as in (1); (3) of the union of two stems so as to form a single new one.

I. *Stems formed from the root alone** are such as Skr. *ê* in *êmi* (I go), *i* in *imas* (we go), from R. *i*, the guṇa of which is *ê*, Gr. ὀπ in ὄψ from R. ὀπ, &c. We find many examples of nominal stems consisting of the mere root, such as Gr. ὀπ, the vowel of the root being sometimes lengthened as in Skr. *vák'* (the voice), from R. *vak'* (to speak). Thus in Skr. we have *yudh* (a fight), *kshudh* (hunger), *mud* (joy), *bhî* (fear), *drs'* (the eye), *vis'* (a man), &c., from the verbal roots *yudh, kshudh*, &c. In Greek we have φλογ (φλόξ) from R. φλεγ, &c. In Latin we have *ped* (*pēs* = *pĕds*) from I. E. *pad* (to go), *vōc* (*vōx*) = Skr.

---

* Consult Schleicher Compendium, pp. 346 seq., 374 seq., and Curtius zur Chronologie, &c., pp. 218 seq.

vák', &c. Curtius supposes that the signification of such stems as these was originally a mean between an infinitive and a participle, and nearly the same as that of English forms in *-ing*; e. g. *vis'* (a man) from *vis'* (to enter), originally meant "the *entering*" person; *drs'* (the eye) from *drs'* (to see) meant "the *seeing*" faculty; &c.

In stems of this first class the root was sometimes reduplicated, as in Skr. *dadámi*= Gr. δίδωμι, &c.

II. *Stems formed from the root + a pronominal suffix*, are such as Skr. *déva* (a god) from *dév*, the guna-form of R. *div* (to shine), and pronominal suffix *a*; Skr. *divya* (celestial) from *div + ya*; Skr. *bhára* (a burden) = Gr. φορο from Skr. *bhár* the guna-form of *bhar* (to bear) = Gr. φερ and pron. suffix *a*; Skr. *bháraya*, the stem of *bhárayati* (he makes to bear) from *bhár + a + ya*, and similar causative forms; &c.

Before nominal stems were formed from roots by means of pronominal suffixes, the root itself must have been used independently as a nominal stem, for the pronominal suffix has merely an *individualizing* force, and is nearly equivalent to an *article*. In the earliest stage of Indo-European, language consisted of roots placed in juxtaposition; at this period there were no stems, no case-endings, no personal endings, no distinction between noun and verb. The root *bhar*, for example, signified "*to bear*," "*bearing*," "*the burden*," "*the bearer*," &c. The next stage through which Indo-European passed was the formation of verbal stems. Nouns were now distinguished from verbs only *negatively*, that is, only by the absence of the pronominal suffixes. This stage again was followed by another, in which nominal stems were formed by the addition of these suffixes in order to individualize the root that had been used as a noun. That the verbal suffixes are older than the nominal ones is shown by the fact, that the latter are preserved in a much more perfect form in the Indo-European languages than the former; thus we find the suffixes *a, an, ma, ta*, &c., still kept perfect in nominal stems, while no single personal ending is found in its original form.* An additional proof that verbal and nominal stems were formed at different periods is supplied by the consideration that, as the same suffixes are in many cases used to form both classes of stems, a considerable period must have elapsed between the use of the same suffix in two such totally different ways. Moreover, as the original meaning of the pronoun is more manifest in the verbal stem than in the nominal, the former must have been older than the latter; thus the pronominal stem *ta* (he, she, it) is employed to form the 3 pers. sing. of the verb, as *bharati* (he bears), and also such nouns as Skr. *sthi-ta-s* (standing) = Gr. στα-τό-ς, Gr. φόρ-το-ς, κοί-τη, L. *secta, doc-tu-s*, &c., and it is obvious that its original meaning can be much more easily discovered from the verb than from the noun.

Pronominal suffixes are twofold, *primary* and *secondary*. The former are employed in forming stems from roots, and the latter in forming stems from other stems. Stems formed directly from roots are called *primary*, and those from stems, *secondary*. In many cases these suffixes agree in form: thus *a* is a primary suffix in Skr. *bhâr-a-s* (a burden) = Gr. φόρ-ο-ς, Skr. *dév-a-s* (a god) = L. *div-u-s*, &c., and a secondary suffix in Skr. *dáuhitr-a-s* (filiæ natus) from St. *duhitar*, Gr. ἡγεμόν-η from St. ἡγεμον, &c.; *ya* is a primary suffix in Skr. *madh-ya-s* = Gr. μέσσος (for μεθ-yo-ς) = L. *med-iu-s*, Gr. μοῖρα = μορ-ya, L. *exim-iu-s*, &c., and a secondary suffix in Skr. *pitr̥-ya-s* = Gr. πάτρ-ι-ος, L. *patr-ia*, &c.

III. *Stems formed by the union of two other stems* are such as Gr. λογο-γράφο-ς, Skr. *ûrṇa-vâbha-s* (a spider), &c. Schleicher supposes that such compound stems existed in Indo-European, and adduces as examples I. E. *svastar* (soror), and *svakura* (socer).

§. 101. As there was a period when Indo-European con-

---

* Curtius zur Chronologie, &c., p. 220.

sisted merely of roots, so there was subsequently another period when it consisted merely of stems.*

The nominal suffixes –*ant* and –*tar* are found in all the I. E. languages, and consequently must have existed in the original Indo-European. Now if *ant* is composed of the two pronominal suffixes *an* and *ta*, and *tar* of the two *ta* and *ra*, *bharanta, dâtara* must have been the original forms of the stems *bharant, dâtar;* and if the case-endings had already existed, we would have found such forms as *bharanta-s* (nom. sing.) in place of *bharanta-s* (= Gr. φέρων, L. *ferens*, &c.), *bharanta-sya* (gen. sing.) in place of *bharant-as* (= Gr. φέροντος, L. *ferentis*, &c.), *dâtara-s* (nom. sing.) in place of *dâtar-s*, *dâtara-i* (loc. sing.) in place of *dâtar-i*, &c. Now although it is possible to suppose that *bharants* came from *bharantas* from analogy with later formations, yet it is impossible to derive the oblique cases *bharantas, dâtari*, &c., from *bharantasya, dâtarai*, &c., and therefore before the oblique case-endings were attached, these stems must have already lost their final vowel.

§. 102. We have remarked that in the earliest stage of Indo-European there was no distinction between the noun and verb. In its latest stage, however, this distinction was sharply marked, firstly, by the *form*, and secondly, by the *syntactical construction* of each, the verb requiring as its complementary case an accusative, and the noun requiring a genitive. In Vedic even still many nouns, following the analogy of the verb, are construed with the accusative.

---

* Consult Curtius, zur Chronologie, &c., p. 223, whom I have here closely followed.

CHAPTER VIII.

SUBSTANTIVES.

§. 103. All the Indo-European words are either nouns or verbs. Nouns include substantives, adjectives, pronouns, and numerals. Prepositions, adverbs, and particles were originally cases of nouns or verbal forms. No nominal stem can be used as a word; the only example of the pure stem being found independently is the vocative case, but this case is not properly a word, being only an interjection. The stem, subject only to euphonic changes, occurs in the beginning of compounds, as the representative of all the cases, and consequently it has been called *casus generalis*: thus we have Skr. *g'alamuch* (a cloud), from St. *g'ala* (water), and *much* (to pour), Skr. *rathas'âla* (a coach-house), from St. *ratha* (a coach) and *s'âla* (a house), Skr. *as'varûpa* (having the form of a horse), from St. *as'va* (a horse) and *rûpa* (shape), Gr. λογογράφος from St. λογο and γράφω, Gr. νυκθήμερον from St. νυκτ and ἡμέρα, Gr. μακρόθυμος from St. μακρο and θυμός, L. *longimanus* from St. *longo* and *manus*, L. *tubicen* from St. *tuba* and *cano*.

In Sanskrit when a noun has two stems, the weaker is always employed in compounds, as in *pitrrâg'a-s* (the God Yama, lit. the king of the Manes) from *pitṛ* the weak form of the stem *pitar*; and when a noun has three stems, strong, intermediate, and weak, the intermediate is the one always employed in these forms. The Sanskrit grammarians treat as the true form of the nominal stem that which is found at the beginning of compounds.

§. 103. There were three numbers in Indo-European,

singular, *dual*, and *plural*. The dual is of later formation than the plural and derived from it, as is proved by the forms of its case-endings. In Pâli the dual is found only in the words for *two* and *both*, while in Prâkrit it is entirely lost. It did not occur in Æolic Greek, and is lost in Modern Greek. In Latin it is only found in *duo* and *ambo* (nom. and acc. masc. and neut.); the feminine and the other cases of these two words are treated as plurals: even *duos* and *ambos* are found in the oldest poets, beside *duo* and *ambo*; the neuter *dua* was used in vulgar Latin, and finally crept into the literary language, as in *post dua lustra* (Orestis trag. 26). There is no trace of the dual in Umbrian; N. U. *dur* (two) has assumed the plural ending.

§. 104. There were three genders in Indo-European, *masculine*, *feminine*, and *neuter*; the last was called *klíva* (an eunuch) by the Sanskrit grammarians. In Semitic and Hamitic, the latter including Egyptian, Ethiopian, Libyan, and Hottentot, we only find two genders, masculine and feminine, while no distinction* of gender is found in Tataric (Tungusian, Mongolian, Turkish, Samoyedic, Finnic), the monosyllabic languages (Chinese, &c.), the isolated languages (in Europe, Basque, in Asia, Japanese, &c.), the Polynesian, Australian, African, and American languages.

The distinction of gender was of course unknown to the

* "It is not accidental (writes C. R. Lepsius, Standard Alphabet, 2nd Ed. p. 89), but very significant, that as far as I know, without any essential exception, only the most highly civilized races—the leading nations in the history of mankind—distinguish throughout the genders, and that the *gender-languages* are the same as those which scientifically, by linguistic reasons, may be proved as descending from one original Asiatic stock. The development of peculiar forms for the grammatical genders proves a comparatively higher consciousness of the two sexes; and the distinction not only of the masculine and feminine, as in the *Semitic* and *Hamitic* languages, but also of the feminine and neuter gender, exclusively expressed in the *Japhetic* branch, is only a further step in the same direction."

Indo-European in its *radical* stage, just as it is at present unknown to radical languages, such as Chinese, &c. Such a distinction was impossible when language consisted merely of roots placed in juxtaposition. Moreover, at the period when verbal suffixes first made their appearance, the difference of gender was not marked, for had it been so, it would have shown itself in the verb, just as the same distinction appears in the Semitic verb, proving that in this latter case the difference of gender was marked before the introduction of the verbal suffixes. The early introduction of the verbal suffixes in Indo-European also appears from the fact that they must have been introduced before the difference of *number* was marked in the noun, for had there existed at that period a plural suffix, we would have found it in the verb instead of such forms as I. E. *-masi, -tvasi* (or *-tasi*), *-anti*, (or *-nti*)* for the suffixes of the *first*, *second*, and *third* persons plural respectively.

We find traces on all sides that originally there was no distinction between the masculine and feminine gender in Indo-European; e. g. the words for *father* and *mother* are formed with the same suffix (= I. E. *-tar*) in all the Indo-European family of languages. The introduction of the neuter gender took place at a period subsequent to that of the introduction of the masculine and feminine. That these three genders were all, however, introduced before the first separation occurred among the Indo-Europeans, is obvious from the agreement respecting them that pervades the whole I. E. family of languages. Various methods† were adopted of marking the difference of gender as well in Indo-European as in the languages that sprang from it.

* Consult Curtius zur Chronologie der Indo-germanischen Sprachforschung, pp. 214, 222.

† I have here followed chiefly Schleicher's arrangement; see his Compendium, p. 518.

I. *By a Change of Stem.*

While no attempt was made to distinguish the gender of diphthongal and consonantal stems, those in -*a*, -*i*, and -*u*, were lengthened to -*â*, -*î*, and -*û*, to express the feminine, although this method was only very partially carried out in the *i*- and *u*- stems, and there are some important exceptions in those in -*a*. In Sanskrit, where the majority of stems in -*î* and -*û* are feminine, we find many both masculine and feminine as *papî-s* (the sun) *nrtû-s* (a dancer), &c., as well as stems, formed from such roots as *dhî* (to think), *lû* (to cut), &c., such as *s'uddha-dhî-s* (a man of pure thought), *yavalû-s* (a corn-cutter), &c. Besides we find numerous feminine stems, as well as masculine, in -*i* and -*u*; e. g. *mati-s* (fem. thought), *s'uchi-s* (fem. bright), *mrdu-s* (fem. soft). The feminines of adjectives in -*u* may also be formed by adding *î*, as *mrdvî* (nom. fem.), &c., except when two consonants precede, as in *pându-s* (fem. pale), &c. Some adjectives in -*u* lengthen this vowel in the feminine, as *pângû-s* (fem. lame from St. *pângu*), *kurû-s* (a female Kuru) from St. *kuru*, &c. The allocation of the *ă*- stems to the masculine, and the *â*- stems to the feminine, was better carried out than that of the *i*- and *u*- stems; yet we find *ă* in such feminine forms as Skr. *s'ivayâ* (instr. sing. of *s'ivâ*), &c., and *â* in Skr. *s'ivât* (abl. sing. masc. and neut. of *s'iva*), &c. In Greek we find masculine stems in -*a* ($\eta, \bar{a}$) and feminine ones in -*ă* (o). Thus we have as masculines, νεανίας, ἱππότης, πολίτης, &c.; and as feminines, ἡ ὁδός, ἡ κέλευθος, and other names for a road, except ὁ στενωπός; ἡ νῆσος, and the special names of islands, such as ἡ Λέσβος, &c.; names denoting a collection, such as ἡ ἵππος (a body of cavalry), ἡ

---

* We also find in Vedic a nominative plural, both masculine and feminine, in -*âsas* where *â* is common to both genders, e. g. *dhûmâsas* (masc.) from St. *dhûma* (smoke), *yag'nâsas* (masc.) from St. *yag'na* (a sacrifice), *pâvakâsas* (fem.) from *pâvakâ* (pure).

δρόσος (the dew), &c.; ἡ λίθος* (a precious stone); &c. In Latin we also find masculine stems in ā, and feminine ones in ă (o, u). Thus we have as masculines, *poeta, scriba, collega, terrigena*, &c., which originally ended in ā, although in classical Latin this ā has been shortened to ă, just as in Greek we find the Epic forms ἱππότᾰ, νεφεληγερέτᾰ for ἱππότης, νεφεληγερέτης: and as feminines we have *domus, nurus, alvus, carbasus, malus* (the apple tree), *pomus* (id.), *Corinthus, Saguntus*, &c., along with many words borrowed from the Greek, such as *atomus, antidotus, dialectus, diametrus*, &c. There was some irregularity among the Romans in their use of the different genders: two forms of the same word often coexisted, as *ramenta* beside *ramentum, caementa* beside *caementum, vinus* (*vinus mihi in cerebrum abiit*) beside *vinum*, &c.; on inscriptions we find *eum sepulchrum, hunc munimentum, Corinto deleto*, &c., which prove that in vulgar Latin the distinction of the genders was often lost; moreover, in classical Latin many stems in –o are both masculine and feminine, such as *colus* (the distaff), *papyrus, pampinus* (the vine), *barbitos* (the lyre), &c.; *vulgus*, originally a masculine ă- stem, is sometimes masculine but generally neuter.

In Græco-Italic times† the masculine and neuter of adjectives in *-os, -a, -om*, were distinguished from the feminine by the former changing the original *a* into *o*: thus we have Gr. νέος (m.), νέον (n.), L. *novos* (m.), later *novus, novom* (n.), later *novum* beside Gr. νέα (f.) and L. *nova* (f.).

---

* ὁ λίθος is any stone, but Homer twice uses ἡ λ. for ὁ λ. Names of precious stones are in general feminine, but we find ὁ and ἡ σμάραγδος.

† See Grundriss der lateinischen Declination von Franz Bücheler (p. 4), where he remarks that the tendency of feminines to retain the older grammatical forms shows itself also in adjectives whose stems ended in *-ri*, e. g. Fem. *celeris, equestris, salubris*, Masc. *celer, equester, saluber*, where the helping vowel *e* was inserted after the loss of the final *-is*.

II. *By different Case Suffixes.*

S was added to the stem to mark the nominative of the masculine and feminine genders, while the nominative neuter was represented by the mere stem, or in the case of the *a*-stems, by the stem + *m*. In Indo-European times this *s* was already dropped in the nom. fem. of the *a*-stems, as Skr. *navâ* = Gr. νέα = L. *nova*. In Sanskrit it is also dropped in the case of polysyllabic feminine *î*-stems, as *balinî* (fem. strong), except *lakshmî-s* (the wife of Vishnu), *tarî-s* (a boat), *avî-s* (mulier menstrualis, lit. not desiring), *tantrî-s* (a lute), *starî-s* (smoke). In Greek and Latin *s* is also dropped in the nominative of feminine *î*-stems, but new suffixes are introduced in its stead, such as -α, -δς in Greek, -*es* in Latin, &c. *S* is kept in feminine *û*-stems in Sanskrit, Greek, and Latin, as Skr. *vadhû-s* (a wife), *bhû-s* (earth), Gr. δρῦς, σῦς, L. *sûs.**

The nominative neuter of *a*-stems was formed by adding *m* to the stem, as Skr. *navam* = Gr. νέον = L. *novom*, &c. In other cases the mere stem, subject to the euphonic laws peculiar to each language, was used as the nom. neut.: thus the following stems act as nominatives neuter, Skr. *vâri* (water), *mṛdu* (soft), *sumanas* (benevolent), &c., Gr. ἴδρι (expert), γλυκύ (sweet), εὐμενές, γάλα for γαλακτ, σῶμα for σωματ, τέρας for τερατ, &c., L. *mare* for *mari*, *facile* for *facili*, *genu*, *caput*, *cor* for *cord*, *corpus*, &c. Gr. γῆρας is neuter, but the corresponding Skr. stem *g'aras*† (old age) is feminine; similarly in Latin *vulgus* (nearly always neut.) and *virus* (neut.) correspond to Skr. *varga-s* (masc. a multitude), and *visha-s* (masc.

---

* Schleicher considers that neither *î* nor *û* existed in Indo-European, and consequently that we cannot speak of I. E. stems in *î* and *û*. This is a question upon which it is difficult to pronounce a decided opinion, on account of the conflicting evidence, and it may consequently be considered at present an open one.

† The usual form of this stem is *g'arâ*; *g'aras* is defective in those cases, whose case-endings do not begin with a vowel.

poison). In Latin the masc. -s has frequently penetrated into the neut.; thus *prudens* (St. *prudent*), *concors* (St. *concord*), *dives* (St. *divit*), *ferens* (St. *ferent*), are both masc. and neut. The Greek does not permit this confusion of the genders, for we find φέρον for φεροντ, τιθέν for τιθεντ, χαρίεν for χαριεντ beside L. *ferens*, &c. In Greek, however, we find two neuter nominatives lengthened, although no -s could have been lost, viz. πῦρ from St. πῠρ, and πᾶν from St. παντ.

D is used as a neuter suffix in the pronominal declension; it appears as *t* in Sanskrit, but the Latin, Gothic, and German forms prove* that the I. E. form was *d*. In Sanskrit we find this *t* in *yat* (which), *tat* (it), *êtat* (this), *tyat* (this) from *ta* + *yat*, Ved. *kat* (which) = Skr. *kim*, *it* (an old neuter = L. *id*, Goth. *ita*), found in *k'ĕt*† (even, if) = *k'a* (and) + *it*, and in *nĕt* (lest) = *na* (not) + *it*, *anyat* (aliud), *itarat*‡ (aliud). We find on the other hand Z. *nôid* (lest) = Skr. *nêt*, Z. *kad* (quod) = Ved. *kat*, Gr. ὅττι = ὁδ + τι, L. *aliud, alid* (= *aliud*), *istud, id, illud*, Goth. *ita* (it), G. *das, was*, in which *s* points back to an older *t*, which represents an I. E. *d* according to Grimm's law.

A was the Indo-European case-suffix for the nom. pl. neuter: thus we have Z. *madhva* (or *madhava*) = Gr. μέθυα from St. *madhu* = Gr. μέθυ, Z. *namana* = L. *nomina*, Z. *dâta* (gifts) from St. *datĕ*, Gr. δῶρα from St. δωρο, τάλανα from St. ταλαν, ἴδρια from St. ἰδρι, L. *dona, maria, capita*, Goth. *namna* (names) = L. *nomina*, &c. In Sanskrit this *a* became *i*; as in *nâmâni* = L. *nomina*, *madhu-n-i* from St. *madhu*, *dânâ-n-i* from St. *dâna* = L. *dōno*, &c.

The genitive singular of masculine and neuter *ă*-stems ends

---

* Bopp (Kritische Grammatik der Sanskrita-Sprache, p. 173, note) supports the view that the I. E. form of this suffix was *t*, and he considers the Gothic forms to be exceptions to Grimm's law.

† Benfey connects Gr. καί with *k'ĕt*: καί would then be derived from an older καιδ. Wilson derives Skr. *k'ĕt* from R. *k'it* (to think).

‡ Beside *itarat* we also find Ved. *itaram* (nom. neut.), which may be compared with L. *iterum*.

in –*sya*, whereas that of the feminine *â*-stems ends in –*s*; thus we have Skr. *as'vasya* (gen. sing. masc.) from St. *as'va*, Gr. ἵπποιο for ἱπποσιο beside Skr. *as'vâyâs* (gen. sing. fem.) from St. *as'vâ*, Gr. χώρας from St. χωρᾱ.

III. *By a Change of the Stem after the Separation of the various Indo-European Languages from each other.*

Thus Sanskrit masculine and neuter stems in –*i* and –*u* insert an euphonic *n* before *â* the instrumental case-ending, as in *kavinâ*, from St. *kavi* (masc. a poet), *vâriṇâ* from St. *vâri* (neut. water), *bhânunâ* from St. *bhânu* (masc. the sun), *tâlunâ* from St. *tâlu* (neut. the palate) beside *gatyâ* from *gati* (fem. motion), and *dhênvâ* from *dhênu* (fem. a milch cow). Sanskrit *a*-stems also insert an euphonic *n* in the masc. and neut. instr., but they shorten the final *â*, and change *a* of the stem into *ê*, as in *s'ivêna* from St. *s'iva* (masc. the god S'iva), *gâtrêna* from St. *gâtra* (neut. a limb), beside *s'ivayâ* = *s'ivê* + *â* from St. *s'ivâ* (fem. propitious). In the Veda we find instrumental forms without the euphonic *n*, as *mahitvanâ* from St. *mahitvana* (neut. greatness), *madhvâ* from St. *madhu* (neut. honey), &c. We also find in the Veda such instr. forms as *svapnayâ* from St. *svapna* (masc. sleep), *kulis'ênâ* from St. *kulis'a* (masc. and neut. an axe).

In forming the genitive of Sanskrit *i*- and *u*- stems, we gunate these vowels, and add merely *s* for masc. stems, while for fem. stems we either form the genitive as in the masc. or we simply add *âs* to the stem, and for neut. stems we insert *n* before the final *as*; thus we have *kavês*, *gatês* or *gatyâs*, *variṇas*, *bhânôs*, *dhênôs* or *dhênvâs*, *tâlunas* as genitives of the stems *kavi*, *gati*, *vâri*, *bhânu*, *dhênu*, *tâlu*. In the Veda, however, we find sometimes the older form of the genitive, without either the gunation of the vowel, or the insertion of *n*, as *pas'v-as* from St. *pas'u* (masc. cattle), *madhv-as* (= Gr. μέθυ-ος) from *madhu* (neut.), *ary-as* from St. *ari* (an enemy), as in Gr. ἴδρι-ος from St. ἴδρι.

The above insertion of *n* in the instrumental was not Indo-European, for we find in Zend *as'pa* = Skr. *as'véna*, *pas'va* = Ved. *pas'vâ* from St. *pas'u*. Similarly the gunation of *i* and *u* in the gen. of masc. and fem. stems, and the insertion of *n* in neuter ones, was not original, as is proved by the Greek forms πίτυος (fem.) πήχυος (masc.) μέθυος (neut.) ἴδριος (masc. fem. and neut.) πόσιος (masc.); the gunation of the genitives of the *i*- and *u*- stems, however, occurred before the separation of the Sanskrit from the Zend, or else the same course was pursued independently by each of these languages. The Gothic and Lithuanian present the same gunation of *i* and *u*, as in Goth. *sunaus* = Lith. *sūnaus* = Skr. *sûnôs* from St. *sunu* (masc.), Goth. *anstais* from St. *ansti* (favor), Lith. *awēs*, from St. *awi* (a sheep): these forms, on the other hand, support the opinion that the above gunation of *i* and *u* was Indo-European.

IV. *By a Change of Case-endings, originally identical.*

Thus in Indo-European the case suffix of the acc. pl. was -*ns*, while in Sanskrit masc. stems dropped the *s*, and feminine stems the *n*, the preceding vowel in each case, if short, being lengthened to compensate for the loss of the consonant: consequently we have *s'ivân*, *kavîn*, *bhânûn*, as accs. pl. of the masc. stems *s'iva*, *kavi*, *bhânu*, and *s'ivâs*, *gatîs*, *dhênûs*, as accs. pl. of the fem. stems *s'ivâ*, *gati*, *dhênu*.

V. *By the Formation of special Stems, especially for the Feminine Gender.*

Long *i* was perhaps used as a feminine suffix in the Indo-European; in Sanskrit its use as such is very common, as in *dêvî* (nom. fem. a goddess), from St. *dêva* (a god), *dhanavatî* (nom. fem. rich) from St. *dhanavant*, *laghvî* (nom. fem. light), from St. *laghu*, *svâdvî* (nom. fem. sweet), from St. *svâdu*, *dâtrî* (nom. fem. a giver) from St. *dátar*. In Greek this *i* also appears in feminine forms, but its exact signification seems to have been lost, and consequently *a* was added to express the feminine more definitely: thus we have ἡδεῖα for ἡδεϝια beside Skr. *svádvî* from St. ἡδυ = Skr. *svádu*; δύτειρα for δοτερya = δοτερι + a beside Skr. *dâtrî*; σώτειρα for σωτερya; θέαινα (a goddess) for θεανya; λύκαινα (a she-wolf) for λυκανya; τέκταινα, λέαινα,* &c., beside τέκτων, λέων, &c.; δέσποινα = δεσποινya; πότνια beside Skr. *patnî* (nom. fem. a wife); ἄνασσα for ἀνακya beside ἄναξ; &c. We also find δ added in Greek fem. stems to this I. E. *i* to form new stems, as in προδότις, St. προδοτιδ beside προδότης, Σκύθις, St. Σκυθιδ beside Σκύθης, Περσίς, St. Περσιδ beside Πέρσης, καπηλίς,† St. καπηλιδ beside κάπηλος, αἰχμαλωτίς, St. αἰχμαλωτιδ beside αἰχμάλωτος, &c. Many Greek masculines have two feminines of both these classes: as λῃστειρα and λῃστρίς from λῃστής or λῃστήρ; ὀρχηστρία and ὀρχηστρίς from ὀρχηστήρ; ὀλέτειρα and ὀλέτις for ὀλετρις from ὀλετήρ; αὐλήτρια and αὐλητρίς from αὐλητήρ or αὐλητής. In Latin *i* is found in feminine stems, but new stems were formed by the addition of *c*, as *victrix* from St. *victrīc*, *genetrix* from St. *genetrīc* beside Skr. *g'anitrî* (nom. fem. a mother), &c. This formative *c* has been identified by some writers with *k* in Gr. γυναικός, but this is very unlikely. Curtius

---

* The stems of λέων, θεράπων, &c., are λεοντ, θεραποντ, &c., of which the termination -οντ is = I. E. *vant*. The Greek feminines in -αινα = -ανya, and the Sanskrit ones in -*vatî*, therefore point back to an I. E. fem. term. -*vantî*, or else these different feminine forms were developed independently after the separation of Greek from Sanskrit. It is even possible that the Greek form is older than the Sanskrit, and that the Skr. *î* is = I. E. -*yă*.

† Bopp (Sanskrit Grammar, p. 144) adduces as additional proof of the connexion of Gr. -ιδ with Skr. -*î*, the fact that the accent in many Sanskrit feminines in -*î* changes in the same way as in many Greek feminines in -ιδ: thus we have Skr. *kalmâshî* (nom. fem. variegated), *nartakî* (nom. fem. a dancer), Gr. ἡμερίς, καπηλίς, &c., all oxytones, beside Skr. *kalmâ'sha-s*, *n'artaka-s*, Gr. ἥμερος, κάπηλος, &c.

considers that the I. E. stem was *ganaki*, which is very probable, as we find Skr. *g'anaka-s* (a father). Bopp supposes that γυναικ- meant originally "the figure of a woman," and derives it from γυνή and R. ἰκ (to be like), whence come ἔ-οικ·α, ἐ-ίκ-την, ἴκ-ελος, &c. It is very doubtful whether *a* was ever added in Latin to form new feminine stems in *-a* from original ones in *-i*, but some Latin words apparently point to such forms: thus *gallina* appears to bear the same relation to *gallus* that θέαινα does to θέος, and if so, it must be for *gallaina*; *Diana* or *Deana*, which is found on an inscription, may be for *Deaina*, a feminine similarly formed from *deus*; *regina* may likewise be for *regaina*, a feminine of *rex*. If *gallaina*, *Deaina*, *regaina* ever existed, they were probably for *gallantya*, *Deantya*, *regantya*, just as λέαινα is for λεαντγa beside St. λεοντ.

§. 105. There were nine cases in Indo-European. These were the *nominative* (casus* rectus), *accusative*, *locative*, *dative*, *ablative*, *genitive*,† two *instrumentals* and *vocative*. The last of these, though not properly a case, and generally in the singular represented by the mere stem, I nevertheless enumerate among the cases, following the common custom of doing so. These nine cases are only distinguished from each other in the singular: in the dual there are only three different case-endings, one for nom. acc. and voc., another for gen. and loc. and a third for dat. abl. and both inst. s: in the plural the

---

* *Casus* is a translation merely of Gr. πτῶσις, which meant the inclination that one idea had to another, and which was expressed by the case-ending. The nominative was called *rectus* (εὐθεῖα, ὀρθή) because it stood erect at the beginning of the sentence, and did not depend on anything: consequently some grammarians did not consider it to be strictly a *casus*. The Sanskrit term for a case-ending is *vibhakti* (division), Pân. I. 4, 104; v. 3, 1, sq.

† The Greek term for *genitive* is γενική, which meant casus *generalis*. *Genetivus* is properly equivalent to γεννητική and is a mistaken translation of γενική.

P

nom. and voc. agree in form, so do the dat. and abl., while there is only one instr.

The question now suggests itself,* what are the relative ages of these cases? This is a question that in the present state of our knowledge can only be partially answered. The cases at once divide themselves into two groups,† the first consisting of the nominative, accusative, and vocative, and the second of all the rest. That the nom. acc. and voc. are closely connected together, is shown by the facts, that in the neuter they are generally all identical, and that they are never interchanged with any case belonging to the second division, while these latter cases frequently interchange with one another: e. g. in Sanskrit the ablative and genitive frequently agree in form, so do the genitive and locative dual; the instrumental is represented in Greek by the dative, and in Latin by the ablative; –*bi* is locative in L. *ubi*, *ibi*, and dative in L. *tibi*, this connexion of the loc. with the dat. is easily understood, for the sentence, "You gave the book to me" (dative), is equivalent to "The place where you deposited the book was I" (locative); again, the genitive and dative are closely allied, for "she is my daughter" has the same meaning as "she is daughter to me;" &c.‡

* Consult Curtius zur Chronologie der indogermanischen Sprachforschung, p. 250, seq., whose views I have followed in the text.

† Grassmann (über die casusbildung in indogermanischen in K. Z. XII. p. 241, seq.), also divides the cases into these same two groups. The first group are formed from the stem by the addition of what he calls *die deutende anhänge*, and the second, by the addition of *die zeigende anhänge*: *die deutende* are –*s*, –*d*, –*a*, –*am*, and are all of pronominal origin, *die zeigende* are –*as*, –*at*, –*in*, –*ana*, –*bhi*, –*abhi*, –*av*, and are derived from prepositions; these latter, he says, only enter in those cases where a prepositional origin is probable, and where prepositions are used to a great extent in Greek, Latin, German, and almost entirely in the Romance languages and English. Ahrens calls the genitive, dative, and accusative, the three logical cases, and he justifies his use of this name by the relation in which this triad stands to the three chief classes of words, substantives, adjectives, and verbs.

‡ So in Pâli and Prâkrit *mayham dhîtu* and *mama dhîtu* both mean

The vocative is the oldest of all the cases, and was originally merely the stem itself used as an interjection: e. g. Skr. *s'iva* (masc.) is both the voc. and the stem, Gr. πρέσβυ is both the voc. and the stem which is found in πρεσβυ-γενής. Next to the vocative the accusative, called by Curtius the case with the *M-* suffix, was developed; the suffix probably only acted the part of an article, and was merely intended to call attention to the word to which it was attached. That the case with the *M-* suffix is older than the case with the *S-* suffix, (afterwards the nominative) appears firstly from the fact, that the nominative of the pronouns frequently ends in *m*, as Skr. *aham, tvam, ayam, iyam, idam*, Gr. ἐγών, Bœot. τούν, L. *idem*, and secondly from the very extended use of the accusative which is used in so many different relations, and which consequently must have existed for a long period by itself.*

When the case with the *M-* suffix had been for some time in use, the want of a suffix, which should distinguish the ani-

my daughter where *mayham* = Skr. *mahyam* (dative), and *mama* = Skr. *mama* (genitive). In modern Greek also we find the genitive used for the dative, as in σοῦ λέγω (I say to thee); in Constantinople and Athens, however, where the best Modern Greek is spoken, σὲ λέγω is used in this sense, while in printed books σοὶ λέγω is used.

* Madvig, in his Latin Grammar (§ 222, Obs. 1, p. 197, Fourth English Edition), explains the connexion of the accusative with the infinitive, on the ground that the accusative, as the indefinite case, was naturally joined to the indefinite infinitive expression. "The accusative," he writes, "is originally the word without further definition or distinction. In the masculine and feminine a peculiar form, the nominative has been devised, in order to denote the word as a subject (or as the predicative noun), but in the neuter, the accusative is also nominative. The accusative, therefore (as an indefinite case), is used in the most simple way, in which a word is added, to define and complete the predicate expressed in the verb. In the indefinite infinitive expression, where the connexion between the subject and predicate is not of itself asserted, the subject and the predicative noun stand in the accusative, e. g. *hominem currere*, that a man runs; *esse dominum*, to be lord." The derivation of the nominative in the Romance languages from the Latin accusative, as Fr. *père* from L. *patrem*, It. *domino* from L. *dominum*, supports this view of the nature of the accusative.

mate from the inanimate, began to make itself felt, and the *S*-suffix was consequently introduced to satisfy the want. This *S* was used to mark both masculines and feminines, and was evidently derived from the pronominal root *sa* (he, she).

In the same period, during which the *M*- and *S*- suffixes were being developed, also arose the *D*- suffix to mark the neuter of the pronouns. The introduction of this latter suffix probably occurred between that of the *M*- and that of the *S*-suffix.

For a long period the Indo-European was content with the three cases noticed above, the Vocative, Accusative, and Nominative; but gradually there arose the necessity of new case-endings to express different ideas, and the remaining cases began to develope themselves. Among these the genitive singular appears to be the oldest; it originally ended in –*sya*, a suffix which is found in Gr. δημό-σιο-ς, and which, perhaps, arose from an older –*tya*.* This form was evidently of adjectival origin, and it is probable that adjectives in –*sya* were used to denote the notion afterwards expressed by the genitive in early times, even before the introduction of the *M*- and *S*- suffixes: in Greek we find one adjective in –*sya*, viz., δημόσιος, the stem of which δημοσιο is the original of the Epic genitive δήμοιο. The other genitive suffix –*as* is connected by Curtius† with the same pronominal root *sa* from which the nominative suffix *S* is derived, and consequently points back to an older –*asa*: the original form of I. E. gen. *vâk-as* (Skr. *vâk'-as*, L. *voc-is*) was accordingly *vâk-asa*, just as the original form of I. E. nom. *svana-s* (L. *sonu-s*) was *svana-sa*. The compound *vâk-asa*, in Curtius' view, is therefore related to *svana-sa*, as a Tatpurusha compound in Sanskrit

* This is the same pronominal root that appears in Skr. *sya-s* (he), *syâ* (she), *tyat* (it). With this pronoun Bopp connects the Old High German and Anglo-Saxon article; see his Sanskrit Grammar, 3rd Ed. p. 176.

† Consult Curtius zur Chronologie, &c., p. 253.

(i. e. one in which the last word governs the preceding one, as *tatpurusha-s*, his man, where St. *tat* is used for gen. sing. *tasya*, *kumbha-kára-s*, a maker of pots, from St. *kumbha*, a pot) is to a Karmadhâraya (i. e. a compound in which the first part is the predicate of the second part, as *nila-utpalam*, the blue lotus, from St. *nila*, blue), *vâk-a-sa* being thus equivalent to ὁ (τῆς) ὑπός and *svana-sa* to ὁ φθόγγος, the suffix in the first case governing the noun, and in the second, being only in apposition; and consequently *vâkasa sranasa* in conjunction would mean *the sound of the voice*, *vâkasa* being used in an adjectival sense, and literally meaning *vocal*. The two objections that can be brought against this view of the genitive are first, that the *a* which occurs before *sa* in *vâkasa* is left unaccounted for, and second, that, while the combination *vâkasa svanasa* (= vocis sonus) is quite comprehensible, *vâkasa svanama* (= vocis sonum) is not so, but that we should expect *vâkama svanama*. The first of these objections is of little importance, for *a* may be merely an adventitious element similar to *n*, that is inserted so frequently in Skr. gen. pl. as in *devâ-n-âm*, *vadhû-n-âm*, *mâtṛ-n-am*, &c., from the stems *deva*, *vadhû*, *mâtṛ*, &c.; or to *i* that is inserted in the loc. pl. of Skr. *a*-stems, as in *s'iréshu* = *s'iva-i-shu* from St. *s'iva*. The second objection is of more importance, and different methods of obviating it may be adopted: the simplest explanation seems to be that these adjectival forms in *-sya* and *-asa* are relics of that period when language had only arrived at the stage of *stems*, and that, when their true explanation had been lost, they became *genitives* after the introduction of the *M*- and *S*-suffixes, for before these latter suffixes were introduced, the conception of the genitive could not have been formed. Curtius compares this ancient genitive with the L. *cujus*, which is used not only as genitive, but also declined like an adjective, as *cujus puer*, *cuja puella*, *cujum pecus*.

In the present state of our knowledge, it appears impossible to advance farther in the chronological arrangement of the cases.

SANSKRIT CONSONANTAL STEMS.

§. 106. As the case-endings were originally the same for all stems, we properly cannot speak of different declensions, but only of different stems. We therefore, classifying stems according to their final sounds, divide them into *consonantal* and *vocalic*.* The declension of stems, ending in *i*, *î*, *u*, *û*, or a diphthong, agrees in many respects with that of those ending in a consonant; this arises partly from the fact that the vowels *i* and *u* are closely related to the spirants *j* and *v*, and are easily interchanged with them. Consonantal stems in Sanskrit generally end in *n*, *t*, *s*, and *r*; the other consonants are found only in *root-stems* or those of *uncertain origin*.

§. 107. *Guttural Stems.*—These are found much more frequently in Greek and Latin than in Sanskrit. In Greek we find gutturals ending both root-stems and those of uncertain origin, as φλογ, φρικ, ὀνυχ, κορακ, &c.; and in Latin we find the mending not only root-stems, as *duc*, *reg*, *leg*, &c., but also formative suffixes, as *vor-ac*, *ed-ac*, *geni-tric*, *junic*, &c. In Sanskrit we have *sarvas'ak* (omnipotent, nom. sing *sarvas'ak*,†

---

* Grassmann (K. Z. XII. p. 241) divides Indo-European stems into those that end in a consonant or root-vowel and those that add a stem-vowel before the case-endings. The declension of the first class of stems he calls the *first declension*, and that of the second, the *second declension*.

† *Sarvas'ak* (nom. sing.) is for *sarvas'ak + s*, because two consonants are never allowed to end a word in Sanskrit, the last being always rejected, except when the one before the last is *r* (after which every consonant is kept, except *sh* (= *s* of desiderative forms) as *ûrk*, nom. sing. of St. *ûrg'* (strong). The nom. sing. of St. *k'itralikh* is *k'itralik* for *k'itralikh + s*, final *s* being first rejected, and then *kh* becoming *k*, as in Sanskrit only *tenues* are allowed to end a word, aspirates and mediæ consequently having to pass into the corresponding tenues, in the guttural, cerebral, dental, and labial rows, as *kh*, *g*, *gh*, into *k*. No palatal can end a word; *k'*, *g'*, *g'h*, generally become *k*, and *k'h* becomes *t*.

from *sarva*, all, and *s'ak*, to be able), *suvalg* (going well, nom. sing. *suval*, from *su*, well, and *valg*, to go), *k'itralikh* (a painter, nom. sing. *k'itralik*, from *k'itra*, a picture, and *likh*, to paint), *lih* (licking. nom. sing. *lit*), *guh* (covering, nom. sing *ghut*), *upânah* (a shoe, nom. sing. *upânat*, from *upa* = Gr. ὑπό and *nah*, to bind), *duh* (milking, nom. sing. *dhuk*), *druh* (hating, nom. sing. *dhrut* or *dhruk*), &c. No stem ends in *ñ*.

§. 108. *Palatal Stems.*—*Vâk'* (voice, nom. sing. *vâk*), *ruk'* (light, nom. sing. *ruk*), *g'alamuk'* (a cloud, nom. sing. *g'alamuk*, from *g'ala*, water, and *muk'* to shed), *prânk'* (the east, nom. sing. *prân*), *rug'* (disease, nom. sing. *ruk*), *samrâg'* (a king, nom. sing. *samrât*, from *sam* = Gr. σύν and *râg'* to shine), *ûrg'* (might, nom. sing. *ûrk*), *bhug'* (eating, nom. sing. *bhuk*), *khañg'* (lame, nom. sing. *khân*), *prâk'h* (asking, nom. sing. *prât*, from *pra* = Gr. πρό and I. E. *ask*), *vis'* (a man, nom. sing. *vit*, E. *wight*), *dis'* (a region, nom. sing. *dik*), &c. There are no stems which end in *y* or *ñ*.

§. 109. *Cerebral Stems.*—*Dadhrsh* (bold, nom. sing. *dadhrk*), *dvish* (hating, nom. sing. *dvit*), *mrsh* (bearing, nom. sing. *mrk*), *sugan* (a good reckoner, from *su*, well, and *gan*, to number, a denominative verb formed from *gana*, a multitude, for *garna* from I. E. *gar*, to collect, whence Gr. ἀγείρω).

§. 110. *Dental Stems.*—*Marut* (the wind, nom. sing. *marut*), *g'agat* (the world, nom. sing. *g'agat*), *bharant* (= Gr. φέρουν, nom. sing. *bharan* = Gr. φέρων = L. *ferens*), &c., *suhrd* (good-hearted, nom. sing. *suhrt*, from *su* = Gr. εὔ and *hrd* = E. *heart*), *pad* (a foot, nom. sing. *pât*), *kravyâd* (one who eats flesh, nom. sing. *kravyât*, from *kravya*, raw flesh, Gr. κρέας, L. *caro*, E. *raw*, and *ad*, to eat, Gr. ἔδω, L. *edo*), *aranyasad* (living in forests, nom. sing. *aranyasat*, from *aranya*, a forest, and *sad*, to sit), *sad* (found in the dative *â-sad-ê*, used as an infinitive, to place one's self), *agnimath* (fire-lighting, nom. sing. *agnimat*, from *agni*, fire, L. *ignis* and *math*, to agitate), *path* (a way), *s'is'rath* (found in the dative *s'is'rath-ê*, used as an infinitive, from *s'is'rath*, a reduplicated form of *s'rath*, to tie, to loosen, with which Benfey connects Gr. κλώθω, κάλαθος, L. *crates, rete, restis*), *budh* (knowing, nom. sing. *bhut*), *kshudh* (hunger, nom. sing. *kshut*), *yudh* (war, nom. sing. *yut*), *idh* (found in the accusative *sam-idh-am*, used as an infinitive, to set on fire), &c. Stems formed by the suffixes *-as, -is*, and *-us* are common, as *sumanas* (= Gr. εὐμενες), *k'andramas* (the moon, nom. sing. *k'andramâs*), *sug'yotis* (having good light, nom. sing. *sug'yotis*), *suk'akshus* (having good eyes, nom. sing. *suk'ashus*), &c. We also find stems ending in radical *s*, as *piṇḍagras* (an eater of lumps, nom. sing. *piṇḍagras*, from *piṇḍa*, a lump, and *gras*, to eat), *supis* (walking well, nom. sing. *supis* from *su*, well, and *pis* to walk), *sutus* (well sounding, nom. sing. *sutûs*), *dôs* (the fore-arm), &c. Stems ending in *n* are also common, as *s'van* (a dog, nom. sing. *s'vâ*), *maghavan* (a name of Indra, nom. sing. *maghavâ*, from *maghavant*, wealthy), *yuvan* (young, nom. sing. *yuvâ*), *râg'an* (a king, nom. sing. *râ'gâ*), &c. Stems in *r* are also of frequent occurrence, as *gir* (voice, nom. sing. *gîr*), *dvâr* (a door, nom. sing. *dvâr*), *pur* (a town, nom. sing. *pûr*), *pitar* (father, nom. sing. *pitâ*), *dâtâr* (giver, nom. sing. *dâtâ*), &c. No Sanskrit stem ends in *l*.

§. 111. *Labial Stems.—Ap* (water, only used in the plural, nom. pl. *âpas*, acc. pl. *apas*, instr. pl. *adbhis*),* *gup* (guarding), *kakubh* (a summit or a region, nom. sing. *kakup*), *labh* (receiving, nom. sing. *lap*), *rabh* (found in the accusative *rabham*, used as an infinitive, to desire), *div* (heaven, nom. sing. *dyâus* from another stem *dyô*, acc. sing. *divam*), *pras'âm* (mild, nom. sing. *pras'ân* from *pra* = Gr. πρό and *s'am*, to cease, connected by Benfey with Gr. κάμ-νω), *kram* (found in the dative *ati-kram-ê*, used as an infinitive, to step over).

§. 112. *Unchangeable and Changeable Stems.*—Nouns with unchangeable stems have the same form before all the case-ter-

---

* Bopp (Sanskrit Grammar, p. 135), illustrates the change of the labial media in this word into the dental media by the Dor. ὀδελός = ὀβελός.

minations, subject only to the influence of euphonic laws ;*
e. g. *marut* (the wind) belongs to this class, and remains unchanged.

	Sing.	Dual.	Plural.
N.	*marut*	*marut-âu*	*marut-as*
A.	*marut-am*	*marut-âu*	*marut-as*
I.	*marut-â*	*marud-bhyâm*	*marud-bhis*
D.	*marut-ê*	*marud-bhyâm*	*marud-bhyas*
Ab.	*marut-as*	*marud-bhyâm*	*marud-bhyas*
G.	*marut-as*	*marut-ôs*	*marut-âm*
L.	*marut-i*	*marut-ôs*	*marut-su*
V	*marut*	*marut-âu*	*marut-as*

Nouns with changeable stems are divided into two classes; the first class has two stems, the second has three.

The cases of the first class are divided into the *strong* (called by the Indian Grammarians the *Aṅga* cases) and the *weak* (called by the same grammarians the *Pada* and *Bha* cases). The *strong* cases in masculine and feminine† nouns are the nom. and voc. of the three numbers, and the nom. and acc. of the singular and dual, while in neuter nouns the nom. voc. and acc. pl. are the *strong* cases; all the remaining cases are *weak*.

The cases of the second class of nouns are divided into *strong* (or *Aṅga*), *intermediate* (or *Pada*) and *weak* (or *Bha*). The *strong* stem is found in the same cases as in the nouns with only two stems; the *intermediate* stem is found before all case-terminations beginning with consonants, and in the nom. and acc. sing. of neuter nouns.

The strong stem is evidently the oldest form, for it is found in the three oldest cases, nom. acc. and voc. (consult §. 105),

---

* For the special euphonic laws of Sanskrit, consult Bopp's Sanskrit Grammar, pp. 36–68, or Max Müller's Sanskrit Grammar, pp. 9–59.

† Such feminine stems are very rare, and generally occur at the end of compounds, for the feminines of changeable stems are formed by adding *i* to the weak stem.

and in Greek and Latin the strong stems are preserved much more generally than in Sanskrit, as may be seen from a comparison of the declension of the present participle, e. g. Skr. *bharant* (bearing) = Gr. φεροντ = L. *ferent*, the weak form of which stem is *bharat*:

		Skr.	Gr.	L.
Sing.	N. V.	*bharan*	φέρων	*ferens*
	A.	*bharant-am*	φέροντ-α	*ferent-em*
	I.	*bharat-â*	—	—
	D.	*bharat-ê*	φέροντ-ι	*ferent-i*
	Ab.	*bharat-as*	—	*ferent-e*
	G.	*bharat-as*	φέροντ-ος	*ferent-is*
	L.	*bharat-î*	—	—

These Greek and Latin forms at once indicate that the original form of the stem was the *strong* one.

The declension of the participle stem *bharant* (masc.) illustrates that of all stems with two bases;

		Strong cases.	Weak cases.
Sing.	N. V.	*bharan*	
	A.	*bharant-am*	
	I.	—	*bharat-â*
	D.	—	*bharat-ê*
	Ab. G.	—	*bharat-as*
	L.	—	*bharat-i*
Dual.	N. V. A.	*bharant-âu*	
	I. D. Ab.	—	*bharad-bhyâm*
	G. L.	—	*bharat-ôs*
Plural.	N. V.	*bharant-as*	
	A.	—	*bharat-as*
	I.	—	*bharad-bhis*
	D. Ab.	—	*bharad-bhyas*
	G.	—	*bharat-âm*
	L.	—	*bharat-su*

Neuter.

	Strong cases.	Weak cases.
Sing. N. A. V.	—	bharat
Dual. N. A. V.	—	bharat-î
Plural. N. A. V.	bharanti.	—

The feminines of these participle stems* are formed by adding *î* to the weak stem, as *bharatî*, &c.

The declension of the participle of the præterite active illustrates that of stems with three bases; e. g. *rurudvâṅs* (having wept) is the *strong*, *rurudvas* the *intermediate* (the final *s* of which becomes *t* if it be either final or followed by terminations beginning with *s* and *bh*), and *rurudush* the *weak* base.

Masculine.

	Strong.	Intermediate.	Weak.
Sing. N.	rurudvân	—	—
A.	rurudvâṅs-am	—	—
I.	—	—	rurudush-â
D.	—	—	rurudush-ê
Ab. G.	—	—	rurudush-as
L.	—	—	rurudush-i
V.	rurudvan	—	—
Dual. N. A. V.	rurudvâṅs-âu	—	—
I. D. Ab.	—	rurudvad-bhyâm	—
G. L.	—	—	rurudush-ôs
Plur. N. V.	rurudvâṅs-as	—	—
A.	—	—	rurudush-as
I.	—	rurudvad-bhis	—
D. Ab.	—	rurudvad-bhyas	—
G.	—	—	rurudush-âm
L.	—	—	—

---

* For exceptions to this rule consult Max Müller's Sanskrit Grammar, p. 81.

Neuter.

	Strong.	Intermediate.	Weak.
Sing. N. A. V.	—	*rurudvat*	—

[The others are the same as the masculine.]

| Dual. N. A. V. | — | — | *rurudush-î* |

[The others are the same as the masculine.]

| Plur. N. A. V. | *rurudvâṅs-i* | — | — |

[The others are the same as the masculine.]

§. 113. The most important changeable stems in Sanskrit are the following:—

I. *Guttural.*—Compound stems, whose last element is *vâh* (bearing), retain *vâh* in the *strong* and *intermediate* cases, but ruduce it to *ûh* in the *weak* cases; e. g. from St. *vis'vavâh* (the supporter of the world) we have Sing. A. *vis'vavâh-am*, Pl. I. *vis'vavâd-bhis*, but Pl. A. *vis'vâuh-as*: in a similar way are declined *s'âlivâh* (bearing rice), *bhâravâh* (bearing a burden). *S'vêtavâh* (a name of Indra, lit. drawn by white horses) differs from the preceding compounds of *vâh* in forming its *intermediate* cases from *svêtavas*, from which also the nom. and voc. sing. are formed, and in allowing the *weak* cases to be formed from either *s'vêtavâh* or *s'vêtâuh*. The feminine stems of *vis'-vavâh*, &c., are *vis'vauhî*, &c. *Anaduh* (an ox, lit. a waggon-drawer, from *anas*, a waggon and *vâh*) forms the nom. and voc. sing. and the nom. acc. and voc. pl. neut. from *anadvâṅs* (the *â* of which becomes *a* in voc. sing.) and the remaining strong cases from *anadvâh*, the intermediate from *anadut* and the weak from *anaduh*. *Upânah* (fem. a shoe) forms the nom. sing. and the intermediate cases from the stem *upânat*, as Sing. N. *upânat*, Dual. I. *upânadbhyâm*, Pl. I. *upânadbhis*, and the remaining cases from *upânah*: these forms are explained by the fact that the original form of *nah* (to bind) was *nadh*, connected perhaps with Gr. νήθω.

II. *Palatal.*—Compounds of *añk'* (to go) have either two or three stems: e. g. *prâñk* (directed forwards, eastern) and *avâñk'* (directed downwards, southern, from *ava*, down, and *añk'*) have each two stems, *prâñk'* and *avâñk'* for the strong, and *prâk'* and *avâk'* for the weak cases; *pratyañk'* (lying opposite, westward, from *prati* = Gr. προτί and *añk'*), *udañk'* (directed upwards, northern, from *ut*, up, and *añk'*), &c., have each three stems, *pratyañk'*, *udañk'*, &c., for the strong, *pratyak'*, *udak'*, &c., for the intermediate, and *pratik'*, *udik'*, &c., for the weak cases. *Yuñg'* (binding) forms its strong cases from *yuñg'* and its weak from *yug'*.

III. *Cerebral.*—*Sag'ush* (a companion from *sa*, with, and *g'ush*, to love) forms its strong and intermediate cases from *sag'us* (*u* also becoming *û*) and only its weak cases from *sag'ush*.

IV. *Dental.*—The present and future participle stems* end in *ant* in the strong, and in *at* in the weak cases; see §. 112. for the declension of St. *bharant*, in a similar way to which are declined future participles, such as *dâsyant* = Gr. δωσοντ. The present participles of reduplicated verbs use the weak base throughout their whole declension, except in the Nom. Acc. and Voc. Pl. Neut., where either the strong or the weak stem may be used: e. g. *g'âgrat* (waking, from *g'âgar*, to wake) and *dadat* (giving from *dâ*, to give) have as their acc. s. sing. *g'âgratam* and *dadatam* (= Gr. διδόντα). *G'agat* (neut. the world, lit. moving, an old present participle of *gam*, to go) is declined like *dadat* (neut.), except that it only has *g'aganti* as nom. pl. *Brhant* or *vrhant* (great) and *prshant* (m. a deer and n. a drop of water) are declined like *bharant*; these words are however real participles, the first two being

---

* Zend, as well as Greek and Latin, keeps the strong stem all through the declension of participles in -*ant*; in some words we find traces of the weak stem, as in Z. *běrěsant* (great) = Skr. *brhant*, the dat. of which is *běrěsaitě* and the gen. *běrěsatô* from the weak stem *běrěsat*, while the acc. is *běresantěm* from the strong stem.

from *bṛh* or *vṛh* (to increase) and the last, which is used in Vedic Sanskrit as an adjective, meaning *speckled*, being from *pṛsh* (to sprinkle). *Mahant* (great)* is also declined like *bharant*, except that the strong cases are formed from *mahânt*; this word is a participle of *mah* (to be great) = I. E. *magh*, whence Skr. *magha* (power). In Vedic we find other examples of *ant* becoming *ânt*, as in *mahânt* : e. g. Nom. Acc. and Voc. Pl. Neut. of the suffixes *mant* and *vant* and the present participle of *as* (to be); thus we have *pas'umânti* (abounding in cattle), *sânti* = Gr. ὄντα, &c. Stems in *vant* and *mant* are declined like *bharat*, except that the nom. sing masc. ends in *vân* and *mân*, whereas the nom. sing. masc. of the participles ends in *an*, as nom. sing. *agnimân* (having fire), *udanvân* (having water) in opposition to *bharan*. In Greek the vowel is lengthened in the participles, as Gr. φέρων = Skr. *bharan* = L. *ferens* = Z. *barans*. *Arvant*† (m. a horse) is declined like nouns in -*vant*, except that the nom. sing. is *arvâ*, as if from a stem *arvan*. *Kiyant* (now much), *iyant* (so much), *bhavant* (Your Honour) are declined like *udanvant*. In Vedic we find that the vocatives of stems in -*vant* and -*mant* generally end in -*vas* and -*mas*, which point back to an older -*vat* and -*mat*.

Pâd (a foot) at the end of compounds keeps *pâd* in the strong and intermediate cases, but shortens it to *pad* in the

---

* In Vedic we find *mahâm* (acc. sing.) for *mahântam*. Bopp compares to this rejection of *nt*, that of *vr* in the Greek participles τύψᾱς, ἱστᾱς, and he considers μίγας to be for μιγαντς, a similar participial form; he also accounts for the short ᾰ in μίγᾰς by supposing that its participial origin had been so long forgotten by the Greeks that they shortened the α.

† This stem comes from *ar* (to go) and *vant* (possessed of), the horse being so called from his speed: similarly Skr. *as'ra-s* (a horse) = Gr. ἵππος, ἴκκος, L. *equus* is from the same root as Skr. *ás'u-s* (swift) = Gr. ὠκύς, &c.; E. *horse* has also been connected with Skr. *k'ar* (to move), L. *curro*, though it seems better to connect it with Skr. *hrêsh* (to neigh), and to look upon it as an onomatopœic word. L. *armentum* is perhaps connected with Skr. *arvant*.

weak cases. The participle in -váns* of the reduplicated preterite has three stems, as we have already seen from the declension of *rurudváns* in §. 112. Comparative stems in -*íyáns* preserve these forms in the strong cases, but reduce them to -*íyáns* or -*yas* in the intermediate and weak cases; e. g. from *yavíyáns* (younger) we have nom. sing. *yavíyán*, acc. pl. *yavíyasas*, instr. pl. *yavíyóbhis*, &c. The termination of the nom. sing. is -*íyán* = Gr. ίων = L. *iōr* (the *o* of which is only shortened when *r* is final = O. L. -*iōs*), all of which forms point back to -*iyáns* as the termination of the nom. sing. in Indo-European. The feminines of participles in -*váns* and comparatives in *íyáns* are formed by adding *í* to the weak base, as *rurudushí*, *yavíyasí*. *Pumáns*† (a man) forms the strong cases from *pumáns*, the intermediate from *pum* and the weak from *puns*.

* This suffix = I. E. *vant* which meant *having, provided with*, &c. Its use to express the idea of the perfect tense is similar to that of the auxiliary verb *have* in English: *udanvant* (having water, the ocean) is a perfectly similar form to *rurudvant* (having roared). We find -*vant* in Gr. Fιντ (nom. sing. masc. -Fιις, fem. -Fισσα- = -Fιντγα, neut. -Fιν), as νιφο-Fιντ, &c., and in Lat. -*osus* = -*onsus* = -*vant-a-s*, as *formōsus* for *formonsus*, &c. Similarly we find -*vant* in perf. part. in Gr. as λιλοιπ-ώς = λιλοιπ-Fοτ-ς (m.) λιλοιπ-υῖα = λιλοιπ-υσγα = λιλοιπ -Fανrγα (f.) λιλοιπ-ός = λιλοιπ -Fοτ (n.): the only case of -*vant* being used to express the perfect in the Italic languages is the very doubtful one of the Oscan perfect; e. g. *prúfatted*, 3. sing. perf. (probavit), *prúfattens*, 3. pl. perf. (probaverunt) are supposed to be for *prúfat-fed*, *prúfat-fens*, where *fed* and *fens* come from root *fu* (to be) and *prúfat* is supposed to be the participle pret. and = *profa-vot*, *vot* being = Gr. Fοτ. Consult Schleicher's Compendium, p. 834.

† *Pumáns* is derived by Benfey from *api* (= Gr. *ἰπί*, L. ob) and *man* (to think) + *t*. This is a very unlikely account of the word. It is much more probable that it is derived from an old root *pu* (with the suffix -*mant*) whence come Skr. *pu-tra-s* (a son), *pô-ta-s* (the young of any animal). *Pu* meant *to grow*, and from it arose in Sanskrit the secondary verb *push* (to nourish). This root perhaps is the origin of a very numerous class of words in Greek and Latin, as Gr. παῖς (for παF-ιδς) for which παῦς and ποῦς are found on inscriptions, πῶλος (for ποF-λος), ποι-ίω, πό-α, ποίία, L. *pu-er*, *pa-pav-er*, *po-mum* (for *pov-mum*), *præ-pu-tium*, &c.

Stems in -*an*, -*man*, -*van*,* form their strong cases from -*ân*, -*mân*, -*vân*, their intermediate form -*a*, -*ma*, -*va*, and their weak form -*n*, -*mn*, -*vn*: e. g. *râg'ân* (m. a king) and *nâman* (n. a name) are thus declined:

[St. *râg'ân*].

	Sing.	Dual.	Pl.
N.	*râg'â*	*râg'ân-âu*	*râgân-as*
A.	*râg'ân-an*	*râg'ân-âu*	*râg'ñ-as*
I.	*râg'ñ-â*	*râg'a-bhyâm*	*râg'a-bhis*
D.	*râg'ñ-ê*	*râg'a-bhyâm*	*râg'a-bhyas*
Ab.	*râg'ñ-as*	*râg'a-bhyâm*	*râg'a-bhyas*
G.	*râg'ñ-as*	*râg'ñ-os*	*râg'ñ-âm*
L.	*râg'ñ-i*	*râg'ñ-os*	*râg'a-su*
V.	*râg'an*	*râg'ân-âu*	*râg'ân-as*

[St. *nâman*].

	Sing.	Dual.	Pl.
N. A. V.	*nâma*	*nâmn-î*	*nâmân-i*
I.	*nâmn-â*	*nâma-bhyâm*	*nâma-bhis*
D.	*nâmn-ê*	*nâma-bhyâm*	*nâma-bhyas*
Ab.	*nâmn-as*	*nâma-bhyâm*	*nâma-bhyas*
G.	*nâmn-as*	*nâmn-ôs*	*nâmn-âm*
L.	*nâmn-i*	*nâmn-ôs*	*nâma-su*

The locative sing. of these nouns may also be *râg'ani* and *nâmani*; the voc. sing. of *nâman* may also be *nâman* and its nom. acc. and voc. dual also *nâmanî*.

The feminines† of *râg'ân* and similar stems are generally formed by adding *î* to the weak stem, as *râg'ñî* (a queen). Nouns in -*vân* form their feminines in -*varî*, as *pivân* (m. fat) = Gr. πίων, *pivarî* (f.) = Gr. πίειρα, Πιερία, &c. Feminine stems in -*an*, such as *dâmân* (f. a rope) are declined like *râg'ân*.

---

* For special peculiarities in the declension of these stems consult Bopp's Sanskrit Grammar, p. 129, seq., or Max Müller's Sanskrit Grammar, p. 85, seq.

† For special rules see Max Müller's Sanskrit Grammar, p. 87, seq.

S'van (m. a dog), *yuvan* (m. young), and *maghavan* (m. a name of Indra, lit. mighty) form their strong cases from *s'ván yuván, maghaván;* their intermediate from *s'va, yuva, maghava;* and their weak from *s'un, yûn, maghôn.*

For other examples of changeable stems in *–n* Bopp's Sanskrit Grammar (pp. 130-134) may be consulted.

Stems in *-tar* and *-tár* form their strong cases from *-tar* and *-tár,* and the remainder from *-tr* and *-tr̥*: e. g. *dátár* (m. a giver), *pitar* (m. father), *mátar* (f. mother) are thus declined.

Singular.

N.	dátá	pitá	mátá
A.	dátár-am	pitar-am	mátar-am
I.	dátr-á	pitr-á	mátr-á
D.	dátr-é	pitr-é	mátr-é
Ab. G.	dátur	pitur	mátur
L.	dátar-i	pitar-i	mátar-i
V.	dátar	pitar	mátar

Dual.

N. A. V.	dátár-áu	pitar-áu	mátar-áu
I. D. Ab.	dátr̥-bhyám	pitr̥-bhyám	mátr̥-bhyám
G. L.	dátr-ós	pitr-ós	mátr-ós

Plural.

N. V.	dátár-as	pitar-as	mátar-as
A.	dátr̥-n	pitr̥-n	mátr̥-s
I.	dátr-bhis	pitr-bhis	mátr-bhis
D. Ab.	dátr-bhyas	pitr-bhyas	mátr-bhyas
G.	dátr̥-nám	pitr̥-nám	mátr̥-nám
L.	dátr-shu	pitr-shu	mátr-shu

The locatives *pitari* and *mâtari* are treated as strong cases, while the corresponding Greek datives πατρί and μητρί have become weak.

Bopp considers that the term. of the abl. and gen. sing. *-ur* is for *-urs*, and that this is derived by metathesis from *-rus*, which represents an older *-ras*: *pitr-as* would be exactly = Gr. πατρός. This view is supported by Zend, in which we find *dâthrô* (gen. sing.), which has arisen from *dâthras*.

V. *Labial.*—*Âp* (f. water), only used in the plural, forms its strong cases from *âp*, and its weak from *ap*, which becomes *ad* when followed by *bh*. *Div* (f. sky) forms its nom. and voc. sing. from *dyô*, its intermediate cases from *dyu*, and all the rest from *div*.

§. 114. The division of cases into strong and weak manifests itself remarkably in the accentuation of monosyllabic nouns, of which the strong cases retain the accent on the stem, while the weak have it on the case-ending. In this law of accentuation Greek in general agrees with Sanskrit, and it has consequently been inferred by Bopp that the division of the cases into the strong and the weak had already partially begun in Indo-European times. As far as the accentuation is concerned, the accusative plural ranks as a strong case: this fact points back to the time when the acc. pl. was in every respect strong, as it must have been in early times on account of its being older than all the other cases (except the vocative). In the Veda we also find traces of its having been strong, as in the acc. pl. *pitáras* (= Gr. πατέρας) for which in later Sanskrit we find *pitṛ́n*. The declension of the Sanskrit stems *nâu* and *vâk'*, as compared with that of the Greek stems *ναυ* and *ὀπ*, illustrates the agreement of Sanskrit and Greek in the accentuation of the cases:

Singular.

N. V.	nâ'us	ναῦς	vâ'k	ὄψ
A.	nâ'vam	νῆα	vâ'k'am	ὄπα
I.	nâvâ'	—	vâk'â'	—
D.	nâvê'	—	vâk'ê'	—
Ab.	nâvás	—	vâk'a's	—
G.	nâvás	ναός	vâk'a's	ὀπός
L. (Gr. D.)	nâví	ναί	vâk'í	ὀπί

Dual.

N. A. V.	nâ'vâu	νᾶε	vâ'k'âu	ὔπε
I. D. Ab. (Gr. G. D.)	nâubhyâ'm	ναοῖν	vâgbhyâ'm	ὀποῖν
G. L.	nâvô's	—	vâk'ô's	—

Plural.

N. V.	nâ'vas	νᾶες	vâ'k'as	ὄπες
A.	nâ'vas	νᾶας	vâ'k'as	ὄπας
I.	nâubhís	—	vâgbhís	—
D. Ab.	nâubhyás	—	vâgbhyás	—
G.	nâvâ'm	ναῶν	vâk'â'm	ὀπῶν
L. (Gr. D.)	nâushú	ναυσί	vâkshú	ὀψί

In the declension of ναῦς given above I have used generally the Doric forms as being nearer to the Sanskrit, on account of their having kept the original ā, except in the acc. sing., where the Ionic νῆα is nearer to nâ'vam than the Doric ναῦν or νᾶν.

There are some exceptions to the foregoing law of accentuation in Sanskrit: e.g. gô (m. f. an ox, cow), s'van (m. a dog), kruñk' (m. a plover) always keep the accent on the stem-syllable. The same is the case with râg' (m. a king), kṛt (making), and roots in â, such as dhmâ (to blow), when occurring at the end of compounds, except in the vocative, where the accent is thrown as far back as possible, as in sáṅkhadh-

más, voc. sing. of St. *s'aṅkhadhmá* (m. a shell-blower). In the Greek stems βου and κυν, corresponding to Skr. *gó* and *s'ran*, the accent, however, follows the general rule: thus we have κυνί = *s'únê*, κυνός = *s'únas*, κυνοῖν = *s'vábhyâm*, κυνῶν = *s'únâm*, κυσί = *s'vásu*, βοί = *gávi*, βοοῖν = *góbhyam*, βοῶν = *gávâm*, βουσί = *góshu*. In *div* (f. heaven) the accent is kept on the stem in the intermediate cases, as in the instr. pl. *dyúbhis;* in the intermediate cases of *nar* (m. a man), the accent may fall either on the stem or on the case-ending, as in dat. pl. *nṛ'bhyas* or *nṛbhyás*. In the Greek ἀνήρ, corresponding to Skr. *nar*, the accent is kept on the ε whenever it appears as in ἀνέρι, ἀνέρα, ἀνέρων, but in the weak cases, when the ε is lost, the case ending is accented as in Sanskrit; thus we have Gr. ἀνδρί = Skr. *narí*, &c.

The following Sanskrit monosyllabic stems accentuate the case-ending of the accusative plural, like those of the other weak cases: *ap* (f. water), *dat* (m. tooth), *div* (f. heaven), *nas* (f. nose), *nis'* (f. night), *pad* (m. foot), *puṅs* (m. man), *mâs* (m. month), *path* (m. path), *math* (m. churning-stick), *râi* (f. riches), and *ûh* (for *váh* at the end of compounds), *suhṛd* (m. friend), and other compounds of *hṛd* (n. heart). The Greek presents an older form than the Sanskrit in πόδας = Skr. *padás*, while in the other cases the accentuation is the same, as in ποδί = *padí*, ποδός = *padás*, ποδῶν = *padā́m*, ποσσί = *patsú*.

It has been already remarked that the opinion is maintained that the distinction between the strong and weak cases in monosyllabic stems had already begun in Indo-European times. Now, if such a distinction had then manifested itself, and if it had begun in a difference of accentuation, it would be quite natural to expect that the Greek stems βου and κυν should be accented in the same way as the Skr. stems *gó* and *s'van*, but this, as we have seen, is not the case; for in Sanskrit these *stems* are accented throughout their whole declension, whereas in the Greek corresponding stems the accent is placed on the case-endings of the weak cases. It is then safer to suppose that, when the Greek and Sanskrit separated from each other, there was no distinction (as far as monosyllabic stems were concerned) between the accentuation of the strong and that of the weak cases, and consequently, as we shall see, only one form of the stem (i. e. the strong one) existed. It is, however, evident that certain latent tendencies already existed in Indo-European, which afterwards bore similar fruits in Sanskrit and Greek.

Before the first separation of any Indo-European language from the parent stock, the only law of accentuation that existed was this, that the root-syllable should always have the accent. Consequently in the declension of monosyllabic stems the accent always fell upon the stem, which preserved the strong form in every case. In process of time, but not till after the first separation that occurred in the Indo-European, the accent began to move towards the termination, and consequently, as generally happens to unaccented syllables, the stem became shortened in form. The initial consonants* (*bh* and *s*) of the intermediate case-endings preserved the accent on the stem in these cases for a longer period than it remained on the stem in the weak cases, and consequently these cases frequently preserve a stronger form of the stem than is found in the weak cases. The accentuation of the intermediate cases of *div* (e. g. instr. pl. *dyúbhis*, &c.) is a relic of the

---

* Oxytone stems of the part. pres. active allow the accent to fall on the case-ending in the weak cases, while in the intermediate cases the accent is kept where it originally was, as the consonantal combinations *dbh* and *ts* prevent it passing over them: thus from St. *tudánt* (striking) we have instr. pl. *tudádbhis*, loc. pl. *tudátsi* beside instr. sing. *tudatá'*, &c. Similarly the consonantal conjunction *nt* prevents the accent moving on to the final syllable in nom. and acc. dual neuter *tudánti*, whereas in the side form of the same cases *tudati'* the accent advances. In participles such as *bhárant* (bearing) the accent remains on the root syllable throughout the whole declension.

time when the accent in these cases still remained on the stem; while that of *nṛ́bhyas* or *nṛbhyás* (dat. pl. of *nar*) points to the time when the accent in the same cases was moving on from the stem to the case-ending. The monosyllabic pronouns and the numeral *two* also retain the accent on the stem in Sanskrit in the weak cases: thus we have *té'shu* = Gr. τοῖσι *tá'su* = Gr. ταῖσι, *yé'shu* = Gr. οἷσι, *máhyam* = L. *mihi*, *túbhyam* = L. *tibi*, *máma* (gen. sing. of *ahám*, I), *dvá'bhyâm* = Gr. δυοῖν, which latter has become weak beside the nom. δύο, which is still strong.

Sanskrit Vocalic Stems.

§. 115. Stems ending in *a* (m. and n.) and *â* (f.) are very numerous; e. g. *s'iva* [which as an adjective means *prosperous*, while as a noun *S'ivá* (m.) is the god *S'ivá*, *s'ivấ* (f.) *his wife*, and *s'ivam* (n.) *happiness*] is thus declined:

Singular.

	Masc.	Fem.	Neut.
N.	s'ivas	s'ivấ	s'ivam
A.	s'ivam	s'ivấm	s'ivam
I.	s'ivéna	s'ivayấ	s'ivéna
D.	s'ivấya	s'ivấyâi	s'ivấya
Ab.	s'ivất	s'ivấyâs	s'ivất
G.	s'ivasya	s'ivấyâs	s'ivasya
L.	s'ivé	s'ivấyâm	s'ivé
V.	s'iva	s'ivé	s'iva

Dual.

	Masc.	Fem.	Neut.
N. A. V.	s'ivấu	s'ivé	s'ivé
I. D. Ab.	s'ivấbhyâm	s'ivấbhyam	s'ivấbhyâm
G. L.	s'ivayós	s'ivayós	s'ivayós

Plural.

	Masc.	Fem.	Neut.
N. V.	s'ivás	s'ivás	s'ivâni
A.	s'iván	s'ivás	s'ivâni
I.	s'ivâis	s'ivábhis	s'ivâis
D. Ab.	s'ivébhyas	s'ivábhyas	s'ivêbhyas
G.	s'ivânâm	s'ivânâm	s'ivânâm
L.	s'ivéshu	s'ivâsu	s'ivéshu

The declension of these stems corresponds to that of *malus, mala, malum* in Latin, and ἀγαθός, ἀγαθή, ἀγαθόν in Greek.

Stems ending in *â*, both masculine and feminine, are derived from verbal roots ending in *â*, as *s'ankhadhmâ* (m. f. a shell-blower), from *s'ankha* (a shell, Gr. κόγχη) and *dhmâ* (to blow). The strong and intermediate cases of this stem are formed from *s'ankhadhmâ*, and the weak from *s'ankhadhm*. The neuter stem is *s'ankhadhma*, which is declined as *s'iva* (n.).

§. 116. Stems in *i, î, u, û*. We find masc. fem. and neut. stems in *i* and *u*; e. g. *kavi* (m. poet), *gati* (f. motion), *vâri* (n. water), &c.; *bhânu* (m. the sun), *dhênu* (f. a milch-cow), *tâlu* (n. the palate), &c. We find stems in *î* and *û*, both masc. and fem., derived from verbal roots such as *krî* (to buy), *lû* (to cut), &c.; these stems are of course monosyllabic. We find other polysyllabic stems in *î* and *û*, also masc., such as *papî* (m. the sun), *nṛtû* (m. a dancer), &c. In general stems in *î* and *û* are feminine, such as *bhî* (f. fear), *bhû* (f. earth), *vadhû* (f. a wife), &c.

§. 117. The chief diphthongal stems are *rái* (m. f. wealth, L. *res*), *gó* (m. an ox, f. a cow), *dyó* (f. heaven), *nâu* (f. a ship), *gláu* (m. the moon).*

---

* For the special rules respecting all Sanskrit Vocalic stems consult Max Müller's "Sanskrit Grammar," pp. 96-115, and Bopp's "Sanskrit Grammar," pp. 109, *seq.*

GREEK CONSONANTAL STEMS.

§. 118. Guttural Stems.

The nom. sing of these stems ends in ξ.

I. *Stems ending in* κ: κορᾰκ (m. a crow), δρᾱκ (f. the hand, connected with δράσσομαι, δραχμή, δράγμα, δάρκ-ες, meaning *bundles* according to Hesychius), θωρᾱκ (m. a corslet), βλᾱκ (weak, connected with μαλακός), ἀλωπεκ (f. nom. sing. ἀλώπηξ, where ε irregularly becomes η; this word is perhaps derived from ἀλωπός which meant *craft*, Hesych.), σφηκ (m., derived from Curtius from the same root as L. *vespa*, by the addition of the individualizing suffix κ, which is found in ἱέραξ beside ἱερός, μύρμηξ = μύρμος, an ant, ἀλώπηξ beside ἀλωπός, &c.; the stages through which the original *vaspa* passed were accordingly Fεσπα, Fεσπακ, σπᾱκ, Ion. σπηκ, σφηκ, as π is aspirated through the influence of σ), χοινῑκ (f.), φοινῑκ (m. and f. nom. sing. φοῖνιξ, where the ι is irregularly shortened as in κῆρυξ from St. κηρῡκ), γυναικ* (f. nom. sin. γυνή, voc. γύναι; this noun is also declined as an α-stem, as acc. sing. γυνήν acc. pl. γυνάς, &c.), &c. These κ-stems are very common in Greek, and are either root-stems such as πτᾰκ (f. acc. sing. πτάκα, a hare, found in Æsch. Ag. 135) from R. πτᾰκ, whence ἔ-πτακον, πτήσσο = πτηκ-γω, πτώξ, or stems of uncertain origin such as κορᾰκ, νεᾱκ (m. a young man), &c. The κ of these latter stems may however have arisen from an older κο = I. E. *ka*, a very common suffix; thus μαλακός became μαλακς, and then μλαξ, and finally βλάξ, as βροτός from μροτος. Many κ-stems exist side by side with ones in κο or κη: thus οἰκ in

---

* Γυναικ is accented in the oblique cases like monosyllabic stems, such as ὀπ, see §. 114; thus as the strong cases we have γυναῖκα, γυναῖκι, γυναῖκες, γυναῖκας; and as the weak, γυναικός, γυναικί, γυναικοῖν, &c.: γυναικ may either be for γυνακι = I. E. *ganaki*, the fem. of *ganaka*, whence Skr. *g'anaka* (a father); and as the accent generally is placed on the fem. termination -*i*, it may be kept here on it, although transposed, or else it may be derived from γυνα + R. ικ (to be like), and declined as a root-stem. This latter derivation is improbable, as the R. ικ was originally Fικ.

οἴκ-α-δε beside οἶκο, ἀλκ in ἀλκί for ἀλκῇ from ἀλκή, ἰωκ in ἰῶκα for ἰωκήν from ἰωκή, κρόκ-α for κρόκην from κρόκη, λάκ-ας (φάραγγας, Hesych.) beside λάκκο-ς (m. a lake). Moreover in the dialects we find a similar connexion between the κ-and the κο-stems : thus we have Ion. φύλακο-ς = φύλαξ, Ion. φρίκη = φρίξ, Æol. ἱέρακο-ς = ἱέραξ, γλαῦκο-ς = γλαῦξ, αὔλακο-ς = αὔλαξ.

II. *Stems ending in* γ: ἁρπάγ, ῥᾱγ (f. a berry), μαστῑγ (f. a whip; Homer uses μαστι as the stem whence dat. μάστι, acc. μάστιν), φλογ (f. from R. φλεγ = Skr. *bhrâg*, to shine), διζῡγ (m. f. having two yokes), Σφιγγ (f. the Sphinx, lit. the strangler: this stem becomes Φικ in Bœotic, nom. sing. Φίξ), αἰγ (m. f. for ἀγι = I. E. *agi*, a she-goat, beside Skr. *aga-s*, a he-goat, from R. *ag* = Skr. *ag*, to move, when Gr. ἄγ-ω, L. *ago*), &c. &c.* There appears to be some connexion between the γ-stems and those in -γο and -γη, but not so close as the connexion between the κ-stems and those in -κο and -κη ; thus we find φυγ in φύγ-α-δε beside φυγή, ἅρπαξ (f. = ἁρπαγή in Hesiod), Æol. ἅρπαγος = ἅρπαξ, αἰγο- (= αἰγ) found in Bœot. ἤγυς, i. e. αἴγοις for αἰξί.

III. *Stems ending in* χ: βηχ (f. a cough), τριχ (f. nom. sing. θρίξ), ὀρνιχ (m. f. Doric for ὄρνιθ, beside which in Pindar we find stem ὀρνι), στιχ (f. a row), πτυχ (f. a fold), ὀνυχ (m. a nail), &c.† There appears also to be some connexion between these stems and those in -χυ and -χη ; thus we have πτύξ beside πτυχή, στίξ beside στίχο-ς, ἀγχοῦ (the gen. of an old χο-stem) beside ἄγχ-ι (the loc. of an old χ-stem) ; ὀνυχ is probably derived from an older ὀνυχο = I. E. *nagha*, whence Skr. *nakha-s* (m. a nail), L. *ungui-s*, Lith. *naga-s* (id.).

---

* Πύξ (with the fists) may be a shortened dat. pl. from a stem πυγ, connected with πυγ-ών (an ell), πυγ-μή (the fist), L. *pug-nus*, *pug-il*, &c. Consult Curtius, Grundzüge, &c., p. 258.

† Πλίξ (f. βῆμα), appears to be from the stem πλιχ ; compare πλιχ-άς (interfeminium). Ἄγχ-ι may be the loc. of an old stem αγχ, connected with ἀγχω, ἄχος, L. *angustus*, *anxius*, &c.

§. 119. Dental Stems.

I. *Stems ending in τ*: γαλακτ (n. nom. sing γάλα), νυκτ (f. nom. sing. νύξ), μελιτ (n. nom. sing. μέλι), τερατ (n. nom. sing. τέρας), δαιτ (f. nom. sing. δαίς), κερᾱτ* (n. horn, nom. sing. κέρᾰς, dat. pl. κέρᾱσι, but κέρᾱτος, κέρᾱτι, &c.), κρεατ (n. meat, nom. sing. κρέας), χρωτ (m. nom. sing. χρώς), ἱρωτ (m.), χαριτ† (f. nom. sing. χάρις), ὀνειρατ (n. found in gen. sing. ὀνείρατ-ος, nom. pl. ὀνείρατ-α beside nom. sing. ὄνειρο-ς, m. a dream), προσωπατ (n. found in dat. pl. προσώπα-σι beside πρόσωπο-ν, n.), γονϝατ (n. the knee, nom. sing. γόνυ, gen. sing. γούνατος and γόνατος = γονϝατος, &c.: γόνυ is also declined as an υ-stem, from which the former stem γονϝατ has been derived by means of the individualizing suffix ατ, thus, gen. sing. γούνος = γονυος, acc. pl. γοῦνα = γονυα), δορϝατ (n. a spear, nom. sing. δόρυ, gen. sing. δούρατος and δόρατος = δορϝατος, &c., δόρυ is also declined as an υ-stem, thus gen. sing. δουρός = δορνος, &c., and as a ρ-stem, thus gen. sing. δορ-ός, dat. sing. δορ-ί, and perhaps as a σ-stem, thus dat. sing. δόρει = δορεσ-ι, acc. pl. δόρη = δορεα = δορεσ-α), ὠτ (n. the ear, Ion. οὐατ, nom. sing. οὖς,‡ Ion. οὖας, gen. sing. ὠτ-ός, Ion. οὔατ-ος : Curtius supposes that the ori-

---

* The stems κερᾱτ, κρεατ, χρωτ, ἱδρωτ, γελωτ, &c., appear to have side forms ending in ς : thus κιρως (gen. sing. of κερας) = κεραος = κερασ-ος, κιρᾳ (dat. sing.) = κιραῖ = κερασ-ι, χροῖ (dat. sing. of χρώς) = χροσ-ι, γιλω (acc. sing. of γελως) = γελοα = γελοσ-α, &c. Beside ιρωτ we find the stem ιρο, whence comes acc. sing. ἴρον.

† Beside such stems as χαριτ and other dental stems ending in -ιδ, -ιθ, -υδ, -υθ, which are *not* oxytone in the nom. sing., other stems are found ending in -ι and -ν ; thus we find χάριτ-α = χάρι-ν, ἰριδ-α = ἰρι-ν, Θίριδ-ος = Θίρι-ος, &c. : in the case of oxytone stems no such side forms exist, and we only find such forms as ἰλπίδ-α, χλαμύδ-α, λαμπάδ-α, &c.

‡ Οὖς may be connected with Skr. αυ (to desire), Gr. ἀ-ίω (I hear), ἀ-ιτι (ἀκούετι, Hesych.), L. αυ-eo, αυ-dio, &c. The suffix ατ appears also in stem ἀλατ (salt), whence dat. pl. ἀλασιν.

ginal form of ὠτ was αὐσ-ατ, ατ being the same suffix that appears in δορυ-ατ and γονυ-ατ, and he connects with it L. *aur-is* for *aus-is*, cf. *aus-culto*, Goth. *aus-o*, the ear, Lith. *aus-is*, id.); δεσμaτ* (n. bonds, nom. pl. δέσματ-a beside δεσμος, m.), σωματ (n. nom. sing. σῶμα), ὀμματ (n. for οπ-ματ, Æol. ὀππατ, nom. sing. ὄμμα), εἱματ (n. for ἐσ-ματ, Æol. ἑμματ, nom. sing. εἱμα), &c.; participial stems in -αντ, -εντ, -οντ, -υντ, such as βιβαντ, βαντ, τυψαντ, τιθεντ, θεντ, βληθεντ, τυπτοντ, διδοντ, δεικνυντ, &c.; stems, which perhaps were originally participles, such as Fεκοντ (willing, from R. Fεκ = Skr. *vas′*, to wish), θεραποντ, λεοντ, Ἀτλαντ (lit. the bearer, from R. ταλ = Skr. *tul*, to bear, cf. τλῆ-ναι, τάλα-ς, &c.), λυκαβαντ (the year, lit. the course of light), ὀδοντ (lit. the eater, from R. ἐδ, to eat, nom. sing. ὀδούς, cf. διδούς, nom. sing. of participial stem διδοντ), &c.; φωτ (m. a man, nom. sing φώς) may be an old participle of R. φυ (to produce), and = φοFατ (lit. the producer), cf. Skr. *bhavat* (being) from R. *bhû* (to be); participial stems in οτ = Fοτ, such as ἑσταFοτ (nom. sing. ἑσταώς), λελυκοτ (nom. sing. λελυκώς), &c.; stems in -Fεντ (nom. sing. m. -Fεις, n. -Fεν, f. -Fεσσα = -Fετya from the weak form of the stem -Fετ = Skr. *-vant*† (full of, provided with), such as

* Stems in -μaτ are very common, and have arisen perhaps from older forms in -μaντ, traces of which are found in the cognate adjectival and other stems in -μον, and in verbs ending in -μaινω; thus we have εὔ-ειμον (well clad) beside εἱματ, ὀνοματ, beside ὀνομαίνω = ὀνομαντyω, χειματ beside χείμων and χειμαίνω (compare Skr. *hêman*, m. winter, and *hêmanta*, m. and n. id.). That verbs in -αινω originally possessed τ appears not impossible if we compare ὔφασμα and μίασμα, which arose from ὐφατμα and μιατμα, with ὐφαίνω and μιαίνω. This connexion of -μaτ with -μaντ is supported by comparing ὀνοματ with L. *cognomen* and *cognomentum*, *tegumen* with *tegumentum*, &c.

† Παντ (nom. πᾶς, πᾶσα, πᾶν) appears to contain this suffix, and to point back to an I. E. *kvâ-vant* or *kvâ-vanta*, whence L. *quantu-s*, U. *panta*. *Kvávan* meant "how much," just as Skr. *távant* meant "so much" (cf. L. *tantus*) and *yávant*. "how much." Πᾶσα (Æol. παῖσα) arose from παντya through the steps παντ-σα, παντ-σα, παν-σα: α in πᾶν is irregularly lengthened; it is short in ἄπαν.

βροτοϜεντ (full of blood), δολοϜεντ (crafty), &c.; stems in -αρτ (the nom. sing. of which ends generally in -ap, and sometimes in -ωρ, whereas the oblique cases reject ρ*, and are formed from stems in -ατ, except δάμαρ, f., the oblique cases of which are δάμαρτ-ος, δάμαρτ-ι, &c., compare δόμορτι-ς = δάμαρ, Hesych.), such as φρεᾶρ for φρεαρτ (n. a well, gen. sing. φρέᾱτος and φρητός, nom. pl. Hom. φρείᾱτα, Att. φρέᾱτα), ἧπατ for ἧπαρτ = Skr. *yakṛt* (n. the liver), σκατ (n. dung, nom. sing. σκώρ) = Skr. *s'akṛt* (n. id.), στεατ for στεαρτ (n. fat, beside τὸ σταῖς, gen. σταιτ-ός, dough), ὕδατ for ὕδαρτ (n. nom. sing. ὕδωρ), ἀλειατ (n. meal), κυατ (n. a hole), &c.; stems in —τητ†, all feminine, such as φιλοτητ (love, nom. sing. φιλότης), &c.

11. *Stems ending in* -δ (which is lost in nom. sing.)‡: λαμπαδ (f.), δρομαδ (m. f.) &c.; Θεμιδ (f. beside Θεμι, Dor. Θεμιτ, and Ep. Θεμιστ), Ἀρτεμιδ (f. beside Dor. Ἀρτεμιτ), Θετιδ (f. beside Θετι), ἐλπιδ (f.), ἀϊδ (m. only used in the oblique cases); ποδ (m. nom. sing. πούς, the compounds of which can also form their acc. sing. like stems in ου, e. g. Οἰδίποδα and Οἰδίπουν, τρίποδα and τρίπουν, &c.); χλαμῡδ (f.), δαγῡδ (f. a doll); φῳδ (f. a blister); παιδ (m. f.); κλειδ§ (f. acc. sing. κλεῖν and κλεῖδα, acc. pl. κλεῖς and κλεῖδας), &c.

---

* We find other instances of the omission of r; thus ποτί = Kret. πορτί = προτί = Skr. *prati* (πρός), δρύφακτος for δρυφρακτος from R. φραγ, whence φράσσω = φραγγω, L. *pedo* = Gr. πέρδω, E. *speak* = G. *sprechen*, &c.

† This stem-termination arose from an I. E. -*tāti*, which is found in Skr. *śivatāti* (f. benevolence), *sarvatāti* = Gr. ὁλοτητ, &c., and in the Latin plural genitives, *civitati-um, ætati-um, voluptati-um*, &c.

‡ In Æolic ι is also lost in acc. sing.: thus we find in this dialect such forms as κνᾶμιν, σφρᾶγιν, κλᾶϊν, πάϊν, χλάμυν, for κνημῖδα, σφραγῖδα, κληῖδα, παῖδα, χλάμυδα.

§ Beside κλεις we find the Doric form κλάξ, which Ahrens ("De Dialecto Dorica," pp. 94, 140, 141), considers to have arisen from κλαῖς, ις being changed into ξ. This explanation is very doubtful, and it is much more likely that the final guttural in κλάξ arose from the dental in κλαιδ. If this

III. *Stems ending in* -θ (which is lost in nom. sing.):
Παρνηθ (m. a mountain in Attica); ὀρνῖθ (m. f. beside ὄρνι and Dor. ὄρνιχ); κορῦθ (f.), κωμῦθ (f. a sheaf of hay); ἑλμινθ (f. a worm, beside ἕλμι and ἑλμιγγ), πειρινθ (f. a wicker basket); Τιρυνθ (f.); &c.

IV. *Stems ending in* -ς (preceded by any vowel).

1°. *Stems in* -ας: σελας (n. gen. sing. σέλαος for σέλασος), κνεφας (n. gen. sing. κνέφαος and κνέφους, the latter being from a stem κνεφες), βρετας (n. an image), κωας (n. a fleece), οὐδας (n. the ground), γηρας (n.), δεπας (n.), &c. These stems appear to be closely connected with others in -ες: thus βρέτας, κῶας, οὐδας, &c., form their oblique cases from βρετες, κωες, οὐδες, &c. It has been suggested that stems in -ας have arisen from older forms in -ατ, and accordingly they have been compared with such stems as κερατ (n. a horn, whence nom. sing. κέρας, gen. sing. κέρᾱτ-ος and κέρως = κεραος, τ being thrown out), κρεατ (n. flesh, for κρεϜγατ, whence nom. sing. κρέας and κρεῖας, gen. sing. κρέως).

2°. *Stems in* -ες: adjectival stems in -ες such as σαφες, &c., of which the nom. sing. masc. and fem. ends in -ης; substantival masc. stems in -ες, of which the nom. sing. also ends in -ης, as Σωκρατες, Ἄρες, &c., while the acc. sing. may either come from these stems (Σωκράτη = Σωκρατεσ-α), or from stems in -α (Σωκράτην); substantival neuter stems in -ες, which becomes -ος in the nom. sing.; e. g. γενες, nom. sing. γένος, gen. sing. γένους = γενεσος = L. *generis* for *genesis*, from St. *genes*, &c. These latter stems have frequently side forms ending in -ο: thus we have σκοτες (n.) and σκοτο (m.), ὀχες (n.) and ὀχο (m.), κλαδες (found in dat. pl. κλάδεσι) beside κλαδο (m.), δενδρες (n.) beside δενδρο (n.), ἀνδραποδες

be so, κλάξ bears nearly the same relation or κλεις (for κλειδς), that Dor. ὀρνιχ does to ὀρνιθ. Θ and χ appear to be interchanged in Mod. Gr. Λιθαδό -νησα from Λιχάδες and Mod. Gr. ἤρχα from ἦλθον. Compare also Dor. ψάφαξ (m.) from St. ψαφᾱκ with ψηφίς (f. dim. of ψῆφος) from St. ψηφιδ.

(found in dat. pl. ἀνδραπόδεσσι) beside ἀνδραποδο (n.), and many others.

3°. *Stems in* -ος: αἰδος (f. nom. sing. αἰδως, gen. sing. αἰδοῦς = αἰδοσ-ος), ἠχος (f. nom. sing. ἠχώ, gen. sing. ἠχοῦς = ηχυσ-ος), ἠος (f. nom. sing. ἠώς), χρος (m. nom. sing. χρώς, gen. sing. χροός = χροσ-ος, beside Attic stem χρωτ), πειθος (f. nom. sing. πειθώ, gen. sing. πειθοῦς), &c. The vocative singular of these stems ends in -οῖ, as αἰδοῖ, ἠχοῖ, πειθοῖ, &c., and various theories have been proposed to account for these forms. One writer suggests that the original form of these stems ended in -ονι; another that they ended in -ον, and that ν was merely vocalized into ι, as in Æol. μέλαις for μέλανς, &c., τίθεις for τιθενς, &c.; another that they ended in -ονι; another that they ended in -ο; another that they ended in -οι, inasmuch as we find such nominative forms as Λητώ, Σαπφώ, &c., and, lastly, another that σ is vocalized into ι. Whatever may be the true explanation of this vocative in -οι, it apparently bears a remarkable resemblance to the Sanskrit vocative in *ê* of feminine nouns in -*â*, e. g. *s'ivê* from *s'ivâ*; for ω : *â* : : οι : *ê* (*ai*).

4°. *Stems in* -υς: μῦς (m. nom. sing. μῦς, gen sing. μυός = μυσ-ος).

5°. *Stems in* -ως: θως (m. a jackal, nom. sing. θώς, gen. sing. θωός = θωσ-ος), ἡρως (m. gen. sing. ἥρωος), μητρως (m. avunculus), ἁλως (f. the threshing-floor, found in acc. sing. ἅλωα = ἁλωσ-α, Arat. 940), καλως (m. a rope), &c. Some of these stems have side forms in -ων, and most of them can also be declined according to the Attic second declension.

V. *Stems ending in* -ν (preceded by any vowel).

1°. *Stems in* -αν: ταλᾰν (nom. sing. m. τάλας, f. τάλαινα = ταλανya, n. τάλαν), and similarly μελᾰν, the only other adjectival stem in -αν; Πᾱν (m. Pan, nom. sing. Πάν), παιᾱν (m. nom. sing. παιάν).

2°. *Stems in* -εν: adjectival stems in -εν, such as ἀρσεν (nom. sing. m. and f. ἄρσην, n. ἄρσεν), τερεν (nom. sing. m.

τέρην, f. τέρεινα, n. τέρεν); φρεν (f. nom. sing. φρήν); ποιμεν (m. nom. sing. ποιμήν); κτεν (m. a comb, nom. sing. κτείς), ἑν (nom. sing. m. εἷς, n. ἕν); &c.

3°. *Stems in* -ην (nom. sing. -ην) : μην (m. beside Ion. μείς = μεν + ς; Curtius considers that the original form of this stem was μηνς, whence comes Æolic μῆννος for μηνσος, cf. L. *mens-i-s*), χην (m. beside χηνο found in χηνο-βοσκός; Curtius considers that this stem was originally χενς, or a fem. stem χενσι beside Skr. *hansî* = I. E. *ghansî*, Ch. Sl. *gansĭ*), Ζην (m. Jove), Ἕλλην (m.), πευθην (m. an inquirer), πυρην (m. a fruit-stone), ψην (m. the gall-insect), &c.

4°. *Stems in* -ιν : ρῖν (f. the nose, nom. sing. ῥίς, and later ῥίν), θῖν (m. f. a heap, nom. sing. θίς, and later θίν), ἰκτῖν and κτῖν (m. a weasel), δελφῖν (m.), &c.

5°. *Stems in* -ον : χθον (f. perhaps for an older χθομ, compare χαμαί, χθαμ-αλός, Z. *zem*, earth, L. *humu-s*, Ch. Sl. *zem-lja*, land); adjectival stems in -ον (nom. sing. m. f. -ων, n. -ον), such as μειζον and other comparatives, in which ν may be thrown out, and the vowels contracted as in μείζους for and beside μείζονες, while other adjectival stems in -ον, as σωφρον, εὐδαιμον, cannot throw out ν; δαιμον (m.), ἡγεμον (m.), χιον (f.); ἀηδον (f. nom. sing. ἀηδών, gen. sing. ἀηδόνος and ἀηδοῦς), χελιδον (f. nom. sing. χελιδών, gen. sing. χελιδόνος and χελιδοῦς), εἰκον (f. nom. sing. εἰκών, gen. sing. εἰκόνος and εἰκοῦς), Γοργον (f. nom. sing. Γοργώ and Γοργών, gen. sing. Γοργόνος and Γοργόος, Dor. Γοργώς, Æol. Γόργως), &c. These feminine stems in -ον partly agree in their declension with feminine stems in -ος : e. g. πειθοῦς (gen. sing. of St. πειθος) is similar to εἰκοῦς (gen. sing. of St. εἰκον). This similarity is, however, not a sufficient basis on which to build the theory that all these stems in -ον and -ος, such as αιδος, πειθος, εἰκον, &c., were originally identical.

6°. *Stems in* -υν : μοσσυν (m. a tower, nom. sing. μόσσυν), Φόρκυν (nom. sing. Φόρκυς), Γορτυν (nom. sing. Γόρτυς). The oblique cases of κύων (m. f.), with the exception of the vocative κύον, are formed from St. κῠν.

7°. *Stems in* -ων : Ἀπολλων, Ποσειδων, κλων (m. a branch, nom. sing. κλών), αἰων (m.), ἡρων (m. found in Syracusan ἡρώνεσσι,* beside St. ἥρως), ταων (m. a peacock, nom. sing. ταὼς, which is generally declined according to the Attic second declension), ἁλων (f. nom. sing. ἅλως, also declined according to Attic second declension), τυφων (m. nom. sing. τυφών and τυφώς), &c.

8°. *Stems in* ν preceded by a consonant : ἀρν (m. f. a lamb, without nom.), Πυκν (f. the Pnyx, nom. sing. Πνύξ).

VI. *Stems ending in* -ρ (preceded by any vowel).

1°. *Stems in* -αρ (nom. sing. -αρ): νεκταρ (n.), ψαρ (m. the starling), μακαρ (m. happy, nom. sing. μάκαρ, Æol. μάκαρς), ὀαρ (f. a wife, from ὀ = Skr. *sa*, with, and a root σαρ, to join, whence σειρά, a rope ; or from ὀ = Skr. *sa* and Fαρ = L. *vir* ; in the former case ὀαρ would be for ὁσαρ, and in the latter for ὁFαρ).

2°. *Stems ending in* ερ : χερ (f. nom. sing. χείρ, Æol. χέρς, beside St. χειρ), αἰθερ (m. nom. sing. αἰθήρ), πατερ (m.), ἀνερ (m.), &c.

3°. *Stems in* -ηρ : θηρ (m. a wild beast), κρατηρ (m.), &c.

4°. *Stems in* -ορ : ῥητορ (m. nom sing. ῥήτωρ), ἡτορ (n. nom. sing. ἧτορ, the heart), ἀορ (n. a sword), &c.

5°. *Stems in* υρ : πῠρ (n. nom. sing. πῦρ), μαρτῠρ (m. nom. sing. μάρτυς, and later μάρτυρ), Λιγῠρ (m.), Κερκῠρ (m.).

6°. *Stems ending in* -ωρ : φωρ (m. a thief), πελωρ (n.), ἰχωρ (m.), &c.

VII. The only Greek stem in -λ is ἁλ (m. salt, f. the sea, nom. sing. ἅλς).

---

* Consult Ahrens " De dialecto Dorica," p. 241.

§. 120. Labial Stems.

I. *Stems ending in* -π : λαιλᾰπ (f. a storm, nom. sing. λαῖ-λαψ), θερᾰπ (m. found in acc. sing. θέραπα for θεράποντα); ρῑπ (m. nom. sing. ρίψ, a mat), κνῑπ (m. an ant); ὀπ (f.), 'Αιθιοπ (m.), καλαυροπ (f. a shepherd's crook); γῦπ (m. a vulture); ὠπ (m. f.), &c.

II. *Stems ending in* -β : 'Αρᾰβ (m.), λῐβ (m. a drop, from same root as λείβω), Λῐβ (m. the south-west wind, lit. the moist wind, connected with last stem), χερνιβ (f.), χαλυβ (m. steel).

III. *Stems ending in* -φ : νιφ (f. snow, found only in oblique cases), κατηλιφ (f. an upper story, nom. sing. κατῆλιψ), λιφ (f. nom. sing. λίψ, ἐπιθυμία Hesych.).

§. 121. Strong and Weak Stems.

The strong form of the stem is kept in Greek in many places where we find in Sanskrit the intermediate or the weak form (consult §. 112). We however find several examples where there is a change of stem in Greek.

The adjectival suffix Fεντ = I. E. *vant* assumes frequently the weak form Fετ, as in μητιόεσσα = μητιοFετya, fem. of μη-τιόεις = μητιοFεντ-ς, χαρίεσσα = χαριFετya, fem. of χαρίεις = χαριFεντ-ς, &c. The weak form of the stem is also found in the dat. pl. masc. χαρίεσι = χαριF ετσι, &c., and in the comparative and superlative of such adjectives, as χαρίεσ-τερος, χαρίεσ-τατος = χαριFετ-τερος, χαριFετ-τατος, &c.

The above I. E. suffix *vant* also assumes the weak form Fοτ in participles in -ως, as λελυκώς = λελυκ-Fοτ-ς, λελυκυῖα = λελυκ-Fοτ-ya, &c.: when a vowel precedes Fοτ, it generally becomes Fωτ, as in ἑστεώς (gen. sing. ἑστεῶτος) = ἑστα-Fοτ-ς, τεθνεώς = τεθνα-Fοτ-ς, &c. This suffix *vant* is also supposed to appear in κύων = I. E. *kû-vant*, from *kû* (to howl, c. f. Gr. κω-κύ-ω), which has two stems, the strong κυον and the weak κυν. In Latin we find this stem appearing as *can* in *can-is*,

R

and *cat* in *cat-ulus*, and in Goth. we find it as *hund* in *hund-s*, E. *hound*.

The I. E. suffix *mant* appears in the strong form μαντ and the weak μαν, ματ, μον: thus we have ἱμαντ (m. a strap, nom. sing. ἱμάς from R. ἱ = Skr. *si*, to bind, whence *sîman*, f. a boundary, and *sîmanta*, m. a separation of the hair on each side, so as to leave a distinct line on the top of the head), beside ἱματ (whence ἱμάσσω = ἱματγω and ἱμάσθλη = ἱματθλη, a whip), and ἱμον (whence ἱμονιά, the rope of a well), ὀνοματ (n. nom. sing. ὄνομα) beside ὀνομαν (whence ὀνομαίνω = ὀνομανγω), which point back to an older stem ὀνομαντ, c. f. L. *cognoment-um*, &c.; σπερματ beside σπερμαν (whence σπερμαίνω), &c. Stems in -μῖν are also connected with those in ματ, as ῥηγματ (n. a breach) with ῥηγμῖν (m. breakers), &c.

The oblique cases of participles whose stems end in οντ and αντ retain the strong form: but we find a few examples where the weak stem apparently shows itself; thus we have Æol. ἴασσα and ἴσσα (fem. of ὤν, being) which must be for ἐσατγα and ἐτγα, σατ being the weak form of participial stem οντ = I. E. *sant* = L. *sent* in *ab-sent-em*, &c. This weak form of the participle of εἰμὶ appears also to be found in ἐτεός (true) = Skr. *satyas* (id.), ἔτυμος, ἐτήτυμος.

Nouns of relationship in τηρ, such as πατήρ, μήτηρ, have two stems ending in τερ and τρ, and may form their oblique cases from either, e. g. gen. sing. πατέρος and πατρός, μητέρος and μητρός, dat. sing. πατέρι and πατρί, μητέρι and μητρί, &c.; but in acc. sing. we only find πατέρα and μητέρα, &c., while in dat. pl. the stem ends in τρα, as πατράσι, &c.

§ 122. Vocalic Stems.

I. *Stems in* -a, -η, *and* -o (= I. E. *ă* and *ā*).

1°. *Stems in* -o (m. f. n.), as ἱππο (m. f.), φορο (m.), νοσσο (f.), ζυγο (n.), &c.

Many consonantal stems have side-forms in o, especially in Æolic, where we find the stems αγωνο, φυλακο, μαρτυρο,

COMPARATIVE GRAMMAR. 243

ἑκατυνχειρο, γεροντο, παθηματο, &c. In Bœotic we find ἥγυς = αἴγοις from stem αιγο.*

2°. *Stems in* -ᾰ, -ᾱ, -η, as μουσᾰ (f. nom. sing. μοῦσα), χωρᾱ (f. nom. sing. χώρα), πολιτᾱ (m. nom. sing. πολίτης), νεανιᾱ (m. nom. sing. νεανίας), Ἑρμη (m. nom. sing. Ἑρμῆς) ἱππoτᾰ (m. nom. sing. Ep. ἱππότᾰ), &c.

II. *Stems ending in* -ι, as ποσι (m. for ποτι = Skr. *pati*), δηρι (f. strife), πολι (f.), κῑ (m. a worm), σιναπι (n. mustard), ἰδρι (m. f. knowing), &c. Some stems in -a and -o became ι-stems by throwing out these vowels, as Dor. Δεῖνι-ς, = Δειυία-ς and in later Greek Δημῆτρι-ς = Δημήτριο-ς, Διονῦσι-ς = Διονύσιο-ς.

III. *Stems* in -υ, as ιχθυ (m.), πηχυ (m.), ἐγχελυ (f.), δακρυ (n.), ἀστυ (n.), γλυκυ (m. n.), &c.

IV. Diphthongal stems, as ναυ (f.), γραυ (f.), φονευ (m.), βασιλευ (m.), υἱευ (m. beside υἱο), Ἀρευ (m. beside Ἀρες and Ἀρη), Ζευ (m.), &c.; οἱ (m. f. a sheep, the only diphthongal stem in οι; it is also an ι-stem, ὀï); βου (m. f.), χου (m. *conguis*).

The original stem of λᾶας or λᾶς (m. a stone), was probably λαϝ: its declension is very similar to that of ναῦς, thus we have gen. sing. λᾶος (beside λάου, as if from an α-stem λᾶα), dat. sing. λᾶϊ, acc. sing. λᾶα (beside λᾶαν and λᾶν from St. λᾶα), &c. That λᾶας originally contained a digamma may be inferred from the words λεύω (I stone), λευσμύς, &c. Bopp and Benfey connect it with Skr. *grâvan* (m. a stone).

LATIN STEMS.

§. 123. *Guttural Stems.*

I. *Stems in* -c (nom. sing. m. f. n. *x* and *c*): *făc* (f. a torch), *păc* (f.) *ferāc* (m. f. n. fruitful), *něc* (f.), *halēc* (nom. sing. f. *halex*, and n. *halec*, brine of fish), *salĭc* (f. a willow),

* Consult Ahrens de Dialectis Æolicis et Pseudæolicis, pp. 120, 236.

supplĭc (m. f. n.), *radĭc* (f.), *felĭc* (m. f. n.), *Cappadŏc* (m.), *præcŏc* (m. f. n.) *vōc* (f.), *atrōc* (m. f. n.), *crŭc* (f.), *trŭc* (m. f. n.) *Pollūc* (m.), &c.

II. Stems in -g (nom. sing. *x*) : *grĕg* (m.), *rēg* (m.), *remĭg* (m.), *Allobrŏg* (m.), *conjŭg* (m. f.), *frūg* (f.), &c.,

§. 124. Dental Stems.

I. Stems in -*t* (which is lost before the nom. sing. *s*, the preceding vowel being frequently lengthened in compensation): *anăt* (f. a duck), *ætāt* (f.), *abiĕt* (f.), *quiĕt* (f.), *milĭt* (m.), *lĭt* (f.), *cōt* (f. a whetstone), *virtūt* (f.), &c. *Oss* (n. a bone), *mell* (n.), *fell* (n.), were originally *t*-stems, for *oss* = *ost* (as *messis* = *mes-tis* = *met-tis* from R. *met*, cf. Gr. ὀστ-οῦν), *mell* = *melt* (c. f. Gr. μελιτ, Goth. *milith*, *honey*), *fell* = *felt*, and this perhaps for *fel-ti*.

II. Stems in –*d* (which is lost before the nom. sing. *s*, the preceding vowel being frequently lengthened in compensation) : *văd* (m. a surety), *pĕd* (m.), *herēd* (m. f.), *obsĭd* (m. a hostage), *custōd* (m.), *pecŭd* (f.), *palūd* (f.), &c.

III. Stems in –*s* : *măs* (m. a male), *văs* (n. a vessel), *genĕs* (n. nom. sing. *genus*, gen. sing. *generis* = *genesis*), *cinĭs* (m. gen. sing. *cineris* = *cinisis*, the second *i* becoming *e* through the influence of the succeeding *r*), *glĭs* (m. a dormouse), *arbŏs* (f. nom. sing. *arbor* and *arbos*), *corpŏs* (n. nom. sing. *corpus*), *mŏs* (m.), *ōs* (n.), *Lemŭs* (m. ghosts, found only in plural *Lemūres*), *Ligŭs* (m.) *s*, *jūs* (n.), *mūs* (m.), &c. *Farr* (n. corn) is probably for *fars*, *rs* becoming *rr*, as in *ferre* for *ferse*, and as *ls* becomes *ll* in *velle* for *velse*. *Văs* (n. gen. sing. *vasis*), is the only stem that retains *s* throughout its whole declension ; in other stems it becomes *t* between two vowels. The Latin infinitive in -*re* is perhaps the dative of an old stem in -*as*; *legere* would then be for *leg-es-e*, just as in Vedic similar datives are used as infinitives, such as *sahasē* (to strengthen, lit. for strengthening, Rig. I. 16, 6), &c.

IV. *Stems in -n*: *rĕn* (m. the kidney), *liĕn* (m. the spleen, beside *lieni*); stems in *-min* = I. E. *-man*, nom. sing. (*-men*), as *nomin* (n.), *agmin* (n.), &c.; *flamin* (m. nom. sing. *flamen*), *tibicin* (m.), *tubicin* (m.), *pectin* (m.), *sanguin* (nom. sing. m. *sanguis*, and n. *sanguen*), *homin* (m. nom. sing. *homo*), from an older *homōn* which is found in O. L. acc. sing. *homōnem* and *hemōnem*, *cardin* (m. a hinge, nom. sing. *cardo*), *prædōn* (m. nom. sing. *prædo*), *carn* (f. nom. sing. *caro*), for *caron*, &c. The stems of *canis* and *juvenis* were originally *n*-stems, as we see from the gen. pl. *can-um* and *juven-um*, and the corresponding Sanskrit stems *s'van* and *yuvan*, nom. sing. *s'vâ* and *yuvâ*.

V. *Stems ending in -r*: *baccăr* (n. a kind of berry), *calcūr* (n. a spur), *carcĕr* (m.), *vēr* (n.), *æquŏr* (n.), *dolōr* (m.), *fulgŭr* (n.), *fŭr* (m.), &c.

VI. *Stems ending in -l*: *săl* (m. n. salt), *animăl* (n.), *pugĭl* (m.), *sōl* (m.), *consŭl* (m.), &c.

§. 125. Labial Stems.

I. *Stems ending in -p*: *dap* (f.), *adip* (m. f. nom. sing. *adeps*, fat); compounds, the latter part of which is derived from. R. *cap* (to take), as *princip* (m. nom. sing. *princeps*), *aucup* (m. nom. sing. *auceps*), &c.

II. *Stems ending in -b*: *urb* (f.), stems in *-b* are generally short forms of other stems, as *pleb* (f. nom. sing. *plebs*), is for *plebi* (gen. pl. *plebi-um*), *scrob* (m. f. a ditch), is for *scrobi*, &c.

III. There is only one stem in *m*, viz., *hiem* (f. nom. sing. *hiems* and *hiemps*).

IV. There is only one stem in *-v*, viz., *nigv* (f. snow, nom. sing. *nix*, gen. sing. *nivis*) beside *ningui*.

§. 126. Strong and weak Stems.

The distinction between strong and weak stems has only manifested itself in Latin in a few cases: thus *patr* is the weak form of St. *pater*, and from it in Classical Latin the oblique cases of *pater* are formed, whereas in Old Latin *e* was retained, as in the gen. sing. *Diespiter-is*, *Opiter-is*, &c., similarly *ventr*, *mater*, are the weak forms of the stems *venter* and *mater*.

Carn is the weak form of *carŏn* (nom. sing. *caro*) and may be compared with Skr. *râg'ñ*, the weak form of St. *râg'ân*.

The participles in *-ant* and *-ent* retain their strong forms throughout their declensions, but it is possible that the weak form may show itself in the following examples: *pariĕt* (m. a wall, nom. sing. *paries*) from *par* = Skr. *pari* = Gr. περί and *ient* (going), and therefore, meaning literally, "what goes round," *abiet* (f. the fir), from *ab* and *ient*, and meaning literally "what goes up," *teget* (f. a mat, lit. "what covers" for *tegent*, part. of *teg-o*), *potestat* for *potet-tat* = *potent-tat*, *egestat* for *eget-tat* = *egent-tat*, while we have the strong form of the participial stem in *voluntat*, O. *herentat*.

§. 127. Vocalic Stems.

I. *Stems ending in -a (a, e, o).*

1°. *Stems in -a* (which lose the final *s* of the nom. sing. although it originally existed there, as in *paricidas* found in the law of Numa, and *hosticapas*, i. e. *hostium captor*), as *equă* (f. originally *equā*), *incolă* (m.), *formă* (f. but *formā* on the inscription on the tomb of the Scipios), *aquilă* (f. but *aquilā* in Ennius), &c. Greek nouns in -ας lose the final ς when borrowed by the Latin, as *Pintia* (for Φιντίας), *Apella*, *Mena*, &c., Gr. ποιητής (m.) becomes *poeta* and χάρτης (m.) becomes *charta* (f.)

2°. *Stems ending in -e* (all of which are feminine except *dies*, which is either masculine or feminine, while *meridies* is always masculine): *re* (nom. sing. *res*), *fide* (f.), *plebe* (f.) &c. These stems are closely connected with those in *-a*, and we frequently find two forms of the same stem existing beside each other, one ending in *-a* and another in *-e*, as *barbaria* and *barbarie*, *materia* and *materie*, *effigia* and *effigie*, &c.

3°. *Stems in o: equo* (m. nom. sing. *equos*, later *equus*), *alvo* (f. the stomach, nom. sing. *alvos*, later *alvus*), *jugo* (n. nom. sing. *jugom*, later *jugum*), &c. We frequently find stems in *-a* beside stems in *-o*, as *transfuga* beside *profugo*, *collega* beside *sacrilego*, *Graiugena* beside *Asiageno* and *privigno* (= *privigeno*), &c. When r preceded o, the latter was generally dropped and e inserted in the nom. sing. when another consonant immediately preceded, as in *caper* = Gr. καπρό-ς, *ager* = Gr. ἀγρός, &c.: this inserted e was not retained in the oblique cases, as in gen. sing. *capri*, *agri*, &c., except where it belonged to the root, as in *corniger*, *armiger*, *prosper* (from *pro* and R. *sper*, whence *sper-o*, *spes*, O. L. acc. pl. *sper-es*), &c., and in some other cases as O. L. *magisteres* = *magisteri*, *dexteri* beside *dextri*, &c. In many cases o is retained in the nominative after r, as in O. L. *socerus* = *socer*, O. L. *puerus* = *puer* (= *poverus*, which also became *por* in the proper names, *Marcipor*, *Publipor*, &c., and was then declined as a stem in *-r*), O. L. *vulturus* = *vultur*, *numerus*, *umerus*, *uterus*, *prosperus* = *prosper*, *herus*, *verus*, *laurus*, *taurus*, *severus*, *serus*, *mirus*, *virus*, *-parus* (*oviparus*), *-vorus* (*carnivorus*), *purus*, *murus*. After *l* o is only omitted in *famul* beside *famulus*, and *nihil* = *nihilum*, just as in N. U. *katel* = L. *catulus* and O. O. *Mutil* = *Mutilos*.

O is also lost in nom. sing. in O. L. *damnas* for *damnats* = *damnatos*, just as in N. U. *taçez* = L. *tacitos*, O. O. *hurz* = L. *hortos*, &c. In Old Latin o was lost after *i*, and then the nom. sing. *s* was itself frequently lost, as in *Clodis* and *Clodi* = *Claudius*, *Cornelis*, and *Corneli* = *Cornelius*, &c.

O was written in the nom. sing. of all *o*-stems until about the middle of the third century, B. C., when *u* took its place, except in stems ending in *-vo*, in which o was still written, as in *servo-s*, *equo-s*, &c.

II. *Stems ending in -i* (nom. sing. m. f. *-is*, and *-es*, n. *-e*): *amni* (m. nom. sing. *amnis*), *torqui* (m. f. nom. sing. *torquis* and *torques*), *avi* (f. nom. sing. *avis*), *scrobi*

(f. a ditch. nom. sing. *scrobs* and *scrobis*), *sinapi* (mustard, nom. sing. f. *sinapis*, and n. *sinape*), *mari* (n. nom. sing. *mare*, pl. *mari-a*), *sali* (n. the sea, nom. sing. *sale* beside St. *sal*), *ossi* (n. a bone, nom. sing. *osse* beside St. *oss*), *lacti* (n. milk, nom. sing. *lacte* beside St. *lact*), &c. In nouns formed with suffix *-ti* the stem of the nom. sing. generally ends in *-t* as *menti* (f. nom. sing. *mens* = *ments*), *morti* (f. nom. sing. *mors* = *morts*), *juventuti* (f. nom. sing. *juventus* = *juventuts*), *civitati* (f. nom. sing. *civitas* = *civitats*), &c. Stems ending in *-ri* often lose the final *i* and insert *e* before *r*, like stems in *-ro*; *imbri* (m. nom. sing. *imber*), *acri* (m. f. n. nom. sing. m. *acer* and *acris*), *silvestri* (m. f. n. nom. sing. m *silvester* and *silvestris*), &c. Similarly *i* is sometimes lost when preceded by *l* as in *vigili* (m. f. n. nom. sing. m. *vigil*), *pugili* (m. nom. sing. *pugil*), &c. *I* is frequently added to adjectival stems in *-u*, and thus new stems in *-i* are formed, as *brevi* = *bregu-i* from *bregu* = Gr. βραχυ, *gravi* = *garu-i* from *garu* = Gr. βαρυ = Skr. *guru*, *levi* = *legu-i* from *legu* = Gr. ἐλαχυ = Skr. *laghu*, *suavi* = *suadu-i* from *suadu* = Gr. ἡδυ = Skr. *svâdu*, *pingui* from *pingu* = Gr. παχυ, *tenui* from *tenu* = Gr. ταυυ = Skr. *tanu*. *I* is also frequently employed to lengthen consonantal stems, as in *voc-i-bus*, *duc-i-bus* for *voc-bus* *duc-bus*, *amant-i-a*, *amant-i-um*, *amant-i-bus*, &c. *Vates* is for *vats* (gen. pl. *vat-um*), from a root = Z. *vat* (to speak); *canis* (and *canes*) is for *cans* (gen. pl. *can-um*); *navis* is for *navs* = Gr. ναῦς = Skr. *nâus*; O. L. *Jovis* (nom. sing.) = *Jovs* = Gr. Ζεύς = Skr. *dyâus*, *bovis* or *bos* = *bovs* = Gr. βοῦς = Skr. *gâus*.

III. *Stems ending in* -u: *fructu* (m.), *lacu* (m.), *socru* (f.), *manu* (f.), *cornu* (n.), *genu* (n.). These stems are often interchanged with others in *-o*: thus beside the stems *senatu, tumultu, cupressu, penu* (provisions), &c., we also find the stems *senato, tumulto, cupresso, peno* (n.), &c. In some cases we find consonantal side forms of *u*-stems, as *pecūd* (f.), and *pecos* (n.) beside *pecu* (n.), *impet* (m.) beside *impetu* (m.), *penos* (n.) beside *penu* (f.).

No Latin stem ends in a diphthong.

The Cases.

§. 128. *The Nominative Singular.*

The nominative singular masculine and feminine is formed from the stem by the addition of *s*, which is derived from the pronominal root *sa* (*sa* = Gr. ὁ, *sâ* = Gr. ἡ). The nominative singular neuter is identical with the acc. sing. and consequently adds *m* to the stem in the case of *a*-stems, while in all others it is identical with the stem itself, subject only to the euphonic laws peculiar to each language.

I. *Sanskrit Nom. Sing.* In all consonantal stems *s* is omitted, and in some cases the vowel of the final syllable is lengthened in compensation for this omission, and in others not: thus *durmanás* = *durmanas* + *s*, is nom. sing. of St. *durmanas* = Gr. δυσμενες, whereas *bharan* = *bharant* + *s*, is nom. sing. of St. *bharant* = Gr. φεροντ. Masc. and fem. stems in -*âr* and -*ar* reject both *r* and *s*, and form their nom. sing. in -*â*: thus *pitâ* is nom. sing. of St. *pitar* = Gr. πατερ, and *dâtâ* is nom. sing. of St. *dâtâr* = Gr. δοτηρ. Masc. and fem. nouns in -*an* and -*in* reject both *n* and *s*, and lengthen preceding vowel: thus, *râgâ* is nom. sing. of St. *râg'an* (m. a king), and *dhanî* is nom. sing. of St. *dhanin* (rich). In all vocalic stems *s* is retained, except in feminine ones which end in -*â* or -*î*, if the latter are polysyllabic. When *â* however belongs to the root, *s* remains as in *vis'vapâ-s* (m. and f. all preserving, from *vis'va*, all, and *pâ*, to preserve), *dhanadâ-s* (m. and f. wealth-giving, from *dhana*, wealth and *dâ* to give).*

II. *Greek Nom. Sing.* In the case of guttural and labial stems, *s* is simply added, and the nom. sing. ends in ξ and ψ, as ψύλαξ from St. ψυλακ (m.), φλόξ from St. φλογ (f.), ὄψ from St. ὀπ (f.), &c. In dental stems τ and δ are never kept

---

* For further particulars as to forming the nom. sing. in Sanskrit, consult §. 104, and §. 107-113; also Bopp's and Max Muller's "Sanskrit Grammars."

before ς, but always disappear, and the preceding vowel is generally lengthened in compensation: thus we have χάρις from χαριτ (f.), λαμπας from λαμπαδ (f.), πούς from ποδ (m.), τετυφώς from τετυπϜοτ, νύξ from νυκτ, &c. In δάμαρ from δαμαρτ (f.) both τ and σ disappear. Stems in -ντ sometimes lose both consonants before σ, as in τύψᾱς from τυψαντ, δούς from δοντ, θείς from θεντ, &c., and sometimes lose τ and ς, retaining ν, as in φέρων from φεροντ, &c. The Æolic dialect kept ν before ς, as in τιθένς = τιθείς, and in this respect is similar to Zend, Latin, Lithuanian, and Old Prussian; thus we have Z. *barans* = L. *ferens* = Gr. φέρων, Lith. *degans* (burning), O. P. *sidans* (sitting), &c. In ν-stems the nasal is sometimes thrown out and the preceding vowel lengthened, as in τάλᾱς from ταλαν, κτείς from κτεν, &c., while in other cases the nasal is retained and the preceding vowel lengthened to compensate for the loss of ς, as in τέρην from τερεν, φρήν from φρεν (f.), μείζων from μειζον, χθών from χθον (f.), &c. We often find a later nominative in ν beside an older one in ς, as θίν beside θίς, δελφίν beside δελφίς, &c. Σ is lost after ρ, as in χείρ from χερ (f.), πατήρ from πατερ (m.), &c.: whereas in Æolic both consonants are kept, as in χέρς = χείρ, μάκαρς. In μάρτυς from μαρτυρ, ρ appears to be lost before ς. The solitary λ-stem (ἅλς) retains both λ and ς. In ς-stems ς is lost, and the preceding vowel lengthened as in δυσμενής from δυσμενες.

In vocalic stems ς is simply added to stem, as in ἀγρός from ἀγρο (m.), ταμίας from ταμιᾱ (m.), πόλις from πολι (f.), ἴδρις from ἰδρι, βοητύς from βοητυ (f.), &c. Σ is lost in feminine stems in ᾱ (η) as χώρα, κορη, &c., and in the Homeric forms, ἱππότᾰ (m.) for ἱππότης, αἰχμητᾰ (m.) for αἰχμητής, &c.

III. *Latin Nom. Sing.* In guttural and labial stems *s* is simply added to the stem, as in *vox, halex, lex, auceps, urbs,* &c., from the stems *voc* (f.), *halec* (f.), *leg.* (f.), *aucup* (m.), *urb* (f.), &c. In the case of adjectival stems this *s* is also retained in the neuter nom., as *audax* (m. f. n.), *ferox* (m. f. n.),

&c.: *atriplex* (the orach) is also neuter, and *halec* (n.) is a side-form of *halex* (f.) In dental stems *t* and *d* disappear before *s*, and the preceding vowel was originally lengthened in compensation; this lengthening is only found in Classical Latin, in monosyllables, and where the preceding syllable ends in *i*, as in *pēs = pĕd + s*, *vās = văd + s*, *ariēs = ariĕt + s*, *pariēs = pariĕt + s*, *abiēs = abiĕt + s;* in other cases the vowel has become short as in *milĕs = milet + s*, *pedĕs = pedet + s*, &c. Participial stems in *–nt* only reject *t*, as in *amans = amant + s*, &c. In Old Latin and in the vulgar dialect we find *n* also lost in *infas, sapies*, &c. for *infans, sapiens*, &c.: compare Gr. τύψας for τυψαντ + ς. In these stems in *-nt s* is also retained in the neuter nom. as *sapiens* (m. f. n.), &c. In *s*-stems *s* is lost, and the preceding vowel, although originally lengthened as in Greek, is generally short in Classical Latin. Traces, however, of its having been originally lengthened still remain, as in *Cerēs* (f.) from St. *Cerĕs*, *arbōs* (f.) from St. *arbŏs*, &c. In the declension of these stems the final *s* became *r* in the oblique cases, except in *vas;* and in the case of masculine and feminine nouns this *r* often supplanted the final *s* of the nominative, especially in later Latin; thus we have *puber* (m.) beside *pubes*, *arbor* (f.) beside *arbōs*, *sudor* (m.) for *sudōs* = Gr. ἰδρώς, *honor* (m.) beside *honos*, *vomer* (m. a ploughshare) beside *vomis* (m.), *lepor* (m. wit) beside *lepos* from St. *lepōs* (gen. sing. *lepōr-is*) &c. The nom. sing. ends in *-us* in *lepus* (m. a hare), from St. *lepŏs*, and in *vetus* (m. old) beside *veter* (m. id.) used by Ennius. Neuter stems in *-os* retain the final *s* in nom. sing., yet we find *robur* (n.) = Skr. *rádhas* (n. strength) and *calor* used as a neuter in Plautus Merc. 660, *nec calor nec frigus metuo*. Masculine and feminine stems in *–n* lose the final *-ns* in the nom.: thus we have *homo* for *homōns*, *combibo* (m.) for *combibōns*, &c. In some cases *n* is retained, as in *pecten* (m.), *flamen* (m.), &c., and in *sanguis* for *sanguins*, *s* is kept and *n* lost. *S* is always lost after *r* and *l*, but the preceding vowel was originally lengthened in compensation as in Greek: thus we have *lector* (m.) for *lector + s, mater* (f.) for *mater + s, sol* (m.) for *sol + s, pār* (m.) for *pār + s, sāl* (m.) for *sāl + s*, &c.

In the *i*- and *u*-stems *s* is kept, as in *amni-s* (m.) *fructu-s* (m.), &c. In stems ending in *-ti, i* is frequently lost before *s*, as in *mens* (f.) for *ment + s = menti + s, mors* (f.) for *mort + s = morti + s, vetustas* (f.) for *vetustat + s = vetustati + s, senectus* (f.) for *senectut + s = senectuti + s*, &c. After *r* and *l, is* was lost in masculine stems and *e* was inserted before *r*, when another consonant immediately preceded, as *acer* for *acri + s*, *equester* for *equestri + s*, &c.: the full form is kept in the fem. nom. *acris, equestris*, &c. Similarly we have *vigil* for and beside *vigilis*. In neuter stems *i* was sometimes lost and sometimes changed into *e*, as in *animal, calcar*, &c., and *mare, exemplare* (also *exemplar*), &c. Stems ending in *-o* also retain *s*, as *servo-s* (m.), *equo-s* (m.), &c., except when *r* precedes, in which case *-os* (*-us*) is often lost, as in *ager* for *agro + s, puer* for *puero + s*, &c. *O* (*u*) was sometimes lost after *t*, and then *t* disappeared, as in *damnas* for *damnato-s* ; similarly we find O. U. *pihaz*, N. U. *pihos* = L. *piatus*, O. O. *hurz* = L. *hortus*, N. U. *taçez* = L. *tacitus*. After *i o* was sometimes lost, as in *Cornelis* for *Cornelius, Clodis* for *Clodius*, &c., and then *s* sometimes disappears, as in *Corneli*, &c., which occur as nom. s. on inscriptions : similarly in Oscan we find *Heïrennis* for *Herennius*, in which *u* first became *ï* or *i* (as in *Püpidiis* = L. *Popidius, Vïunikiis* = L. *Vinicius*) and then *ïi* or *ii* became *i*. We also find *o* (*u*) lost after *n* in Umbrian, as in *Ikuvins* = L. *Iguvinus*, and in Oscan, as in *Bantins* = L. *Bantinus, Pümpaiians* = L. *Pompeianus*. *O* is lost after *k* in O. O. *tiuvtiks* = L. *tuticus*. Feminine stems in *-ā* have entirely lost *s*, and *-ā* has become *-ă* in Classical Latin : Bücheler suggests that the change of final *-ā* of nom. sing. into *-ă* was contemporaneous with that of final *-ād* of abl. sing. into *-ā*. In Old Umbrian this *ā* sometimes became *u*, and in New Umbrian it always became *o*, as in O. U. *tuta, tutu*, N. U. *toto* = *tuta* (a city); similarly in Old Oscan it became *ü*, and in New Oscan *o*, as in O. O. *viü* = L. *via*, O. O. *tüvtü*, N. O. *tovto* = *tuta*. Masculine stems in -*a*, such as *incola*, *nauta*, &c., have also lost *s*, but that they once had it is shown by the forms *paricidas*, *hasticapas* (see page 246).

§. 129. The Nominative Plural.

The sign of the nom. pl. appears to have been originally the reduplication of that of the nom. sing. Its oldest form, accordingly, must have been -*sasa*, whence came firstly -*sas* and then -*as*. *Sas*, as the sign of the nom. pl., occurs in Vedic Sanskrit in the declension of the *a*-stems: thus we have, as nom. pl. *dhûmâ-sas* from *dhûma* (m. smoke), *dêvâ-sas* from *dêva* (m. a god), *pâvakâ-sas* from *pâvakâ* (f. pure). Traces of this -*sas* also appear in Zend, in which such forms of the nom. pl. as *vĕhrkâonhô* (m. wolves) = I. E. *varkâ-sas*, &c., point back to older forms in -*sas*. The nom. pl. neuter is the same as the acc. pl. neuter.

1. *Sanskrit Nom. Pl.* Masculine and feminine stems form this case always in -*as*, before which *ĭ* and *ŭ* are gunated; thus we have *marut-as* from *marut* (m. the wind), *mâtar-as* from *mâtar* (f. a mother), *nâdy-as* from *nâdî* (f. a river), *s'ivâs* for *s'iva* + *as* from *s'iva* (m. fortunate) or for *sivâ* + *as* (f. id.), *kavay-as* from *kavi* (m. a wise man), *dhênav-as* from *dhênu* (f. a milch cow). In the Veda we find nom. s. of stems in -*ĭ* and -*ŭ* without gunation of these vowels, as *ary-as* from *ari* (m. an enemy), *mumukshv-as* from *mumukshu* (m. a sage abstracted from all human passion). In Vedic we also find nom. pl. of polysyllabic *ĭ*-stems formed by simply adding *s* to the stem, as *dêvî-s* from *devî* (f. a goddess).

II. *Greek Nom. Pl.* Masculine and feminine stems form this case by adding -ες to the stem; thus we have φλέβ-ες from φλεβ (f. a vein), ποιμέν-ες from ποιμήν (m.), πατέρ-ες from πατερ (m.), ἰχθύ-ες from ἰχθυ (m.), κί-ες from κι (m. a worm).

Stems ending in *ĭ* and *ŭ* may either gunate the final vowel or not, before adding -ες: thus we have as examples of -ες being added to unchanged stem, μάντι-ες from μαντι (m.), οἴ-ες from ὀι (m. f.), ἴδρι-ες from ἰδρι (m. f.), νέκυ-ες from νεκυ (m.), &c.; and as examples of gunated stems we have, πόλεις, πόληες, πόλεες = πολεy-ες from πολει, the gunated form of πολι (f. a city), whence also we have without gunation, Ion. πόλι-ες, πολεῖς = πολεϝ-ες from πολευ, the gunated form of πολυ, ταχεῖς = ταχέες = ταχεϝ-ες from ταχυ, ἐγχέλεις = ἐγχελεϝ-ες from ἐγχελυ (f.) beside Ion. ἐγχέλυ-ες, &c. Masculine and feminine stems in *o* and *a* (= Skr. *ă*) form their nom. pl. in -οι and -αι, as ἵπποι from ἱππο (m.), and χῶραι from χωρα (f.) These forms originally ended in ς and were not developed till after the Greek and Latin languages separated from each other. The loss of the final ς may have occurred first in the nom. pl. of the pronominal stems ὁ or το, ἁ or τα. Schleicher suggests that τοί (= οἱ), and ταί (= αἱ) may have arisen from *ta-y-as* and *tâ-y-as*, the pronominal stems *ta* and *tâ* having been increased by *y* (*i*) before the addition of –*as*, and that *tayas* and *tâyas* became *tai* and *tâi* by the loss of the final syllable. In Sanskrit we find *s* lost only in the nom. pl. masc. of some pronominal stems, while the fem. retains *s*: thus *yê* (m.), beside *yâs* (f.) from *ya* (who), *tê* (m.), beside *tâs* (f.) from *ta* (he, she), *tyê* (m.), beside *tyâs* (f.), from *tya* (this), &c. This similarity between the nom. pl. masc. of the pronouns in Sanskrit and Greek is not sufficient to prove that these nominatives were already developed in Indo-European times. All that can be asserted is that it is just possible that the final *s* of the nom. pl. was lost in some pronouns before the first separation occurred in the Indo-European family of languages.

III. *Latin Nom. Pl.* Masculine and feminine consonantal stems originally formed this case by the addition of -*ĕs* = Gr. ἕς. Final *s* was frequently lost in Old Latin, as we see from Inscriptions, on which we find such forms as *Pisaurese* for

Pisaurenses. Even *ĕ* itself was also lost, so that the nom. pl. was reduced to the mere stem, as in U. *frater* (fratres), O. *censtur* (censores), L. *quattuor* for *quattuor-es*, *Luceres* for *Lucerenses*, *Tities* for *Titienses*, *Ramnes* for *Ramnenses*. Consonantal stems, however, perhaps during the third century, B. C. ceased to form their nom. pl. by the addition of *–ĕs*, but, assuming the form of the *i*-stems, formed this case by adding *–ēs*, as in *leg-ēs, bov-ēs, ferent-ēs*. The nom. pl. of the *i*-stems ends in *–ēs*, as *ovēs* from *ovi*, *hostēs* from *hosti*, &c. : *ē* here may be explained in either of two ways, either as being for *ie* (*ovēs* = *ovi* + *ĕs*, as πόλι-ες from πολι, without gunation of stem-vowel) or as being for *ĕĕ* (*ovēs* = *ovĕĕs* = *ovey* + *ĕs* as πύλεις for πολεy + ες from πολι, with gunation of stem-vowel). *I*-stems also form their nom. pl. in *–eis* and *–īs*, which are probably of later formation than *–ēs*, although some writers hold that *–īs* (= *-iis* = *-iĕs*) was the oldest form. The nom. pl. of the *u*-stems ends in *–ūs*, as *fructūs* from *fructu* : *fructūs* may either be for *fructu* + *ĕs* (as νέκυες from νεκυ, without gunation of stem-vowel) or for *fructov-es* (as πήχεις = πηχεϝ-ες from πηχυ, with gunation of stem-vowel). The nom. pl. of the *a*-stems ends in *–ai*, the original termination was *–ās*, as may be inferred from the O. U. *urtas* = L. *ortæ*, N. U. *ivengar* = L. *juvencæ*, N. O. *scriftas* = L. *scriptæ*, N. O. *pas* = L. *quæ*. Final *s* was then lost, as we see from inscriptions, on which we find as nom. pl. *matrona*, &c., and then after the analogy of the pronominal declension, *i* was added, and the nom. pl. of these stems ended in *–ai*, as in *tabelai, datai* (Sc. de Bacc.), which finally became *ae*. In Classical Latin the nom. pl. of the *o*-stem ends in *–ī*, but originally *–es* was attached immediately to the stem, so that the original termination was *–oes*. This termination appears in various forms : thus we find as nom. pl. *pilumnoe poploe* (in Carmen Saliare, explained by Festus as Romani pilis uti assueti), *fesceninæ* (qui depellere fascinum credebantur), *modies, ques, ploirumē, leibereis, oinvorsei, ministrīs*, &c. Final *s* is retained in Oscan and Umbrian : thus we have O.O. *Nùvlanùs* = L. *Nolani*, *putùrūs* = Gr. πότεροι, O. U. *Ikuvinus*, N. U. *screitor* = L. *scripti*, &c. In Latin *ē*-stems *s* is kept as in *diēs*, &c., but in some cases the pl. is formed from a corresponding *a*-stem, as nom. sing. *intemperies* or *intemperia*, nom. pl. *intemperiæ*.

§. 130. THE NOMINATIVE DUAL.

The original termination of the masculine and feminine nominative dual was *–sâs*, which was merely the lengthened form of the nom. pl. *-sas;* similarly *ī*, the case-ending of the nom. dual neuter, is the lengthened form of *-ĭ*, the case-ending of the nom. pl. neuter, and *–bhyâm* (for *–bhyâms*), the case-ending of the dat. abl. and instr. dual, is the lengthened form of *-bhyas* (for *–bhyams*), the case-ending of the dat. and abl. pl. As *-sas* became *–as*, so *-sâs* became *–âs*. That the dual nom. ended in *-âs* is proved by the Zend. nom. dual, which sometimes ends in *-âo*, which represents an I. E. *-âs*. The nom. acc. and voc. dual have the same case-ending.

I. *Sanskrit Nom. Dual.* Masculine and feminine stems form this case by the addition of *âu*, as *marut-âu* from *marut* (m.), *nady-âu* from *nadî* (f.), *s'ivâu* from *s'iva* (m.), &c. In Vedic we find *â* for *âu*, as in *ubhâ* (both), *as'vinâ* (the two As'vins), &c. Masculine and feminine stems in *-ĭ* and *-ŭ* omit *-âu*, and in compensation lengthen the final vowel, as in *kavî* from *kavĭ* (m.), *dhênû* from *dhênŭ* (f.). Feminine stems in *-â* merely change this vowel into *-ê*, as in *s'ivê* from *s'ivâ* (f.). Bopp* considers that the original form of *s'ivê* was *s'ivay-âu* and that, when the final *u* had been lost, *s'ivayâ* became *s'ivê*, as Skr. *k'intayâmi* (I think), has become *h'intêmi* in Prâkrit. The nom. neuter is formed by adding *-î* to the stem as *s'ivê* for *s'iva + î* from *s'iva* (n.), *vâri-ṇ-î* from *vâri* (n. water),

---

* Consult Bopp's "Comparative Grammar," vol. I., p. 418, and Bopp's "Sanskrit Grammar," p. 93.

balint from *balin* (n. strong): stems ending-in -*i* and *ŭ* insert *n* before -*î*.

II. *Greek Nom. Dual.* The sign of this case for the three genders is ε for all stems except those ending in -*a* (ο, α): thus we have μέλανε (m. n.) from μελαν, ἤδίε (m. n.) = ἤδεϝε from ἤδυ, πόλιε from πολι (f.) beside πόλεε and πόληε = πολεγ-ε, &c, In the *a*-stems the dual case-ending coalesces with the stem-vowel: thus we have ἴππω from ἱππο (m.), κόρᾱ from κορᾱ (f.), &c.

III. *Latin Nom. Dual.* There are only two dual nom. s. in Latin, *duŏ* and *ambŏ*: *duō* = Skr. *dváu* = Gr. δύω, *ambo* = Skr. *ubháu* = Gr. ἄμφω.

§. 131. THE ACCUSATIVE SINGULAR.

This case in all masculine and feminine nouns ended in –*m*, which was attached immediately to the stem if it ended in a vowel, or by means of –*a* if it ended in a consonant. In the *a*-stems the neuter acc. sing. was formed by adding -*m*, but in all other neuters the stem and the acc. sing. were identical. The acc. sign. -*m* or -*am* is perhaps connected with the pronominal root which is found in Skr. *am-u* (that), *i-mê* (those), &c.

I. *Sanskrit Acc. Sing.* Masculine and feminine consonantal stems add -*am*, as *marut-am* (m.), *bharant-am* (m.), *pitar-am* (m.), &c. The acc. sing. neut. is merely the stem itself, subject to the euphonic laws of Sanskrit, as *bharat* (n.) from St. *bharant*, *hṛt* (n.) from St. *hṛd*, &c. Vocalic stems add -*m*, as *s'iva-m* (m.), *s'ivâ-m* (f.), *kavi-m* (m.), *nadî-m* (f.), &c. Monosyllabic vocalic stems, however, except those in -*ô*, add -*am*, as *nâv-am* from *nâu* (f.), *bhiy-am* from *bhî* (f. fear), *bhuv-am* from *bhû* (f. the earth), &c. The acc. sing. neut. of stems in -*i* and -*u* is merely the stem, but in the *a*-stems *m* is added, as in *s'iva-m* from *s'iva* (n.). The nom. sing. neut. and the acc. sing. neuter are the same.

s

II. *Greek Acc. Sing.* Masculine and feminine consonantal stems add -α for -αν = I. E. *-am*, as in λαμπάδ-α (f.), φέροντ-α (m.), πατέρ-α (m.), &c. Masculine and feminine vocalic stems, except those ending in ευ, add -ν, as μάντι-ν (m.), νέκυ-ν (m.) ἀγρό-ν (m.), φυγή-ν (f.), &c.: those in -ευ add -α, as βασιλῆ-α and βασιλέ-α = βασιλεϜ-α (m.), ἱερῆα and ἱερέ-α = ἱερεϜ-α (m.). Beside ναῦ-ν (f.) we find Hom. νῆϜ-α and νέϜ-α; beside ὀφρύ-ν (f.), we find the later form ὀφρύ-α; from εὐρυ we have both εὐρύ-ν and εὐρέ-α = εὐρεϜ-α, &c. In consonantal stems and those ending in -ι and -υ, the acc. neuter is merely the stem, subject to the euphonic laws of the Greek language, while in o-stems it ends in -ν; thus we have τέρας (n.), for τερατ, φέρον (n.) for φεροντ, μέλι (n.) for μελιτ, ἴδρι (n.), γλυκύ (n.), σοφό-ν (n.), &c. Stems ending in -ιο (= I. E. -ya) sometimes lose o in later Greek, as in μάρτυρι-ν for μαρτύριο-ν, &c.; similarly in Umbrian we find *terti-m* = *tertio-m*, &c., and in modern Greek παιδί for παιδιν = παιδίον, μάρτι for μαρτιν = μάρτιον, &c.

III. *Latin Acc. Sing.* Masculine and feminine consonantal stems form this case in *-em*, thus agreeing in form with the *i*-stems: thus we have *voc-em* (f.), *ferent-em* (m. f.), *patr-em*, &c. This *-em* does not represent an I. E. *-am*, as has been suggested by some writers, but the consonantal stems were lengthened by *i*, which became *e* before the acc. sing. *-m*. Masculine and feminine vocalic stems add *-m*, as *fructu-m*, (m.), *bona-m* (f.), *bono-m* (m.), &c. In the *i*-stems the stem-vowel generally becomes *e*, as this vowel is more easily pronounced with *m* than *i*; but we nevertheless find *i* retained in many feminine stems, as *febri-m*, *siti-m*, *tussi-m*, *Tiberi-m*, *vi-m*, *navi-m* (also *nave-m*), &c. The acc. s sing. of *su-s* (f.) and *gru-s* (f.) are *su-em* (compare Gr. σῦ-ν and ὗ-ν) and *gru-em*. In neuter stems the acc. sing. is merely the stem, subject to the euphonic laws of Latin: thus we have *lac* for *lact*, *mel* for *mell* = *melt*, *cor* for *cord*, *mare* for *mari*, *nomen*, &c. In some cases the acc. sing. neuter agrees with the nom. sing.

masc., as in such forms as *feren-s* for *ferent-s*, *audac-s*, &c. In Umbrian and Oscan the acc. sing. ends in -*m*, as in Latin, and this *m* very often disappears, as in Old Latin: thus in Umbrian we have O. U. *puplum* = N. U. *poplom* = L. *populum*; O. U. *tutam* = N. U. *totam*, N. U. *Fisim* = *Fisiom*, N. U. *tertim* = L. *tertiom*, &c.; and in Oscan, O. O. *hurtum* = L. *hortum*, *viam* and *via* = L. *viam*, &c. Consonantal stems in Umbrian do not go over to the *i*-declension, as in Latin, but form their acc. in -*um* or -*u*, and -*om* or -*o*, as O. U. *ûhtûru* = L. *auctorem*, N. U. *curnaco* = L. *cornicem*, &c.

§. 132. The Accusative Plural.

The accusative plural of masc. and fem. stems appears to have been formed by adding *s* to the acc. singular; its ending was, therefore, originally -*ns* (= -*ms*), the labial *m* becoming the dental *n* on account of the following dental *s*. Traces of this -*ns* are found in Sanskrit, Zend, Greek, and Latin; but it is kept perfect in Gothic vocalic stems, for the euphonic laws of this language did not forbid such a combination as *ns*, occurring at the end of a word. The acc. pl. neuter and the nom. pl. neuter were formed by adding -*a* to the stem.

I. *Sanskrit Acc. Pl.* Masculine and feminine consonantal and monosyllabic vocalic stems form this case by adding -*as* to the stem, as *marut-as* from *marut*, *bhiy-as* (f.) from *bhî*, &c. Masculine vocalic stems, ending in a short vowel, form their acc. sing. by adding *n*, and lengthening the stem-vowel: thus we have *s'ivân* = *s'iva-ns* from *s'iva* (m.), *kavîn* = *kavi-ns* from *kavi* (m.), &c. The acc. pl. of masc. stems in -*tar* ends in *tṛn*, as *pi-tṛn*, &c.; but an older termination was -*tar-as*, as in Vedic *pitar-as* from *pitar*. Feminine vocalic stems form their acc. pl. by adding *s*, and lengthening the stem-vowel, when it is short, as in *gatîs* = *gati-ns* from *gati* (f. motion), *s'ivâs* = *s'ivâ-ns* from *sivâ* (f.), &c. We find traces of the termination -*ns* still appearing in Sanskrit, as in *kâns*, the acc.

pl. of *ka* (m. who), which occurs only before *kán*, the regular form: thus *káns kan* = O. Pr. *kans kans*, compare Gothic acc. pl. *hvans*, found in *hvans-uh* (quoscunque).* In Vedic also masc. stems in -*i* and -*u* form their acc. pl. in -*iñr*, -*uñr*† before vowels, and occasionally before *y*, *v*, and *h*, as in *giriñr* from *giri* (m. a mountain), *ṛtuñr* from *ṛtu* (m. a season), *vasuñr* from *vasu* (m.); we also find in Vedic *nṛ̃nh* and *nṛ̃nr* as the acc. pl. of *nar* (m. a man): in these cases -*ñr* and -*ñh* represent an original -*ns*; compare the Gothic acc. s pl. *gasti-ns*, *sunu-ns* from *gasti* and *sunu*, and Z. *nĕr-a-ṅs*. Neuter vocalic stems form the acc. pl. by lengthening the stem-vowel, and adding *ni;* neuter consonantal stems add *i*, and insert *n* before the final consonant, except in the case of stems ending in a nasal, or *y*, *r*, *l*, and *v*: thus we have *s'ivâ-ni* from *s'iva* (n.), *vârî-ni* from *vari* (n. water), *tâlû-ni* from *tâlu* (n. the palate), *g'aganti* from *g'agat* (n. the world), *hṛndi* from *hṛd* (n. the heart), &c. Stems ending in -*s* or -*n* also lengthen the preceding vowel, as in *manâṅsi* from *manas* (n. the mind), *balîni* from *balin* (n. strong), &c. This final *i* is probably a weakened form of an older *a*, and was obviously introduced in Sanskrit after the other Indo-European languages had separated from the parent stock. In the Vedas we find for the acc. pl. terminations -*âni*, -*îni*, and -*ûni*, -*â*, -*î*, and -*û*, as in *vanâ* for *vanâni* from *vana* (n. a wood), *vis'vâ* for *vis'vâni* from *vis'va* (n. all), *vârî* for *vârini* from *vâri* (n. water), *purû* for *purûni* from *puru* (n. much).‡ *Vanâ* and *vis'vâ* are formations similar to Gr. κακά and L. *bona*, where the final *a* was originally long; but in *purû* for *puru-a*, and *vârî* for *vâri-a*, the final *a* has been assimilated to the preceding vowels, whereas in Greek and Latin this is never done, as in Gr. ἴδρια, γούυα for γονυα, L. *maria*, *pecua*.

II. *Greek Acc. Pl.* This case was formed by adding ς to

---

* Consult Bopp's "Sanskrit Grammar," p. 97.

† The sound of the Anunâsika is represented by *ñ*.

‡ We also find in Vedic as acc. s pl. *madhu*, *vâri*.

the acc. sing., but the full termination -νς was only kept in the Argive and Cretan dialects; when ν was lost, the preceding vowel was originally lengthened in compensation, traces of which still remain; thus we have ἰχθύ-ας and ἰχθῦς = ἰχθῦνς from ἰχθῠ (m.; compare acc. sing. ἰχθύα and ἰχθύν), γλυκεῖς = γλυκεϝ-ας, from γλυκυ (m.), πόλεις = πολεy-ας beside πόλι-ας, πόλη-ας, and πόλῖς = πολῖνς from πολῐ (f.), &c. The full term -νς is found in Arg. and Cret. τόνς = τους, πρειγευτάνς = πρεσβευτάς. In Lesbian -ονς and -ανς became -οις and -αις, just as we find in the same dialect, τάλαις = τάλανς for τάλας, κινήσαις = κινήσανς for κινησαντς, &c. : thus we have κάλαις = κάλας, σόφαις = σύφας, ἀλλάλοις = ἀλλήλους, &c. In Doric -ονς became ως, as ἵππως = ἵππους. The acc. pl. neuter is formed by adding a to the stem, as in φέροντ-α, γένη = γενεσ-α, ἴδρι-α, ἄστη = ἀστεϝ-α from ἀστυ, &c.

III. *Latin Acc. Pl.* In masculine and feminine stems this case always ends in -*s*, the vowel preceding which is always long, the consonantal stems, as usual, assuming the form of those in -*i*: thus we have *leg-ēs, ferent-ēs, patrēs, artūs = artu-ns* from *artu* (m.), *turreis, turrīs,* and *turrēs* from *turri* (f.), *bono-s* from *bono* (m.), *bona-s* from *bona* (f.). With such forms as *turreis, fineis, tristeis,* compare Gr. πόλεις, and with *turrīs, ignīs, hostīs,* compare Gr. πόλῖς. The acc. pl. neuter is formed by adding -*a*, as *cornu-a, corpor-a* for *corpos-a, bona* for *boṇā = bona-a*, &c. Participial stems in -*nt* assume *i* before adding *a*, as *ferentia* from *ferent, amantia* from *amant*, &c.; yet *silenta* from *silent* occurs. In Oscan we find -*ss* for -*ns, n* being assimilated to *s*, as in *via-ss* = L. *vias* for *via-ns*, &c. In Umbrian the acc. pl. ends in *f*, as in O. U. *avef, avif*, N. U. *avif, aveif* = L. *avēs, avīs, aveis,* O. U. *apruf*, N. U. *aprof* = L. *apros,* &c. No satisfactory explanation has as yet been suggested for this *f*: some writers consider it to be the remains of a postposition before which final *s* has disappeared, in which case *avef* would be for *aves-f;* others connect it with I. E. -*bhi*, which is used to form some other cases, but this explanation is just as improbable as the preceding one. It is more likely that *f* arose merely from a provincial pronunciation of the original *s*, and *s* may have become *f* in Umbrian, just as *-as* passed through the stage *-af* in becoming *-ô* in Sanskrit (consult §. 34).

§. 133. THE ACCUSATIVE DUAL.

This case has the same termination as the nom. dual.

I. *Sanskrit Acc. Dual.* The masc. and fem. acc. dual, being the same as the nom. dual, has been already noticed under that case. Neuters have as their ending *î-*, which is merely the lengthening of the nom. pl. neuter sign *-ĭ*, as *balin-î* from *balin* (n. strong), *vári-ṇ-î* from *vári* (n. water), *madhu-n-î* from *madhu* (n.), *s'ivê* = *s'iva* + *î* from *s'iva* (n.).

II. *Greek Acc. Dual.* This case has the same termination as the nom. dual. Greek differs from Sanskrit in having the same termination in the three genders, as κόρακ-ε from κορακ (m.), φλέβ-ε from φλεβ (f.), σώματ-ε from σωμα (n.), λόγω from λογο (m.), νόσω from νοσο (f.), ξύλω from ξυλο (n.), &c.

III. *Latin Acc. Dual.* In *duo* and *ambo* the acc. masc. is either *duo* and *ambo*, or *duo-s* and *ambo-s*, following the analogy of the plural. The feminine is formed only as a plural, nom. *duæ, ambæ*, acc. *dua-s, amba-s*. In vulgar Latin *dua* was used for the neuter beside *duo*.

§. 134. THE INSTRUMENTAL SINGULAR.

In Indo-European two forms of the instr. sing. existed, one ending in *-â*, and another in *-bhi*. Now, as the instrumental has two meanings, the one *comitative*, and the other *instrumental proper*,[*] it is likely that each of the above terminations was limited to one special meaning, although finally this limitation was lost. The termination *-â* is perhaps con-

---

[*] So E. *with* has both these meanings, as in "I went with him," and "I cut the bread with a knife." See Schleicher, "Compendium," &c. p. 577.

nected with the pronominal root *a*, of which it is the guna: *bhi* has been connected by some writers with the preposition Skr. *abhi* = Gr. ἀμφί; but then how is *abhi* itself to be explained? It is generally supposed to be the instrumental of the pronominal root *a*. Besides, if *bhi* be of prepositional origin, how are the terminations -*bhy-as*, *bhy-âm*, to be accounted for? Such forms as Skr. *vâg-bhy-as* cannot be compared to such as L. *vobiscum*, for in the latter the preposition comes last; they would rather require *vo-cum-bis* as a parallel case. Curtius* suggests that -*bhi* is connected with the root *bhu* (to be); from *bhu* was formed the nominal stem *bhu-ya*, whence came *bhya*, and finally *bhi*. *Bhuya* and consequently *bhi* in this view meant *existence*, and being added to another nominal stem expressed coexistence; hence we have the *comitative* instrumental.

I. *Sanskrit Instr. Sing.* In consonantal stems and feminine ones ending in -*i*, -*î*, -*u*, and -*û*, this case is formed by simply adding -*â*, as in *vâk'-â* from *vâk'* (f.), *marut-â* from *marut* (m.), *nady-â* from *nadî* (f.), *dhênv-â* from *dhênu* (f.), &c. Feminine stems in -*â* alter the stem-vowel to -*ê* before adding -*â*; hence we have *s'ivay-â* from *s'ivâ*, &c. In Vedic, however, we find such forms as *dhârâ* (= *dhârâ-â*) for *dhâray-â* from *dhârâ* (f. a shower), &c. Masculine and neuter stems ending in -*i* and -*u* insert *n*, as in *bhânunâ* from *bhânu* (m. the sun), *vârinâ* from *vâri* (n. water), &c. In the Vedas we find other forms of this case without *n*, as *pas'vâ* from *pas'u* (m. cattle), *madhvâ* from *madhu* (n. honey); also with guna, as *prabâhavâ* from *prabâhu* from *bâhu* (m. the arm); and also with euphonic *y*, as *uruyâ* from *uru* (great). Even in later Sanskrit we find *patyâ* from *pati* (m. a master), and *sakhyâ*

* Consult Curtius "zur Chronologie," &c., p. 257. *Bhi* appears to be connected with other suffixes beginning with *bh*, as Skr. -*bha* = Gr. -φο in *karabha-s*, *karam-bha-s*, Gr. ἰλα-φο-ς, στρίφο-ς, &c. As Curtius connects *bhi* with R. *bhu*, so he connects the Greek suffixes -θα, -θι, -θεν, with the I. E. *dha* (to place), whence perhaps also the suffix -θο in μισ-θό-ς (from R. μεδ), &c.

from *sakhi* (m. a friend). Masculine and neuter stems in -*a* also insert *n*, but change the stem-vowel into *ê*, and shorten the final *â*, as *s'ivéna* from *s'iva* (m. n.), &c. In the Vedas we find the final *â* sometimes retained, as in *kulis'ênâ* from *kulis'a* (m. n. an axe); also without the euphonic *n*, as *mahitvâ* from *mahitva* (n. greatness); and also with an euphonic *y*, as *svapnayâ* from *svapna* (m. sleep).

The other instrumental termination, -*bhi*, does not occur in Sanskrit, unless the preposition *abhi* be the instr. of the pronominal root *a*. It is, however, much more probable that *abhi* was originally a locative, meaning "on both sides of;" compare Skr. *abhitas*, which still retains this sense.

II. *Greek Instr. Sing.* The form ending in -*â* appears probably in the adverbial forms, ἅμἄ, Dor. ἀμᾶ, δίχα, Dor. διχᾶ, τάχα, πῆ, φή (found in Il. 2, 144; 14, 499, perhaps for σφη = Goth. *svê*, as), ἀλλαχῆ, δή (for *dyâ* = *yâ*, from pronominal stem *ya*, whence we have the locative form in L. *jam*), πάντῃ, Dor. παντᾶ, &c. Ἴνα may be the instr. of pronominal stem *i* = I. E. *ya*, with *ν* inserted, as in τινός from τί-ς.

The other instrumental ending, -φι, is used also in an ablative and locative signification. It is an instrumental proper in βίηφι, ἦφι, &c.; and comitative in (ξὺν) ὄχεσφι, (ἅμ' ἠοῖ) φαινομένηφι, &c.

III. *Latin Instr. Sing.* Neither form of the instr. is found in Latin or any other Italic language.

§. 135. The Instrumental Plural.

In Indo-European this case ended in -*bhis*, the plural form of the sing -*bhi*.

I. *Sanskrit Instr. Pl. Marudbhis* from *marut* (m.), *kavibhis* from *kavi* (m.), *s'ivâbhis* from *s'ivâ* (f.), &c. Masculine and neuter stems in -*a* change the stem-vowel into *ê* in Vedic, as in *as'vêbhis* from *as'va* (m.); whereas in ordinary Sanskrit *a* becomes *â*, and *bh* is thrown out, as in *s'ivâis* from *s'iva* (m. n.). The oldest form of the instr. of the *â*-stems ended in

-*ábhis*, as we see from the pronominal instr. forms *asmábhis* and *yushmábhis*, from *asma* and *yushma*. The Prâkrit instr. pl. of the *á*-stems ends in -*êhiṅ* = Ved. -*êbhis*, as in *kusumêhiṅ* = Ved. *kusumêbhis* beside Skr. *kusumáis* from *kusuma* (n. a flower). In Old Persian this case in these stems ends in -*aibhish* = Ved. -*êbhis*.

II. *Greek Instr. Pl.* The final ς was lost, and consequently the form of the instr. pl. is the same as that of the instr. sing.; i. e. -φι or -φιν, as in ναῦφιν (Il. 2, 794). The form -φιν probably belonged originally to the dual, and corresponded to Skr. -*bhyâm*.

III. *Latin Instr. Pl.* There is no trace of this case in Latin or the other Italic languages.

§. 136. THE INSTRUMENTAL DUAL.

See the section on the dative plural, which is identical in form with this case.

§. 137. THE DATIVE SINGULAR.

In Indo-European this case was formed by adding -*ai* to the stem. The origin of this termination is very doubtful. Some writers consider it to be the guna of the locative termination -*i*; others derive it from the preposition *abhi*, *bh* being lost, as in Skr. *s'ivâis*, instr. pl. of *s'iva* (m. n.), &c., and in Lith. *vilkais* (for *vilkamis*) instr. pl. of *vilka*, &c., and as φ is lost in Doric ἐμίν = Skr. *mahyam* for *mabhyam*, and Homeric τεΐν =Skr. *tubhyam*. *Bh* also appears in these pronominal datives; and as the pronouns generally preserve more archaic forms than the noun, it is likely that here also they point back to the oldest form of the dative. We may compare with this use of *abhi* to form the dative the use of the Latin preposition *ad* to express the dative idea in the expression *te ad carnuficem dabo*, which occurs in Plautus. Bopp identifies *ê*, the termination of the Sanskrit dative, with the demonstrative stem *ê*, whence *ay-am* = *ê* + *am*, and which *ê* he considers to be only another form of the stem *á*.

I. *Sanskrit Dative Sing.* The dative of the consonantal stems is formed by the addition of -*ê*, as *marut-ê* from *marut*, &c. Polysyllabic feminine stems in -*î* and -*û* form the dative by adding *âi*, while monosyllabic feminines in -*î* and -*û*, and all feminines in -*i* and -*u* may form this case in either -*ê* or -*âi*. All masculine and feminine stems in -*i* and -*u* gunate the final vowel before -*ê*, as *gatay-ê* from *gati* (f. motion), *bhânav-ê* from *bhânu* (m. the sun), &c. Neuter stems in -*i* and -*u* insert *n*, as *vâri-n-ê* from *vâri*, &c. Masculines and neuters in -*a* add -*aya*, as *s'ivâya* from *s'iva*, &c., while feminines in -*â* add -*yâi*, as *sivâyâi* from *s'ivâ*, &c.

II. *Greek Dative Sing.* The true dative termination in Greek is only found in stems ending in -*a* (*a*, *η*, *o*): thus we have οἴκῳ = οικο + οι, θεᾷ = θεα + αι, &c. In other stems the locative is used as the dative.

It is a disputed question whether Greek infinitives in -αι, -μεναι, -εναι, -ναι, are datives of consonantal stems, or locatives of feminine stems in -*ā*. In favour of the first view we have the analogy of the Sanskrit, in which datives are used as infinitives; and in favour of the second view we have the fact that no Greek dative ends in -αι, whereas this termination is found in χαμαί, loc. of St. χαμα. Thus λῦσαι, τεθνάμεναι, λελοιπέναι, δεικνύναι, may be either datives of the stems λυ-ς, τεθνα-μεν, λελοιπ-εν, δεικ-νυ-ν, or locatives of the stems λυ-σα, τεθνα-μενα, λελοιπ-ενα, δεικ-νυ-να. The infinitive in -σθαι is either the dative of a feminine stem in -*i*, corresponding to the Sanskrit dative of stems in -*dhi*, which is used as an infinitive, as *piba-dhyâi* (to drink, Rigv. 4, 27, 5), or it has assumed the termination -αι, following the analogy of other infinitives.

III. *Latin Dative Sing.* The dative of cons. stems ends in -*i*, which probably represents the I. E. -*ai*. In the fifth century A. U. C. the termination of this case was -*ē*, as in the Umbrian forms *nomn-e* = Skr. *nâmn-ê*, *patr-e* = Skr. *pitr-ê*. In the sixth century A. U. C. *ē* became *ei*, as in Oscan: thus find L. *patr-ei*, *Diov-ei*, &c., beside O. *pater-ei*, *Diuv-ei*, &c. Finally *ei* became *i*, as in *voc-i*, &c. The *u-stems* follow the analogy of the cons. stems, as in *senatu-ei* (SC. de Tiburtibus) : here also final *ei* became *ī*, as in *ostentu-i*, and at last *-u-i* became *-ū*, a change which began early, as in *visū* (Lucr. 5, 101), &c. In the *a*-, *e*-, and *o*- stems the initial vowel of the termination *-ai* united itself to the stem vowel, and final *i* while it remained an independent syllable was long. Thus in the *a*-stems we have *terrā-ī* (Enn. Ann. 479) = *terra-ai*, later *terræ*, &c. ; final *ī* sometimes entirely disappeared in early times, as in the datives *Matuta*, *Tuscolana*, and similar forms dating from the sixth century, just as in Greek we have θεᾷ for θεᾶι, &c. ; *-āi* sometimes became *e*, as in the datives *Diane*, *Victorie*, &c., just as in Umbrian we have the datives O. U. *tute Ikuvine* = N. U. *tote Ijoveine*, O. U. *ase* = L. *aræ*. In Oscan we find the dative ending in *aí*, as in *aasaí* = L. *aræ*. In the *e*-stems we have the dative ending in *-ēī* = *-e + ei*, as *fidē-i*, *spē-ī*, &c. ; and later in *-ē*, *i* being lost, as *fidē*. The dative of the *o*-stems ended originally in *-ōi*, as *populōi* = *populo-oi*, later *populō*, *i* being lost, as in Gr. ἵππῳ = ἵππωι, &c. In Umbrian this dative ended in *e*, as *pople* = L. *populoi*, *Martie* = L. *Martioi ;* similarly in Volscian we have *deve* = L. *divoi*, *Declune* = L. *Declunoi*. In Oscan *o*-stems this case ends in *-uí*, as in O. O. *hurtúí* = L. *horto*, &c. The Latin infinitive in *-re* is probably the dative of an abstract noun in *-as*, just as similar datives are used as infinitives in Sanskrit, as Skr. *k'akshas-ê* (to see), &c. : *legere* would therefore be for *legese*—final *e*, though originally long, as representing *ai*, being shortened. This shortening of final *e* is not surprising, as the Romans forgot that the infinitive had been originally a dative ; and moreover, we have an analogous case in the loss of the final αι in Greek infinitives in -μεναι, as ἔμεν = ἔμεναι, &c.

§. 138. THE DATIVE PLURAL.

We have already seen that in Sanskrit *bhyam* (= *bhi* + *am*), is used to form the dative singular of the pronouns, as in *tubhyam*, *mahyam*. This termination, with the addition of *s*, was therefore most probably the original termination of the dative plural in Indo-European. The Old Prussian supplies us with a positive proof that this supposition is correct, as in it the dat. pl. ends in -*mans*, which represents an I. E. -*bhyams*. In Lithuanian this case ended in -*mus*, which also must have arisen from the same form, as the presence of the nasal is shown by *u*; for had the original form been -*bhyas*, we would have found -*mas*.

I. *Sanskrit Dat. Pl.* Here -*bhyams* becomes -*bhyas*, as in *marud-bhyas*, *naubhyas*, &c. Final *a* becomes *é*, as in *s'irébhyas* from *s'iva* (m. n.), &c.

II. *Greek Dat. Pl.* The locative plural is used as the dative in Greek.

III. *Latin Dat. Pl.* Here -*bhyams* became -*beis*, and later -*bis* in the pronouns, as in *vobeis*, later *vobis*, &c.; and -*bos* (?), and later -*bus* in the nouns, as in *navebos*, *ovibus*, &c. The consonantal stems add *i* to the stem, as in *fratribus*, *hominibus*, from the stems *frater*, *homin*. It is possible that originally in Latin -*bus* was added immediately to the stem, and perhaps *bōbus* or *būbus* = *bov-bus*, is a relic of this stage. In the *i*-stems *i* in Old Latin became *e*, as in *tempestatebus*. In the *u*-stems, *u* sometimes became *i*, as in *fructibus*. In the *e*-stems -*bus* only occurs in Classical Latin in *diebus* and *rebus*; *speciebus* is censured by Cicero as not correct. In the *o*-stems -*bus* only occurs in *duobus* and *ambobus*. In feminine *ā* stems -*bus* often occurs, as in *filiābus*, *deābus*, &c. The dat. pl. of the *a*- and *o*-stems ends in -*is*. Two different explanations have been suggested to explain this termination. Schleicher supposes that *equis*, for example, arose from *equois*, and that *equois* again represents an older *equo-hios* = *equo-fios*, in which -*fios* = -*bhyas*. This explanation is most improbable, and it is much more likely that here,* as in the Greek dat. pl., we have the old lo-

---

* Consult Schleicher, "Compendium," &c., p. 587; and "Grundriss der lateinischen Declination von Franz Bücheler," p. 66.

cative: *silvais, agrois,* would then be for *silvaisi, agroisi,* just as Gr. ὕλαις, ἀγροῖς, are for ὕλαισι, ἀγροῖσι. The loss of final *i* is very common in Latin; thus we have *est* = Gr. ἐστί, *tremunt* = O. L. *tremonti,* &c. The oldest form of the Latin dative, without the addition of *i* to the stem-vowel, as in *mensa-i-s,* &c., is found on an inscription (C. I. L. 1, n. 814), where we read *devas Corniscas sacrum,* where *devas* and *Corniscas* correspond to the old Attic datives ταμίασι, ὥρασι, &c. That the dative plural of the *a-* and *o-*stems originally ended in the diphthongs *-ais* and *-ois* is proved by the forms noticed by Festus, *oloes* (= *illis*), *privicloes* (= *priviculis*), and by the cognate Italic languages. On an old inscription, perhaps of Latin origin, we find *suois* and *cnatois* = L. *suis* and *gnatis.* In Oscan we find *Nuvlanuis* (m.) = L. *Nolanis, ligatuis* (m.) = L. *legatis, diumpais* (f.) = L. *lymphis.* In Umbrian the dat. pl. of the *a-* and *o-*stems ends in *-eis, -es, -is,* and in later Umbrian in *-eir, -er, -ir*; thus we have O. U. *termnes* (= L. *terminis*), O. U. *veskles* (= L. *vasculis*), O. U. *tekuries* = N. U. *dequrier* (= L. *decuriis*), O. U. *Treplanes* = N. U. *Treblaneir* or *Treblanir,* N. U. *toter* (= L. *tutis*), N. U. *alfir* (= L. *albis*), &c. In the *i-*stems this case ends in *-eis, -es,* following probably the analogy of the *a-* and *o-*stems; Schleicher, however, explains this form in the same way as Latin datives in *-is,* and deduces *aves, aveis,* from *avi-fos,* &c. The dative pl. of the consonantal stems ends in *-us,* as *fratrus* (*fratribus*), *dupursus* (bipedibus), &c. Schleicher considers that the oldest form of *fratrus* was *fratr-o-fos,* whence came *fratrus* through the stages *fratrufos, fratrufs, fratruss.*

§. 139. THE DATIVE DUAL.

This case in Indo-European perhaps ended in *-bhyâms,* a lengthened form of the pl. *-bhyams.*

I. *Sanskrit Dat. Dual.* The I. E. termination here became *-bhyâm,* as in *marud-bhyâm* from *marut* (m.), *s'ivâ-bhyâm* from *s'iva* (m. n.) and *s'ivâ* (f.), &c. The *ă-*stems lengthen the stem-vowel before adding this suffix.

II. *Greek Dat. Dual.** The dative and genitive dual have the same form in Greek: -*bhyâms* first, probably, became -φιν, and then -ιν, φ being lost. Stems ending in -ι, -υ, or a consonant, follow the analogy of the *a*-stems: thus we have γενέοιν and γενοῖν = γενεσ-ο-φιν, ματέροιν = ματερ-ο-φιν, νεκύοιν = νεκυ-ο-φιν, γλυκέοιν = γλυκεϝ-ο-φιν from St. γλυκυ with guna of the stem-vowel, Ion. πολίοιν = πολι-ο-φιν, πολέοιν = πολεγ-ο-φιν from St. πολι with guna of the stem-vowel, ἵπποιν = ἱππο-φιν, &c. In the Homeric forms τοῖιν, ὤμοιιν, ἀλλήλοιιν, βλεφάροιιν, &c., from the stems το, ὠμο, ἀλληλο, βλεφαρο, &c., ι appears to have been added to the stem, and consequently τοῖιν = το-ι-φιν, &c. This ι, perhaps, represents an older *a*, by which the *ă*-stems were lengthened as in Sanskrit; τοῖιν would then be identical with Skr. *tâbhyâm* (from St. *ta*) = *ta-a-bhyâms*. It has been suggested that the second *a* here is not a mere lengthening of the stem, but that it belongs to the termination: consequently the word should be thus divided, *ta-abhi-âms*, *abhi* being in this view the preposition. We find in some Greek consonantal stems datives similar to τοῖιν; thus we have ποδοῖιν = ποδ-ο-ι-φιν from St. ποδ, Σειρήνοιιν = Σειρην-ο-ι-φιν from St. Σειρην.

III. *Latin Dat. Dual.* There is no trace of the termination -*bhyâms* in any Italic language.

§. 140. THE ABLATIVE CASE.

In Indo-European this case was formed by adding -*t*† to the vocalic stems, with gunation of the stem vowel, or -*at*

---

* Consult Schleicher, "Compendium," &c., p. 590; and Leo Meyer, "Gedrängte Vergleichung der griechischen und lateinischen Declination," p. 64.

† As the abl. sing. ends in Zend in *đ* (written *ţ* by Schleicher), and in Latin in *d*, it is likely that *d* was the original form of the case-ending. This *d* may be connected with the pronouns *ad-as* (n. that) and *id-am* (n. that). Bopp considers that the *d* in these pronouns is derived from an older *t*, but it is quite possible that here we may have an independent pronominal stem.

with or without this gunation: in consonantal stems -*at* was simply added. This -*t* or -*at* is of pronominal origin, and was probably connected with the pronominal stem *ta*.*

I. *Sanskrit Abl. Sing.* The original *t* only occurs in the *ā*-stems, as in *s'ivât* from *s'iva* (m. n.). Benfey† adduces one ablative of an *u*-stem ending in -*t*, *vidyôt* from *vidyu*. In all other stems -*t* has become -*s*, and the ablative agrees in form with the genitive. The change of final *t* into *s* is common in Greek, as in τετυφός = τετυφοτ, &c., ὁμῶς for ὁμωτ = Skr. *samât* (abl. of St. *sama*, similar), &c. That final -*s* of the abl. has sprung from -*t* is proved by the Zend, where we still find the abl. termination $\d$: thus we have Z. *patôiḍ* (abl. of *pati*) = Skr. *patês* (abl. of *pati* = Gr. ποσι), which is found in compounds, beside Z. *patôis* (gen.) = Skr. *patês* (gen.).

II. *Greek Abl. Sing.* The I. E. *t* is found in Greek adverbs in -ως, where final σ = I. E. *t*, as no Greek word can end in *t*: moreover, -*at* has become -*ât* = -ωτ = -ως, just as in Zend.‡ Thus we have πῶς, Ion. κῶς = I. E. *kvât* from *kva*, πάντ-ως = παντ-ωτ, ταχέ-ως =ταχεϝ-ωτ, &c.

III. *Latin Abl. Sing.* In Old Latin and Oscan the abl. ends in -*d*, which is lost in Classical Latin and in Umbrian. Thus in Old Latin we find *dictator-ed, convention-id, senatu-d, navale-d, mari-d, alto-d, Gnaivo-d, praida-d, sententia-d*, &c. From *facilumed*, which is found in the S. C. de Bacc., we see that all adverbs in -*e* are of ablatival origin, and spring from adjectives in -*us*, -*a*, -*um*; the adverbial ablative ending in -*ed*, so as to be distinguished from the masc. and fem. ablatives of the adjective, which ended in -*od* and -*ad*. This *ē* was originally long, but gradually became short, as the adverbs were words in constant use. In Oscan -*d* is also found: thus we have

---

* Consult Curtius "Zur Chronologie der Indogermanischen Spachforschung," p. 255.

† Benfey's Practical Grammar of the Sanskrit Language for the use of early Students, §. 237, p. 197.

‡ Consult Bopp's "Comparative Grammar," vol. I., pp. 347, 348.

from *a*-stems, *sukaraklú-d* (sacello), *aragetu-d* = L. *argento*, *preivatu-d* = O. L. *preivato-d*, *suva-d* = O. L. *sova-d* (suâ), *ehtra-d* = O. L. *exstra-d* (in S. C. de Bacc., *exstrad urbem*), *Akudunnia-d* = L. *Aquiloniâ*, &c. ; from an *i*-stem, *slaagi-d* (fine); the *u*-stems follow the analogy of those in -*i*, as *castri-d* from St. *castru*, which appears in Latin as an *a*-stem *castro;* the consonantal stems partly follow the *i*-stems, and partly end in -*ud*, as *præsent-id* = L. *præsente*, *lig-ud* = L. *lege*. The Oscan also supplies us with additional proof that adverbs in -*e* were originally ablatives ; for we find *amprufi-d* (= L. *improbe*), which is either from an *i*-stem or from an *a*-stem, as L. *improbe*. Perhaps the stem vowel was lengthened by *a*, as in the Latin adverbs ; in the latter case O. -*id* and L. -*ed* would both point back to an older -*eid* = -*oid* = -*a-i-d* = -*a-a-d* or -*a-a-t*. This lengthening of *ă*-stems by adding *ă* is, as we have already seen, of frequent occurrence in Sanskrit. In Umbrian -*d* has been lost, as in the *a*-stems, *puplu* = O. L. *poplod* (populo), *vinu* = O. L. *veinod* (vino), *termnu* = L. *termino*, *mefa* = L. *mediâ*, *tuta* = O. *touta-d*, *mestru* = L. *magistro*, &c. ; in the *i*-stems, *ukri*, &c. ; in the *u*-stems, which, however, as in Oscan, follow the analogy of the *i*-stems, as *mani* = L. *manu*, &c. ; in the consonantal stems, as *kvestur-e* = L. *quaestore*, &c.*

---

* In Sanskrit, Greek, and Latin, we find the suffixes, Skr. -*tas*, Gr. -θεν, L. -*tus*, employed to form adverbs with an ablative meaning, and which in some cases actually take the place of the ablative, especially in the pronominal declension. Thus in Sanskrit we have *svarga-tas* (from heaven) from *svarga*, *ku-tas* (whence) from *ku* = *kva* (who), *itas* (from here), also used as abl. of *id-am* (n. this), &c. The Skr. pronouns of the 1st and 2nd pers. attach -*tas*, not to the true stem, but to the abl., as *mat-tas*, *tvat-tas*. In Latin -*tus* corresponds to Skr. -*tas*, as in *cœli-tus*, &c. This termination has also a locative meaning in Latin, as in *in-tus*, *sub-tus*. The Greek θεν is from a different root; for Gr. θ = Skr. *dh*, and not *t* ; πό-θεν, τό-θεν, ὄ-θεν, do not therefore correspond exactly to Skr. *ku-tas*, *ta-tas*, *ya-tas*, but would require such forms as *ku-dhas*, &c. We find -*dhas*, however, in Skr., *adhas* (down), with which Benfey connects Gr. ἐν-θεν. We also find the exact representative of Skr. -*tas* in Gr. ἐν-τός, ἐκ-τός, which have a locative meaning. It is possible that in

§. 141. The Ablative Plural.
This case agrees in form with the dat. pl.

§. 142. The Ablative Dual.
This case agrees in form with the dat. dual.

§. 143. The Genitive Singular.

In Indo-European the gen. sing. of the *a*-stems ended in -*sya*, and that of all other stems in -*s* or -*as*. The origin of these suffixes has been already discussed in §. 105.

I. *Sanskrit Gen. Sing.* In consonantal stems and monosyllabic ones ending in any vowel except *ô*, this case ends in -*as*, as *marut-as* from *marut* (m.), *nâv-as* from *nâu* (f.), *bhiy-as* from *bhî* (f. fear), &c. The gen. sing. of monosyllabic stems in -*î* and -*û* may also end in -*âs*, as *bhiy-âs*, &c. ; stems in -*ar* originally formed their gen. in -*as*, as we see from the Vedic genitives *pitr-as*, *nar-as*, from the stems *pitar*, *nar* (m. a man); but in later Sanskrit we find the remarkable forms, *pitur*, *mâtur*, *dâtur*, &c., as gen.s of the stems *pitar*, *mâtar*, *dâtâr*, &c. Bopp considers that -*ur* here arose from -*urs* = -*rus* = -*ras*, and consequently that the old form *pitras* passed through the stages *pitrus* (= Gr. πατρός) and *piturs* in becoming *pitur*. According to this view the final *r* is the stem -*r* transposed ; but it is more natural to suppose that the old form *pitras* became *pitrs* (*a* being lost, and *r* treated as a vowel), and that from *pitrs* arose *pitus* (as this gen. ought properly to be written), *r* becoming *u*, as is very common in Prâkrit.* The Zend supports the view that these gen.s originally ended in -*as*: thus we have Z. *dathrô* (for *dathr-as*) = Skr. *dâtus*, Z. *nafĕ-*

Indo-European these suffixes had at first a merely locative signification, and that -*ta-s* marked the direction *whither*, and -*dha-s* the place *where*, the former being from the verbal root *ta* (to stretch), and the latter from *dha* (to place), and the final *s* coming from the pronominal stem *sa*.

* The form *pitus* may also be accounted for by supposing that the gen. sing. was originally *pitâras* (= Gr. πατέρος), and that this, through the influence of the accent, became, firstly, *pitârs*. and then *pitûs*.

T

dhró (euphonically for *naptró*) = Skr. *naptus*, final *-as* becoming *ó*, as usual. In Z. *áthras'-k'a* (ignisque) we find the gen. still ending in *-as*, from St. *átar*. In Vedic the gen. of the *i*- and *u*-stems was formed by adding *-as* directly to the stem-vowel, as in *pas'v-as* from *pas'u* (m. cattle), *madhv-as* = Gr. μέθυ-ος from *madhu* (n. honey), *ary-as* from *ari* (m. an enemy), as Gr. ἴδρι-ος from ἴδρι. We find traces of this formation in later Sanskrit, as in *paty-us* for *paty-as* from *pati* (m. a master), *sakhy-us* for *sakhy-as* (m. a friend). The original genitive in *-as* was supplanted by other forms; and with the exception of Skr. *paty-us*, and *sakhy-us* no traces of it are found except in Vedic. Masculine stems in *-i* and *-u* gunate the stem-vowel, and add *s*, as *katê-s* from *kavi* (m. a poet), *bhânô-s* from *bhânu* (m. the sun), &c. Neuter stems are lengthened by *n*, as *vâri-n-as* from *vâri* (n. water), &c. Feminine stems in *-i* and *-u* either follow the analogy of the masc. stems in *-i* and *-u*, or attach *-âs* directly to stem, while feminine stems in *-î* and *-û* can form their genitive only in the latter way: thus we have *gatê-s* or *gaty-âs* from *gati* (f.), but only *nady-âs* from *nadî* (f.), &c. Feminines in *-â* change the stem-vowel into *-âi* before *-âs*, as *s'ivây-âs* from *s'ivâ*, &c. Masculines and neuters in *-a* form the gen. by adding *-sya*, as *s'iva-sya* from *s'iva* (m. n.), &c.; *-sya* occurs in no other stems except in the pronominal stem *amu*, the gen. of which is *amushya*.

II. *Greek Gen. Sing.* In consonantal stems this case is formed by adding -ος to the stem, as in ποδ-ός, μένους = μενεσ-ος, αἰδόος and αἰδοῦς (Æol. αἴδως) = αἰδοσ-ος, ἐρέβους (Hom. ἐρέβευς) = ἐρεβεσ-ος, Γοργύος (Dor. Γοργῶς, Æol. Γόργως) = Γοργον-ος, πατρ-ός and πατέρ-ος, &c. The gen. of stems ending in a diphthong, or ι or υ, is formed in a similar way, as ναϝ-ός, βοϝ-ός, ὕβρι-ος, ἀχλύ-ος, γουνός = γυνυ-ος, δουρός = δορυ-ος, &c.: the stem-vowels ι and υ can also be gunated before -ος, as πόλε-ως,* πόλε-ος, and Hom. πόλη-ος

---

* The lengthening of -ος here is analogous to the lengthening of -*as* in the gen. sing. of Skr. feminine stems in -*â*, -*î*, and -*û*.

= πολεγ-ος, beside Ion. πόλι-ος, Hom. μάντη-ος = μαντεγ-ος, beside μάντι-ος, γλυκεϝ-ος, ἄστεϝ-ος and ἄστε-ως, πολέϝ-ος from πολυ. In feminine a-stems the gen. sign -as was immediately added to the stem-vowel, as in σοφίας, φυγῆς. The gen. of the masculine and neuter a-stems ended originally in -σyo ; the Hom. gen. s in -οιο and -οο are derived at once from -ο-σyo ; thus κταμένοιο = κταμενο-σyo, ἀγρόο = ἀγροῖο = αγρο-σyo. The ordinary gen. in -ου, Æol. -ω, arises from -οο simply by contraction. The Hom. gen. in -αο is probably derived from an older form in -α-σyo, as in Ἀτρείδᾱο, &c.; -ᾱο sometimes become -ω, as in Αἰνείω, &c.; and final -ο is sometimes lost, as in the Æol. Ἀΐδα, Κρονίδα, &c. In the Arcadian dialect -αο becomes -αυ, as in Ἀπολλωνίδαυ, Ἔαυ, &c. Curtius* deduces the gen. ending -αο from -αος = Skr. -âyâs, but the former explanation is much more probable. Such genitives as ποιήτου, πολίτου, &c., are derived from older forms in -ᾱο: thus πολίτου = πολιταο, &c. In the Thessalian dialect † the gen. sing. of the o-stems frequently ended in -οι. Ahrens considers, and rightly I believe, that this -οι represents the older -οιο, final o being merely lost, as in gens. in ᾱ. In opposition to this view it has been suggested that this gen. in -οι is properly an old locative, which is here used in the genitive signification, just as in Latin the gen. in -i is supposed to have been also originally a locative.

III. *Latin Gen. Sing.*—The I. E. gen. suffix -as appears in Latin in the forms -os, -us, -is, -es. The gen. of consonantal stems is formed by adding the suffix immediately to the stem: thus we have *ped-is, gener-is* for *genes-is, nomin-is, patr-is,* &c. The I. E. -as in becoming -is first became -os (which is found in the u-stems), and then -us (which is found on inscriptions up to the middle of the seventh century A. U. C.

---

* Curtius, "Grundzüge der griechischen Etymologie," p. 646.

† Ahrens, "De Dialectis Æolicis," &c., p. 221 ; and "De Dialecto Dorica," p. 528, *seq.*

in *homin-us*, *Vener-us*, *Cerer-us*, *patr-us*, &c.). In Old Latin we also find the gen. of consonantal stems ending in *-es*, as in *Salut-es*, *Apolon-es*, *Cerer-es*. In late Latin this gen. in *-es* again appears as in the gens. *Cæsar-es*, *campestr-es*. This *-es* either arose from *-is*, or else preceded it, the I. E. *-as* becoming first *-es*, and then *-is*; or perhaps we can detect here the influence of the *i*-stems, and *-ĕs* may be equal to *-eis* or *-īs*. Final *s* was often lost in old and vulgar Latin, as in *Cæsar-u* (C. I. L. 1, n. 696), *Palæstrion-i* (Pl. Mil. Glor. 387), &c.; and in many cases, where it was written, it was not pronounced, as in *militīs qui amicam* (Pl. Bacch. 574), &c.* As the gen. of the *i*-stems ends in classical Latin is *-īs*, it agrees in form with that of the cons. stems; thus *ovīs*, *piscis*, &c., would have had the same form, if they had been derived from the stems *ov*, *pisc*, &c. But this gen. ending *-īs* was perhaps originally long (*-īs*), and arose from *-i-os*, just as *alis* = *alios*. The close connexion of the consonantal stems with those in *-i* is shown by the gen. form *part-us* (Tab. Bant.), from St. *part* beside *parti-s* from St. *parti*. The gen. of the *u*-stems was formed by adding *-os* to the gunated stem; thus, *senatu-os* (S. C. de Bacc.) = *senatov-os*, *magistratu-os*, &c.; *-os* afterwards became *-us*, as in *domu-us*, *exercitu-us*, *conventu-us* (all on inscriptions); and from *-u-us*, by contraction, arose the usual gen. in *-ūs*, and in Old Latin *-ū*, final *s* being lost. Beside these gens. in *-u-os*, *-u-us*, *-ūs*, we also find another form in *-u-is* in use up to Cicero's time, as in *senatu-is*, *domu-is*, &c., cited by Gellius, *anu-is* (Ennius), *metu-is* (Cicero), &c.: *su-is* and *gru-is* always kept this form. The *u*-stems are also declined like those in *-o*, as gen. *sumpti* beside *sumptus*, *quæsti* beside *quæstu-is* (Ter. Hec. 735), and *quæstus*, *senati*, *gemiti*, *geli*, &c. The gen. of neuter *u*-stems followed the analogy of the masculine, as *cornu-is*, *cornūs*, and *cornū* (final *s* being lost, as in gen. *senatu*, C. I. L. 1, n. 1166),

---

* Bücheler, "Grundriss der lateinischen Declination," p. 30, *seq.*

from St. *cornu*. The gen. of the *o*-stems, masc. and neut., ends in *ī*, in late Latin *-ei*. Three different ways of explaining this form have been suggested : one is, that this case is really the locative, which has here supplanted the old genitive ; another is, that we find here a trace of the termination *-asya*, e. g. *agri* = *agroi* = *agro-sya ;* the last is, that the gen. originally ended in *-o-is*, e. g. *agri* = *agro-is*. This last explanation is much the most likely, for in Umbrian and Oscan the final *s* is still retained ; thus we have O. O. *súveís* = L. *sui*, O. O. *Púmpaiia-neís* = L. *Pompeiani ;* O. U. *puples, puple*, and N. U. *popler* = L. *populi ;* O. U. *katles* and *katle* = L. *catuli*, &c. These forms point back to an Italic gen. in *-ois*, whence came O. O. *-eís*, O. U. *-ēs*, *-ē*, and L. *-i*, final *s* being lost. This *-ois* may be explained in three different ways : either the stem was lengthened by *y* (= *i*), and *-as* added, as to the consonantal stems, *agrois* representing therefore an older *agra-y-as ;* or the analogy of the *i*-stems was followed here, and *-is* added directly to the stem ; or, more simply, *-as* was added to the stem without the intervention of *y*, and, consequently, *-o-is* = *-a-is* = *-a-as*. Final *i*, though essentially long, was sometimes shortened by Plautus ; and disappeared in *Nœpor* for *Nœi* (= *Gnœvi*), *por* and *Marpor* = *Marcipor*. The gen. sing. of the fem. *ā*-stems ended originally in *-ās*, as *terras* (Næv.), *vias* (Enn.), *fortunas* (Næv.), &c. ; the same ending is found in O. *eituas* (pecuniæ), O. *múltas* (= L. *mulctæ*), U. *tutas*, &c. ; in classical Latin it is still found in (*pater-*, *mater-*) *familias*. The gen. sing. of these stems also ends in *-āī* (in Ennius, Plautus, Lucretius, &c.), later *-æ*. This *-āī* arose perhaps from *-ais* = *-ay-as*, the stem being lengthened by *y* (= *i*) ; *-ais* is found in the gen. *Prosepnais* (C. I. L. 1, p. 554) = *Proserpinæ*, and it appears as *-æs* in *Faustæs, Dianæs, Lepidæs*, &c. This form in *æs* belonged entirely to vulgar Latin, and is not found before the seventh century A. U. C. It penetrated even into the masc. *a*-stems, as in *Messalæs, Midæs*. We may also explain the form *-ais* in the same way as we explained the masc. *-ois*, without supposing the stem to be lengthened by *y*: thus, by adding *-as* directly to the stem we get, on the one hand, *-ā-is* = *-ā-as*, the second *a* being weakened to *i* to diminish the weight of the termination, as in *-o -is* = *-ā-as*, while on the other hand we obtain by simple contraction the other form of the gen. *-ās* = *-ā-as*. A third explanation has been suggested: it is supposed that the *ā*-stems formed their gen. by adding *-sya*, following the analogy of those in *-ā*, and that consequently *-āī* = *-ā-sya*; but this theory is extremely improbable, for no trace of the I. E. *-sya* is found in the corresponding Oscan and Umbrian stems. The gen. of the *e*-stems is formed similarly to that of those in *-ā*: thus corresponding to the gen. in *-ās*, we find the gen. in *-ēs*, as *rabies* (Lucret.), *fides* (Plaut.), *dies* (Enn.), &c.; this gen. perhaps appears in *Diespiter* (the father of day). Corresponding also to the gen. in *-āī*, we find the gen. in *-ēī*, later *-ěī*, except when immediately preceded by a vowel; and then still later corresponding to *-ae*, we find *-ei* contracted into a diphthong: thus we have *fidēi* (Enn.), *rēī* (Plaut.), &c.; then *rěī* (Pl.), *fiděi*, &c.; but always *aciēi*; then in the Comedians, *rei*, *spei*, are frequently monosyllables. The gen. of the *e*-stems also ends in *ē*, which may be derived either from *-ēs*, *s* being lost; or from *-ei*, *i* being lost; as *perniciē*, *fidē*, *aciē*, *diē*. Finally, we find a gen. in *-i* after the analogy of the *o*- and *u*- stems, as *fami* (Cato), *plebi* (Tab. Bant.); and even when *i* immediately precedes, as in *pernicii* (Cic. according to Gellius), *progenii* (Pacuv.), &c., where we might have expected final *e* to be retained to avoid the conjunction of two *i*'s: this *i* evidently arose from the diphthongisation of the original *-ēi*, as in the monosyllabic *rei*. In Oscan the gen. of the consonantal stems is formed by adding *-eis*, as *Jŭv-eis* = L. *Jovis*, *maatr-eis* = L. *matris*. The gen. of the *i*-stems also ends in *-eis*, as *Herentateïs*, from St. *Herentati*, *Liuvkanateïs* from St. *Liuvkanati*. We find only one example of an *u*-stem, viz., *castrous* from St. *castru*; here *-s* appears to have been simply added to the gunated stem, as in Sanskrit. We have already noticed the Oscan and Umbrian *a*-stems. In Umbrian the consonantal stems form their gen. in -*es*, N. U. -*er*, following the analogy of the *i*-stems, as N. U. *nomn-er* from St. *nomn* beside N. U. *ocrer* from St. *ocri*. In the *u*-stems we find *o* instead of the old *u*, as in N. U. *trifo-r* (from St. *trifu*) = L. *tribu-s*.

§. 144. THE GENITIVE PLURAL.

The oldest form of the termination of the gen. pl. in Indo-European was probably -*as-am-s*, -*as* being the sign of the gen. sing., -*am* the pronominal element which is found in -*bhi-am*, &c., and -*s* the sign of the plural. From -*asams* came first -*asâm*, then -*sâm*, and finally -*âm*. We find traces of the first of these forms in the Sanskrit pronominal declension, as *têshâm* (horum) = *ta-âsam* from St. *ta* (hic), *yêshâm* (quorum) = *ya-âsam* from St. *ya* (qui), &c.; and in the Latin *o*-stems, as *equôrum* (from St. *equŏ*) = I. E. *akva-asâm* (from St. *akva*), &c.

I. *Sanskrit Gen. Pl.* The gen. ending -*sâm* is only found in the pronominal declension: in the nominal declension this case was formed by attaching -*âm* immediately to stems ending in a consonant or diphthong, as *marut-âm*, *manas-âm*, *bharat-âm*, *nâv-âm*, &c., from the stems *marut* (m.), *manas* (n.), *bharant* (m.), *nâu* (f.), &c. Pollysyllabic vocalic stems lengthen the stem by *n*, as in *gatî-nâm*, *vârî-nâm*, *s'ivâ-nâm*, *nadî-nâm*, &c., from the stems *gati* (f.), *vâri* (n.), *s'iva* (m. n.), *nadî* (f.), &c.: short stem-vowels are always lengthened before this *n*. Monosyllabic feminine stems in *î* and *û* may either add *n* or not; thus from *bhî* (f.) we have *bhiy-âm*, or *bhî-nâm*, &c. Stems in -*ar* form their gen. pl. from the weak stem in -*r̥*, and add *n*, as *pitr̥-nâm*, *mâtr̥-nam*, *dâtr̥-nam*, &c., from the stems *pitar*, *mâtar*, *dâtâr*, &c. In Vedic we find older forms of these genitives without *n*, as *dêvâm* from St. *dêva* (m. a god), *nar-âm*, *svasr-âm* from stems *nar* (m. a man), *svasâr* (f. a sister).

II. *Greek Gen. Pl.* This case is formed by adding -ων to all stems, except those ending in -$\bar{a}$; ι- and υ- stems are sometimes gunated. Thus we have ποδ-ῶν, δεπά-ων = δεπασ-ων, στηθῶν and στηθέων = στηθεσ-ων, μακάρ-ων, ναϝ-ῶν, βασιλή-ων = βασιλεϝ-ων, συ-ῶν, γενύ-ων, γούν-ων = γονυ-ων, πολῶν and πολέ-ων = πολεϝ-ων from St. πολυ gunated, πολίων beside πόλε-ων = πολεγ-ων from St. πολι gunated, ἀγρῶν = ἀγρο-ων, χωρῶν = χωρᾱ-σων. The gen. pl. of the ā-stems generally ends in Homer in -ā-ων = -ā-sâm; thus we find θεᾱ́-ων = θεᾱ-σων from St. θεᾱ, τᾱ́-ων = τᾱ-σων = Skr. tâ-sâm from St. ta, &c. This -ā-ων became -ε-ων in Ionic.

III. *Latin Gen. Pl.* This case is formed by adding -*um*, O. L. -*om* (found in the *u*-stems and in the *o*-stems after *v* or *u*), to stems ending in a consonant or -*i* or -*u*. Thus we have *princip-um, fulmin-um, can-um, matr-um,* &c.; *avi-um, ovi-um,* &c.; *magistratu-om* perhaps for *magistratov-om, fructu-um,* &c.; and with -*u-um* contracted, as in *passum* (Pl.), *currum* (Virg.), but in vulgar Latin also after the analogy of the *o*-declension, *verso-rum, spirito-rum,* &c. Many consonantal stems are lengthened by *i*, and so their gen. pl. termination agrees in form with that of the *i*-stems: thus we have *merc-i-um, radic-i-um, forcip-i-um, penat-i-um, amant-i-um* beside *amant-um, ferent-i-um* beside *ferent-um,* &c. Stems ending in -*n*, -*r*, or -*s*, seldom permit this addition of *i*; we find, however, *vir-i-um* and *complur-i-um*. We find some examples of consonantal stems following the analogy of those in -*u*: thus we have *alit-u-um* (Lucr. and Virg.) beside *alit-um*, and on inscriptions *virtut-u-um, fratr-u-um,* &c.

The masc. and neut. *o*-stems form their gen. pl. in two ways: by adding either -*om* (or -*um*) = I. E. -*ăm* or -*ŏrum* = I. E. -*asâm*. Thus we find in Old Latin the forms in -*om*, *Romanom* (C. I. L. 1, n. 1), *sovom* (C. I. L. 1, n. 588) = *suorum, divom* (Lucr.) &c.; later in -*um*, as in *virum, deum, meum, nummum, modium, talentum, fabrum,* &c. Similarly in Oscan we find *Abellanum, Tiiatium, Nuvlanum,* and in Umbrian *puplum,* later *poplom* (populorum), &c. The other gen. pl. ending in -*ŏrum,* (m. n.) and -*ārum* (f.) is the usual form, as in *bonōrum* = *bonŏ* + *ŏrum*, *bonārum* = *bonā* + *ărum*, &c. In Oscan the gen. pl. of the *ā*-stems ends in -*azum*, and in Umbrian in -*arum*, -*aru*, as in O. *eisa-zun-c egma-zum* (illarum rerum), U. *menzaru* = L. *mensarum*, &c. The *ē*-stems follow the analogy of the *ā*-stems, as *dierum*, *rerum*, &c. Masc. stems in -*a* form their gen. pl. in -*rum*, but in the poets we find the form in -*um* in compounds of -*gena* and -*cola*, and in the patronymics in -*des*, as *agricolum*, *terrigenum*, *Æneadum*, &c. Two feminine stems in -*ā* form their gen. pl. also in -*um*—namely, *amphorum* and *drachmum*, but these forms were probably borrowed from the Greek. We find other traces of the gen. pl. ending -*sum* in the forms (noticed by Varro and Charisius) *boverum*, *nucerum*, *regerum*, *lapiderum*, which are supposed by Bopp to have been formed from the *i*-stems *bovi*, *nuci*, *regi*, *lapidi*, and consequently to be for *bovirum*, &c., thus proving that -*rum* was also originally attached to the *i*-stems. These forms have been also explained by supposing them to have been formed from the stems *bover*, *nucer*, &c., the original stems *bov*, *nuc*, &c., being lengthened by the addition of -*er*, because this *r* appears also in some stems in the gen. sing., and consequently is not peculiar to the plural: thus we find *sueris*, *puberis*, *acipenseris*, *cucumeris*, beside *suis*, *pubis*, *acipensis*, *cucumis*.*

The Oscan and Umbrian form the gen. pl. of stems ending in -*i* or a consonant in the same way as the Latin.

§. 145. THE GENITIVE DUAL.

This case agrees in form with the locative dual.

§. 146. THE LOCATIVE SINGULAR.

In Indo-European the sign of this case was probably -*in*, which was added directly to the stem. This -*in* was connected

---

* Consult Bopp's "Comparative Grammar," 1., p. 490; and Bücheler "Grundriss der lateinischen Declination," p. 40.

with the pronominal root -*am*, which was reduced firstly to -*an* (*n* being weaker than *m*), and then to -*in* (*i* being weaker than *a*). From -*an* are derived the prepositions, Gr. ἐν, L. *in*. The oldest form (-*am*) of this suffix is still perhaps found in -*âm*, the locative ending of Skr. fem. stems.

I. *Sanskrit Loc. Sing.* Stems ending in a consonant or diphthong form this case by adding -*i* to stem, as *marut-i*, *bharat-i*, *pitar-i*, *nâv-i*, *gav-i*, from the stems *marut*, *bharat*, *pitar*, *nâu*, *gó*. Masc. stems in -*i* and -*u* add -*âu*, before which the stem-vowel disappears, as in *kavâu*, *bhânâu*, from *kavi*, *bhânu*: the stem-vowel is still kept in *paty-âu* and *sakhy-âu* from *pati* and *sakhi*. This -*âu* perhaps represents -*âm*, the gunated form of -*am*. Fem. stems in -*i* and -*u* either follow the analogy of the masc. in -*i* and -*u*, or else add -*âm*, as *gat-âu* or *gaty-âm* from *gati*. Polysyllabic fem. stems in -*â*, -*î*, or *û*, always add -*âm*, as *s'ivâ-y-âm*, *nâdy-âm*, *radhv-âm*, from *s'ivâ*, *nadî*, *vadhû*. Monosyllabic fem. stems in -*î* and -*û* add either -*i* or -*âm*, as *bhuv-i* or *bhuv-âm* from *bhû*. Neuter stems in -*i* and -*u* lengthen the stem by *n*, as *vâri-ṇ-i* from *vâri*. Masc. and neut. stems in -*a* add -*i*, as *s'ivê* from *s'iva* (m., n.).

In Vedic we find the loc. of the *u*-stems formed by simply adding -*i*, as *tanv-i* (from *tanu*, f. the body) = Z. *tanv-i* (loc. of *tanu*, f. id.); this form corresponds to Gr. dat., as νέκυ-ι, &c. We also find in Vedic -*i* added to the gunated *u*-stem, as *sûnav-i* (from *sûnu*, m. a son) = Ch. Sl. *sŭnov-i*. The loc. of the fem. *â*-stems also ends sometimes in -*ê* in Vedic. The loc. ending -*in* is only found in Sanskrit in the pronominal declension, as in *ya-sm-in* from *ya* (who), *ta-sm-in* from *ta* (that), &c.

II. *Greek Loc. Sing.* The Gr. dat. sing., except in the case of the *ā*-stems, is properly a loc., being formed simply by the addition of ι: thus we have ποδ-ί, γέροντ-ι, μητέρ-ι, χρο-ί for χροσ-ι, βέλε-ϊ for βελεσ-ι, λᾶϜ-ι, νηϜ-ί, συ-ί, νέκυ-ι, δουρ-ί for δορυ-ι, γλυκε-ϊ for γλυκεϜ-ι, πόλε-ι for πολεy-ι, &c.

The loc. meaning is still frequently found, as in Δωδῶν-ι, Μαραθῶν-ι, Σαλαμῖν-ι, νυκτ-ί, &c.

In the *a*-stems we find the loc. and dat. both in existence beside each other, as dat. ἀγρῷ = ἀγρο + οι beside loc. οἴκοι = οἰκο + ι, dat. τιμῇ = τιμᾱ + ᾳι beside loc. χαμαί = χαμα + ι. Χαμαί is the only example of the loc. of an ᾱ-stem, unless the preposition ὑπαί (ὑπό) be the loc. of a stem ὑπᾱ, just as ὑπείρ (ὑπερ) appears to be the loc. of a stem ὑπερ, and to be for ὑπερι = Skr. *upari* and Z. *upairi*. Besides οἴκοι we find many other examples of locs. of o-stems, as Πυλο-ι (found in Πυλοιγενής—compare χαμαι-εύνης), πέδο-ι (Æsch. Prom.), Æol. μέσσο-ι or μέσο-ι (Alc.), Æol. ἔνδο-ι (ἔνδον), Æol. ὕψο-ι (beside ὑψοῦ), ποῖ = πο + ι, &c. In Æolic we frequently find this loc. termination -ο-ι becoming -υ-ι: thus we find μέσυ-ι = μέσο-ι, τυῖδε (here) for το-ι-δε, πήλυ-ι (τήλοσε), ἄλλυ-ι, ἀτέρυ-ι (ἑτέροσε) = ἑτερο-ι. In Doric we find -οι represented by -ει, as in εἶ (οἶ), πεῖ (ποῖ), τηνεῖ, τουτεῖ, τεῖδε, Lac. ἔξει (ἔξω, Syrac. ἔξοι). We also find in common Greek this same loc. in -ει, as in ἐκεῖ = ἐ-κο-ι from St. κο = I. E. *kva*, ἀμαχεί, πανοικεί, ἀμισθεί, πανστρατεί: -ει sometimes became -ι, as in ἀμαχί. Ἄγχ-ι is perhaps for ἄγχε-ι from·an o-stem ἀγχο, whence ἀγχοῦ: comp. Hom. ἀγχέ-μαχος, where ἀγχε = ἀγχι-ι, ι being lost. 'Αιεί may also be the loc. of a stem, αιϜο = Skr. *êva* = L. *ævo*: in Lesbian Æolic this particle appears also in the forms αἶιν, ἄιν, where final ν is perhaps the original loc. *n*. The datives μοί, σοί = Dor. τοί, are probably locatives, and correspond to the Skr. loc.s *may-i*, *tvay-i*, from the stems *ma*, *tva*; *may-i* being = *ma-i-i* = *ma-a-i*, the stem being lengthened by *a*, and then this *a* being weakened to *i*, and similarly *tvayi* = *tva-a-i*.

III. *Latin Loc. Sing.* The locative of the consonantal stems ended in -ῑ, later -ĕ: the loc. ending was properly ῐ; but the consonantal stems were lengthened by *i*, and so followed the analogy of the *i*-stems, and thus ῑ = -ῐ + ῐ arose; thus we find *loc-ī* (Pl. Amph. 165), *rur-ī* (Pl. Most. 799), and *rur-i̯, vesper-i* and *vesper-e, infelic-i, arbor-i* (Liv. 1, 26, infelici arbori reste suspendito), *her-i* for *hes-i* from *hes* (= Gr. χθές) which appears in *hes-ternus, Anxur-i, Acherunt-i, Sicyon-i,* &c. *Mane* is the loc. of an *i*-stem, and *domu-i* of an *u*-stem; for *domu-i* we generally find *domī* and *domī* after the analogy of the *o*-stems.* The loc. of the *o*-stems ends in -*i* (Old Latin also -*ei* and -*e*) = -*o-i*, as *humi* (from St. *humo*) = *humo-i, belli, foci, Ephesi, Corinthi*, &c. This case is also found in *postri-die, quoti-die, pri-die*; and in Old Latin we find *die quinte* and *die quinti, die septimei, die crastini*, &c. Similarly the loc. of the *a*-stems is formed by adding -*i*, as *Roma-i*, later *Romæ, militiæ*, &c. In Oscan the loc. of the *o*- and *a*-stems is formed in the same way as in Latin: thus we have *múnikei terei* (in communi agro), *tero-* being a neuter stem, and *esai viai mefiai* (in ea via media). The loc -*n* has nearly disappeared, but it probably still exists in -*en* (lo!) loc. of St. *i*, and in *peren-die, peren* being loc. of St. *pero* = Skr. *para* (another), which is also found in *per-egre*, from *pero* and *agro*. In Oscan we find this *n* in *hortin Kerriiin* (in horto Cercali), *hortin* being probably for *hortein* from St. *horto*. In Sabellian we also find it in *esmen-ek asin* (on this altar), from stems *esmo* and *asa*: *esmen* is identical with Skr. *asmin*, except that it still retains the stem-vowel, which is lost in Sanskrit. *Jam* is also supposed to be a loc. from a stem *ja*, and is identified with Skr. *yasmin*, loc. of *ya*. In Umbrian we find two peculiar locative suffixes, -*mem* or -*me* in sing., and -*fem* or *fe* in pl. No satisfactory explanation of these forms has as yet been suggested: Aufrecht and Kirchhoff consider that *mem* and *fem* were originally identical,† and connected with Skr.

---

* *Domus* was originally an *o*-stem = Gr. δόμος.

† Lottner agrees with Siegfried's view that the suffixes -*mem*, -*fem* originally began with *mbh*; see Siegfried's remarks on the Gaulish inscription of Poitiers, arranged and edited by C. F. Lottner.

bhyâm, while Bopp* considers that they arise from a postposition added to the acc.s sing. and pl. In Umbrian we also find traces of a loc. in -*i*, as in O. U. *sve* (if) = O. O. *svai* = L. *si*, O. U. *pre* = L. *præ* for *pra-i*, from a St. *pra* ; N. U. *perne* (from the front), N. U. *postne* (from the rear).

§. 147. The Locative Plural.†

Schleicher considers that the original termination of this case in Indo-European was -*sva-sa*, -*sva* being of pronominal origin, and *sa* the mark of the plural. From -*svasa* are derived the Vedic loc. ending -*susu*, the Zend -*shva*, -*shû*, -*shu*, -*hva*, -*hû*, -*hu*, the old Persian -*suvâ*, the Skr. -*su*, -*shu*, and the Gr. -σσι, -σι.

I. *Sanskrit Loc. Pl.*—This case is formed by adding -*su* (or -*shu*) to the stem, final *ă* becoming *ê* ; thus we have *s'ivê-shu*, *s'ivâ-su*, *kavi-shu*, *marut-su*, &c., from *s'iva* (m., n.), *sivâ* (f.), *kavi* (m.), *marut* (m.), &c.

II. *Greek Loc. Pl.*—This case ends in -σσι or -σι, from -σϜι, before which stems in -*ā* are lengthened by the addition of *i*, as is the case with *ă*-stems in Sanskrit. This -σσι or -σι is added to some consonantal stems and some ending in -ι and -υ, by means of the helping vowel ε : thus we have ποσ-σί for ποδ-σι, κτήμα-σι for κτηματ-σι, δεπά-εσσι for δεπασ-εσσι, βελέ-εσσι for βελεσ-εσσι, βόϜ-εσσι, and βου-σί, κύν-εσσι and κυ-σί, φέρου-σι for φεροντ-σι, νεκύ-εσσι and νέκυ-σσι, πολί-εσσι, πόλι-σι and πόλε-σι = πολεγ-εσσι from πολι, πόλε-σσι for πολεϜ-εσσι from πολυ-, ἵππο-ι-σι, χώρα-ι-σι, &c. The lengthening of the *ā*-stems by *i* was probably much later than that of the *ă*-stems ; for we still find fem. loc.s without this *i*, as θύρᾱ-σι, 'Αθήνη-σι, &c.

III. *Latin Loc. Pl.* This case agrees in form with the dat. and abl. pl. A trace of the Indo-European loc. termi-

---

* Consult Bopp's " Comparative Grammar," vol. I., p. 400, *seq.*

† Consult Schleicher, " Compendium," &c., p. 573 ; and Bopp, " Comparative Grammar," pp. 494, 545.

nation is supposed by some to be found in the plural ending -*is*, which is also used for the dat. and abl. in the *a*- and *o*-declensions: thus we find *foris*, *Athenis*, *Cumis*, *Delphis*, &c., all used as locatives.

§. 148. The Locative Dual.

I. *Sanskrit Loc. Dual.* This case is formed by adding -*ôs* to the stem, final -*ă* becoming -*ê* and neuter stems in -*i* and -*u* being lengthened by *n*: thus we have *marut-ôs*, *kavy-ôs*, *vâri-ṇ-ôs*, *sivay-ôs*, &c., from *marut* (m.), *kavi* (m.), *vâri* (n.), *s'iva* (m., n.), and *s'ivâ* (f.), &c.

II. and III. This case is not found in either Greek or Latin.

§. 149 The Vocative Singular.

The vocative singular consisted of the mere stem in Indo-European.

I. *Sanskrit Voc. Sing.* Masc. and fem. stems in -*i* and -*u* gunate the stem-vowel in this case, as *kavê*, *dhênô*, &c., from *kavi* (m.), *dhênu* (f.), &c. Polysyllabic fem. stems in -*î* and -*û* shorten the stem-vowel, as in *nadi*, *vadhu*, from *nadî* (f.), *vadhû* (f.); fem. stems in -*â* change the stem-vowel into *ê*, as *s'ivê* from *s'ivâ* (f.). Monosyllabic stems ending in a vowel use the nominative for the vocative, as *bhîs*, *nâus*, &c., from *bhî* (f.), *nâu* (f.), &c. Neuter stems in -*i* and -*u* may either gunate the stem-vowel or leave it unchanged, as *vâri* and *vârê* from *vâri* (n.), &c. Neuter stems in -*n* may either retain or lose this consonant, as *nâma* or *nâman* from *nâman* (n.), &c. In all other stems the vocative consists of the mere stem, as *s'iva*, *marut*, *vâk*, &c., from *s'iva* (m., n.), *marut* (m.), *vâk* (f.), &c. In all Skr. vocatives the accent is always placed on the first syllable, as *nádi*, *bálin*, &c, from *nadî*, *balín*, &c.

II. *Greek Voc. Sing.*—In guttural and labial stems the vocative is the same as the nominative, as φύλαξ, Κύκλωψ, &c.; we find, however, γύναι from γυναικ. In dental stems the vocative generally is identical with the mere stem, subject to the euphonic laws of the Greek language, as παῖ for παιδ, ἄνα for ἀνακτ, Ἄρτεμι for Ἀρτεμιδ, γέρον for γεροντ, κύον, πάτερ (with accent thrown back as in Skr. Voc. *pítar*), δυσμενές, &c.; we find, however, πούς used as the voc.; and in participles ending in -ας, -εις, -ους, and -ων, the voc. is the same as the nom. The voc. of masc. o-stems ends in -ε generally; but we also find voc. θεός (beside Θεέ μου, Θεέ μου, Matth. xxvii., 46), φίλος (Od. 3, 375), &c. Masc. stems in -ā (-η) form the voc. in a and η, as πολῖτα, Κρονίδη, &c. Fem. stems in -ā form voc. in ā generally, as θεά, κούρᾱ (Æol. κοῦρα), &c.; and this ā often becomes ă, as in the nom., as μοῦσα, ἀνασσα. In stems ending in -ι, -υ, or a diphthong, the voc. is the mere stem, as μάντι, ταχύ, γραῦ, &c. The fem. voc.s in -οι, such as αἰδοῖ, appear to be related to the nom.s in -ω as the Skr. voc. of fem. *â*-stems is to the nom.; for -οι (= I. E. -*ai*) : -ω (= I. E. -*â*) : : -*ê* (= I. E. -*ai*) : -*â*.

III. *Latin Voc. Sing.* The voc. in Latin is always the same as the nom., except in the case of the masc. o-stems, where it ends in -*e*, as *bone*, *puere* (Pl. Most. 947), from *puerus* = *puer*, *filie* (in Livius Andronicus), and later *fili*, &c. So in Umbrian the voc. of the o-stems ends in -*e*, as *Sançie*, &c.

§. 150. The Vocatives Plural and Dual.

In Sanskrit and Greek the voc. pl. and the voc. dual are the same as the nom. pl. and the nom. dual, except that in Sanskrit the accent is always placed on the first syllable of the voc. In Latin the nom. pl. and the voc. pl. are the same.

§. 151. Paradigms* of the Nominal Declension.

I. *Consonantal Stems.*

I.—I. E. *vâk-* (f.), &c.

	Skr.	Gr.	L.
Stem.	*vâḱ-* (f.)	ὀπ (f.)	*vōc-* (*voc-i*, f.)
Sing. N. V.	*vâḱ.*	ὄπ-ς.	*vōc-s.*
A.	*vâḱ-am.*	ὄπ-α.	*vōc-em.*
I.	*vâḱ-â*	—	—
D.	*vâḱ-ê.*	—	*vōc-i.*
Ab.	*vâḱ-as.*	—	*vōc-ê(d).*
G.	*vâḱ-as.*	ὀπ-ός.	*vōc-is.*
L. (Gr. D.)	*vâḱ-i.*	ὀπ-ί.	—
Plur. N. V.	*vâḱ-as.*	ὄπ-ες.	*vōc-ēs.*
A.	*vâḱ-as.*	ὄπ-ας.	*vōc-ēs.*
I.	*vâg-bhis.*	—	—
D. Ab.	*vâg-bhyas.*	—	*vōc-i-bus.*
G.	*vâḱ-âm.*	ὀπ-ῶν.	*vōc-um.*
L. (Gr. D.)	*vâk-shu.*	ὀπ-σί.	—
Dual. N. A. V.	*vâḱ-âu..*	—	—
,,	Ved. *vâḱ-â.*	ὄπ-ε.	—
I. D. Ab. (Gr. G. D.)	*vâg-bhyâm.*	ὀπ-ο-ῖν.	—
G. L.	*vâḱ-ôs.*	—	—

II.—I. E. *bharant-* (m., f., n.), &c.

	Skr.	Gr.	L.
Stem.	*bharant-* (m., n.)	φεροντ- (m., n.)	*ferent-* (*ferent-i.*) (m., f., n.)
Sing. N. V.	*bharan* (m.)	φέρων (m.)	*ferens* (m., f., n.)
	bharat (n.)	φέρον (n.)	—
A.	*bharant-am* (m.)	φέροντ-α (m.)	*ferent-em* (m., f.)
,,	*bharat* (n.)	φέρον (n.)	*ferens* (n.)
I.	*bharat-â.*	—	—
D.	*bharat-ê.*	—	*ferent-i.*
Ab.	*bharat-as.*	—	*ferent-ê(d).*
G.	*bharat-as.*	φέροντ-ος.	*ferent-is.*
L. (Gr. D.)	*bharat-i.*	φέροντ-ι.	—

* Consult Bopp's "Comparative Grammar," vol. I., pp. 449-519; and Schleicher's "Compendium," &c., pp. 524-623.

COMPARATIVE GRAMMAR: 289

	Skr.	Gr.	L.
Plur. N. V.	bharant-as (m.)	φέροντ-ες (m.)	ferent-ēs (m., f.)
,,	bharant-i (n.)	φέροντ-α (n.)	ferent-i-a (n.)
A.	bharat-as (m.)	φέροντ-ας (m.)	ferent-ēs (m., f.)
,,	bharant-i (n.)	φέροντ-α (n.)	ferent-i-a (n.)
I.	bharad-bhis.	—	—
D. Ab.	bharad-bhyas.	—	ferent-i-bus.
G.	bharat-âm.	φερόντ-ων.	ferent-i-um.
L. (Gr. D.)	bharat-su.	φέρου-σι.	—
Dual. N. A. V.	bharant-âu (m.)	—	—
,,	Voc. bharant-â (m.)	φέροντ-ε.	—
,,	bharant-î (n.)	—	—
,,	bharat-î (n.)	—	—
I. D. Ab. (Gr. D. G.)	} bharad-bhyâm.	φερόντ-ο-ιν.	—
G. L.	bharat-ôs.	—	—

III. a.—I. F., manas- (n.), durmanas- (n.), &c.

	Skr.	Gr.	L.
Stem.	manas- (n.)	μενες- (n.)	genes-.
,,	—	—	(gener-i-) (n.)
Sing. N. A. V.	manas.	μένος.	genus.
I.	manas-â.	—	—
,,	—	κράτεσ-φι.	—
D.	manas-ê.	—	gener-î.
Ab.	manas-as.	—	gener-ē (d.)
G.	manas-as.	μένους (-νεσ-ος.)	gener-is.
L. (Gr. D.)	manas-i.	μένει (-νεσ-ι.)	—
Plur. N. A. V.	manâns-i.	μένη (-νεσ-α.)	gener-a.
I.	manô-bhis.	ὔχεσ-φι.	—
D. Ab.	manô-bhyas.	—	gener-i-bus.
G.	manas-âm.	μενῶν (-νεσ-ων.)	gener-um.
L. (Gr. D.)	manas-su.	μένεσ-σι.	—
,,	—	μένε-σι.	—
Dual. N. A. V.	manas-î.	μένη (-νεσ-ι.)	—
I. D. Ab. (Gr. D. G.)	} manô-bhyâm.	μενοῖν (-νεσ-ο-ιν.)	—
G. L.	manas-ôs.	—	—

III. b.—I. E., dusmanas- (m., f.), &c.

	Skr.	Gr.	L.
Stem.	durmanas- (m., f.)	δυσμενες- (m., f.)	vetes-
,,	—	—	(veter-i-) (m., f., n.)
,,	—	—	arbos-
,,	—	—	(arbor-i-) (f.)
Sing. N. V.	durmanâs.	δυσμενής.	vetus (m., f., n.)
,,	—	—	arbos (f.)
A.	durmanas-am.	δυσμενῆ (-νεσ-α).	arbor-em.
I.	durmanas-â.	—	—
D.	durmanas-ê.	—	arbor-ī.
Ab.	durmanas-as.	—	arbor-ĕ (d).
G.	durmanas-as.	δυσμενοῦς (-νεσ-ος).	arbor-is.
L. (Gr. D.)	durmanas-i.	δυσμενεῖ (-νεσ-ι).	—
Plur. N. V.	durmanas-as.	δυσμενεῖς (-νεσ-ες).	arbor-ēs.
A.	durmanas-as.	δυσμενεῖς (-νεσ-ας).	arbor-ēs.
I.	durmanô-bhis.	—	—
D. Ab.	durmanô-bhyas.	—	arbor-i-bus.
G.	durmanas-âm.	δυσμενῶν (-νεσ-ων).	arbor-um.
L. (Gr. D.)	durmanas-su.	δυσμενίσ-σι.	—
Dual. N. A. V.	durmanas-âu.	—	—
,,	durmanas-â.	δυσμενῆ (-νεσ-ε).	—
I. D. Ab. (Gr. G. D.)	durmanô-bhyâm.	δυσμενοῖν (-νεσ-ο-ιν).	—
G. L.	durmanas-ôs.	—	—

IV. a.—I. E. akman- (m.), &c.

	Skr.	Gr.	L.
Stem.	as'man- (m.)	δαιμον- (m.)	homin-.
,,	—	—	(homin-i) (m.)
Sing. N.	as'mâ.	δαίμων.	homŏ.
A.	as'mân-am.	δαίμον-α.	homin-em.
I.	as'man-â.	—	—
D.	as'man-ê.	—	homin-ī.
Ab.	as'man-as.	—	homin-ĕ (d).
G.	as'man-as.	δαίμον-ος.	homin-is.
L. (Gr. D.)	as'man-i.	δαίμον-ι.	—
V.	as'man.	δαῖμον.	homŏ.
Plur. N. V.	as'mân-as.	δαίμον-ες.	homin-ēs.
A.	as'man-as.	δαίμον-ας.	homin-ēs.
D. I.	as'ma-bhis.	κοτυληδον-ό-φιν.	—

COMPARATIVE GRAMMAR.

	Skr.	Gr.	L.
D. Ab.	aś'ma-bhyas.	—	homin-i-bus.
G.	aś'man-âm.	δαιμόν-ων.	homin-um.
L. (Gr. D.)	aś'ma-su.	δαίμο-σι.	—
Dual. N. A. V.	aś'man-âu.	—	—
,,	Ved. aś'man-â.	δαίμον-ε.	—
I. D. Ab. (Gr. D. G.)	aś'ma-bhyâm.	δαιμόν-ο-ιν.	—
G. L.	aś'man-ôs.	—	—

IV. b.—I. E. gnâman- (n.), &c.

	Skr.	Gr.	L.
Stem.	nâman- (n.)	ταλαν- (n.)	nōmen-
,,	—	—	(nōmin-i-) (n.)
Sing. N. A.	nâma.	τάλαν.	nōmen.
I.	nâmn-â.	—	—
D.	nâmn-ê.	—	nōmin-ī.
Ab.	nâmn-as.	—	nōmin-ē (d).
G.	nâmn-as.	τάλαν-ος.	nōmin-is.
L. (Gr. D.)	nâmn-i.	—	—
,,	nâman-i.	τάλαν-ι.	—
V.	nâman.	τάλαν.	nōmen.
,,	nâma	—	—
Plur. N. A. V.	nâmân-i.	τάλαν-α.	nōmin-a.
I.	nâma-bhis.	—	—
D. Ab.	nâma-bhyas.	—	nōmin-i-bus.
G.	nâmn-âm.	ταλάν-ων.	nōmin-um.
L. (Gr. D.)	nâma-su.	τάλα-σι.	—
Dual. N. A. V.	nâmn-î.	τάλαν-ε.	—
I. D. Ab. Gr. G. D.	nâma-bhyâm.	ταλάν-ο-ιν.	—
G. L.	nâmn-ôs.	—	—

V. a.—I. E. mâtar- (f.), patar- (m.), &c.

	Skr.	Gr.	L.
Stem.	mâtar- (f.)	μητερ- (f.)	māter-
,,	—	—	(mātr-i) (f.)
Sing. N.	mâtâ.	μήτηρ.	māter.
A.	mâtar-am.	μητέρ-α.	mātr-em.
I.	mâtr-â.	—	—
D.	mâtr-ê.	—	mātr-ī.

	Skr.	Gr.	L.
Sing. Ab.	mátu-s.	—	mātr-ē (d).
G.	mátu-s.	μητρ-ός.	mātr-is.
„	—	μητέρ-ος.	—
L. (Gr. D.)	mátar-i.	μητέρ-ι.	—
„	—	μητρ-ί.	—
V.	mátar.	μῆτερ.	māter.
Plur. N. V.	mātar-as.	μητέρ-ες.	mātr-ēs.
A.	mātr̥-s (f.)	—	—
„	pitr̥-n (m.)	—	—
„	Ved. pitar-as.	μητέρ-ας.	mātr-ēs.
I.	mātr̥-bhis.	—	—
D. Ab.	mātr̥-bhyas.	—	mātr-i-bus.
G.	mātr̥-n-ām.	—	—
„	Ved. svasr-ām.	μητέρ-ων.	mātr-um.
L. (Gr. D.)	mātr̥-shu.	μητρά-σι.	—
Dual. N. A. V.	mātar-āu.	—	—
	Ved. mātar-ā.	μητέρ-ε.	—
I. D. Ab. (Gr. G. D.)	mātr̥-bhyām.	μητέρ-ο-ιν.	—
G. L.	mātr-ōs.	—	—

V. b.—I. E. dātár- (m.), &c.

	Skr.	Gr.	L.
Stem.	dātár- (m.)	δοτηρ- (m.)	datōr-.
„	—	—	(datōr-i-) (m.)
Sing. N.	dātā́.	δοτήρ.	datōr.
A.	dātār-am.	δοτῆρ-α.	datōr-em.
I.	dātr-ā́.	—	—
D.	dātr-é.	—	datōr-ī.
Ab.	dātu-s.	—	datōr-ē (d).
G.	dātu-s.	δοτῆρ-ος.	datōr-is.
L. (Gr. D.)	dātar-i.	δοτῆρ-ι.	—
V.	dā́tar.	δοτηρ.	datōr.
Plur. N. V.	dātár-as.	δοτῆρ-ες.	datōr-ēs.
A.	dātr̥-n.	δοτῆρ-ας.	datōr-ēs.
I.	dātr̥-bhis.	—	—
D. Ab.	dātr̥-bhyas.	—	datōr-i-bus.
G.	dātr̥-n-ām.	δοτηρ-ων.	datōr-um.
L. (Gr. D.)	dātr̥-shu.	δοτῆρ-σι.	—
Dual. N. A. V.	dātār-au.	—	—
„	Ved. dātār-ā.	δοτῆρ-ε.	—

	Skr.	Gr.	L.
I. D. Ab. (Gr. D. G.)	dâtŗ-bhyâm.	δοτήρ-ο-ιν.	—
G. L.	dâtr-ôs.	—	—

VI. a.—I. E. akva- (m.), yuga- (n.)

	Skr.	Gr.	L.
Stem.	aś'va- (m.)	ἱππο- (m.)	equo- (m.)
„	yuga- (n.)	ζυγο- (n.)	jugo- (n.)
Sing. N.	aś'va-s (m.)	ἵππο-ς (m.)	equu-s (m.)
„	yuga-m (n.)	ζυγό-ν (n.)	jugu-m (n.)
A.	aś'va-m (m.)	ἵππο-ν (m.)	equu-m (m.)
„	yuga-m (n.)	ζυγό-ν (n.)	jugu-m (n.)
I.	aś'vê-na.	—	—
„	Ved. aś'vâ.	αὐτό-φι.	—
D.	aś'vâ-ya.	ἵππῳ.	equoi, equo.
Ab.	aś'vâ-t.	—	equô-d.
G.	aś'va-sya.	ἵππο-ιο (-ο-σyο).	equî.
„	—	ἵππου.	—
L.	aś'vê.	οἴκο-ι, μο-ί.	domî.
V.	aś'va.	ἵππε, ζυγόν.	eque, jugum.
Pl. N. V.	aś'vâ-s (m.)	ἵππο-ι (m.)	eque-i, equî (m.)
„	Ved. aś'vâ-sas (m.)	—	eque-is.
„	—	—	U. Ikuvinu-s.
„	—	—	O. Nuvlanu-s.
„	yugâ-ni (n.)	—	—
„	Ved. yugâ (n.)	ζυγά (n.)	juga (n.)
A.	aś'vâ-n (m.)	ἵππο-υς (m.)	equô-s.
„	—	Kret. πρειγυτά-νς.	—
„	yugâ-ni (n.)	—	—
„	Ved. yugâ (n.)	ζυγά (n.)	juga (n.)
I.	aś'vâ-is.	—	—
„	Ved. aś'vê-bhis.	θεό-φιν.	—
D. Ab.	aś'vê-bhyas.	—	equî-s, duô-bus.
G.	aśvâ-nâm.	ἵππων (-πο-ων).	(equu-m.)
„	—	—	equô-rum.
L. (Gr. D.)	aś'vê-shu.	ἵππο-ι-σι.	—
„	—	ἵππο-ι-ς.	—
Dual. N. A. V.	aś'vâu (-va-au) (m.)	—	—
„	Ved. aś'vâ (m.)	ἵππω (m.)	duo (m., n.)
„	yugê (n.)	ζυγώ (n.)	—
I. D. Ab. (Gr. G. D.)	aś'vâ-bhyâm.	ἵππο-ιν.	—
L. G.	aś'va-y-ôs.	—	—

VI. b.—I. E. *akvâ* (f.), &c.

	Skr.	Gr.	L.
Stem.	*as'vá-* (f.)	χωρα- (f.)	*equa-* (f.)
Sing. N.	*as'vá.*	χώρα.	*equa.*
A.	*as'vá-m.*	χώρᾱ-ν.	*equa-m.*
I.	*as'va-y-á.*	—	—
,,	Ved. *as'vá.*	—	—
,,	—	βίη-φι.	—
D.	*as'vá-y-ái.*	—	—
,,	Ved. *as'vá-i* (*-vá-ai*.)	χώρᾳ (*-ρα-αι*)	*equá-i* (*-vá-ai*)
,,	—	—	*equae.*
Ab.	*as'vá-y-ás.*	—	*praedā-d.*
,,	—	—	O. *tovtā-d.*
G.	*as'vá-yás.*	χώρα-ς.	*familia-s.*
,,	—.	—	*Proserpna-is.*
,,	—	—	*Diana-es.*
,,	—	—	*equa-i, equae.*
L. (Gr. D.)	*as'vá-y-ám.*	χαμα-ί.	*Romae.*
,,	—	—	O. *via-í.*
V.	*as'vé.*	—	—
,,	Ved. *as'va.*	χώρα.	*equa.*
Pl. N. V.	*as'vá-s.*	χῶραι.	*equai, equae.*
,,	—	—	O. *scrifta-s.*
,,	—	—	U. *urta-s.*
A.	*as'vá-s.*	χώρᾱ-ς.	*equa-s,* O. *vía-ss.*
I.	*as'vá-bhis.*	—	—
D. Ab.	*as'vá-bhyas.*	—	*equá-bus, equi-s.*
,,	—	—	O. *diumpa-is.*
G.	*as'vá-n-ám.*	χωρά-ων.	*equá-rum.*
,,	Ved. *as'vá-m.*	χωρῶν.	—
L. (Gr. D.)	*as'vá-su.*	χώρα-ι-σι.	—
,,	—	χώρα-ι-ς.	—
Dual. N. A. V.	*as'vé.*	χώρα.	—
I. D. Ab. (Gr. G. D.)	*as'vá-bhyám.*	χώρα-ιν.	—
G. L.	*as'vá-y-ós.*	—	—

VII.—I. E. avi- (m., f.), &c.

	Skr.	Gr.	L.
Stem.	avi- (m., f.)	πολι- (f.), κι- (m.)	ovi- (f.), fasci (m.)
,,	vâri- (n.)	—	mari- (n.)
,,	s'uk'i- (m., f., n.)*	ἰδρι- (m., f., n.)	levi (m., f., n.)
Sing. N.	avi-s (m., f.)	πόλι-ς (f.)	ovi-s (f.)
,,	vâri (n.)	ἰδρι (n.)	mare (n.)
A.	avi-m (m., f.)	πόλι-ν (f.)	ovi-m (f.)
,,	vâri.	ἰδρι (n.)	mare (n.)
I.	avi-n-â (m.)	—	—
,,	avy-â (f.)	—	—
,,	vâri-ṇ-â (n.)	—	—
D.	avay-ê (m., f.)	—	—
,,	avy-âi (f.)	—	ovi.
,,	vâri-ṇ-ê (m.)	—	—
Ab.	avê-s (m., f.)	—	ovê-d, mari-d.
,,	avy-âs (f.)	—	—
,,	vâri-ṇ-as (n.)	—	—
G.	avê-s (m., f.)	πόλε-ως.	ovi-s.
,,	avy-âs (f.)	Hom. πόληος.	—
,,	vâri-n-as (n.)	πόλι-ος.	—
L. (Gr. D.)	av-âu (m., f.)	πόλε-ϊ.	—
,,	avy'âm (f.)	πόλει, πόλῑ.	—
,,	vâri-n-i (n.)	Hom. πόλη-ϊ.	—
V.	avê (m., f.)	πόλι (f.)	ovi-s (f.)
,,	vâri (n.), varê (n.)	ἰδρι (n.)	mare (n.)
Pl. N. V.	avay-as (m., f.)	Hom. πόλη-ες (f.)	ovê-s (f.)
,,	—	πόλι-ες (f.)	—
,,	—	πόλει-ς (f.)	—
,,	vâri-ṇ-i.	ἰδρι-α (n.)	mari-a (n.)
A.	avi-n (m.)	πόλι-ας (f.)	ovê-s (f.)
,,	avi-s (f.)	πόλει-ς (f.)	—
,,	—	Hom. πόλη-ας (f.)	—
,,	vâri-ṇ-i.	ἰδρι-α.	mari-a (n.)
I.	avi-bhis.	—	—
D. Ab.	avi-bhyas.	—	ovi-bus.
G.	avi-n-âm.	πυλί-ων.	ovi-um.
,,	—	πόλι-ων.	—

* Neuter adjectives in -i in Sanskrit in the D. Ab. G. and L. sing., and in the G. and L. dual may follow the declension either of vâri (n.), or of avi (m.).

	Skr.	Gr.	L.
L. (Gr. D.)	avi-shu.	πόλι-σι.	—
,,	—	πόλε-σι.	—
,,	—	Hom. πολί-εσσι.	—
Dual. N. A. V.	aví (m., f.)	πόλι-ε.	—
,,	vári-ṇ-í (n.)	πόλε-ε.	—
I. D. Ab. (Gr. D. G.)	avi-bhyâm.	πολέ-ο-ιν.	—
G. L.	avy-ós.	—	—
,,	vári-ṇ-ós.	—	—

VIII.—I. E. sûnu- (m.), &c.

	Skr.	Gr.	L.
Stem.	sûnu- (m.)	νεκυ- (m.)	fructu- (m.)
	dhénu- (f.)	συ- (f.)	manu- (f.)
	tálu- (n.)	μεθυ- (n.)	cornu- (n.)
	mṛdu- (m., n.)*	γλυκυ- (m., n.)	—
Sing. N.	sûnu-s (m.)	νέκυ-ς (m.)	fructu-s (m.)
,,	tálu (n.)	μέθυ (n.)	cornu- (n.)
A.	sûnu-m (m.)	νέκυ-ν (m.)	fructu-m (m.)
,,	tálu (n.)	μέθυ (n.)	cornu (n.)
I.	sûnu-n-â (m.)	—	—
,,	dhénv-â (f.)	—	—
,,	tálu-n-â (n.)	—	—
D.	sunav-ê (m.)	—	fructu-i.
,,	dhênav-ê (f.)	—	fructu.
,,	dhênv-âi (f.)	—	—
,,	tálu-n-ê (n.)	—	—
Ab.	sûnô-s (m.)	—	magistratû-d.
,,	dhênô-s (f.)	—	—
,,	dhênv-âs (f.)	—	—
,,	tálu-n-as (n.)	—	—
G.	sûnô-s (m.)	νέκυ-ος.	fructu-os.
,,	dhênô-s (f.)	γλυκέ-ος.	fructû-s.
,,	dhênv-âs (f.)	ἀστε-ως (n.)	O. castrou-s (n.)
,,	tálu-n-as (n.)	—	U. trifo-r.
L. (Gr. D.)	sûn-âu (m.)	νέκυ-ι.	—
,,	dhên-âu (f.)	ἀστει.	—
,,	dhênv-âm (f.)	—	—

* Neuter adjectives in -u in Sanskrit in the D. Ab. G. and L. sing., and in the G. and L. dual may follow the declension either of *tálu* (n.), or *sûnu* (m.).

	Skr.	Gr.	L.
L. (Gr. D.)	tálu-n-i (n.)	—	—
V.	súnó (m.)	νέκυ.	fructu-s (m.)
,,	dhénó (f.)	—	—
,,	táló (n.)	—	—
,,	tálu (n.)	μέθυ.	cornu (n.)
Pl. N. V.	súnav-as (m.)	γλυκεῖς(-κεϜ-ες)(m.)	fructu-s (m.)
,,	dhénav-as (f.)	ἐγχέλεις (f.)	—
,,	tálû-n-i.	γλυκέ-a (n.)	cornu-a (n.)
,,	—	ἄστη (-τεϜ-a) (n.)	—
Plur. A.	súnú-n (m.)	νέκυ-ας.	fructū-s (m.)
,,	Vod. súnv-as (m.)	γλυκεῖς (-κεϜ-ας).	—
,,	dhénú-s (f.)	ἐγχελεῖς (f.)	—
,,	tálû-n-i (n.)	γλυκέ-a (n.)	cornu-a (n.)
,,	—	ἄστη (n.)	—
I.	súnu-bhis.	—	—
D. Ab.	súnu-bhyas.	—	fructi-bus.
,,	—	—	portu-bus.
G.	súnú-n-ám.	νεκύ-ων.	fructu-um.
,,	—	γλυκέ-ων.	—
L. (Gr. D.)	súnu-shu.	νεκύ-εσσι.	—
,,	—	νέκυ-σσι.	—
,,	—	νέκυ-σι.	—
,,	—	γλυκέ-σι.	—
Dual. N. A. V.	súnú (m.)	νέκυ-ε.	—
	dhénú (f.)	γλυκέ-ε.	—
	tálu-n-í.	—	—
I. D. Ab. (Gr. D. G.)	súnu-bhyám.	γλυκέ-ο-ιν.	—
G. L.	súnv-ós.	—	—

IX.—I. E. nâu- (f.), grau- (m., f.), &c.

	Skr.	Gr.	L.
Stem.	nâu- (f.)	νᾶυ- (f.), Ion. νευ-	nav-i-* (f.)
,,	gó- (m., f.)	βου- (m., f.)	bo- (bov-), bov-i- (m. f.)

* There were no diphthongal stems in Old Latin; diphthongs were avoided either by the addition of i, as in nav-i, or by dropping the second vowel, as in bo-. Greek diphthongal stems, such as 'Αχιλλεύς, &c., when introduced into Latin, became, in early times, Aciles, &c.; while in later times either the Greek de-

		Skr.	Gr.	L.
Sing.	N.	nâu-s, gâu-s.	ναῦ-ς, βοῦ-ς.	nari-s, bo-s, bov-i-s.
	A.	nâv-am.	νῆ-α, ναῦ-ν, νέ-α.	nave-m.
	,,	gâ-m.	βοῦ-ν.	bove-m.
	I.	nâv-â, gav-â.	—	—
	,,	—	ναῦ-φι.	—
	D.	nâv-é, gav-é.	—	navî, bovî.
	Ab.	nâv-as, gô-s.	—	navē- (d), borë (d).
	G.	nâv-as.	νη-ός, νε-ώς, νε-ός.	navi-s.
	,,	gô-s.	βο-ός.	bovi-s.
	L. Gr. D.	nâv-i, gav-i.	νη-ί, νε-ί, βο-î.	—
	V.	nâu-s, gâu-s.	ναῦ, βοῦ.	navi-s, bovi-s.
Plur.	N. V.	nâv-as, gâv-as.	νῆ-ες, νέ-ες, βό-ες.	navē-s, bovē-s.
	A.	nâv-as.	νῆ-ας, ναῦ-ς, νέ-ας.	navē-s.
	,,	gâv-as, gâ-s.	βό-ας, βοῦ-ς.	bovē-s.
	I.	nâu-bhis, gó-bhis.	ναῦ-φιν.	—
	D. Ab.	nâu-bhyas.	—	navi-bus.
	,,	gó-bhyas.	—	bō-bus, bū-bus.
	G.	nâv-âm.	νη-ῶν, νε-ῶν.	navi-um.
	,,	gav-âm.	βο-ῶν.	bo-um.
Plur.	L.	nâu-shu.	νή-ε-σσι, νην-σί.	—
	,,	—	ναυ-σί, νέ-ε-σσι.	—
	,,	gó-shu.	βό-ε-σσι, βου-σί.	—
Dual.	N. A. V.	nâv-âu, gâv-âu.	—	—
. . . . . .		nâv-â, gâv-â.	νῆ-ε, βό-ε.	—
I. D. Ab.	}	nâu-bhyâm.	νη-ο-ῖν.	—
(Gr. D. G.)	}	gó-bhyâm.	βο-ο-ῖν.	—
	G. L.	nâv-ós, gav-ós.	—	—

clension was followed, or the diphthong was resolved into its two constituent elements, and the word passed over to the o- declension; thus we find N. *Achilleus, Orphe-us*, &c.; G. *Achille-ï, Orphe-ï, Ulixe-ï*, &c.

CHAPTER IX.

ADJECTIVES.*

§. 152. THE COMPARATIVE DEGREE.

THE stem of the comparative degree was formed in Indo-European either by the addition of -*yant* (= *yan-ta*), or by that of -*tara* to the stem of the positive. *Yant* and *tara* may be derived either from verbal or from pronominal roots. Those writers who connect them with verbal roots derive -*yant* from I. E. root *ya* (to go), whence come Skr. *yâ* (id.), Gr. *ἰέ-ναι*, &c.; and -*tara*, from I. E. root *tar* (to cross over); whence come Ved. *tiras* (across), Z. *tarô* (id.), Kelt. *tair* (id.), L. *trans*, Goth. *thair-h*, E. *through*. These roots signify a *progression*, and consequently their addition to the positive heightens the idea implied by it. It is, however, better to derive these suffixes from pronominal roots, and to connect -*yant* with the common suffixes -*ant*, -*m-ant*, -*v-ant*, and to resolve -*tara* into the elements *ta* and *ra*—the latter of which by itself sometimes expresses the idea of the comparative, as in Skr. *avara* (posterior), *apara* (id.), Goth. *afar*, G. *aber*, L. *sup-er-us*, &c. As regards the relative age of these suffixes, it is probable that -*yant* is the older of the two, for it is a primary suffix, i. e. it must be attached immediately to the root, whereas -*tara* is a secondary suffix, and consequently must be of later introduction than those primary suffixes to which it is attached. We find, however, traces of -*tara* being used as a primary suffix in Skr. *antara* (interior, other), *antar* (within), L. *inter*, Goth. *anthar* (other), E. *other*, all from pronominal root *an*, Gr. *φίλ-τερος*, &c.

---

* The declension of the adjectives has been already noticed in Chapter VIII., and consequently we have here only to do with the degrees of comparison.

§. 153. THE SANSKRIT COMPARATIVE.

I. *The form in -yâns and -îyâns.* We find *-yâns* (f. *-yasi*, n., *-yas*) in Ved. *nav-yâns*, from *nava* (new), Skr. *sthê-yâns*, from *sthira* (firm) ; *sphê-yâns*, from *sphira* (swollen) ; *s'rê-yâns*, from *s'rila* (lucky) ; *prê-yâns*, from *priya* (dear) ; *g'yâ-yâns*, from R. *g'yâ* (to grow old, overpower), the positive of which is not found, but which is supposed by Bopp to have been *g'yâ-yin*, formed from *g'yâ*, as *yâ-yin* (going), from *yâ;* *bhû-yâns*, from *bhûri* (much), according to Bopp, or from *bahu* (much), according to Benfey. In *sthêyâns, sphêyâns, s'rêyâns*, and *prêyâns* the *i* of the positive is *gunated;* but we may also explain the *ê* in the first two of these forms by adding *-îyâns* to what were probably the original forms of their positives (omitting the ending *-ra*) *sthara* (from R. *sthû* = L. *sta*), and *sphara* (from R. *sphâ-y*, c. f. Gr. σφαίρα = σφαρya) : this latter explanation is, however, more improbable than the preceding one, for the stem-vowel of the positive, if it be *i* or *u*, is gunated when final *-ra* is lost, as we shall see further on ; and it is also possible that the form *-îyâns* had not been developed from *-yâns* before *sphara* and *sthara* had become *sphira* and *sthira*. The form *-îyâns* arose from *-yâns* through the influence of *y*, which has a tendency to generate *i* before it, as in the Pâli *nadiyâ* = Skr. *nadyâ*, Instr. of *nadî*. That *-yâns* is older than *-îyans* appears at once from the cognate languages ; thus, beside Skr. *mah-iyâns*, from Ved. *maha* (great), we find Z. *mas'-yas*, Gr. μειζον = μεγ-yov, L. *majôr* = *mag-yôr*, from I. E. *magh* (to be mighty); beside Skr. *âs'-îyâns*, from *âs'u* (swift), we find Z. *âs'-yas*, Gr. ὤκιον = ὠκ-yov, L. *ôc-iôr*. Before *-îyâns* the final vowel of the positive stem is suppressed, and the vowel of its first syllable, if susceptible of gunation, receives it, except this vowel be *r*, which becomes *ra*, or *a*, which is unaltered. Thus we have *alp-îyâns*, from *alpa* (small), *pâp-îyâns* (= Gr.

κακ-ιον), from *pápa* (bad), *var-îyâns* (= Gr. ἀρε-ιον), from *vara* (good), &c.; *sádh-iyáns*, from *sádhu* (good), *lagh-îyáns* (= Gr. ἐλασσον = 'ἐλαχ-yov), from *laghu* (light), *gar-îyáns* (= Gr. βαρ-ιον), *mrad-îyáns* (= Gr. βραδ-ιον), from *mṛdu* (soft), *prath-îyáns*, from *pṛthu* (= Gr. πλατυ), &c.; *-ra* is lost in *kshêp-îyáns*, from *kshipra* (swift), &c.; as in Gr. αἰσχ-ιον, from αἰσχρο, &c.; *-la* is lost in *s'rê-yâns*, from *s'rî-la* (lucky); *-ya* is lost in *prê-yáns*, from *priya* (dear); adjectives in *-mant*, *-vant*, *-vin*, and *-tár* lose these suffixes before *-îyáns*.

II. *The form in -tara.* This suffix is attached immediately to the positive stem, as in *puṇya-tara*, from *puṇya* (pure), *bali-tara*, from *balin* (strong), final *n* being lost, beside Ved. *supathin-tara*. In words with two stems *-tara* is attached to the weak form, and in words with three, to the intermediate one, as *mahat-tara*, from *mahat*, the weak form of *mahânt* (strong), and *vidvat-tara*, from *vidvat*, the intermediate form of *vidvâns* (Gr. ειδοτ), beside Ved. *vidush-tara*, from the weakest form of *vidvâns*, &c. In the pronoun we find this suffix constantly employed, as in *ka-tara* (uter), from *ka* (= I. E. *kva*, L. *qui-s*), *ya-tara* (uter), from *ya* (= Gr. ὁ-), *i-tara*, from *i* (= L. *i-s*, whence *i-terum* = Ved. *i-taram*), *êka-tara* (one of two), from *êka* (one), &c. From the preposition *ut* (up) is formed *ut-tara* (higher) = Gr. ὑσ-τερο.

§. 154. THE GREEK COMPARATIVE.

I. *The form in -ιον.* In adding this termination to the stem of the positive final, ο, υ and ρο are omitted, as in φιλ-ιον, from φιλο, κα-κ-ιον, from κακο; ὀλιζον = ὀλιγ-yov, from ὀλιγο; ἡδ-ιον, from ἡδυ; θασσον = ταχ-yov, from ταχυ; ἐλασσον = ελαχ-yov, from ἐλαχυ; γλυκ-ιον, and γλυσσον (σσ = κy), from γλυκυ, βραδ-ιον and βρασσον (σσ = δy), from βραδυ; παχ-ιον and πασσον (σσ = χy), from παχυ; μασσον = μακ-yον, from μακ-ρο; αἰσχ-ιον, from αἰσχ-ρο, &c.

II. *The form in -τερο.* In adding this termination to the

stem of the positive, the stem-vowel is generally retained, -τερο being a secondary suffix, as in φιλω-τερο, from φιλο (the stem-vowel here being lengthened as the penult is short), κουφο-τερο, from κουφο ; γλυκυ-τερο, from γλυκυ ; χαριεσ-τερο, from χαριετ, the weak form of χαριεντ, &c. In φιλ-τερο this suffix is primary, being attached directly to the root.

By adding -τερο to the preceding form of the comparative suffix -ιον = yan-s, we obtain the forms -εσ-τερο, -ισ-τερο, and -αι-τερο ;* as in ἀφθον-εστερο, from αφθονο ; λαλ-ιστερο, from λαλο ; φιλ-αιτερο, from φιλο, &c. ; the stem-vowel being lost in these cases. In -αι-τερο it is possible that a may belong to the stem, and so represent the original a from which o was developed ; Benfey, however, considers -αι to be an old locative termination, to which the comparative suffix was attached. We find the two forms -ιον and -τερο combined also in ἀσσο-τέρω, from ἀσσον = αγχ-yον, and in the Hom. ἐπασσύτεροι from the same root. The suffix -τερο is added also to prepositions, numerals, and pronouns ; as προ-τερο, from προ ; δευ-τερο, from δύο ; ἑ-τερο, from ἱ ; πο-τερυ and κο-τερο, from I. E. *kva*, &c. It is also employed in other cases where only opposition in space is implied, as in δεξι-τερο, ἀρισ-τερο, &c. In ἀλλό-τριο-ς we find -τερο augmented by the suffix -ιο = I. E. -*ya*.

§. 155. The Latin Comparative.

I. *The form in -iōs* (m. f. n.), later *-iōs* (m. f.), *-ius* (n.). The masc. *-ior* and the neut. *-ius* were both originally *-iōs;* the neuter *-ius* is still found in Plautus. This suffix is both primary and secondary in Latin; in adding it to vocalic positive stems the stem-vowel is always lost. Thus we have *sapient-ior*, from *sap-ient; prob-ior*, from *prob-o ; lev-ior*, from *lev-i = leg-u-i; major = mag-jor, ma-jus*, and *mag-is = mag-ius*,

---

* From this form is probably derived the Modern Greek comparative in -ητερος, as καλ-ήτερος from καλός, κακ-ήτερος from κακός, &c.

from R. *mag*, whence *mag-nus* ; *min-or* = *min-jor*, from R. *min* ; *plūs* = *plo-jus*, from I. E. *par* or *pra* (to fill), whence *ple-nus, ple-rique*; Gr. πλε-ίων, &c.

II. *The form in -tero*. This suffix is not used in Latin to form regular comparatives. It is, however, of frequent occurrence: as in *dexter* = Gr. δεξιτερό-ς ; *u-ter* = Goth. *hva-thar* (which of two), from I. E. *kva* (who); *neu-ter, al-ter*, from the same root, as Gr. ἄλλυ-ς = ἀλ-γος, L. *al-iu-s*, &c.; *ce-teru-s* from same root as L. *-ce* in *hi-ce, ci-s, ci-tra;* Gr. ἐ-κεῖ, ἐ-κεῖ-νο-ς. We find *-ter* also employed to form prepositions : as in *præ-ter, prop-ter, in-ter;* and adverbs, as in *sub-ter, audac-ter, pari-ter*, &c. It appears as *-trō* in *ul-trō* and *-intrō;* and as *-trā* in *ex-trā, in-trā, con-trā*, &c. These forms in *-trā* are supposed by some to be old instrumentals, just as in Skr. the instr. *antarēṇa* is used adverbially; this view is, however, wrong, for they are really old ablatives, as we see from O. L. *exstrād* = *extrā*.

In many cases both forms of the comparative suffix are united in Latin. Thus in *sin-is-tero-, min-is-tero-, mag-is-tero-,* we have *-is-tero* = I. E. *-yāns* + *tara ;* and in *dex-ter-ior, in-ter-ior, ci-ter-ior*, &c., we have *-ter-ior* = I. E. *-tara* + *yāns*. With *sin-is-tero*, &c., may be compared the Gr. λαλ-ισ-τερο, &c.

§. 156. The Indo-European Superlative.

In Indo-European the idea of the superlative was expressed by adding either *-ma* or *-ta* to the stem of the positive. After the first separation that occurred in the I. E. family of languages, these suffixes were either used separately, or united together, or doubled, or *ta* and *tata* were added to *-yāns*. Thus we find *-ta* in the stems Skr. *shash-tha* = Gr. ἕκ-το, L. *quar-to*, &c. : *-ma* in Skr. *nava-ma* (= L. *no-no* by assimilation for *nomo*), Skr. *ava-ma* (low) from *ava* (down), which is, perhaps, connected with Gr. αὖ, αὐ-τός, L. *au-t*, *au-tem*, Skr. *agri-ma* (first), from *agra* (a point), L. *sum-mo* for *sup-mo*, &c.; *-tama** in Skr. *puṇya-tama* from *puṇya* (holy), and other superlatives, in *pra-thama* (beside Gr. πρω-το, L. *pri-mo*), &c., L. *op-timo*, &c.; *-mata* in Gr. ἑβδο-ματο† (beside ἑβδο-μο), πυ-ματο (for πυσ-ματο, from πυς, an Æolicised form of a root πος which is connected with Skr. *paśk'át*, after, Gr. ὀ-πίσ-ω, L. *pos-t*, *po-ne* = *pos-ne*, O. *pos-mo-m* = L. *postremum*), and especially in the Irish ordinals, as *secht-mad* (the 6th), *ocht-mad* (the 8th), &c.; *-mama*, also in the Irish forms *uaisli-mem*, from *uasal* (high); *doir-bem*, from *dóir* (a slave), with *b* for *m*, &c.; *-tata* in Gr. κουφο-τατο, and other superlatives; *-yâns + ta = ish-tha*, in Skr. *mah-ishtha* (= Gr. μεγ-ιστο, &c., and = ισ-το in Gr. ὠκ-ιστο, &c.; *-yâns + ta + ta = -ισ-τα-το, -εσ-τα-το, -αι-τα-το* in Gr.

§. 157. THE SANSKRIT SUPERLATIVE.

The form in *-ta* is found in some ordinal numbers, as *k'atur-tha* = Gr. τεταρ-το, &c. *Ish-tha-* is of common occurrence, and is added to the stem in the same way as the comp. suffix *îyâns*, as in *pap-ishtha* (= Gr. κακ-ιστο), &c. *Ma*-is found in *ashta-ma* (the 8th), *nava-ma* (the 9th), *madhya-ma* (middle), &c. *Tama-* is the usual superlative suffix, as in *mahat-tama*, &c.; it is also found in the ordinals, as in *vinśati-tama* (the 20th), &c. From the superlative *g'yêshtha* (eldest) is also formed the double superlative *g'yêshtha-tama*.

---

* Bopp derives *-tama* from *-tara + ma*, and *-τατο* from *-ταρο + το*; he had previously suggested *tan* (to stretch) as the root of both forms; but it is much more probable that they arise from the pronominal roots *ta* and *ma*, as these roots are separately found expressing the idea of the superlative.

† Lottner and others consider that initial *m* of the suffixes *-ma* and *-mata* belongs sometimes to the stem, and that the words noticed in the text should be divided thus: Skr. *ashṭam-a, navam-a;* Gr. ἑβδομ-ο, ἑβδομ-ατο; Ir. *sechtm-ad*, &c.

§. 158. The Greek Superlative.

The form in -το is found in some ordinal numbers, as τεταρ-το, &c. Ισ-το is added to stem in the same way as the comp. suffix -ιον, as in ἡδ-ιστο, from ἡδυ, &c. Τα-το is the usual superlative suffix, as in φιλ-τατο, &c.; added to the comparative suffix -yáns, it appears as -αι-τατο, -εσ-τατο, -ισ-τατο, in ἡσυχ-αι-τατο, σωφρον-εσ-τατο, πτωχ-εσ-τατο, &c. from ἡσυχο,σωφρον, πτωχο, &c. We find -μο in ἑβδο-μο and προ-μο and -μα-το in ἑβδο-ματο and πυ-ματο.

§. 159. The Latin Superlative.

The form in -to is found in some ordinal numbers, as quin-to-, &c.; also in quo-to-, from I. E. kva. Mo- is found in i-mo-, sum-mo-,* &c. In min-i-mo- and plur-i-mo-, it is added to the comparative suffix -ios, of which the vowel i alone is left; and we find it added to the other comparative suffix -ter in ex-tre-mo- beside ex-timo-, pos-tre-mo- beside pos-tu-mo-. The form -timo or -tumo is found in op-timo-, and op-tumo-, dex-timo-, maximo- = mag-timo-, pessimo- = pep-timo-, proximo-† = prop-timo-, liberrimo- = liber-timo-, facillimo- = facil-timo-, &c. This suffix is also used in other words without expressing any superlative idea, as in fini-timo-, mari-timo-, &c. Timo is added to the comparative suffix -ios, which here becomes is, and -is-timo becomes -issimo-, as in prob-issimo-, levissim-o, pot-issimo-, &c.

---

* I-mo is a superlative stem formed from the preposition in, and summo is a superlative of sub.

† This is Benfey's view, who connects the word with Skr. pâpa (bad), L. peccare ; pejor is, in his view, for pepjor. Lottner, however, connects it with an I. E. root pi (to hate), whence E. fiend, &c.

CHAPTER X.

NUMERALS.

§. 160. THE CARDINAL NUMBERS.*

I.—Ind. Eur.: the idea of unity was probably marked by the demonstrative stem *i-* or its gunated form *ai-*.

Sanskrit: *é-ka-* from *é-* = I. E. *ai-*, the gunated form of the demonstrative stem *i-*, and *ka-* .†

Greek: nom. sing. m., εἷς = ἑν-ς, f. μία, n. ἕν; ἑν may be = I. E. *sam*, or *sa*, whence Gr. ἅ-παξ, Kret. ἄμ-ακις (once), Tarent. ἄμ-ατις (id.), Skr. *sa-kṛt* (id.), L. *sem-el*, *sim-plex*, *sin-guli*, and μία would then be = *sam-ya*. In Hesiod we find ἕεις for εἷς, where the initial ε must represent a lost digamma; and if this be so, then it is possible that Ϝεν may be an older form of the stem, with which we may compare the Lith. *vḗna-s* (one), and E. *one* (as pronounced). If Bopp's explanation of Lith. *vḗnas* (Comp. Gram. II., p. 57) be correct, then it is also possible that Gr. Ϝεν may be = an older μεν, whence μέν. In ἰῷ (= ἑνί), and ἴα (= μία), the demonstrative stems *i* and *a* are united. Gr. οἰ-Ϝο- (whence οἶο-ς) is identical with Z. *aeva* (one). Gr.

---

* For the declension of the Sanskrit numerals, consult Bopp's "Sanskrit Grammar," pp. 157-161.

† *Ka-* (one) is found, according to Bopp, in L. *cocles* (one-eyed), from *ca*, and *oculus* and *cæcus* = *ca-icus*, from *ca* and a supposed *ocus* (eye), whence *oculus*, a diminutive; and in Goth. *halta-* (lame), from *ha* = I. E. *ka*, and *lith* (to go); *halba-* (half), from *ha*, and *leiban* (to remain); *haihs* (one-eyed). Curtius connects L. *cæcus* and Goth. *haihs* with I. E. root *ska* to shade); whence Skr. *k'hâyâ* for *skâyâ*, Gr. σκι-ά, σκο-ιά (σκοτεινά, Hesych.) = I. E. *skaya*, σκη-νή, σκό-τος, E. *shade*, *sky*, &c.: *cocles* he considers to be a diminutive from the same root.

οἰ-νό-ς, οἰ-νή (one) correspond also exactly to O. L. oino-s, Goth. ain-s; οι- in οἰνός and οἶος, being from the stem i-.

Latin: uno-s = O. L. oino-s, from stem i-.

II.—Ind.-Eur.: dva-.*

Sanskrit: dva-, dvi- (in compounds); dvis (twice).

Greek: δύο, δυώ, G. δυοῖν, δυώ, Att. δυεῖν, Dor. δυῶν, Mod. Gr. δυονῶν, D. δυοῖν, δυώ, Dor. δυσί, Æol. δύεσσι; δίς (twice) for δϝίς; δισσό-ς for δϝι-τγο-ς; δι-ά (originally meaning *between* and then *through*), for δϝι-α, Instr. of stem δϝι, as E. *between* is from *twain;* δοιώ, δοιοί (two), from stem δϝι-ο; δι- (in compounds); δέ (lit. *secondly*).

Latin: m. duo, f. duae, n. duo (and dua in vulgar Latin), Acc. m. duo, duos; f. duas; bini for dvini; bis for dvis;

---

* Various methods of explaining the numerals have been suggested; but, except in the case of the first numeral, which is probably derived from a demonstrative stem, none of these explanations are satisfactory. Thus *tri-* is derived from I. E. *tar* (to cross); but how is the idea of *crossing* connected with the idea of *three* more than with that of *four?* *Kvankva* is supposed to be the reduplication of a root *kvan*, which is said to mean *to seize*, whence are derived Skr. *śvan* (a dog), Gr. κυον, &c., and therefore to have originally meant the five fingers, as that part of the body with which we seize anything; but what proof have we that such a root ever existed? Skr. *pañk'an* is again connected with *pâṇi* (the hand), but *pâṇi* is probably for *par-ni* from *par* (to fill). The I. E. form of *ten* is said to be *dva-kvan* from *dva-* (2), and *kvan-* (5); but there are no traces of the two *v* s in any I. E. language. Again, it is suggested that the root of *dakan* is I. E. *dak* (to point out), whence come Gr. δείκνυμι, δάκτυλος; L. *digitus*, Skr. *diś* (to point out), &c. *Kantam* probably meant *host, multitude;* but its origin is obscure. Other methods of explaining the numerals have been suggested, but so absurd as scarcely to deserve notice; thus Skr. *tisar* (fem. three) is derived from *tri* (3), and *strí* (a woman)! *Ashṭâu* (8) is for *as'vâu* (two horses), &c.! It is also impossible to connect the I. E. numbers with the Shemitic; the likeness that exists between the names of numbers *six* and *seven* is merely accidental.

du-plum, du-plex. N. U. *duf* (duos), *duir* (duobus), O. U. *tuves* (duobus), N. U. *du-* (in compounds), L. *bi-* (id.).

III.—Ind. Eur.: *tri-*.

Sanskrit: m. n. *tri-*, f. *tisar-* for *titar-*, according to Bopp, a reduplicated form of *tri-*; *tri-s* (thrice).

Greek: m. f., τρεῖς, Dor. τρῖ-ς; n. τρί-α, from τρι-; τρί-ς.

Latin: m. f., *tres*, n. *tri-a*, from *tri-*; *ter*; O. U. *tri-* in *tribriçu* (triplicatio).

IV.—Ind.-Eur.: *kvatvar-*.

Sanskrit: m. n., *k'atvâr-*, *k'atur-*; f. *k'atasar-* (according to Bopp, from *ka*, one, and *tasar*, three); *k'atur* (four times).

Greek: m. f., τέσσαρες, τέτταρες; n., τέσσαρα, τέτταρα; Dor. τέτορες (o = Fa), Bœot. πέτταρες, Æol. πέσσυρες, Hom. πίσυρες (ε becoming ι through the influence of υ); New Ion. and Mod. Gr. τέσσερες; τετρά-κις.

Latin: *quatuor* and *quattuor, quadru-* (in compounds), *quater*; U. *petur-* (in compounds), O. *petor-a*, whence *Petr-ejus, petiro-* (in compounds).

V.—Ind.-Eur.: *kvankva-*.

Sanskrit: *pañk'an-*.

Greek: πέντε for πεντα found in πεντά-κις, for I. E. -an becomes -a in Greek; Æol. πέμπε, the gen. of which occurs in μαχέων ἀπὺ πέμπων* (Alcæi fragmenta, 26).

Latin: *quinque*, O. *pomtis*, whence *Pontius* (= L. *Quinctius*), *Pomp-ejus*: *p* = I. E. *kv* as in W. *pump* (5), &c.

VI.—Ind.-Eur.: *ksvaks-*; from this complicated form alone can be deduced the various words expressing the idea of *six*, in the Indo-European languages. Thus in Z. *khsva-s* we find the initial *ksv* still preserved; *ks* is found in Ossetian *achsaz*† and the initial *sh* in Skr.

---

* "Ahrens de Dialectis Æolicis et Pseudæolicis," p. 245.

† The *a* in *achsaz* is merely prosthetic, as ε in ἰχθίς.

shash arises from *s* through the influence of the preceding *k*; *sv* is found in Afghan *spash* (Afgh. *sp* = Skr. *sv*), and in Welsh *chwech* (W. *chw* = Skr. *sv**); *s* is found in Gr. ἕξ (aspirate = *s*), L. *sex*, Ir. *sé*; *v* is found in Dor. Ϝέξ, Armenian *weż*.

Sanskrit: *shash-*.
Greek: ἕξ, Dor. Ϝέξ, Mod. Gr. ἕξι.
Latin: *sex*.

VII.—Ind.-Eur.: *saptam-* or *saptan-*.
Sanskrit: *saptan-*.
Greek: ἑπτά, Mod. Gr. ἐφτά.
Latin: *septem*. Bopp supposes that the final *m* in *septem*, *novem*, and *decem* is due to the influence of the corresponding ordinal numbers, *septimo-* = Skr. *saptama-*, &c.

VIII.—Ind.-Eur.: *aktam-*, or, according to Bopp, *aktâu-*.
Sanskrit: *ashṭan-* (after analogy of *saptan-*), nom. *ashṭâu*, apparently a dual form, as *s'ivâu* from *s'iva* (m.), 8 being equal to twice 4, and therefore being the dual of 4.
Greek: ὀκτώ, Dor. ὀκτώ (the aspirate being added as in Fr. *huit*, from L. *octo*, New Pers. *hest* = Skr. *ashṭâu*), Mod. Gr. ὀχτώ.
Latin: *octo*.

IX.—Ind.-Eur.: *navam-* or *navan-*.
Sanskrit: *navan-*.
Greek: ἐννέα, Dor. ἐννέα, Mod. Gr. ἐννιά.
Latin: *novem*.

X.—Ind.-Eur.: *dakam-* or *dakan-*.
Sanskrit: *das'an-*.
Greek: δέκα.
Latin: *decem*, U. *deçem*.

XI.—Ind.-Eur.: *ai-* (?) *dakam-* (this and the other I. E. numbers up to XIX. were probably two separate words).

---

* Thus we have W. *chwegyr* = Skr. *s'vas'rû* (where *s'v* = I. E. *sv*), W. *chwaer* (O. W. *chwior*) = Skr. *svasar*.

Sanskrit: *ékâ-das'an-*.
Greek: ἕν-δεκα, δέκα εἷς.
Latin: *un-decim*.

XII.—Ind.-Eur.: *dva-dakam-*.
Sanskrit: *dvá-das'an-*.
Greek: δώ-δεκα, δυώ-δεκα, δυο-κάι-δεκα (gen. δυοκαιδέκων, Alcæi Fragmenta,* 98), δέκα δύο.
Latin: *duo-decim*, U. *desen-du-f* (acc. pl.).

XIII.—Ind.-Eur.: *tri- dakam-*.
Sanskrit: *trayô-das'an-*.
Greek: τρις-καί-δεκα, δεκα-τρεῖς.
Latin: *trĕ-decim*.

XIV.—Ind.-Eur.: *kvatvar- dakam-*.
Sanskrit: *k'atur-das'an-*.
Greek: τεσσαρες-καί-δεκα, τεσσαρα-καί-δεκα.
Latin: *quatuor-decim*.

XV.—Ind.-Eur.: *kvankva- dakam-*.
Sanskrit: *pañk'a-das'an-*.
Greek: πεντε-καί-δεκα.
Latin: *quin-decim*.

XVI.—Ind.-Eur.: *ksvaks- dakam-*.
Sanskrit: *shô-das'an-*.
Greek: ἑκ-καί-δεκα.
Latin: *se-decim, sex-decim*.

XVII.—Ind.-Eur.: *saptam- dakam-*.
Sanskrit: *sapta-das'an-*.
Greek: ἑπτα-καί-δεκα.
Latin: *septem-decem*.

XVIII.—Ind.-Eur.: *aktam- dakam-*.
Sanskrit: *ashṭû-das'an-*.
Greek: ὀκτω-καί-δεκα.
Latin: *decem et octo* [*duo-de-viginti*].

XIX.—Ind.-Eur.: *navam- dakam-*.

---

* "Ahrens de Dialectis Æolicis et Pseudæolicis," p. 255.

Sanskrit: *nava-das'an-* [*ûna-viṅs'ati-*].
Greek: ἐννεα-καί-δεκα.
Latin: *decem et novem* [*un-de-viginti*].

XX.—Ind.-Eur.: *dvi-dakan-ta-* or *dvi-dakan-ti-*.
Sanskrit: *viṅs'ati-* = *dvin-das'a-ti-*. The nasal in *dvin* is probably the remains of the nom. pl. case-ending of a neuter stem *dvi-*.
Greek: ἐϜείκοσι, εἴκοσι, Bœot. Ϝίκατι, Lacon. βείκατι. Hesychius notices ἴκαντιν (εἴκασιν), which is remarkable on account of the retention of the ν before τ.
Latin: *viginti*, *g* taking the place of the original *c*, which is retained in *vicesimus, vicies*.

XXX.—Ind.-Eur.: *tri-dakan-ta-*, or *tri-dakan-ti-*.
Sanskrit: *triṅs'ati-* or *triṅs'at-*.
Greek: τριάκοντα (gen. τριηκόντων, Hes. Op. et D. 694) a neuter pl. the first *a* being lengthened. The remaining decades XL.-XC. are also neuters pl.
Latin: *triginta* for *triāginta*, a neuter pl., as are also the remaining decades.

XL.—Ind.-Eur.: *kvatvar-dakan-ta-*, or *kvatvar-dakan-ti-*.
Sanskrit: *k'atvâriṅs'at-*.
Greek: τεσσαράκοντα, Ion. τεσσαρήκοντα, Dor. τετρώκοντα; Ion. -η- and Dor. -ω- = -ā-.
Latin: *quadrāginta*.

L.—Ind.-Eur.: *kvankva-dakan-ta-*, or *kvankva-dakan-ti-*.
Sanskrit: *pañk'âs'at-*.
Greek: πεντήκοντα. -η- = -ā-.
Latin: *quinquāginta*.

LX.—Ind.-Eur.: *ksvaks-dakan-ta*, or *ksvaks-dakan-ti-*.
Sanskrit: *shashṭi-*.
Greek: ἑξήκοντα. -η- = -ā-.
Latin: *sexāginta*.

LXX.—Ind.-Eur.: *saptan-dakan-ta-*, or *saptan-dakan-ti-*.
Sanskrit: *saptati-*.

Greek: ἑβδομήκοντα from ordinal stem ἑβδομο- ; -η- = -ᾱ-.
Latin: *septuāginta* for *septumāginta* from ordinal stem *septumo-*.

LXXX.—Ind.-Eur.: *aktâu-dakan-ta-*, or *aktâu-dakan-ti-*.
Sanskrit: *as'îti-*.
Greek: ὀγδοήκοντα from ordinal stem ὀγδοο-, with -η- for -ᾱ- ; Hom. ὀγδώκοντα.
Latin: *octo-ginta*.

XC.—Ind.-Eur.: *navan-dakan-ta-*, or *navan-dakan-ti-*.
Sanskrit: *navati-*.
Greek: ἐνενήκοντα, Hom. ἐννήκοντα, from an ordinal stem ἐνενο- = L. *nono-* ; -η- = -ᾱ-.
Latin: *nonāginta* from ordinal stem *nono-*.

C.—Ind.-Eur.: *kantam*.
Sanskrit: *s'ata-m*.
Greek: ἑκατό-ν, ἑ being = ἕν (one).
Latin: *centu-m*.

CC–DCCCC.—Ind.-Eur.: here no compound forms were found, but the constituent numerals were kept separate, as in E. *two hundred*, &c.
Sanskrit: here also the constituent numerals were either kept separate, as in *dvê s'atê* (200), or the compound numeral was formed in usual way, as *dvis'ata-* (200), &c.
Greek: διᾱκόσιο- (m. -οι, f. -αι, n. -α) ; Ion. διηκοσιο-, Dor. διακατιο-, &c.
Latin: *ducento-* (m. -i, f. -æ, n. -a) ; *trecento-, quadringento-, quadrin-* being formed after the analogy of *septin-* ; *quingento-* for *quinc-gento-* ; *sexcento-, septingento-, octingento-*, where *octin-* is either formed after analogy of *septin-*, or else = I. E. *aktan-* ; *nongento-* from ordinal stem *nono-*.

M.—Ind.-Eur.: ——— ?
Sanskrit: *sahasra-* (m. and n.).
Greek: χῑλιο- (m. -οι, f. -αι, n. -α), Lesb. χελλιο-, Bœot. χειλιο-, Dor. χηλιο-. Bopp suggests that this stem

may be connected with Skr. *sahasra-*, the original Greek form having been σαχιλιο-, then ἀχιλιο-, and finally χιλιο- ; *r* became λ, and the preceding *s* was assimilated in the Lesb. form, or became ι, as in Bœot., and a new suffix -ιο = Skr. -*ya* was added. Schleicher, on the other hand, considers χελyo- to have been the original stem, which would be identical with an I. E. *ghar-ya-*.

Latin : *milli-* (*mille, milli-a*).

§. 161. THE ORDINAL NUMBERS.

In Indo-European the ordinals appear to have been formed by adding either -*ta* or sometimes -*ma* to the cardinal stems ; *pra-ta-* or *pra-ma-* (1st), *dva-ta-* (2nd), *tri-ta-* (3rd), *kvatvar-ta-* (4th), *kvankva-ta-* (5th), *ksvaks-ta-* (6th), *sapta(m)-ma* or *saptan-ta* (7th), *akta(m)-ma-* or *aktâv-(m)a-* (8th), *navan-ta-* or *nava(m)-ma-* (9th), *dakan-ta-* or *dakan(m)-ma-* (10th). The ordinal decades were formed in a similar way. The ordinals from 11 to 19, &c., were formed of two separate words, as *prata- dakanta-* (11th = 1st + 10th), &c.

In Sanskrit we have *prathama-* (1st), from preposition *pra* and superlative suffix -*tama* ; *dvitîya-* (2nd) for *dvitya* (Gr. δισσο-), = *dva-ta-ya-* ; *tṛtîyâ-* (3rd) for *tritya-* (Gr. τρισσο-) = *tri-ta-ya-*; *k'aturtha-* and *turîya-* (4th) = (*k'a*)*turîya-*, perhaps for (*k'a*)*turtîya-*, the second *t* being thrown out to distinguish this form more completely from *tṛtîya-*, unless *ya-* is used here by itself instead of *ta-ya-* ; *pank'ama-*, Ved. *pank'atha-* (5th) ; *shashtha-* (6th), *saptama-*, Ved. *saptatha-* (7th), *ashṭama-* (8th), *navama-* (9th), *das'ama-* (10th).* In the numerals compounded with *das'an* final -*an* is lost, and the suffix *a*- added ; thus we have *êkâdas'a-* (11th), &c. The cardinal stems end-

---

* Lottner considers that the ordinals, Skr. *saptama-, ashṭama-, navama-, das'ama-*, Gr. ἑβδομο-, L. *septimo-, decimo-*, &c., are formed simply by the addition of *a* to the cardinal stems, *saptam, ashṭam*, &c.

ing in -*ti* or -*t* either add -*tama* or -*a;* in the latter case *viṅs'ati* and the numerals ending in -*t* lose *t*- with the preceding vowel, while *shashṭi, saptati, as'īti,* and *navati* only lose final *i:* thus *viṅs'atitama*- or *viṅs'a*- (20th); *triṅs'attama*- or *triṅs'a*- (30th); *k'atvâriṅs'attama*- or *k'atvâriṅs'a*- (40th); *pañk'âs'attama*- or *pañk'âs'a*- (50th); *shashṭitama*- or *shashṭa*- (60th), &c. From *s'ata* and *sahasra* we have *s'atatama*- (100th), *sahasratama*- (1000th).

In Greek we have πρωτο- (1st), Dor. πρατο-, Ep. προμο-, from πρό (whence πρίν = προ-ιον, πρόσσω = προτψω, πρότερος, &c.), δευτερο- (2nd) = I. E. *dvatara*-; τριτο-, τριτατο-, Æol. τερτο- (3rd); τεταρτο-, τετρατο- (4th); πεμπτο- (5th); ἑκτο- (6th); ἑβδομο-, ἑβδοματο- (7th); ὀγδοο- (8th) = ογδοϜο- from ὀκτοϜ = I. E. *aktâv*: ἐνατο-, ἐννατο-, εἰνατο- (9th); δεκατο- (10th); ἐνδεκατο- (11th); δωδεκατο-, δυοδεκατο- (12th); τρισκαιδεκατο-, τριτο- και δεκατο- (13th), &c.; εἰκοστο- (20th); τριᾱκοστο- (30th); τεσσαρακοστο-, Dor. τετρωκοστο- (40th), &c.; ἑκατοστο- (100th); χιλιοστο- (1000). The termination -στο is, perhaps, connected with the superlative ending -ιστο, initial ι being lost. The same ending is found in ἕκαστο-, ποστο-, ὁποστο-.

In Latin we have *primo*- (1st) for *pro-imo*-, according to Curtius, or for *pris-mo*-, according to Pott, *pris* being for *prius; secundo*- (2nd), from R. *sequ* (to follow), whence *sequor; tertio*- (3rd); *quarto*- (4th), for *quatuorto*-; *quinto*- (5th), for *quincto*-; *sexto*- (6th); *septimo*- (7th); *octavo*- (8th), from *octav* = I. E. *aktâv; nono*- (9th), for *novimo*-, *m* being assimilated to the preceding *n; decimo*- (10th); *undecimo*- (11th); *duodecimo*- (12th); *tertio- decimo*- (13th), &c.; *vigesimo*-, *vicesimo*-, (20th), for *vicensimo*- = *vicent-timo*-; *trigesimo*-, *tricesimo*- (30th), for *tricensimo*- = *tricent-timo*-, &c.; *centesimo*- (100th) following the analogy of the preceding decades, &c.; *millesimo*- (1000th).

CHAPTER XI.

§. 162. PRONOUNS.

IN the pronouns of the first and second person we find no distinction of gender in any of the Indo-European languages.* This may be accounted for by supposing that they were developed at a period preceding the introduction of this distinction, as is probable, for they express ideas that are among the first to suggest themselves to man. Their antiquity also accounts for the fact, that there is such a variety in the different pronominal roots employed to express these ideas, and also for the fact that these pronominal roots have become so disguised in various ways, that it is impossible to analyze the greater portion of them, and consequently impossible to reproduce the original Indo-European forms from which they are derived.†

No distinction of gender is found also in the reflexive pronoun; all the other pronouns have three genders.

No vocative case is found in the pronouns.

In Sanskrit in all the pronouns the real stem is not used in compounds, but in the pronouns of the first and second person the abl. sing. or pl. is used, and in the others the nom. sing. neut.

---

* In Sanskrit the pronouns in their acc.s. pl. *asmân, yushmân*, and their Vedic nom.s pl. *asmê, yushmê*, appear to be masculine *in form*. In the White Yag'ur-Veda (XI., 47) we find a remarkable exception in the fem. acc. pl. *yushmâs*.

† Consult an Essay by Dr. C. Lottner, "On the Forms and Origin of the Pronouns of the First and Second Persons," in the Transactions of the Philological Society (1859, Part I.).

§. 163. The Pronoun of the First Person.

The stem of this pronoun was originally *ma-*, connected either with the I. E. verbal root *ma* (to think), whence Skr. *man* (id.), or with the pronominal root *ma-* (this), whence Skr. *i-ma-* (id.). *Ma* is of universal occurrence in the verbal inflexion, as in Skr. *as-mi* (I am), *i-ma-s* (we go), &c.; Gr. εἶ-μι, ἴ-με-ν, &c.; L. *su-m*, *i-mu-s*, &c.

Beside the stem *ma-* we also find in Indo-European a stem *agham(a-)*, whence Skr. *aham* (I.), or *agam(a)*, whence Goth. *ik* (I.), Gr. ἐγώ. As *ma-* has been connected with the verbal root *ma* (to think), so *agam(a-)*, from which, after the separation of the European branches of the Indo-European from the Asiatic, the Sanskrit *agham*, and finally *aham*, was developed, has been derived from the I. E. verbal root *ag* (to move),[*] whence Skr. *ag'* (id.), Gr. ἄγω, &c.: *agam-a* would then be divided thus: *ag* (a verbal root) + *a-* (a pronominal demonstrative root) + *ma-* (the preceding stem of *I*). Bopp, however, considers that in Skr. *aham* an initial *m* has been lost, and supposes that the first portion of the word is merely the stem *ma-* (I.).

The other explanation, suggested by Bopp, is much preferable to either of the preceding, viz.: that the initial *a-* is

---

[*] In this case *agama-* would mean "*I the mover*," and hence "I," as the first idea we have of *a mover, a cause,* is derived from the power we have of *willing*. The I. E. root *ag* also meant "to *speak*," whence Skr. *ah* (which also passed through the stage *agh*); L. *ad-ag-ium*, *ajo* = *ag-io*, Goth. *af-aik-a* (I deny); and here *agama-* would mean "*I the speaker.*" Although it is possible that both forms of this stem, *agama-* and *aghama-*, existed in Indo-European, it is nevertheless more probable that *aham* is a special Sanskrit form developed from *agama-*, through the stage *aghama-*. We find a few other examples of a Skr. *h* being = an I. E. *g*; thus we have Skr. *hanu-s* (the jaw), Gr. γένυ-ς, L. *gena*, Goth. *kinnu-s*: Skr. *maha-t* (great), Gr. μέγα-ς, Goth. *mikil-s*.

the demonstrative stem * a- (this). A-ga-ma- (or a-gha-ma-) would then be resolved into the three pronominal stems, a- (this); ga- (or gha-), which is connected with Ved. ghâ, gha, hâ; Skr. ha, Gr. γε, γα (in Dor. ἔγωνγα, Bœot. ἴωνγα); Goth. -k in the acc.s sing. mik (me), thuk (te), sik (se), O. H. G. -h in the acc.s pl. unsih (nos), iwih (vos), and ma- (the other stem of the first person).

Nominative Singular.

Ind.-Eur.: agam(a-).†

Skr.: aham.

Gr.: ἐγώ, Dor. ἐγών, ἐγώνη, ἐγώνγα; Bœot. ἰών, ἰώνει, ἰώνγα. Here ω = I. E. ă, but the cause of this change is unknown.

L.: egō (with ō as in Greek), and later egŏ.

---

* So in the Sanskrit Dramas we find ayañ g'anah (lit. this person) used to express the first personal pronoun. Compare also the use of L. hic, and of *this* in vulgar English.

† Lottner (in the essay quoted in p. 315) considers that there were two periods in prehistorical Indo-European times: firstly, a period when *M* was solely the characteristic of the first person; secondly, a period when *M* became restricted to the oblique cases of the singular. Both periods had been gone through before our ancestors separated. "In the historical times," he writes, "the difference of singular and plural, and of the nominative '*I*,' as opposed to the oblique case *Me* is, upon the whole, preserved; but here and there we observe a tendency to come back to the preprimitive—if I may say so—simplicity." . . . . The tendency, that *M* has to return to the nom. sing. we find "in some of the English dialects which partly replace *I* by *me*, in the *moi* of the French, in the *men* of the New Persian . . . . in the *mé* of the Old Irish." . . . . "Secondly, we find the *m* of the first person extended to the plural. This we have in some German and Norse dialects (*mer*, *mir* for *wir* is common about Thuringia; *mer* is also sometimes used in Old Norse), in the New Iranian languages almost throughout (*we* is in New Persian *mâ*, Armenian *meq*, Ossetian *max*), and in Modern Greek μεῖς." I have observed similar phenomena in the Italian dialect of San Remo.

Accusative Singular.

Ind.-Eur.: *mă-m*.

Skr.: *mâ-m*, *mâ*. *Mâm* in form is a fem. acc. Bopp suggests either that *â* was first developed in *mâ* to compensate for the loss of the final *m*, and that it was borrowed by *mâm* from *mâ*, or that *mâm* is for *ma-ha-m*, *ha* being = Gr. γε.

Gr.: με, ἐμέ (the first ε being only prosthetic), Dor. ἐμέι.

L.: *mē* for *mem* = *mim* from stem *mi*-, final *ĕ* being lengthened to compensate for loss of *m*. In Old Latin *med* was used for *me*, as in *Novios Plautios med Romai fecid* (C. I. L. I. n. 54). *Mehe* was also written in Old Latin for *me*. Büchcler suggests that *mehe* may be = Gr. ἐμέγε, Goth *mik*.

Instrumental Singular.

Ind.-Eur.: ——— ?

Skr.: *mayâ* = *ma* + *i* + *â* = *ma* + *a* + *â*.

Dative Singular.

Ind.-Eur.: *ma-bhyam*.

Skr.: *ma-hyam*.

Gr.: Dor. ἐμῖν, ἐμίνη, ἐμίνγα; -ῖν = -ε-φῖν = -*a-bhyam*.

L.: *mi-hei*, *mi-hi*, from St. *mi*-; U. *me-he*.

Ablative Singular.

Ind.-Eur.: *ma̤-d* or *ma-t*.

Skr.: *ma-t*, Ved. *mama-t*, a reduplicated form.

L.: *mē*, O. L. *mē-d* from St. *mi*-.

Genitive Singular.

Ind.-Eur.: ——— ?

Skr.: *mama*, a reduplication of stem, with loss of case-ending.

Gr.: μοῦ, ἐμοῦ; Ep. ἐμεῖο (= ἐμε-σyo); Ion. ἐμέο; Dor. ἐμεῦ, μεῦ; Lacon. ἐμεύνη; Syrac. ἐμίο, ἐμίω. In Dor. ἐμέος, ἐμοῦς, ἐμεῦς; Syrac. ἐμῶς; the gen. case-ending ς appears to be added to the old genitive.

Locative Singular.

Ind.-Eur.: *ma-i.*

Skr.: *mayi = ma + i + i = ma + a + i*, the stem *ma-* being lengthened by *a*, as in the instrumental. Skr. *mê* which is used for gen. and dat. sing. is properly a loc.; compare *s'ivê*, loc. of *s'iva*.

Gr.: μοί, ἐμοί from St. μο- = I. E. *ma-*.

L.: Bopp considers gen. *mei* to be a loc. = *met-ï* = *mat-ï* = Skr. *mayi*.

Nominative Plural.

Ind.-Eur.: the stem of this case was probably formed by adding *sma-* to the demonstrative stems *ma-, a-, va-*; consequently it may have appeared in the forms *masma-, asma-, vasma-*. Initial *m* is found in Lith. *mēs*, O. Sl. *mŭ*, Arm. *meq̊*; initial *v* in Skr. *vayam*, Goth. *veis* (E. *we*); initial *a* in Ved. *asmê*. Bopp considers that Skr. *vayam* is for *mayam*, and that *v* represents an original *m*. This is possible, for initial *m* and *v* are sometimes interchanged; thus we find* Basque *maguina* from L. *vagina*, Sp. *mimbre* from L. *vimen*, Sp. *milano* from L. *villus*. In Pâli we find *mayam* (we) from Skr. *vayam*. In all these cases, however, *v* is older than *m*, so that it is just as likely that *m* is derived from *v*, as *v* from *m* (consult §. 95, p. 187).

Skr.: *vayam = va + i + am = va + a + am*; Ved. *asmê*; Pâli *mayam, amhê*.

---

* Diez, "Grammatik der Romanischen Sprachen," vol. I., pp. 250, 357.

Gr.: ἡμεῖς from St. ἡμι- (not from ἡμο- = Ved. asma-, for then the nom. pl. would be ἡμοι), Æol. ἄμμες, Dor. ἀμές, Ion. ἡμέες (-εῖς = Ion. -έες = -εγες).

L.: nōs; nōs is, perhaps, an old accusative used as a nom., and follows the analogy of *equōs* from *equo-*. Bopp, however, considers that the final *s* here belongs to the stem, as it occurs in *nos-ter*, and accordingly he connects it with *-sma*, from which he also derives *-me-t* in *egomet, memet, tumet, nosmet*, and *-mmo* in *immo** = *ismo* from St. *i-*. The final *s* of Skr. nās is also considered by Bopp to belong to the stem, as it is used for the acc. dat. and gen. pl., and is explained in the same way. In Z. nâo = nâs we find the vowel lengthened, as in L. nōs. Nōs may be connected with the pronominal root *na-*, as has been already suggested in §. 95, or it may be derived from *ma-*, as initial *m* and *n* are sometimes interchanged: thus we find It. *nespolo* from L. *mespilum, nicchio* from L. *mitulus;* Sp. *nespera* and *nispola* from L. *mespilum, marfil* from Arab. *nabfil, mueso* from L. *noster, mastuerzo* from L. *nasturtuim, naguela* from L. *magalia*, O. Sp. *nembrar* from L. *memorare;* Fr. *nappe* from L. *mappa, natte* from L. *matta, nèfle* from L. *mespilum;* Wall. *nalbe* from L. *malva*.†

Accusative Plural.

Ind.-Eur.: *asma-ns* and *ma-ns*.

Skr.: *asmân* = *asma-ns* and *nās* = *ma-ns*. Schleicher considers that *nas* is for *ma-sma-ns*, initial *m* becoming *n* through dissimilation on account of following *m*.

Gr.: ἡμᾶς, Ion. ἡμέας from St. ἡμι-; Æol. ἄμμε, Dor.

---

* I prefer to connect *immo* with the superlative stem *imo-* for *immo-* = *in-mo-*.

† Diez, "Grammatik der Romanischen Sprachen," vol. I., pp. 199, 357.

ἀμέ, either following the analogy of acc. sing. μέ, or being the mere stem for ἀμμι-, ἀμι-.
L.: *nōs.*

Instrumental Plural.

Ind.-Eur.: *asma-bhis.*
Skr.: *asmâ-bhis.*

Dative Plural.

Ind.-Eur.: *asma-bhyams.*
Skr.: *asma-bhyam, nas,* Ved. *asma-bhya.*
Gr.: ἡμῖν, Æol. ἄμμιν, ἄμμι; Dor. ἀμίν; (-ιν = -ι-φιν).
L.: *nō-bis* perhaps for *nos-bis, nos* appearing as the stem, as in *nos-ter.*

Ablative Plural.

Ind.-Eur.: ———?
Skr.: *asma-t,* following analogy of abl. sing.
L.: *nō-bis.*

Genitive Plural.

Ind.-Eur.: ———?
Skr.: *asmâkam,* properly an adjective in acc. sing. neuter; Ved. *asmâka,* with loss of final *m; nas.*
Gr.: ἡμῶν, Ion. ἡμέων, Ep. ἡμείων from St. ἡμι-, Æol. ἀμμέων, Bœot. ἀμίων, Dor. ἀμῶν, ἀμέων.
L.: *nostrum,* gen. pl. of possessive stem *nostro-,* for *nostrorum,* which occurs in Plautus; *nostri,* gen. sing. of the same stem. Some writers consider *nostrum* to be an acc. sing. neuter.

Locative Plural.

Ind.-Eur.: *asma-sva.*
Skr.: *asmâ-su.*
Gr.: Æol. ἄμμε-σιν.

Nominative and Accusative Dual.

Ind.-Eur. : ———?

Skr. : *ávám* from St. *áva-* = *á* + *tva-* (*I* + *thou*), according to Bopp, or = *á* + *dva-* (*I* + numeral *two*) according to Schleicher, as in Old Lith. *vedu* (m.), *redvi* (f.); New Lith. *mùdu* (m.), *mùdvi* (f.); and Goth. *vi-t* (*we two*). We also find as acc. *nâu*, for *nâs* according to Bopp, a lengthened form of pl. *nâs*. *Nâu* is also used for gen. and dat., and therefore *-âu* belongs probably to the stem; it corresponds to Gr. *νώ* in which *ω* also appears to belong to the stem (c. f. Skr. *ashṭâu* = Gr. *ὀκτώ*). In form *nâu* is a regular acc. dual of St. *na-*, as *s'iváu* from *s'iva-*.

Gr. : νῶϊ, νώ; Bœot. νῶε.

Instrumental and Ablative Dual.

Ind.-Eur. : ———?
Skr. : *ávábhyám.*

Dative Dual.

Ind.-Eur. : ———?
Skr. : *ávábhyám, nâu.*
Gr. : νῶϊν, νῷν.

Genitive Dual.

Ind.-Eur. : ———?
Skr. : *ávayós, nâu.*
Gr. : νῶϊν, νῷν.

Locative Dual.

Ind.-Eur. : ———?
Skr. : *ávayós.*

§. 164. The Pronoun of the Second Person.

Nominative Singular.

Ind.-Eur.: *tvam* for *ta** + *va* + *ma* (see §. 95, p. 187)
Skr.: *tvam*.
Gr.: σύ, Dor. τύ, Bœot. τούν (= Z. *tûm*), τού, τύνη, Lacon. τύνη.
L.: *tu*.

Accusative Singular.

Ind.-Eur.: *tva-m*.
Skr.: *tvâm, tvâ*, which Bopp explains in the same way as *mâm, mâ*.
Gr.: σέ, Dor. τέ, τύ, τέι; Cret. τρέ, Bœot. τίν.
L.: *tē* for *tvem*, from St. *tvi-*; O. L. *ted* (an ablatival form used as an accusative by Plautus), U. *tiom* for *tuom* = *tvam*; or, according to Corssen, for *tvio-m* from St. *tvi-* lengthened by *a*.

---

* Lottner (in his essay quoted in p. 315) remarks, that "whatever the actual nature of the *Thou* may be, it cannot be overlooked, that in a mere abstract metaphysical point of view it is but one of the many cases of the non-ego, and that therefore it is not altogether unreasonable to expect that language should treat it as such; in other words, that the pronoun of the second person should somehow be a variety—strongly marked indeed by individual characteristics—of the pronoun of the third person."

Thus in the Indo-Eur. languages *ta* is the stem of Skr. *ta-m* (eum), Gr. τόν, L. (*is-*) *tum*, Sl. *tŭ*, Goth. *thana*, O. H. G. *den*, &c.

Also in the Semitic languages the stem of the second person is either *tha* or *ta*, to which the syllable *an* or *en* is prefixed, and this same *tha* or *ta* with the same prefix *an* or *en* is also used as the stem of the pronoun of the third person. Thus we have Egyptian *ento-k* (thou, m.), Coptic *entho-k* (thou, m.), &c., beside Egyptian *ento-f* (he), Coptic *entho-f*, &c.

Those writers who derive the pronouns from verbal roots connect *tvam* with I. E. *tan* (to stretch).

Instrumental Singular.

Ind.-Eur. : ——— ?
Skr. : *tvayâ* = *tva* + *i* + *â* = *tva* + *a* + *â*.

Dative Singular.

Ind.-Eur. : *tva-bhyam*.
Skr. : *tu-bhyam*, Ved. *tu-bhya*.
Gr. : Hom. τείν, Dor. τίν, Tarent. τίνη.
L. : *tibi* (final *m* being lost, as in Ved. *tubhya*); U. *tefe*.

Ablative Singular.

Ind.-Eur. : *tva-d* or *tva-t*.
Skr. : *tva-t*.
L. : *tē*, O. L. *tĕd* from St. *ti-*.

Genitive Singular.

Ind.-Eur. : ——— ?
Skr. : *tava* for *tvatva*, a reduplication of stem, with loss of case ending.
Gr. : σοῦ, Ion. σέο, σεῦ ; Ep. σεῖο, τεοῖο (= *tava-sya*), Dor. τέο, τεοῦ, τεῦ, τίω. In Dor. τέος, τεοῦς, τεῦς, τίος, τίως, the gen. case-ending ς appears to be added to the old genitive.
L. : *tui*, the gen. sing of the possessive stem *tuo-*.

Locative singular.

Ind.-Eur. : *tva-i*.
Skr. : *tvayi* = *tva* + *i* + *i* = *tva* + *a* + *i*. Skr. *tē*, Ved. *tvê*, which is used for dat. and gen. sing. is properly a locative.
Gr. : σο-ί, Dor. το-ί.

Nominative Plural.

Ind.-Eur. : *tvasma-* was probably the stem.
Skr. : *yûyam* for *tva* + *i* + *am* = *tva* + *a* + *am* ; Ved. *yushmê*; Pâli *tumhê* (= *tus-mê*).

Gr.: ὑμεῖς from St. ὑμι-, Æol. ὕμμες, Dor. ὑμές, Bœot. οὑμές, Ion. ὑμέες.

L.: vōs (compare nōs).

Accusative Plural.

Ind.-Eur.: *tvasmă-ns* or *tvă-ns*.
Skr.: *yushmán* = *tvasmăns*, Ved. *yushmás* (f.); *vas* = *tvăns*.
Gr.: ὑμᾶς, Ion. ὑμέας from St. ὑμι-; Æol. ὕμμε, Dor. ὑμέ (compare ἄμμε, &c.).

Instrumental Plural.

Ind.-Eur.: *tvasma-bhis*.
Skr.: *yushmá-bhis*.

Dative Plural.

Ind.-Eur.: *tvasma-bhyams*.
Skr.: *yushma-bhyam*, *vas*.
Gr.: ὑμῖν = ὑμι-φιν, Æol. ὕμμι, ὕμμιν; Bœot. οὑμῖν.
L.: vō-bis (compare nō-bis).

Ablative Plural.

Ind.-Eur.: ———?
Skr-: *yushma-t* (compare *asma-t*).
L.: nō-bis.

Genitive Plural.

Ind.-Eur.: ———?
Skr.: *yushmákam*, Ved. *yushmáka*; *vas*.
Gr.: ὑμῶν, Ion. ὑμέων, Ep. ὑμείων from St. ὑμι-; Æol. ὑμμέων, Bœot. οὑμίων.
L.: vostrorum, vostrum (ves-), vostri (ves-).

Locative Plural.

Ind.-Eur.: *tvasma-sva*.
Skr.: *yushmá-su*.
Gr.: Æol. ὕμμεσιν probably, after analogy of ἄμμεσιν.

Nominative and Accusative Dual.

Ind.-Eur. : ———— ?

Skr.: *yuvâm* from St. *yuva-* = *tva + tva-* (thou + thou), or *tva + dva* (thou + numeral two), compare Lith. *yù-du* (m.), *yù-dvi* (f.); Ved. *yuvăm*. We also find as acc. *vâm* for *vâv* (according to Bopp) = *vâu* = *vâs*, (compare *nâu*).

Gr. : σφῶϊ, σφώ.*

Instrumental and Ablative Plural.

Ind.-Eur. : ———— ?

Skr.: *yuvâ-bhyâm*. In Vedic we also find *yuvat* as abl.; compare *mat*, &c.

Dative Dual.

Ind.-Eur. : ———— ?

Skr.: *yuvâ-bhyâm, vâm*; Ved. *yuva-bhyâm*.

Gr. : σφῶϊν, σφῷν.

Genitive Dual.

Ind.-Eur. : ———— ?

Skr.: *yuva-yós*, Ved. *yuvôs, vâm*.

Gr. : σφῶϊν, σφῷν.

Locative Dual.

Ind.-Eur. : ———— ?

Skr.: *yuva-yós*.

§. 165. THE REFLEXIVE PRONOUN.

There is no distinction of gender in this pronoun, except in Gr. nom. and acc. pl. σφέα. The Ind.-Eur. stem was *sva-*, which in Sanskrit only occurs in compounds, as in *sva-yam* (self) = *sva + i + am* = *sva + a + am*, *sva-tas* (by one's self),

---

* Σφ in these forms implies an original *sv*, which may represent an I. E. *tv*.

sva-dhá (spontaneity), *sva-bhû* (self-existent), &c. In Sanskrit the stem *sva-* is also used as a possessive; Skr. *sva-s* = Gr. σφό-ς, L. *suus*. This stem is found in Gr. ἴδιος = σϜε-διος, ἔτης = σϜε-της, ἔθος and ἦθος = σϜε-θος (compare Skr. *svadhá*); Hom. φή = σφη (initial σ being lost, as in Lac. φίν = σφίν, Lac. κουτάλα = σκυτάλη, Lac. κυρσάνιον = σκυρθάνιον, Lac. φαιρίδδειν = σφαιρίζειν, Bœot. Φίξ = Σφίγξ; L. *funda* beside Gr. σφενδόνη, L. *fīdes* beside Gr. σφίδες, L. *fallo* = Gr. σφάλλω, L. *figo* = Gr. σφίγγω, whence φῑμός = σφιγ-μος); and in L. *si*, *si-qua* = U. *sve-pu*, *si-ne* (?), *sed* (an ablative form), *sē-voco*, *sed-itio*, *sē-orsum*, *sue-sco*, *sŏ-dālis* (from *sodā* = Skr. *sva-dhâ*). Bopp connects *-pse* in *ipse* with *sva-*, *v* becoming *p* when transposed, as in Dor. ψίν = σφίν ; but this is wrong, for *ipse* = *i-pte* (compare *sua-pte*), and *-pte* is, probably, connected with Skr. *pati-* (master) = Gr. ποσι-, L. *pot-is*, Lith. *pati-s* (self).

Nominative Singular.

This case is not found in Greek and Latin.

Accusative Singular.

Ind.-Eur.: *svă-m*.

Gr.: ἕ, Æol. Ϝέ = σϜε, Hom. ἑέ = σεϜε, Dor. σφέ. Ep. μίν, Dor. νίν, which are used for ἕ, are, perhaps, for ἰμ-ιμ,* a reduplicated accusative of St. ι; compare the Latin reduplicated accusatives *sese*, O. L. *em-em* (eundem).

L.: *sē* = *sve* = *svi-m* from St. *svi*, O. L. *sed* (*inter sed* in SC de Bac., *apud sed* in tab. Bant.); Osc. *siom*† for *suom* = *sva-m*. Corssen explains *siom* as a lengthened form from St. *si-* by the addition of *a*, and consequently as = *svi-o-m* (compare *e-u-m* = *i-u-m*, Osc. *i-o-n-c* from St. *i-*).

---

* Curtius, "Grundzüge der Griechischen Etymologie," p. 477.
† Schleicher, "Compendium," &c., p. 644.

Dative Singular.

Ind.-Eur.: *sva-bhyam*.
Gr.: Bœot. ἕἴν (Corinna), Dor. ἵν, contracted from ἕἴν = ἑ-φιν.
L.: *sibi*, U. *sibe*, O. *sifei*, from St. *svi-*.

Ablative Singular.

Ind.-Eur.: *sva-d* or *sva-t*.
L.: *sē*, O. L. *sēd* for *seid*, from St. *svi-*.

Genitive Singular.

Ind.-Eur.: ——— ?
Gr.: οὗ, Ep. εἷο = σϜε-σyo, Ion. ἕο, Dor. εὗ, ἑοῦ, Bœot. ἑοῦς.
L.: *sui*, the gen. sing. of the possessive stem *suo-*.

Locative Singular.

Ind.-Eur.: *sva-i*.
Gr.: οἷ, Æol. Ϝοῖ, Bœot. Ϝῡ.

Nominative Plural.

Ind.-Eur.: ——— ?
Gr.: σφεῖς, σφέα (n.), from St. σφι-.

Accusative Plural.

Ind.-Eur.: ——— ?
Gr.: σφᾶς, σφέα (n.); Ion. σφέας, σφεῖας, Dor. σφέ, Syrac. ψέ, Æol. ἄσφε.
L.: same as in sing.

Dative Plural.

Ind.-Eur.: *sva-bhyams*.
Gr.: Dor. σφίν, Syrac. ψίν, Lacon. φίν, Æol. ἄσφι.
L.: same as in sing.

Ablative Plural.

Ind.-Eur.: ——— ?
L.: same as in sing.

Genitive Plural.

Ind.-Eur.: ———?
Gr.: σφῶν, Ion. σφέων, Æol. σφείων, Syrac. ψῶν and ἕων.
L.: same as in sing.

Locative Plural.

Ind.-Eur.: *sva-sva.*
Gr.: σφί-σι.

Nominative and Accusative Dual.

Ind.-Eur.: ———?
Gr.: σφωέ, σφώ.

Dative and Genitive Dual.

Ind.-Eur.: ——— ?
Gr.: σφωῖν = σφω-φιν.

§. 166. THE PRONOUNS IN WHICH THE GENDER IS MARKED.

An examination of all the pronouns of this class found in each language belongs to the special grammar of each, and we here limit our investigation to the declension of these pronouns, selecting the I. E. demonstrative stem *ta* as the one of which the declension will be given in full. In the three following sections we merely notice the chief points of difference between the declension of the pronouns and that of the nouns, omitting some exceptions which will be found in the special grammars of each language.

§. 167. THE SANSKRIT PRONOMINAL DECLENSION.

The nom. sing. masc. generally ends in *-s*, as in the noun, except in *sa* (nom. sing. masc.), where the final *s* was omitted, because it was perhaps a repetition of *sa* itself. The same omission is found in Goth. *sa* and Gr. *ὁ*. We also find the peculiar nominatives *ayam* (m.), *iyam* (f.), which are analogous to the personal pronoun *aham;** also the nom. *asáu* (m. f.), which, perhaps, arose from an older *asás*. The nom. and acc. neut. sing. ends in *d* or *t*, and this form is used as the true stem in compounds. The nom. pl. masc. ends in *-é*, which, perhaps, arose from *-a-i-as* = *-a-a-as*, the stem being lengthened by *a*, which afterwards became *i*, and the final *as* being lost; thus *té* = *ta-i-as* = *ta-a-as*. In the dat., abl., and loc. sing. the masc. and neut. *a-* stems are lengthened by the addition of *sma;* and in the same cases the fem. *á-* stems are lengthened by *sí* (= *smí*, according to Bopp). The gen. pl. ends in *-sám*.

§. 168. The Greek Pronominal Declension.

The nom. sing. mas. ends in -ς, as in the noun, except in ὁ = Skr. *sa*. The nom. sing. neut. ends in -ο = -οτ, final τ (or δ?) being lost. In other respects the pronominal is the same as the nominal declension.

§. 169. The Latin Pronominal Declension.

Final *-s* of nom. sing. masc. is sometimes lost, as in *ipse* (beside *ipsus*), *iste* (beside *istus*), *ecqui*, *siqui*, *qui* (beside *quis*) = O. *pis*, *hic*. *Qui* is probably for *quoi* (whence O. L. *quei*) = U. *poi*, *poei*, *poe*, and *hic* for *hoi-ce*, the stems in both cases being lengthened by *-i*. The nom. sing. fem. ends in *-a* except in *quæ* = O. *pai*, *hæc*, *illæc* (beside *illa*), *istæc* (beside *ista*), the stems of these pronouns being also lengthened by *-i*. *Quis* is used as a nom. fem. in Plautus (*quis mulier est*), as Gr. τίς. This *-i* that is added to the stem in *quæ* is of common occurrence, as in U. *pir-i*, *pir-e* = L. *quid + i*, &c.; Gr. οὑτοσ-ί, &c.: Bœckh con-

---

* The neuter termination *-m*, which is used as masculine and feminine in *ayam* (m.), *iyam* (f.), and *aham*, dates from a time when the distinction of gender had not yet been developed.

siders that it is also found in the forms τοί (= τύ), ταί (= τά), which occur in the "Fœdus Eleorum et Heracensium," but Ahrens ("de Græcæ Linguæ Dialectis," I., p. 280) opposes this view, and considers τοι and ται to be for τῷ and τᾷ. The fem. sometimes occurs without this addition, as in *aliqua*, *numqua*, *siqua* = U. *svepu*. The nom. and acc. sing. neut. are formed by adding *d* to the stem, as in *id* = O. *ĭd*, *quod* = O. *pŭd*, *quid* = O. *pĭd*, O. L. *alid* = *aliud*, U. *pir̩* (-*i*) = *quid*, &c. In the second century B.C. this *d* had a very weak sound, and was sometimes almost imperceptible, just as in Gr. τί and ἄλλο the suffix vanishes. Beside *aliud* we find *alium* (Fabr. 95, 211), as in Gr. τοσοῦτον beside τοσοῦτο. *Ipsum* is neut. of *ipse*. *Hoc*, O. L. *hoce* is for *hod-ce*. The nom.s pl. masc. and fem. are formed in the same way as in the noun: as in the masc. forms *eeis*, *ieis*, *eis*, *ei*, *ques*, *quei*, *qui*, *heis*, *hisce*, *hei*, *hi*, and the fem. *quæ*, *istæ*, &c. The O. *pas* (= L. *quæ*) is analogous to Skr. nom. pl. fem. The nom. and acc. pl. neut. is the same as in the noun, except in *hæc*, O. L. *haice*, *quæ* = O *paĭ*, *istæc* (beside *ista*, *illæc* (beside *illa*), where the stems are lengthened by *i*. This *i* is not found in *aliqua* and *siqua*.

The dat.s sing. (m. f. n.) *illi*, *ipsi*, *toti*, *alteri* = O. L. *alterei* for *altero-i*, &c., are, probably, old locatives: such as *humi* and *domi*. In the O. L. *quoiei* we find the stem lengthened by *i* and then the true dative suffix -*ei* = I. E. -*ai* was added. It is possible that *isti*, &c., may have been formed as *quoiei*, and accordingly that they may have arisen from the true dative forms *istoiei*, &c. We also find the dat. sing. masc. ending in -*o*, as in *nullo usui*, in Cæsar, &c., and the fem. ending in -*æ* in Plautus, &c. In the Umbrian datives *e-smei*, *pu-sme*, we find the stem lengthened by -*sma*, as in Sanskrit.

The gen.s sing. *istīus*, &c., were formed by adding -*ius* to the stem lengthened by *i*: *istīus* would then be for *isto-i-ius*. The ending -*ius* is supposed by Bopp to have arisen merely by transposition from the gen. ending -*sya*, but it is much more probable that *isto-i-ius* is for *isto-i-siu-s*, *-siu* being = *-sya*, and *-s* being added, as in the Doric gen. sing. of the first and second personal pronouns, ἐμέος, ἐμοῦς, τέος, τεοῦς. Meunier considers *istīus*, &c., to have arisen from *istī-ius*, &c., *istī* being the usual genitive in *-i* and *i-us*, an enclitic genitive of the pronominal stem *-i*.*

The adverbs *hic* = O. L. *heic* and *qui* are old locatives, and = *hoi-c* and *quoi*. Similarly in Oscan we find loc. *exei-c* from pronominal stem *exo-*. Corssen considers *qui* to be an ablative form for *quei-d*; *quicum* is used for both *quocum* and *quacum*.

Beside *quorum*, gen. pl. of stem *quo-*, we find *cuium* as gen. pl. of stem *qui* (Charisius II., 136).

§. 170. The Declension of the Stem *ta-* (m. n.)

	Skr.	Gr.	L.
Stem.	*ta-*.	το-.	*is-to-*.†
Sing. N.	*sa, sa-s* (m.), *ta-t* (n.)	ὁ (m.), τό (n.)	*iste* (m.), *istu-d* (n.)
A.	*ta-m* (m.), *ta-t* (n.)	τό-ν (m.), τό (n.)	*istu-m* (m.), *istu-d* (n.)
I.	*tê-n-a*.	—	—

* Consult Meunier's Essay " De quelques anomalies que présente la déclinaison de certains Pronoms Latins" (" Mémoires de la Société de Linguistique de Paris." Tome I., pp. 14-62). Beside these genitives in *-ius* we also find in Old Latin the gen.s *ei, quoi, cui, qui*, &c.: as in *Ei rei argumenta dicam* (Pl. Trin. 522) *Quoi fides fidelitasque amicum erga æquiperet tuam* (Pl. Trin. 1126), *Perii quot hic ipse annos vivet, cui filii tam diu vivont* (Pl. Mil. 1081), &c. In Plautus Pers. 83, Meunier reads *Set eccum parasitum quoi mi ius auxiliost opus*, and considers that here we find existing separately the two genitives (*quoi* from stem *quo-*, and *ius* from stem *i-*), which afterwards coalesced into *quoius*.

The dative *quoiei* (which occurs on the fourth inscription on the tomb of the Scipios, *Qvoiei vita defecit, non honos, honoreis*), is, according to Meunier, a double locative from *quoi* loc. of *quo-*, and *ei* loc. of *i-*. Similarly the dat. *eiei* (as in Lucr. III., 555, *Sive aliud quidvis potius connexius eiei*) is a double loc. of *i-*.

† L. *is-to-* is compounded of the three stems *i-*, *sa-* and *ta-*. In addition to the declension of *isto-* I also give some other pronominal forms to illustrate the original declension of the pronouns.

COMPARATIVE GRAMMAR. 333

		Skr.	Gr.	L.
	D.	ta-smái.	τῷ.	istī, U. pu-sme.
	Ab.	ta-smâ-t.	τώς = τω-τ.	istō-d.
	G.	ta-sya.	το-ῖο, τοῦ.	istīus.
	L.	ta-sm-in.	—	—
Plur.	N.	té (m.), tá-n-i (n.)	τοί, οἱ (m.), τά (n.)	istī, U. pur-e (m.)
		—	—	ista, qua-e (n.)
	A.	tá-n (m.), tá-n-i (n.)	τόνς, τούς (m.), τά (n.)	istō-s (m.), ista (n.)
	I.	táis.	—	—
	D. Ab.	té-bhyas.	—	istīs.
Plur.	G.	té-sham.	τῶν.	istō-rum.
	L.	té-shu.	τοῖ-σι, τοῖς.	—
Dual.	N. A.	táu, tá (m.), té (n.)	τώ.	—
	I. D. Ab.	tá-bhyám.	το-ῖν.	—
	G. L.	ta-y-ós.	—	—

§. 171. THE DECLENSION OF THE STEM tâ- (f.).

		Skr.	Gr.	L.
	Stem.	tâ.	τα-.	is-ta-.
Sing.	N.	sâ.	ή.	ista, qua-e.
	A.	tâ-m.	τά-ν, τή-ν.	ista-m.
	I.	ta-y-â.	ή-φι.	—
	D.	ta-sy-âi.	τῇ.	istī.
	Ab.	ta-sy-âs.	—	istā-d.
	G.	ta-sy-âs.	τῆ-ς.	istīus.
	L.	ta-sy-âm.	—	—
Plur.	N.	tâ-s.	ταί, αἱ.	istæ, O. pa-s.
	A.	tâ-s.	(τά-νς), τά-ς.	istā-s.
	I.	tâ-bhis.	—	—
	D. Ab.	tâ-bhyas.	—	istīs.
	G.	tâ-sâm.	τά-ων, τῶν.	istā-rum.
	L.	tâ-su.	τῇ-σι, ταῖς.	—
Dual.	N. A.	té.	τά.	—
	I. D. Ab.	tâ-bhyám.	τα-ῖν.	—
	G. L.	ta-y-ós.	—	—

APPENDIX.

THE SANSKRIT CEREBRALS OR LINGUALS.

Dr. GEORGE BÜHLER, in his essay "On the Origin of the Sanskrit Linguals," has attempted to demonstrate that these sounds were not borrowed from the Dravidian races of India, but that they were for the most part developed within the limits of the Sanskrit. As Bühler's essay is very instructive, I have condensed his chief arguments in this Appendix, and frequently employed his own words.*

The borrowing of sounds by one language from another is a phenomenon that has never been proved to have occurred in languages that have been influenced by others in historical times. Thus, take the case of English; though it was under Norman influence for so many centuries, and though traces of that influence are seen on all sides in borrowed words, loss of the old Saxon inflexions, &c., yet not a single Norman sound was introduced into it. Neither the French *a* nor *u* nor *nasals* were adopted by the English; and it is just as difficult for an Englishman of the nineteenth century to pronounce these sounds as it was for a Saxon of the tenth century. But the case of such nations as the Irish, the Germanised Sclavonians, &c., demonstrate the same fact still more manifestly; for, while these nations have almost completely lost their original language, and adopted that of their conquerors, they still retain their native sounds, and have adapted their new language to them.†

---

* Bühler of course is not responsible for *all* the examples and comparisons adduced here.

† Thus the initial sound heard in the Irish pronunciation of E. *car* is not *ky*, as is commonly supposed, but the hard aspirate *kh*, which, with the other hard aspirates, is still found in Irish.

Moreover, before we can assert that the Skr. cerebrals are borrowed from the Dravidian languages, we must prove that the conditions under which alone sounds can be borrowed, existed in the case of Skr.; i. e. we must prove that a great many foreign words containing the sound in question were first borrowed and that thus the new sound became perfectly familiar to the people. Therefore it has first to be demonstrated that Sanskrit in very early times already possessed, as loans, a number of Dravidian words containing these cerebrals. Dr. Caldwell, who strongly supports the theory of the Dravidian origin of these sounds, enumerates only sixteen nouns containing cerebrals which he supposed to have been borrowed. Only two of these, *áṇi* (the pin of the axle of a cart), and *kaṭuka* (sharp), are found in the Rigveda, and even these can be easily deduced from ordinary Sanskrit roots. *Áṇi* is for *arṇi*, from R. *ar* (to fit); and consequently may mean "a thing to be fitted (into some other thing"), compare *ara* (a spoke); *kaṭu* (sharp) is for *kartu* from *kṛt* (to cut). Even supposing that these sixteen words were borrowed, they would be far too few in number to cause the introduction into Sanskrit of the cerebral sounds which they contain.

As Zend, however, contains three cerebrals, the consonantal and vocalized *r* and *sh*, and as it can be shown that nearly all the Skr. cerebral mutes and nasal are produced by the direct change of *r* and *sh* into them, or by the change of dentals into the corresponding cerebrals through the influence of *ṛ*, *r* and *sh*, we must surely infer that cerebralization is not due to the influence of foreign tongues, but solely due to the genius of the language itself. As proof of this, we have the following facts:—

A dental *n* is frequently changed into *ṇ*, when it is immediately succeeded by a vowel or *y* or *v*, under the influence of a preceding *ṛ*, *ṝ*, *r* or *sh*, provided no palatal, cerebral, dental, sibilant, or *l* intervene; thus *k'ikîrsha* with suffix *mána* forms *k'ikîrshamáṇa*, *bhrahmáṇan* comes from *bhrahman*, &c.* *Anadvah* (an ox) is for *anarvah*, from *anas* (a cart), and *vah* (to draw); the change of *-as* into *ar* be-

---

* Consult Bopp's "Kritische Grammatik der Sanskrita-Sprache," pp. 60, 61.

fore a soft consonant is found in the Vedas as *usharbudh* (early awake) for later *ushóbudh*, *vanargu* (a thief) for *vanógu*. *R*, when followed by *ṇ*, is assimilated to it sometimes in Sanskrit and always in Prakrit. In Sanskrit the first of these *ṇ*'s may be dropped, and the preceding vowel lengthened, as *dūṇáś'a* (imperishable) for and beside *durṇáś'a*, *dūṇas'a* (difficult to obtain) for and beside *durṇas'a*. *Páṇi* (the hand) = *parṇi* from *pṛ* (to fill). *Aṇu* (small) = *arṇu* from I. E. *ar* (to hurt, grind), whence Skr. *arus* (n. a wound), and Gr. ἀλέω (I grind), ἄλευρον* (flour); *aṇu* would accordingly mean literally "ground down." *Paṇ* (to buy) is for *parṇ* from *pṛ* (to fill) beside Gr. πέρνημι, πόρνη (cf. Skr. *paṇya-strī*), πρίαμαι, &c.; the obscure *baṇig'* or *vaṇig'* (a merchant) may be connected with this root. Bühler illustrates this change of *p* into *b* or *v* by *pibámi* or *pivámi* (I drink) for *pá* and *sphávaya* for *sphápaya*, the causal of *spháy* (to swell). We also find *vishṭapa* (a world) for and beside *pishṭapa*, *váṇa* and *báṇa* (an arrow) beside *parṇa* (a leaf, a feather).

In Prâkrit, Pâli, and the modern vernaculars, mute dentals have become cerebrals through the influence of *r*. Thus Skr. *tálavṛnta* (a leaf of a palm tree, a fan), *vṛddha* (old), *kṛta* (made), *bhartá* (nom. sing. a husband), *gardabha-s* (nom. sing. an ass), &c., become respectively *talaveṇṭa*, *vuḍha*, *kaṭa*, or *kiṭa*, *bhaṭṭá*, *gaḍḍaho*, &c. This influence of *r* shows itself even in Vedic as in *dúḍhi* for *durdhi*, *kuṭa* for *kṛta*, &c. In Classical Sanskrit we find many similar examples, as *náṭaka* (a dancer) for and beside *nartaka*; *bhaṭa* (a soldier), derived by Benfey from *bhar*, and therefore being for *bharta*; *bhátaka* (wages) for *bhartaka*; *vaṭa* (a circle, rope) for *varta* from *vṛt* (to turn), cf. L. *verto*; *paṭṭa* (a table, seat), from *patra*, according to Benfey; *paṭu* (skilful) from *paṭ* (to divide), for *part*, cf. L.

---

* Curtius deduces these Greek words from a R. Fελ or Faλ = I. E. *val* or *var*, whence Skr. *úrmi-s* (a wave), Gr. ἐλύω (I roll), οὐλαί (unground barley), ὅλμος (a mortar, a round stone), ἀλοάω (I thresh), ἀλωή, Att. ἄλως (a threshing floor), μάλευρον (= ἄλευρον, Hesych.) from Faλευρον, &c., L. *volvo*, Goth. *valrjan* (to roll). The final sound in Gr. ἐλυ-, L. *volo*-, Goth. *valv*- is a shortened form of reduplication; the F is represented by *o* in ὀλοοίτροχος (a rolling stone) = ὀλFοιτροχος, and in ἀλοάω = ἀλFαω. We find similar cases of short reduplicated forms in Greek, as φό-β-ο-ς, φί-β-ο-μαι beside Skr. *bhí* (timere), φέρ-β-ω, beside φέρ-ω, Skr. *bhar*, πόρ-π-η beside περ-άω, L. *por-ta*, &c.

Z

par(t)-s; *vaṭa* (an enclosure) for *varta*, from *vṛ* (to enclose), cf. L. *vallum*; *kaṇṭaka* (a thorn) for *karntaka*, according to Benfey, from *kṛt* (to cut); *taṭa* (horizon, bank of a river, mountain) for *tarta* from *tṛ* (to cross), as *pára** (ripa opposita) comes from *par* (to cross), cf. Gr. πόρος, περαίνω, πέραν, L. *per*; *taḍ* (to strike) for *tard*, with which Bopp connects Goth. (*us-*)*thrut* (molestiam facere); *taḍit* (fulmen), *taṇḍula* (granum frumenti, præcipue oryzæ) from *tad*; *paṭh* (to recite) from *prath* (to celebrate), cf. L. *inter-pret-ari*; Benfey, however, considers it to be a demonstrative derived from *pashṭa* for *spashṭa* (evident); *puródás'a* (a cake made of rice meal, offered to the gods) from *dás'* (to make oblations). In these two last examples the dental is influenced by *r*, although a vowel intervenes. Bühler considers that a dental has become a cerebral in the following cases through the influence of a succeeding *r*; *k'aṇḍa* (flaming, passionate) for *k'andra*† (the moon, glowing); *daṇḍa* (a stick) for *dantra* from *dam* (to coerce, tame), and *tra* (a suffix signifying the instrument); *méṭha* (an elephant-driver) beside *mahámátra* (id.).

Sh, when it is original or a substitute for *k'h*, *g'*, *s'*, *ks*, becomes *ṭ*, whenever it ends a word or precedes either the termination (*-su*) of the loc. pl. or hard consonants except *t*, *th*, and *s*: while before a soft consonant it becomes *ḍ*, and if *d* or *dh* immmediately follow, then these become *ḍ* or *ḍh* respectively.‡ Thus we have from the stems *dvish* (hating), *rág'* (a king), *vis'* (entering), *viviksh* (desirous to enter) = *viviks*, *prák'h* (asking), *nis'* (night), as nom. sing. *dviṭ*, *ráṭ*, *viṭ*, *viviṭ*, *práṭ*, *niṭ*; as instr. pl. *dviḍbhis*, *ráḍbhis*, *viḍbhis*, *viviḍbhis*, *práḍbhis*, *niḍbhis*; and as loc. pl. *dviṭsu*, *ráṭsu*, *viṭsu*, *viviṭsu*, *práṭsu*, *niṭsu*. We have also such verbal forms as *dviḍḍhi* (2 sing. imper. Par.) from *dvish* (to hate), *diḍḍhvam* (ye ruled) from *is'* (to rule), &c. We find one of the soft cerebrals formed in accordance with this rule sometimes rejected, and then a preceding *a*

---

* Bopp ("Gloss. Comp. Ling. Sanskr.," p. 238) suggests that *pára* may come from *para* (alius).

† Bopp connects *k'aṇḍa* with Goth. *hata* (I hate).

‡ There are some exceptions to this law; from St. *mṛsh* (enduring) we have *mṛk* (nom. sing.) *mṛgbhis* (instr. pl.), &c.

becomes o, and i or u becomes í or ú. Thus shódas'an (sixteen) = shash (six) + das'an (ten), shódha (sixfold) = shash + dha, shódant (a young ox with six teeth) = shash + dant. Nídha (a nest) = nishda = ni + sada (what lies under); píḍ (to press) = pishd = api + sad (to sit upon). Again, n becomes ṇ when preceded by sh under the same conditions as when preceded by r, ṛ or ṝ, as has already been remarked. Lastly, when sh immediately precedes a hard dental, it changes it into the corresponding cerebral, as dvéshṭum (to hate, infin.), dvéshṭi (he hates), dvishṭha (ye hate), dvishṭa (hated), ushṭha (ye desire) from vas', ashṭáu (eight) for as'tau from an original aktáu = L. octo, shashṭha (sixth), shashṭa (sixtieth), &c. In a few cases s after a becomes sh, and then changes a following t or th into ṭ or ṭh, thus from ava and stambh (to prop) we get avashṭambha (relying on), avashṭabhnati (he supports himself), áshádha (the old name of a month, partly June and partly July, or a staff carried in that month by an ascetic), g'aṭhara (the belly) for gastara beside Gr. γαστήρ.

H can also become a cerebral and change a neighbouring dental into a cerebral: thus we have from St. líh (licking) we have líṭ (nom. sing.), líḍbhis (instr. pl.), líṭsu (loc. pl.): from lih (to lick) we have léḍhi (he licks), líḍha (licked), líḍhvé (ye licked); from ruh (to grow) we have ródhum (to grow, infin.) rúḍha (grown), &c.

Cerebrals also arise from the assimilative force of neighbouring cerebrals, thus from íḍ* (to praise) we have íṭṭé (he praises) from íḍ + ṭé, áiḍḍhvam (ye praised) from áiḍ + dhvam; gaṇṭi (calculation) from gaṇ (to number) + ti, gaṇ is a denominative derived probably from gaṇa (a multitude) connected with Lith. gana (satis), ganau (pasco greges), according to Bopp, but it is better to treat gaṇa as for garna from I. E. gar (to collect) when ἀγείρω; phánṭa (easily

---

* According to Benfey, íḍ is a denominative verb based on ish (to wish, chose), and accordingly it is for ísht = is + t; compare Gr. ἴστης, ἵμερος (?) from same root. In the Vedas we find il for id, as in tvám .... martasa ilaté (te hominos celebrant); consult Bopp's "Skr. Gloss.," p. 48. It is possible that il is the original form, and that íḍ is derived from it, as we frequently find d representing l in the Romance languages, as in Sardinian pedde from L. pellis, poddhige from L. pollex, casteddu from L. castellum, and Sicilian cavaddu from L. caballus, beddu from bellus, &c.

prepared) from *phaṇ* (to produce easily) + *ta; tad dayanam* (this flight) for *tat d., tán diṇḍimán* (these drums) for *tán d.*, &c.

Finally, we find a great number of words where cerebrals have arisen from dentals without any apparent reason, and of many of which we still find side-forms in Vedic still preserving the original dentals. Thus we have Vedic *bhanati* (he praises) beside Skr. *bhaṇ* (to speak), Bühler identifies *bhaṇ* with φων-έω, but wrongly, as φωνέω is from φωνή = φω + νη and φω = Skr. *bhá; pan* and *paṇ* (to praise), &c.

We may conclude then that cerebralisation is a phenomenon that has arisen within the limits of the Sanskrit language, and that it is not due to Dravidic influence. In the course of time this predilection for cerebrals grew rapidly stronger, till it produced the results that manifest themselves so plainly in Prakrit.*

In English the original dentals have all become cerebrals, as we see from the transliteration of English words into the various languages of India. Thus in Tamil *isṭṭar* is written for *Easter*, *kórṭṭu* for *court*, *porṭṭ* for *fort* (initial *f* always becoming *p* in Tamil), *aḍváns* for *advance*, *kalakṭar* for *collector*, *ṭesṭu* for *test*, &c. In Telugu, likewise, we have *kalkaṭaru* for *collector*, *dákṭar* for *doctor*, *ágashṭu* for *August*, &c. These examples completely prove that the English pronounce *t* and *d* as cerebrals, and not as dentals. In other European languages we likewise find cerebrals developed, as in *schtehen*, the High German form of the classical German *stehen*. In *schtehen*, however, Bühler believes that the sound of the *t* is not quite so hollow as that of the Indian *ṭ*, because the G. *sch* is not pronounced so far back in the mouth as the Indian *sh*.

The German *t*-sounds accordingly differ from the English *t*-sounds in this, that the former are pure dentals, while the latter are pure cerebrals or linguals.

* For further information on this subject, consult C. Lassen's most valuable work "Institutiones Linguæ Pracriticae."

ADDENDA ET CORRIGENDA.

Page 12, line 20, for *Inez*, read *Iñes*.
— 34, — 33, for 131, read 110. *seq.*
— 36, — 12, for *bhugh*, read *bhagh*.
— 41, — 23, 24, for *datṛnâm*, read *dâtṛnâm*.
— 48, — 5, for *mṛs'*, read *mṛs'*.
— 49, — 33, *omit* A.
— 52, — 26, for *tubhyan*, read *tubhyam*.
— 59, — 25, omit *Burrus* (= Πύρρυς).
— 63, — 22, for ἰψος, ἴπέρ, read ἴψος, ἴπέρ.
— 69, — 1, for *eð*, read *eð*.
— 70, — 14, *after* aspect, *insert* unless the dangers of the sea are supposed to arise from shoals.
— 73, — 2, for *ghrana*, read *ghraṇa*.
— 125, — 34, *omit* Consult Appendix B.
— 128, — 24, for *kṛs a*, read *kṛs a*.
— 141, — 24, for *spies*, read *spiess*.
— 143, — 34, for *as*, read just *as*.
— 146, — 24, *omit* only.
— 147, — 5, for *meṣtai*, read *meṣtai*.
— 159, — 6, 8, for *Zeud*, read *Zend*.
— 163, — 14, 22, *omit* in line 14, "*Sestius* beside *Sextius*, *mistus* beside *mixtus*; *sescenti* for *sexcenti*;" and *insert* these words in line 22, after "in."
— 179, — 9, for when, *read* whence.
— 186, — 21, *omit* i.
— 189, — 17, *omit* § 99.
— 190, — 6, for *gak'h-ati*, read *gak'k'h-ati*.
— 193, — 24, *omit* § 98.
— 195, — 27, for *dṛs*, read *dṛs'*.
— 198, — 10, for *bharanta-s*, read *bharant-s*.
— 199, — 29, *omit* § 103.
— 202, — 24, for *-a*, read *-â*.
— 208, — 36, for *n'artaka-s*, read *na'rtaka-s*.
— 218, — 13, for *bharat-i*, read *bharat-î*.
— 219, — 31, insert *rurudvat-su* in the intermediate column.
— 220, — 24, for *anadvâns*, read *anadvâns*.
— 226, — 2, 3, for have become, *read* are.
— 227, — 29, for *kṛt*, read *kṛt*.
— 229, — 30, for *tudátsi*, read *tudátsu*.
— 232, — 10, for from, read by.
— 232, — 22, for πτήσυυ, read πτήσσω.
— 240, — 18, *add*, *after* ϸFaρ, "or rather ὑaρ = Skr. *svasâr* (sister), men originally having to marry their sisters."
— 243, — 18, 19, for *congius*, read *congius*.
— 244, — 29, for *l*, read *r*.
— 249, — 29, for ψύλαξ, ψυλακ, read φύλαξ, φυλακ.
— 250, — 8, for Æolic, read Argive.
— 250, — 23 ⎫
— 251, — 13 ⎭ for In σ-stems σ, read In σ-stems the nominatival σ.
— 253, — 4, for *hasticapas*, read *hosticapas*.
— 292, — 10, for *pitṛn*, read *pitṛn*.
— 295, — 23, for *avy'âm*, read *avy-âm*.
— 305, — 18, the reference belongs to *peptimo*, and not to *proximo-*.
— 308, — 24, 25, *omit* "for I. E. *-an* becomes *-a* in Greek."
— 320, — 20, for *nasturtuim*, read *nasturñium*.